OXFORD MONOGRAPHS IN INTERNATIONAL LAW

General Editor: Professor Ian Brownlie QC, DCL, FBA
Chichele Professor of Public International Law in the University of Oxford and Fellow of All Souls College, Oxford.

STATE RESPONSIBILITY AND THE MARINE ENVIRONMENT

OXFORD MONOGRAPHS IN INTERNATIONAL LAW

This new series of monographs will publish important and original pieces of research on all aspects of public international law. Topics which will be given particular prominence are those which, while of interest to the academic lawyer, also have important bearing on issues which touch the actual conduct of international relations. None the less the series is intended to be wide in scope and thus will include the history and philosophical foundations of international law.

ALSO IN THIS SERIES

The Juridical Bay
GAYL WESTERMAN

The Exclusive Economic Zone
DAVID ATTARD

Judicial Remedies in International Law
CHRISTINE GRAY

Occupation, Resistance and Law
ADAM ROBERTS

The Legality of Non-Forcible Counter-Measures in International Law
OMER ELAGAB

The Shatt-al-Arab Boundary Question
KAIYAN KAIKOBAD

State Responsibility and the Marine Environment

THE RULES OF DECISION

BRIAN D. SMITH

CLARENDON PRESS · OXFORD
1988

Oxford University Press, Walton Street, Oxford OX2 6DP
Oxford New York Toronto
Delhi Bombay Calcutta Madras Karachi
Petaling Jaya Singapore Hong Kong Tokyo
Nairobi Dar es Salaam Cape Town
Melbourne Auckland
and associated companies in
Beirut Berlin Ibadan Nicosia

Oxford is a trade mark of Oxford University Press

Published in the United States
by Oxford University Press, New York

British Library Cataloguing in Publication Data
Smith, Brian D.
State responsibility and the marine
environment the rules of decision
1. Maritime Law
I. Title
341.4′5 JX4411
ISBN 0–19–825581–0

Library of Congress Cataloging in Publication Data
Smith, Brian D.
State responsibility and the marine environment:
the rules of decision / Brian D. Smith.
Originally presented as the author's thesis
(Ph.D.)—University of Cambridge, 1985.
Bibliography: p. Includes index.
1. Marine pollution—Law and legislation.
2. Environmental law, International.
3. Maritime law.
4. Government liability (International law)
I. Title.
K3590.4.S57 1988
341.7′62—dc19 87–22915 CIp
ISBN 0–19–825581–0

Set by The Alden Press, Oxford
Printed in Great Britain
at the Alden Press, Oxford

TO MY PARENTS
EDWARD AND FRANCES SMITH

Acknowledgements

THIS work is essentially in the form of a Ph.D. dissertation submitted to the University of Cambridge in 1985. I must note in preface the significant contributions of several people to that dissertation. I wish particularly to express my appreciation to my supervisor, Dr Geoffrey Marston of Sidney Sussex College. Throughout the long process of research and writing, Dr Marston provided consistent guidance, support, and direction well beyond the call of supervisorial duty. My own college, Trinity, was similarly generous in its extension of most welcome economic and administrative assistance. As to the final dissertation product and manuscript revisions, I cannot overstate the contribution of my extraordinary typist, Elizabeth Ansari. Most of all, I want to preface this book with a credit to my wife, Alison; without her patience, humour and strength throughout these years, I have no doubt that this work could never have reached completion.

ACKNOWLEDGEMENTS

[illegible]

Editor's Preface

THE subject of State Responsibility has been relatively neglected in recent decades, and the literature provoked by the work of the International Law Commission has tended to focus upon certain issues only. Dr. Smith's bold and illuminating study addresses a large set of questions involving the intersection of the principles of State responsibility, the law of the sea, and the concept of State jurisdiction. It is difficult territory to negotiate, and at times it may be easier to present the questions than it is to produce definitive answers. The author provides a guide for the wary traveller and, more or less incidentally, shows that a competent handling of the topic of 'international environmental law' necessitates the deployment of the tools of general international law familiar to the legal advisers of States. In other words, the cold-eyed application of legal analysis may be just as fruitful as the invention of a new vehicle such as 'international environmental law'.

All Souls College, IAN BROWNLIE

OXFORD.

26th November 1987.

Contents

Table of Cases

INTERNATIONAL ADJUDICATIONS

INTERNATIONAL ARBITRATIONS

MUNICIPAL DECISIONS

Introduction

INTERNATIONAL environmental law is in the early stages of adolescence. The basic features of a system of responsibility among states for conduct injurious to the environment are taking discernible form. At present, however, they lack the definition, consistency, and sophistication of a mature system able to cope effectively with the complex problems arising out of the interaction of technology and the environment in a society of independent states. The central objective of this work is to analyse the present, rudimentary state of the law of environmental responsibility and to anticipate the direction of the maturation process with reference to the marine environment.

The methodological premise of the work is that the rules of decision in cases of marine environmental injury arise out of the intersection of three sets of international legal principles. The first consists of those rules governing the attribution of state responsibility in all cases, without reference to the content of the specific international duty implicated. These rules, which define in general terms the conditions and consequences of responsibility for violation of duty, will be the subject of Part I. Part II will seek to determine the precise status and character of the international obligations of the state relating to the prevention of injury to the marine environment. The analyses in Parts I and II will demonstrate the significance of the third set of rules, the principles governing the apportionment of state legal authority over the seas, to any decision regarding international responsibility for marine environmental harm. Part III, the final section of the work, will examine the pattern of such authority and venture a synthesis—a definition of the consequential rules of responsibility pertaining to matters in or affecting each of the distinct juridical zones of the sea.

The three component sets of international rules enumerated have in common a dynamic and uncertain character. Analyses of the principles of state responsibility and the regime of jurisdiction over actors upon the sea manifest unresolved questions and insufficient development of particular significance in the context of environmental matters. International law with respect to state environmental duties and the standard of performance applicable to such duties suffers from a similar absence of certainty. The objectives of the present work therefore reside on two planes. It is first hoped to explore and resolve in each body of law those issues essential to the construction of a comprehensive regime of marine environmental responsibility. In certain areas, of course, direct international authority is very limited; the method in such cases will be to articulate a legal structure which proceeds on the logic of available international materials, municipal analogies, and apposite first principles of the interstate system. The paramount objective at all times, however, remains a study of the relationships among the elemental legal regimes so defined. Only out of the interaction of such principles may one deduce the rules of decision to be applied to assertions of international responsibility for damage to the marine environment.

One prefatory definitional note is in order. Chapter 9 will detail the nature and bases of state legal authority. Reference to such authority will occur, however, throughout the work. It is important to explain, therefore, that the 'legal authority' of the state, for the purposes of this work, refers to the competence of the state under international law to render authoritative decisions, i.e. to exercise its legislative, administrative, or judicial powers with respect to given facts or conduct. The phrase is intended to comprehend both of the basic components of such competence: the right to define or prescribe operative rules; and the right to take measures to enforce such rules. It is, moreover, intended to serve interchangeably with the term 'jurisdiction'. 'Jurisdiction', of course, may appropriately be used in several quite different senses.[1] It may denote a spatial region within which legal authority is exercised. In the alternative, it may refer to the legal authority of specific organs of the state endowed and distributed by municipal law.[2] Neither of these meanings, however, is generally employed in this work. As expressed by McDougal, 'In public and private international law, the word "jurisdiction"—in etymological origin, speaking the law—is used to refer to the competence of a state, the authority of a state recognized by international decision-makers and by other states—to make law for, and apply law to, particular events or particular controversies.'[3] State 'legal authority' and 'jurisdiction', therefore, are here used as synonyms referring to the competence of states, defined and limited by international law, to render authoritative legal decisions.

[1] For useful discussions of the semantic issue *see* O'Connell, ii *International Law* (1965) 655; George, 'Extraterritorial Application of Penal Legislation', 64 *Mich. L. Rev.* 609, at 609–12 (1966); Mann, 'The Doctrine of Jurisdiction in International Law', in *Studies in International Law* i, at 3 (1973).

[2] For example, one author notes that three basic usages of the term 'jurisdiction' may be identified in British official literature regarding crimes on board merchant ships: (*a*) the capacity of the legislature; (*b*) the applicability of a body of law; and (*c*) the capacity of the adjudicator. With respect to each of these the term may refer to subject matter or geographical ambit. Marston, 'Crimes on Board Foreign Merchant Ships at Sea: Some Aspects of English Practice', 83 *L.Q. Rev.* 357, at 360 (1972).

[3] McDougal, 'Jurisdiction', 62 *Int'l L. Stud.* 634 (Lillich and Moore eds. 1980).

PART I

State Responsibility: General Principles

I

The Meaning and Elements of Responsibility

THIRTY years ago Garcia-Amador observed that 'it would be difficult to find a topic beset with greater confusion and uncertainty' than state responsibility.[1] Notwithstanding an intervening period of intense doctrinal analysis—including, most notably, the extensive work conducted by the International Law Commission (ILC)—the observation remains strikingly valid.[2] It is perhaps advisable, then, to begin an analysis of this difficult region with a simple proposition. The definition of 'responsibility' operative in the context of the legal relations among states is highly specific. It is not, as in common parlance, a synonym for 'duty' or 'obligation'. Rather, 'responsibility' denotes specifically the juridical position of an obligor-state following its breach of an international obligation.[3] In fact, the condition of such state responsibility itself is one of obligation, It is the duty of a state to make appropriate amends following a breach of an international obligation.[4] Eagleton regards this 'consequential' obligation as axiomatic:

> Historically, the idea of a responsibility between states may be traced back to the vague origins of rights and duties which have always been regarded as fundamental by

[1] Garcia-Amador, 'State Responsibility: Some New Problems', ii *Recueil des cours* 369 (1958).

[2] The ILC has had the codification of the principles of state responsibility on its agenda from its first meeting in 1949. See 4 UN *GAOR* Supp. (no. 10) para. 16, UN Doc. A/925 (1949). To date the Commission has completed its first reading of Pt. I, Arts. 1–315, of its draft text on state responsibility. See 35 UN GAOR Supp. (no. 10), at 59–132; Riphagen, Second Report on the Content, Forms and Degrees of State Responsibility, UN Doc. A/CN.4/344 (1981), at 1. The Commission's agenda called for completion of the second reading of these articles by the end of 1987. See McCaffrey, 'The Thirty-fourth Session of the International Law Commission', 77 *Am. J. Int'l L.* 323, at 337—38 (1983). For a historical view of the ILC efforts—certainly the most comprehensive on the topic—see Ago, First Report on State Responsibility, ii *Yb. Int'l L. Comm'n* 125, at 132, UN Doc. A/CN.4/217 and Add. 1 (1969). See also, Brownlie, *System of the Law of Nations: State Responsibility*, Pt I, 13–18 (1983); Lillich, 'The Current Status of the Law of State Responsibility for Injuries to Aliens', in *International Law of State Responsibility for Injuries to Aliens*, 1, at 17–19 (Lillich ed. 1983) (hereinafter cited as *Injuries to Aliens*).

[3] See generally Garcia-Amador, *supra* n. 1, at 376; Garcia-Amador, Draft Articles on the Responsibility of the State for Injuries Caused in its Territory to the Person or Property of Aliens (hereinafter cited as Garcia-Amador, Draft), reprinted in *Recent Codification of the Law of State Responsibility for Injury to Aliens* 1 (Garcia-Amador, Sohn, and Baxter eds. 1974). Ago, Second Report on State Responsibility, ii *Yb. Int'l L. Comm'n* 177, at 187, UN Doc. A/CN.4/233 (1970).

[4] 'Responsibility is simply the principle which establishes an obligation to make good any violation of international law producing injury, committed by the respondent state.' Eagleton, *The Responsibility of States in International Law* 22 (1928). See Garcia-Amador, Draft, *supra* n. 3, at 8; Riphagen, Second Report on the Content, Forms and Degrees of State Responsibility, UN Doc. A/CN.4/344 (1981), at 15.

mankind. Among these is the conviction that reparation should be made for an injury committed; and this idea of responsibility, whether between persons or states, is as old as morality itself.[5]

In any event, this view of the content of state responsibility for breach of obligation is reflected throughout doctrine and jurisprudence.[6] The language of the Permanent Court in the *Chorzów Factory* Case is at once representative and authoritative: 'It is a principle of international law that the breach of an engagement involves an obligation to make reparation in an adequate form.'[7] In short, state responsibility represents the consequence of, and the sanction against, non-performance by states of their international obligations.

The elements required for responsibility to attach to specific conduct would seem to follow logically from the foregoing definition. First, since the state is conceptually the subject and beneficiary of international obligations, the state must be deemed in law to be the actor.[8] Second, the conduct itself must be in violation of the state's international obligations.[9] This basic dichotomy is reflected in the classic pronouncement on the nature of state responsibility from the arbitral jurisprudence of the Mexico–United States General Claims Commission: 'Under International law, apart from any convention, in order that a State may incur responsibility it is necessary that an unlawful international act be imputed to it, that is, that there exist a violation of a duty imposed by an international juridical standard.'[10] Indeed, Ago, in his work conducted as the Special Rapporteur to the ILC, concludes that there is essential consensus in the literature that these two elements—characterized as 'objective' (breach of obligation) and 'subjective' (state as actor)—constitute the sole prerequisites to state responsibility.[11] The draft text produced by the commission itself reflects this conclusion. State responsibility is said to exist

[5] Eagleton, *supra* n. 4, at 16.

[6] As to the content of the obligation to make reparation see Cheng, *General Principles of Law as Applied by International Courts and Tribunals* 233 (1953); Garcia-Amador *supra* n. 1, at 209; Riphagen, *supra* n. 4, at 15 ff.; Whiteman, i *Damages in International Law* (1937).

[7] The *Chorzów Factory* Case (Indemnity; Jurisdiction) (*Germ.* v. *Pol.*), 1927 PCIJ, Ser. A, no. 9 (Judgment of 26 July 1927), at 21.

[8] See Guerrero, Report to the Council of The League of Nations on the Questions which Appear Ripe for International Regulation: Responsibility of States for Damage Done in Their Territories to the Person or Property of Foreigners, League of Nations Doc. C. 196 M. 70 1927 V (1927), reprinted in Eagleton, *supra* n. 4, at 233, 241. See generally the discussion regarding the state as actor in the text commencing at ch. 3 n. 1 *infra*.

[9] See ch. 2 commencing at n. 1 *infra* for an extensive treatment of this element. See generally Ago, 2nd Rpt., *supra* n. 3, at 191.

[10] *Dickson Car Wheel Co.* Case (1931) (*US* v. *Mex.*), 4 R. Int'l. Arb. Awards 678.

[11] Ago, 2nd Rpt., *supra* n. 3, at 187. See citations *id.* 187–8 nn. 49–54. Subject to variations in language and form, see: Amerasinghe, *State Responsibility for Injury to Aliens* (1967), at 37, Jiménez de Arechaga, 'International Responsibility', in *Manual of Public International Law*, at 534 (Sorensen, ed. 1968), Cheng, *supra* n. 6, at 170; Sohn and Baxter, 'Convention on the International Responsibility of States for Injuries to Aliens (Final Draft with Explanatory Notes)', reprinted in *Recent Codification of the Law of State Responsibility for Injury to Aliens* 135 (Garcia-Amador, Sohn, and Baxter eds. 1974).

when: '(*a*) conduct consisting of an action or omission is attributable to the State under international law; and (*b*) that conduct constitutes a breach of an international obligation of that State.'[12] The following two chapters will be directed to an analysis of these 'objective' and 'subjective' requirements for responsibility.

It should be noted that a number of respected commentators add 'injury' or 'damage' as a third requisite element.[13] For several reasons, it is submitted that this represents a distinction without substance, As noted by one of the proponents of 'injury' as an additional requirement: 'In inter-state relations, the concept of damage does not . . . have an essentially material or patrimonial character.'[14] In addition to the types of physical or economic damage recognized in municipal law, 'moral and political' injury will clearly support the invocation of state responsibility.[15] Critically, there is inherent in the breach of any obligation owed by one state to another sufficient injury to the correlative rights of the latter, albeit of a metaphysical character, to elicit state responsibility.[16] As Ago persuasively argues:

> Every breach of an engagement *vis-à-vis* another State and every impairment of a subjective right of that State in itself constitutes a damage, material or mortal, to that State. As Anzilotti stated in his first work on the topic, international responsibility derives its *raison d'être* purely from the violation of a right of another State and every violation of a right is a damage.[17]

It would appear, therefore, a redundancy to describe 'injury' as an additional requirement for state responsibility; the concept of injury is already embraced within the 'objective' element.

The explanation for the adoption of 'injury' as an independent component by certain authors may lie in the fact that particular obligations of the state may not be breached without the occurrence of injury. This is not at all inconsistent, of course, with the conclusion that injury is not a requisite element of state responsibility. Ago has described the general principles of state responsibility, with which this part is exclusively concerned, as

[12] ILC, Report to the General Assembly, ii *Yb. Int'l L Comm'n* 179, UN Doc. A/9010/Rev. 1 (1973).

[13] See e.g. Amerasinghe, *supra* n. 11, at 37; Jiménez de Arechaga, *supra* n. 11, at 534; De Beus, *The Jurisprudence of the General Claims Commission: United States and Mexico* 125–6 (1938); Sohn and Baxter, *supra* n. 11, at 143.

[14] De Arechaga *supra* n. 11, at 534.

[15] See Garcia-Amador, Draft, *supra* n. 3, at 91–6. See also *The I'm Alone Case* (1935) (*Can.* v *US*), 3 R. Int'l Arb. Awards 1609, at 1618. Note that the dispute regarding the propriety of monetary reparation in the absence of material injury does not call into question the existence of responsibility itself. See generally Parry, 'Some Considerations upon the Protection of Individuals in International Law', ii *Recueil des cours* 657, at 685 (1956).

[16] See Bollecker-Stern, *Le Préjudice dans la theorie de la responsabilité internationale* 36–49 (1973); Ago, Third Report on State Responsibility, ii *Yb. Int'l L. Comm'n* 193, at 223, UN Doc. A/CN.4/246 and Add. 1–3 (1971).

[17] Ago, 2nd Rpt., *supra* n. 3, at 195, Ago's reference to Anzilotti is to the latter's *Teoria generale della responsibilità della stato nel diretto internazionale* (1902)

'secondary' in the sense that they define the consequences of the breach of any 'primary' rule.[18] Yet, a great portion of the literature of state responsibility is in fact limited in inquiry to responsibility arising out of the breach of 'primary' obligations relating to the treatment of aliens.[19] Injury to the alien is a requisite aspect of the breach of certain of these specific primary obligations.[20] Hence, authors may quite accurately identify injury as necessary for state responsibility to arise in this area. This is true, however, only because no breach of the 'primary' obligation—i.e. no satisfaction of the objective element—may occur without it. No general truth about the 'secondary' principles of state responsibility applicable to *all* international obligations is implied. Opinion to the effect that 'injury' is required for responsibility in connexion with the treatment of aliens does not, therefore, threaten the subjective/objective dichotomy.[21]

[18] ILC, Report to the General Assembly, ii *Yb. Int'l L. Comm'n* 269, at 273, UN Doc. A/CN.4/Ser. (1974). The use of such terminology is not intended here or in the ILC materials to suggest that specific obligations are in any sense 'superior' or general principles in any sense 'subordinate'.

[19] See e.g. Amerasinghe, *supra* n. 11; Borchard, *The Diplomatic Protection of Citizens Abroad* (1915); Garcia-Amador, Draft, *supra* n. 3; Sohn and Baxter, *supra* n. 11.

[20] Amerasinghe, *supra* n. 11, at 37; Sohn and Baxter, *supra* n. 11, at 143.

[21] Sohn and Baxter, in fact, specifically acknowledge the inapplicability of their analysis to 'categories' of responsibility other than those arising out of the treatment of aliens. Sohn and Baxter, *supra* n. 11, at 148. Hence, these authors recognize '[t]he responsibility which a State incurs solely as the result of the violation of a duty it owes to a second State under customary international law or a treaty, which violation does not result in direct pecuniary loss to that State or any of its nationals'. *Id.*

2

Breach of Obligation: The Objective Element

THE logic of conditioning state responsibility upon the occurrence of a breach of an international obligation is patent.[1] In the interstate system, each obligation of a state is necessarily corollary to the rights of other states to demand performance.[2] When an obligation is breached, therefore, the rights possessed by other states are, by definition, disturbed.[3] The regime of responsibility is designed specifically to redress, and serve as a disincentive to, such disturbance. Hence, state responsibility may only and must always arise upon the breach of an international obligation. As reported to the General Assembly by the ILC:

> The very essence of wrongfulness, as a source of responsibility, is constituted . . . by the contrast between the State's actual conduct and the conduct required of it under international law, In other words, it is to conduct attributed to the State under international law and representing a breach on its part of an international obligation that the law of nations attaches the emergence of the new legal situations unfavourable to the State in question which are grouped under the common denominator of international responsibility.[4]

The question in each case, then, is whether the state's conduct constitutes a breach of an international obligation. Obviously, one must refer to the content of the primary obligation to determine whether specific conduct constitutes a breach. Nevertheless, one may identify certain generic principles regarding the type of conduct which may place the state in breach of an international duty. A number are of particular relevance to the primary obligations applicable to the marine environment to be described in Part II.

A. NATURE OF CONDUCT

The initial point to be made regarding state conduct in breach of obligation is simply that the significance of such conduct attached by municipal law is not a

[1] See generally Ago, 2nd Rpt., *supra* ch. 1 n. 3, at 191–2.

[2] ILC, Report to the General Assembly, *supra* ch 1 n. 12, at 182. With respect to the 'correlative' character of rights and obligations, see generally Hohfeld, *Fundamental Legal Conceptions as Applied in Judicial Reasoning* (1923), *passim*.

[3] See materials cited at ch. 1 n. 17 *supra*.

[4] Ago, Fifth Report on State Responsibility, ii *Yb. Int'l L. Comm'n* 3, at 4, UN Doc. A/CN.4/291 and Add. 1 and 2 (1976).

factor.[5] Conduct may be permitted, prohibited, or required by the internal law of a state. The acts and omissions of the state violative of international obligations will generate state responsibility regardless of the posture of municipal law *vis-à-vis* such conduct.[6] In the words of Fitzmaurice: 'The principle that a State cannot plead the provisions (or deficiencies) of its constitution as a ground for the non-observance of its international obligations . . . is indeed one of the great principles of international law, informing the whole system and applying to every branch of it . . .'[7]

The conduct of a state which triggers responsibility may have a positive or negative character.[8] It is positive when a state commits an affirmative act violative of an international obligation. It is negative when the state omits to perform an act required of it under international law. In fact, it has been noted that 'the cases in which the international responsibility of a State has been invoked on the basis of an omission are perhaps more numerous than those based on action taken by a State.'[9] In any event there is absolute consensus that a state may breach its international obligations by act or omission depending on the content of the primary obligation.[10]

One of the many contributions of Roberto Ago in this region is the analytic recognition that the violative conduct of the state may consist of several acts or omissions viewed collectively.[11] Ago describes such 'composite' conduct as 'made up of a series of separate actions or omissions which relate to separate situations but which, taken together, meet the conditions for a breach of a given international obligation.'[12] Critically, 'the separate acts which, in the aggregate, would constitute a breach of an international obligation may be internationally lawful.'[13] The principal examples proffered in the ILC materials relate to prohibited 'discriminatory practices' against aliens.[14] An isolated incident of the denial of a professional licence to an alien of a given nationality, for example, would not constitute a 'discriminatory practice'; a persistent pattern of such conduct would.[15] It must be pointed out, however,

[5] See Ago, 3rd Rpt., *supra* ch. 1 n. 16, at 226–33; Amerasinghe, *supra* ch. 1 n. 11, at 39–41 and authorities cited therein.

[6] See the *SS Wimbledon* Case (*Allied Powers* v. *Germ.*), [1923] PCIJ., Ser. A., no. 1 (Judgment of 17 Aug. 1923), at 29–30; *Treatment of Polish Nationals and Other Persons of Polish Origin or Speech in the Danzig Territory* (*Pol.* v. *City of Danz.*), [1932] PCIJ, Ser. A/B, no. 44 (Advisory Opinion of 4 Feb. 1932), at 24.

[7] Fitzmaurice, 'The General Principles of International Law', ii *Recueil des cours* 1, at 85 (1957).

[8] See Guerrero, Report, *supra* ch. 1 n. 8, at 241.

[9] Ago, 2nd Rpt., *supra* ch. 1 n. 3, at 188.

[10] *Id.*, at 188–89 and authorities cited therein.

[11] See Ago, 5th Rpt., *supra* n. 4; Ago, Seventh Report on State Responsibility, ii *Yb. Int'l L. Comm'n* 31 at 47–8, UN Doc. A/CN.4/307 and Add. 1 and 2 (1978).

[12] ILC Report to the General Assembly, ii *Yb. Int'l L. Comm'n* 73, at 93, UN Doc. A/CN.4/Ser. A/1976/Add. 7 (Pt. 2) (1976). See Brownlie, *System*, *supra* ch. 1 n. 2, at 196–8.

[13] Ago, 7th Rpt., *supra* n. 11, at 47.

[14] ILC, 1976 Rpt., *supra* n. 12, at 93–4 (professional licencing) Ago, 5th Rpt., *supra* n. 4, at 23 (expropriation).

[15] See ILC, 1976 Rpt., *supra* n. 12, at 93–4.

that examples of this type unfortunately suggest a limitation of the concept of 'composite' acts to the volation of obligations which may be violated *only* by such acts—as is the case with prohibited 'practices'.[16] This limitation should not exist. An obligation not to damage the territorial resources of another state by pollution, for example, might be violated by a single act of pollution.[17] It might, however, equally be violated, due to the cumulative and synergistic effects of certain types of pollution, by taking the aggregate of several independent acts which, standing alone, might not have constituted a breach. Ago's concept of 'composite' conduct, therefore, appears quite relevant to obligations other than those directed specifically at a pattern of conduct.

State responsibility for 'participation' or 'complicity' in the conduct of another state represents a second aspect of the nature of conduct subjected to thorough analysis for the first time by Ago and the ILC.[18] The issue considered is the legal consequence of acts or omissions which aid or assist another state in the breach of its international obligations. Such assistance, and the character of 'participation' involved, are to be distinguished from acts in concert affecting the breach of an international obligation by both states. As noted by the ILC: 'It is self-evident that the parallel commission of identical offences by two or more States is altogether different from participation by one of those States in an internationally wrongful act committed by the other.'[19] Indeed, the issue of complicity may arise when the conduct of the assisting state, viewed independently, is in breach of *no* primary obligation.[20] For example, the provision of arms or military technology or the siting of foreign forces on state territory may not violate any international obligation.[21] When such conduct facilitates the breach of an international obligation by another State (e.g. aggression), however, the otherwise innocent conduct may trigger state responsibility.[22] The ILC draft Article 27 reflects this conclusion:

[16] Consider the ILC's very limited description of the nature of 'composite' acts: 'The distinctive characteristic of such an act of the State is thus the systematic repetition of actions having the same purpose, content and effect, but relating to specific cases which are independent of one another.' ILC, 1976 Rpt., *supra* n. 12, at 93.

[17] Assume, for present purposes, the existence of such an obligation. See ch. 5 for a discussion of the precise content of such environmental obligations.

[18] See Ago 7th Rpt., *supra* n. 11, at 54; ILC, Report to the General Assembly, ii *Yb. Int'l L. Comm'n* 74, at 99, UN Doc. /CN.4/Ser. A /1978/Add. 1 (Pt 2) (1978); ILC, Summary Records of the 30th Session, ii *Yb. Int'l L. Comm'n* 223, UN Doc. A/CN.4/Ser (1978).

[19] ILC, 1978 Rpt., *supra* n. 18, at 99.

[20] *Id.*, at 103.

[21] On the other hand, of course, such conduct may be in breach of an obligation arising out of contract or custom. This would not, however, alter the analysis of the state's posture *vis-à-vis* the obligation violated by the recipient state. See Ago, 7th Rpt., *supra* n. 11, at 58.

[22] The issue of whether the responsibility of the 'participating' state is of the same character as the responsibility of the recipient state is unresolved. Ago concludes, without extensive reasoning, that the participant's responsibility should be 'ulterior': 'In conclusion, we consider that as a general rule that fact of participation, in the form of aid or assistance— in short, of complicity—in

Aid or assistance by a State to another State, if it is established that it is rendered for the commission of an internationally wrongful act, carried out by the latter, itself constitutes an internationally wrongful act, even if, taken alone, such aid or assistance would not constitute the breach of an international obligation.[23]

It must be submitted that the language of this formulation is wanting in clarity or scope in two minor respects. First, the Article and its accompanying commentary make it quite clear that 'aid or assistance must have been rendered with *intent* to facilitate the commission of that internationally wrongful act by another.'[24] Certainly, responsibility for complicity should arise when 'specific intent' to facilitate a wrong is present. It should arise as well, however, when lesser degrees of intent are present. A state may have been primarily motivated to render aid for reasons unrelated to the breach of the international obligation, e.g. economic rewards. Yet, if the state knew, or perhaps should have known, that such conduct would facilitate the breach, the consequences of complicity ought logically to attach.

The ILC analysis further appears to ignore the circumstance of complicity in another state's breach of obligation by *omission*. The language of 'aid or assistance' certainly suggests limitation to breaches by affirmative conduct. The logic of the principles governing responsibility through participation is not so limited. To use a particularly significant example from the environmental context, one state may provide technology to another with knowledge of the probability of material environmental harm resulting to other states from the use of the technology, due to the characteristics of the technology itself or the patent lack of resources, sophistication, or will of the recipient state to prevent such harm. Such circumstances would seem to be the analytic inverse of the provision of means to engage in an affirmative wrong. Here, the conduct of the providing state has established the situation or 'means' which make possible the occurrence of a wrong by omission, i.e. the later failure of the recipient state to prevent harm to a third state, In the event of such a breach of preventive obligations, it would seem that the regime of 'complicity' should apply.

B. PRESENCE OF 'FAULT'

The introduction into international jurisprudence of the Roman law principle that responsibility depends upon the presence of subjective fault or *culpa* in

the commission of a wrongful act by another must remain under international law, as it does under internal law, an act distinct from such participation, which is characterized differently and does not necessarily have the same legal consequences.' Ago, 7th Rpt., *supra* n. 11, at 60. The final ILC report to the General Assembly expresses no conclusion on the issue. ILC, 1978 Rpt., *supra* n. 18, at 104.

[23] ILC, 1978 Rpt., *supra* n. 18, at 99.

[24] *Id.*, at 104 (emphasis in original).

the conduct of the state is universally attributed to Grotius.[25] With respect to the acts of the state through its representatives, he concluded: 'The liability of one for acts of his servants without fault of his own does not belong to the law of nations, according to which this question has to be settled, but to municipal law . . . '.[26] Similarly, regarding acts of private individuals, he wrote: 'A civil community, just as any other community, is not bound by the act of individuals, apart from some act or neglect of its own.'[27] The notion of *culpa* as the source of and a condition to state responsibility has formed the centrepiece of the traditional jurisprudence of state responsibility. Indeed, it was not until the beginning of this century that serious doctrinal debate commenced with respect to the meaning and relevance of the concept of fault.[28] Since that point, however, the debate has been extremely robust, with the consequence that today it is possible to identify few points of consensus on the issue. Accioly has defined this doctrinal stalemate as essentially one of semantics: 'Il semble que la principale difficulté dans l'acception générale de faute, comme base de la responsabilité internationale, résulte de certaines différences sur le sens précis du mot.'[29] Working from this feasible premise, this section will seek to analyse the problem by considering the dominant perspectives on the content of the term 'fault'.

i. Fault as Culpa

The sense of fault embraced in the orthodox jurisprudence of state responsibility is in many ways quite similar to the notion of 'intention' which operates in tort law.[30] It refers to what is generally described as the 'psychological' attitude of the state with respect to the breach of the international rule.[31] Responsibility may occur, in accord with this concept of fault, only in the presence of the state's malicious intent (*dolus*) or culpable negligence (*culpa*).[32] The conclusion of the *Home Missionary Society* Tribunal is representative of the language found in the numerous cases articulating this

[25] See Eagleton, *supra* ch. 1 n. 4, at 208; *Force majeure* and 'Fortuitous Event' as Circumstances Precluding Wrongfulness: Survey of State Practice, International Judicial Decisions and Doctrine, UN Doc. A/CN 4/315, in ii *Yb. Int'l L. Comm'n* 61, at 190, UN Doc. A/CN 4/Ser.A/1978/Add. 1 (Pt. 1) (1978) (hereinafter cited as *Force maj.* Rpt.); Garcia-Amador, Draft, *supra* ch. 1 no. 3, at 14.

[26] Grotius, *De jure belli ac pacis, libri tres.*, II. c. xvii, xx (1625) trans. Kelsey, at 437.

[27] *Id.*, II. c. xxi, ii, at 523, See ch. 3, text commencing at n. 92.

[28] For a concise history of the debate see Eagleton, *supra* ch. 1 n. 4, at 211; *Force maj.* Rpt., *supra* n. 25, at 190; Garcia-Amador, Draft, *supra* ch. 1 n. 3, at 15.

[29] Accioly, 'Principes genéraux de la responsabilité internationale d'après la doctrine et la jurisprudence', i *Recueil des cours* 353, at 369 (1959).

[30] Accioly in fact views the confusion of tort concepts with the international sense of 'fault' as the source of the principal opposition to 'fault' among publicists. *Id.*, at 366. Nevertheless, the similarities are striking.

[31] *Force maj.* Rpt., *supra* n. 25, at 194–5.

[32] In the literature (and specifically in this work), the term *culpa* comprehends both *dolus* and culpable negligence. See *id.* at 194 n. 724.

perspective: 'It is a well-established principle of international law that no Government can be held responsible for the act of rebellious bodies of men committed in violation of its authority, where it is itself guilty of no breach of good faith, or of negligence in suppressing insurrection.'[33] Language of such import as to the fault of the state is, in fact, almost invariably present in the type of case which provides the greatest fodder for international arbitration: cases in which it is alleged that the state has failed to protect the interests of foreign states from the acts of private individuals.[34] As to the state's obligation to punish offenders harming such foreign interests, the Mexico–United States General Claims Commission, for example, defined the question of responsibility as 'whether what was done shows such a degree of negligence, defective administration of justice, or bad faith, that the procedure falls below the standards of international law.'[35] Although no such specific language is present, the decision in the *Corfu Channel* Case is often interpreted as evidencing the ICJ's adherence to this traditional notion of fault.[36] Lauterpacht and other eminent commentators have submitted that the Court's inquiry into Albania's knowledge of the laying of mines in the strait, actual or constructive, represents clear authority for the requirement of fault in the sense of intentional or negligent conduct.[37] As will be noted below, this reading has often been criticized.[38] Nevertheless, the endorsements of the notion of fault by dissenting judges Krylov and Ečer were unequivocal: 'The responsibility of a State in consequence of an international delinquency presupposes, at the very least, *culpa* on the part of that State.' (Krylov);[39] 'An act of a State injurious to another State is nevertheless not an international delinquency if committed neither wilfully and maliciously nor with culpable negligence.' (Ečer).[40]

Subject to variations in expression, the work of an impressive list of publicists reflects this basic perspective of the meaning of fault.[41] The majority

[33] The *Home Frontier and Foreign Missionary Society* Case (1920) (*US* v. *UK*), 6 R. Int'l Arb. Awards 42, at 44.

[34] See e.g. the *Alabama* Claims Arbitration (1872) (*US* v. *UK*), Moore, i *History and Digest of the International Arbitrations to which the United States Has Been a Party* 495, at 654 (1898) (hereinafter cited as Moore, *Arbitrations*); the *St Albans Raid* Case (1873) (*US* v. *UK*), Moore, iv *Arbitrations* 4042 (1898); the *Spanish Zone of Morocco* Claims (1925) (*UK* v. *Spain*), 2 R. Int'l Arb. Awards 615, at 644; the *Iloilo* Claims (1925) (*UK* v. *US*), 6 R Int'l Arb. Awards 158.

[35] The *Mecham* Case (1929) (*U.S.* v. *Mex.*), 4 R. Int'l Arb. Awards 440, at 443. See also the *Neer* Case (1926) (*US* v. *Mex.*), 4 R. Int'l Arb Awards 60, at 61.

[36] The *Corfu Channel* Case (*UK* v. *Alb.*), [1949] ICJ 4.

[37] See e.g. Oppenheim, i *International Law* 343 (Lauterpacht ed. 1955); M. Garcia-Mora, *International Responsibility for Hostile Acts of Private Persons Against Foreign States* 22 (1962).

[38] See text at n. 61 *infra*.

[39] The *Corfu Channel* Case (*UK* v. *Alb.*), [1949] ICJ 4, at 72 (Dissenting Opinion J. Krylov).

[40] *Id.*, at 128 (Dissenting Opinion J. Ecer) quoting Oppenheim, i *International Law* 311 (Lauterpacht ed. 1948).

[41] See, e.g. Accioly, *supra* n. 29, at 353; Brierly, *The Law of Nations* 289 (Waldock ed. 6th edn. (1963)); Oppenheim, *supra* n. 37, at 343; Rolin, 'Les Principes de droit international public', ii *Recueil des cours* 445 (1950).

of these authors view such *culpa* as the source and a requirement of responsibility for the breach of *any* international obligation.[42] A number of adherents to the same general concept of fault, however, do not agree as to its universal relevance.[43] In the view of Shoen and de Visscher, *culpa* is requisite to a finding of state responsibility only with respect to the obligations of the state to protect foreign interests from the acts of private individuals.[44] Strupp and Garcia-Amador take a somewhat more expansive approach in requiring such fault in all cases of breach by omission.[45] The language of certain arbitral awards also reflects this type of limited view of the role of fault in its traditional sense.[46] As to breaches not requiring such fault, each of these intermediate views accepts as the basis of responsibility the doctrinal foil to *culpa*—'objective' responsibility.

ii. Fault as Breach

The content of the 'objective' doctrine is readily described: it is not subjective *culpa* but simply the fact of a violation of international law that serves as the basis of a state's responsibility.[47] Only fault in the sense of a breach of obligation is required to be present. Hence, fault, from this perspective, becomes equivalent to the objective element of state responsibility itself.[48] Language suggesting this equation of fault with breach of obligation is in evidence at least as early as the *Jamaica* Case (1798): 'Where there is no fault, no omission of duty, there can be nothing whereon to support a charge of responsibility or justify a complaint.'[49] Yet, it was not until the creative and influential work of Anzilotti at the turn of the century that the doctrine of objective responsibility took form.[50] In his words:

La conclusion à laquelle il semble qu'on puisse arriver est donc que, en règle, en droit international l'*animus* de l'individual-organe n'est pas la cause ou la condition de la

[42] *Force maj.* Rpt., *supra* n. 25, at 186–93.

[43] For a summary of such intermediate theories see Garcia-Amador, Draft, *supra* ch. 1 n. 3, at 15; Eagleton, *supra* ch. 1 n. 4, at 212; *Force maj.* Rpt., *supra* n. 25, at 193.

[44] P. Schoen. *Die Völkerrechtliche Haftung der Staaten aus Unerlaubten Handlungen* 51–63 (1917); de Visscher, 'La Responsablité des états, ii *Bibliotheca Visseriana* 86 (1924).

[45] Strupp. *Éléments de droit international public universel, européen et americain* 330 (1930) and *Das Völkerrechtliche Delikt* 60 (1920); Garcia Amador, Draft, *supra* ch. 1 n. 3, at 17, 27.

[46] See e.g., *Différend concernant l'interprétation de l'Article 79* (*Italy* v. *Fr.*), 13 R. Int'l Arb. Awards 422, at 431–3 (1955).

[47] See generally Anzilotti, *Teoria generale della responsabilità dello stato nel diritto internazionale* (1902) (hereinafter cited as Anzilotti, *Teoria*); Anzilotti, 'La Responsabilité internationale des états à raison des dommages soufferts par des étrangers', 13 *RGDIP* 5 (1906) (hereinafter Anzilotti 'Responsabilité'); Anzilotti, *Cours de droit international* 496–501 (Gidel trans., 6th edn. 1929) (hereinafter cited as Anzilotti, *Cours*); Eagleton, *supra* ch. 1 n. 4, at 211; *Force maj.* Rpt., *supra* n. 25, at 188–201; Garcia-Amador, *supra* ch. 1 n. 1, at 15; Garcia-Mora, *supra* n. 37, at 25.

[48] See text at ch. 1 nn. 9–12 *supra*.

[49] The *Jamaica* Case (1798) (*UK* v. *US*), Moore, iv *International Adjudications* 489, at 499 (1931).

[50] See works of Anzilotti cited at n. 47 *supra*.

responsabilité, celle-ci nâit du seul fait de la violation d'un devoir international de l'État.[51]

From these beginnings, the objective doctrine now constitutes a well-established opposition, and perhaps the emerging majority, view among contemporary publicists.[52]

From Anzilotti's perspective, of course, the objective approach served to *replace* the doctrine of fault, not merely to give it new meaning or content. 'Nous pensons, quant à nous, que la théorie de la faut doit être ici mise absolument hors de cause.'[53] Language of this import is echoed in the work of many of his followers. Borchard, for example, states: 'The failure to perform a duty should suffice without a further attempt to prove a vague and uncertain fault.'[54] Jimenéz de Arechaga specifically rejects the need for an inquiry into fault: 'The concept of fault as the violation of a pre-existing obligation is, however, superfluous, because it reiterates the *objective element* of the *internationally wrongful act*.'[55] Nevertheless, the language of fault, limited to an objective sense, appears in many works written by proponents of the objective doctrine.[56] Illustrative is the conclusion of Salvioli: '[S]'il y a acte illicite, il y a faute, la faute consistant dans la violation d'une règle de droit. C'est la même chose.'[57] Consider, too, Cheng's assertion: 'Malice and negligence can neither be identified with, nor are they inherent in, the notion of fault.'[58] Although presenting certain semantic confusion, these two perspectives do not reflect any substantive conflict.[59] Advocates of the objective approach are united in their view that the fact of a breach of obligation, and not *culpa*, is the basis of state responsibility.

It must be submitted, for several reasons, that the objective doctrine appears the preferred approach. The key to its logic is that it does not deny that *culpa* may be a condition to state responsibility in a specific case. A requirement of fault in the subjective sense may arise, however, only out of the 'primary' obligation involved; *culpa* is not a condition imposed by the 'secondary' rules of state responsibility common to all international obligations. As explained by Amerasinghe: 'The basis [of state responsibility] will

[51] Anzilotti, *Cours, supra* n. 47, at 501.

[52] See Amerasinghe, *supra* ch. 1 n. 11, at 44–5; de Arechaga, *supra* ch. 1 n. 11, at 534; Brownlie, *System, supra* ch. 1 n. 2, at 38–46; Brownlie, *Principles of Public International Law* 436 (3rd edn. (1979)), de Beus, *supra* ch. 1 n. 13, at 128; Eagleton, *supra* ch. 1 n. 4, at 213; Kelsen, *Principles of International Law* 201 (2nd edn. (1966)); Personnaz, *La Réparation du préjudice en droit international public* 106 (1939); Starke, 'Imputability in International Delinquencies', 19 *Brit. Yb. Int'l L.* 104 (1938).

[53] Anzilotti, 'Responsabilité', *supra* n. 47, at 287.

[54] Borchard, 'Theoretical Aspects of the International Responsibility of States', 1 *Zeitschrift für Aüsland* (pt. 1), 223, at 226 (1929). See the *Caire* Case (1929) (*Fr.* v *Mex.*), 5 R. Int'l Arb. Awards 516, at 528.

[55] Jiménez de Arechaga, *supra* ch. 1 n. 11, at 535 (emphasis in original).

[56] See *Force maj.* Rpt., *supra* n. 25, at 195.

[57] Salvioli 'Les Règles generales de la paix', iv *Receuil des cours* 5, at 97 (1933).

[58] Cheng, *supra* ch. 1 n. 6, at 226.

[59] See Eagleton, *supra* ch. 1 n. 4, at 213.

vary with the content of the international obligation. This may be a strict basis or the basis of risk in some circumstances, while in others it may involve malice or culpable negligence or, conceivably, malice alone.'[60] It is perfectly consistent with the objective doctrine, then, to speak of a requirement of *culpa* dictated by the content of the specific obligation in question.

With this point in mind, it may be seen that decisions which appear supportive of the *culpa* perspective are in fact reconcilable with the objective theory. The *Corfu Channel* Case is representative. 'The knowledge postulated by the Court was necessary to determine that a pre-existing obligation had been violated, since only a state which knows that a minefield has been located in its territorial waters would be obliged to notify states of its existence.'[61] The condition of knowledge identified by the Court had its source, then, simply in the nature of the primary obligation; no generic requirement of *culpa* is implied.[62] A similar conclusion may be reached with respect to the large number of cases reciting that state responsibility for conduct of private individuals arises only when the state is malicious or negligent, i.e. it fails to exercise due diligence to prevent or punish private conduct.[63] Anzilotti makes the point quite succinctly:

> Le défaut de diligence est une inobservation du devoir imposé par le droit international, sans qu'il y ait alors à parler de faute au sens propre du mot [i.e., *culpa*]. L'Etat qui a usé de la diligence qu'il devait n'est point responsible; mais son defaut de responsabilité ne tient pas à une absence de faute, il vient de ce qu'il n'y a eu aucun acte contraire du droit des gens.[64]

The approach of those theorists taking intermediate courses, rejecting the objective theory and requiring *culpa* with respect to responsibility for failure of such due diligence, would seem, therefore, to arise out of a confusion of primary and secondary rules.[65] The objective doctrine, once again, does not deny that *culpa* may be prerequisite to responsibility; it only denies its universality as a secondary rule.

The analytical attraction of the objective theory lies, however, not only in this capacity to be reconciled with situations in which *culpa* plays a role. Objective responsibility, in fact, works successfully in regions in which the *culpa* perspective either obscures the analysis or, more critically, is simply conceptually inadequate. Cases in which the international obligation itself contains an element of *culpa* illustrate the fashion in which a search for *culpa* may contribute only confusion. Consider, for example, the obligation,

[60] Amerasinghe, *supra* ch. 1 n. 11, at 45.
[61] De Arechaga, *supra* ch. 1 n. 11, at 537.
[62] See Amerasinghe, *supra* ch. 1 n. 11, at 45; Brownlie, *System*, supra ch. 1 n. 2, at 43–4; Brownlie, *supra* n. 52, at 439; Garcia-Amador, Draft, *supra* ch. 1 n. 3, at 16.
[63] See text at ch. 1 nn. 9–11 *supra*. See generally de Beus, *supra* ch 1 n. 13, at 125–6.
[64] Anzilotti, 'Responsabilité', *supra* n. 47, at 291.
[65] See text at nn. 43–6 *supra*.

discussed above, not to aid or assist another state in its breach of international law.[66] By definition, there is no breach unless the state 'intends' to facilitate a violation by the recipient state of its obligations.[67] The conduct of the state constituting a breach, then, subsumes an element of *culpa*. The fact of such conduct inconsistent with the state's obligations suffices to trigger responsibility under the objective doctrine; the *culpa* approach, on the other hand, requires the beach to be intentional or negligent. To speak of such a requirement, external to the content of the obligation itself, would seem, at best, superfluous.[68]

Far more significant than this 'procedural' concern, however, is the failure of the *culpa* theory to account for international obligations which may be breached, with resulting state responsibility, in the absence of any element of *culpa*. As Starke has observed: 'If the original rule or provision of the convention does not envisage malice or culpable negligence, it is difficult to see how this can be invoked as a condition of the imputation and responsibility.'[69] In such cases, only the objective doctrine provides a sufficient and logical basis for responsibility.

The first general category of obligations devoid of any aspect of *culpa* consists simply of obligations breached by the affirmative acts of the state. *Culpa* can not properly be defined as a general condition to state responsibility for the acts of its organs or agents which violate international obligations.[70] The cases, in fact, appear quite uniform in this regard, whether considering the *culpa* of the individual agent or organ of the state or that of the abstract state itself. As to the individual, Meron concludes: 'The cases considered seem to suggest that not only is an element of malice not essential to the establishment of responsibility, but even a total absence of fault [as *culpa*] will not be fatal to the claim.'[71] The language of the *Jessie*, the *Thomas F. Bayard* and the *Pescawha* Case is representative:

It is unquestionable that the United States naval authorities acted *bona fide*, but though their *bona fides* might be invoked by the officers in explanation of their conduct to their own Government, its effect is merely to show that their conduct constituted an error in judgment, and any Government is responsible to other Governments for error in

[66] See text at nn. 18–24 *supra*.

[67] See text commencing at n. 24 *supra*.

[68] In Starke's words there exists no 'general floating requirement of malice or culpable negligence as a condition of responsibility'. Starke, *supra* n. 52, at 114–15.

[69] *Id.*, at 114.

[70] See Anzilotti, *Cours*, *supra* n. 47, at 501. The essence of Anzilotti's logic is that the fact of responsibility for the conduct of organs contrary to internal law proves that *culpa* is not required: how can there be *culpa* of the state when its will, expressed in its law, is violated? There is, on the other hand, always the possibility that a particular obligation may require, by its specific content, *culpa* to exist for a violation.

[71] Meron, 'International Responsibility of States for Unauthorized Acts of Their Officials', 33 *Brit. Yb. Int'l L.* 84, at 96 (1957).

judgment of its officials purporting to act within the scope of their duties and vested with power to enforce their demands.[72]

In short, malice or negligence on the part of the representatives of the state is not required as a condition to responsibility for the positive acts of those representatives.[73]

A parallel conclusion must be reached with respect to the attitude of the state itself, viewed as a collective entity, *vis-à-vis* the positive acts of its agents or organs. Perhaps the best expression of the fact that no *culpa* is requisite is the principle that the state may bear responsibility for the *ultra vires* acts of its representatives. The scope of this principle will be discussed below in the treatment of the subjective element of state responsibility.[74] Suffice it here to note that conduct of officials of the state directly contrary to the instructions of superior officials or in patent violation of the laws of the state may trigger responsibility. Hence, the will of the state, evidenced in its instructions and laws, may be categorically opposed to the conduct for which it is to be deemed responsible. One is left with the conclusion, precisely as Anzilotti argued, that the basis of such responsibility must be objective.[75]

The second category of obligations requiring no element of *culpa* are those obligations entailing 'strict responsibility', responsibility for failure to achieve a required or to prevent a prohibited result without consideration of intent or diligence.[76] The acknowledgment in international jurisprudence of the existence of such regimes is rather recent. Indeed, the place of strict responsibility as a current principle of customary law remains highly controversial. This issue will be treated at some length in Part II, as the doctrinal debate has centred on strict responsibility as an environmental norm.[77] For present purposes, it is sufficient to note the place of strict responsibility in international conventional law.[78] The Vienna Convention on Civil Liability for Nuclear Damage[79] and the Brussels Convention on the Liability of Operators of Nuclear Ships,[80] for example, explicitly impose upon the operators of nuclear installations and vessels, respectively, strict liability for damage arising out of operations. Although these conventions work

[72] *The Jessie, the Thomas F. Bayard, and the Pescawha* (1921) (*UK* v. *US*), 6 R. Int'l Arb. Awards 57, at 59.

[73] See Amerasinghe, *supra* ch. 1 n. 11, at 45; de Arechaga, *supra* ch 1 n. 11, at 535–6; Brownlie, *supra* n. 52, at 440–1; Garcia-Amador, Draft, *supra* ch, 1 n. 3, at 17; Sohn and Baxter, *supra* ch. 1 nbn. 11, at 168–9. *See also* publicists cited at nn. 44, 45.

[74] See ch. 3, commencing at n. 73.

[75] See Anzilotti, *Teoria*, *supra* n. 47, at 172–3.

[76] If one posits a general obligation to prevent state representatives from breaching the more concrete obligations of the state, state responsibility for positive acts of its organs is in a sense a manifestation of strict liability for breach of such obligation.

[77] See ch. 8, text commencing at n. 5.

[78] See *id.*, at n. 22.

[79] Done 21 May 1963, 2 *Int'l Legal Materials* 727 (1963), art. XVIII.

[80] Done 25 May 1962, 37 *Am. J. Int'l L.* 268 (1963), art. II (not yet in force). See Hydeman and Berman, *International Control of Nuclear Maritime Activities* 27 (1960).

principally to unify municipal law regarding civil liability, they each require the licensing state to indemnify the victim for any deficiency in the operator's payments.[81] As Handl persuasively observes: 'It would seem that if states become liable *vis-à-vis* private claimants on a subsidiary basis, they must a fortiori be liable internationally, i.e., *vis-à-vis* the victim State.'[82] In any event, the expression of strict responsibility in the Convention on International Liability for Damage Caused by Space Objects is distinctly direct: 'A launching state shall be absolutely liable to pay compensation for damage caused by its space objects on the surface of the Earth or to aircraft in flight.'[83] Sohn and Baxter in fact appear to view all treaty obligations requiring or prohibiting a result as implicity subject to such a strict regime:

> [L]iability for a violation of a treaty which causes harm to an alien does not necessarily rest upon an intent to cause injury or the creation of an unreasonable risk of injury through failure to exercise due care. . . . If a State has exacted taxes from an alien which it is not entitled to collect by reason of a convention on double taxation, this act is wrongful solely by reason of its being a violation of the treaty.[84]

Putting aside for the moment issues of scope, it should be quite clear that strict responsibility is at least an active principle.[85] Critically, the *culpa* doctrine neither contemplates nor explains the phenonema of responsibility based on a strict standard. The objective theory does do so, precisely because it is unconcerned with the presence or absence of a *culpa* element in the primary obligation.[86]

One further permutation of the objective doctrine should be noted. Certain authorities, though advocating objective responsibility, speak of a requirement that a breach upon which responsibility is based must be 'voluntary' or consistent with the 'will' of the state.[87] Brownlie's language is illustrative: 'Technically, objective responsibility rests on the doctrine of the voluntary act: provided that agency and causal connexion are established, there is a breach of duty by result alone.'[88] Ago views the qualification of voluntariness simply

[81] Vienna Conv., art. 8; Brussels Conv., art 11.

[82] Handl, 'State Liability for Accidental Transnational Environmental Damage by Private Persons', 74 *Am. J. Int'l L.* 525, 530 n. 30 (1980).

[83] Convention on International Liability for Damage Caused by Space Objects, done at London, Moscow and Washington 29 Mar. 1972, entered into force 10 Sept. 1973, 24 UST 2391 (1972), TIAS 7762, reprinted in 10 *Int'l Legal Materials* 965 (1971). See generally Cheng, 'Convention on International Liability for Damage Caused by Space Objects', i *Manual on Space Law* 83 (Jasentuliyana and Lee eds 1979); Foster, 'The Convention on International Liability for Damage Caused by Space Objects', 10 *Can Yb. Int'l L.* 137 (1972); Malik, 'Liability for Damage Caused by Space Activities', 6 *Indian J. Int'l L.* 335 (1966); Theraulaz, *Droit de l'espace ét responsabilite* 229 ff. (1971); Wiewiorowska, 'Some Problems of State Responsibility in Outer Space Law', 7 *J. Space L.* 23 (1979).

[84] Sohn and Baxter, *supra* ch. 1 n. 11, at 169. See Cheng, *supra* ch. 1 n. 6, at 226.

[85] See ch. 8 text commencing at n. 5.

[86] See text at nn. 47–59 *supra*.

[87] See Jiménez de Arechaga, *supra* ch. 1 n. 11, at 544; Brownlie, *supra* n. 52, at 426; the *Corfu Channel* Case (*UK* v. *Alb.*), [1949] ICJ 4, at 65 (Dissenting Opinion Judge Badawi).

[88] Brownlie, *supra* n. 52, at 436.

as a manifestation of the principle of *force majeure*.[89] Yet, it must be submitted that reference to the requirement of a 'voluntary' act as a generic aspect of objective responsibility is not appropriate. First, such references are not necessary. If a breach of an obligation can not occur when conduct is involuntary or caused by *force majeure*, this may be viewed as an aspect of the definition of the specific obligation itself. Cheng puts it succinctly:

> [A]n unlawful act must be one emanating from the free will of the wrongdoer. There is no unlawful act if the event takes place independently of his will and in a manner uncontrollable by him, in short, if it results from *vis major*, for the obligation, the violation of which constitutes an unlawful act, ceases when its observance becomes impossible.[90]

Such a distinction, in fact, seems requisite given the existence of certain obligations which may not be subject to exculpation even in circumstances of impossibility or *force majeure*.[91] Obligations of such 'absolute' character would seem to disprove the existence of any generic condition of voluntariness.[92]

Judge Azevedo, in his dissent in the *Corfu Channel* Case, remarked: 'The notion of *culpa* (faute) is always changing and undergoing a slow process of evolution; moving away from the classical elements of imprudence and negligence, it tends to draw nearer to the system of objective responsibility.'[93] One can only observe that this process seem inevitable. Only a definition of fault in the purely objective sense, equivalent to breach of obligation, appears to serve adequately as the basis of responsibility for breach of the full spectrum of international obligations.[94]

[89] Ago, Eighth Report on State Responsibility, ii *Yb. Int'l L. Comm'n* 3, at 57, UN Doc A/CN 4/318 and Add 1–4 (1979).

[90] Cheng, *supra* ch. 1 n. 6, at 223.

[91] See e.g. Space Objects Convention, *supra* n. 83. See comments noting that certain obligations regarding ultrahazardous activites are not subject to any *force majeure* exception. ILC, Summary Records of the 31st Session, i *Yb. Int'l L. Comm'n* 203, UN Doc A/CN 4/Ser. A/1979.

[92] As to this distinction between 'absolute' and 'strict' liability, see Goldie, 'Liability for Damage and the Progressive Development of International Law', 14 *Int'l & Comp. L.Q.* 1189, at 1215 (1965); Winfield, 'The Myth of Absolute Liability,' 42 *L.Q. Rev.* 37 (1926).

[93] The *Corfu Channel* Case (*UK* v. *Alb.*), [1949] ICJ 4, at 85 (Dissenting Opinion Judge Azevedo).

[94] Ch. 8 will, therefore, consider the issue of whether the specific primary obligations relating to the environment require an element of *culpa*.

3

State as Actor: The Subjective Element

To reiterate, the 'subjective' component of state responsibility refers to the identification of the state as the actor engaged in conduct violative of an international obligation. 'For international responsibility to exist, the damage must be the result of a violation, by the State itself, of some international rule.'[1] The 'state', however, is an abstraction. Conduct, in a material sense, remains the exclusive province of natural persons.[2] To satisfy the subjective element, therefore, the conduct of individuals must be attributed juridically to the state.[3] Analysis of this process of attribution demands first an identification of those individual members of the collective represented by the state whose conduct may be so attributed.[4] That accomplished, there arise certain subsidiary issues relating to the character of attributable conduct. The following discussion will consider these issues, in turn, with respect to the two categories of individuals within the state: those that may be characterized, individually or collectively, as organs or representatives of the state, and private individuals.[5]

A. STATE ORGANS OR REPRESENTATIVES

The Permanent Court in the *German Settlers in Poland* Advisory Opinion acknowledged the truism that the abstract state depends upon individuals charged to act on its behalf to express or realize its will: 'States can only act by and through their agents and representatives.'[6] A central aspect of the

[1] Guerrero, Report, *supra* ch. 1 n. 8, at 241.

[2] 'Being a juridical person, rather than a natural one, the State must act or fail to act through the conduct of persons, whether acting individually or collectively or as members of a collegiate entity.' Sohn and Baxter, *supra* ch. 1 n. 11, at 247.

[3] As to the process of attribution generally, see Accioly, *supra* ch. 2 n. 29, at 371–91; Ago, 2nd Rpt., *supra* ch 1 n. 3, at 189; Amerasinghe, 'Imputability in the Law of State Responsibility for Injuries to Aliens', 22 *R. Égyptienne droit int'l*, 91 (1966); Cheng, *supra* ch. 1 n. 6, at 180–207; Eagleton, *supra* ch. 1 n. 4, at 45; Starke, *supra* ch. 2 n. 52, *passim*.

[4] The term 'attribution' here replaces the term 'imputation' found in most of the traditional literature. Attribution is favoured by the ILC to avoid confusion with imputation in its municipal sense. See Ago, 3rd Rpt., *supra* ch. 1 n. 16, at 214. Perhaps more importantly, imputation connotes a fictional process of attaching responsibility. The international process of attribution involves no fiction; the author of the illegal conduct is the state.

[5] As the discussion below will indicate, this distinction is not absolute. An individual may be deemed an organ or representative of the state for general or specific purposes. The question is the characterization of the individual with respect to the wrongful conduct.

[6] The *German Settlers in Poland* Case (*Germ.* v. *Pol.*), [1923] PCIJ, Ser. B. no. 6, at 22.

subjective element of state responsibility is that the conduct of individuals or groups vested with a part of the public authority of the state, i.e. its organs and representatives, is attributed to the state.[7] In Anzilotti's words: 'L'activité de l'État, c'est en definitive l'activité d'individus dûment autorisées par la loi. L'activité des agents de l'État étant l'activité de l'État, la violation du droit international qu'ils commettant constitue donc une violation commise par l'État lui-même.'[8] Eagleton echoed this conclusion: 'When the State invests such an individual with its authority, his acts become the acts of the State itself, for which the State must accept responsibility under international law.'[9] The threshold question, then, is which individuals or groups are appropriately denominated, from the perspective of international responsibility, the agents or organs of the state.

i. *Municipal Definition*

The starting point for this inquiry is the municipal law of the state. Ago has described it as 'indisputable', based on strikingly consistent practice, that conduct of individuals or collectives designated state organs or agents under the domestic legal order is treated as conduct of the state.[10] Such an acknowledgement by the state that the subject wields authority delegated by and on behalf of the state will not be questioned by international law for the purposes of the attribution of conduct.[11] Thus, the draft articles on state responsibility produced by the ILC provide unequivocally that 'conduct of any State organ having that status under the internal law of that State shall be considered as an act of the State concerned under international law, provided that organ was acting in that capacity in the case in question.'[12]

The work of the ILC reflects a similar consensus that the function of the organ or representative within the structure of the state does not affect its capacity to implicate the responsibility of the state.[13] From the perspective of international law, 'the State is seen only in its unity and not divided into its different powers.'[14] It is this principle, Ago writes, which 'requires that the

[7] See *Case concerning United States Diplomatic and Consular Staff in Tehran* (*US v. Iran*), [1980] ICJ 3, at 29 (Judgment of 24 May 1980). See generally Ago, 3rd Rpt., *supra* ch. 1 n. 16 at 239 ff; Anzilotti, 'Responsabilité', *supra* ch. 2 n. 47, at 164; Borchard, *supra* ch. 1 n. 19, at 189; Guerrero, Report, *supra* ch. 1 n. 8 at 241; Sohn and Baxter, *supra* ch. 1 n. 11, at 247.

[8] Anzilotti, 'Responsabilité', *supra* ch. 2 n. 47, at 291.

[9] Eagleton, *supra* ch. 1 n. 4, at 44–5.

[10] Ago, 3rd Rpt., *supra* ch. 1 n. 16, at 238.

[11] See *id.*, at 238–43; Amerasinghe, *supra* n. 3, at 102; Sohn and Baxter, *supra* ch. 1 n. 11, at 247–57; ILC, Summary Records of the 26th Session, i *Yb. Int'l L. Comm'n* 13, UN Doc. A/CN 4/ Ser. A (1974) (Comments of Kearney).

[12] ILC 1973 Rpt., *supra* ch. 1 n. 12, at 191. The function of the final clause regarding the capacity in which the organ acts is treated below commencing at n. 73 *infra*.

[13] Ago, 3rd Rpt., *supra* ch. 1 n. 16, at 243–53.

[14] *Id.*, at 248. 'It is to be emphasized that the claimant state is unconcerned with the particular agent of whose act complaint is made. The organization of the state and the apportionment of its powers among its various agents is not a matter of interest to the law of nations . . .' Eagleton, *supra* ch. 1 n. 4, at 73–4.

acts or omissions of every individual or collective member of the state machinery be treated in the same way as acts or omissions of the state at the international level, and that, should the occasion arise, they be capable of incurring its international responsibility.'[15] The fashion in which the state elects to organize and delegate its powers is then, in this context, a purely internal matter; attribution for external responsibility may occur with respect to the conduct of individuals wielding any aspect of state authority.[16]

The validity of the foregoing conclusion may be readily demonstrated with respect to each of the basic sectors of governmental power; as shall be demonstrated in Parts II and III, the conduct of each is in fact relevant to the performance of international environmental duties. The attribution of legislative conduct, for example, was held appropriate in the Permanent Court of International Justice in the *Case Concerning Certain German Interests in Polish Upper Silesia*.[17] In the course of its opinion, the Court observed: 'From the standpoint of international law and of the Court which is its organ, municipal laws are merely facts which express the will and constitute and activities of States, in the same manner as do legal decisions or administrative measures.'[18] Eagleton, expressing the consensus of publicists, summarizes: 'The State, then, may be held responsible either for positive acts of legislation in contradiction to international law, or for the failure to provide legislation necessary in order to fulfill its international obligations.'[19] Similar unanimity may be found regarding the conduct of individuals performing the judicial functions of the state.[20] The PCIJ noted specifically in the *Lotus* decision that the actions of the courts of the state may support an asssertion of state responsibility.[21] Sufficient proof of this conclusion may be found in the substantial body of arbitral awards attributing to the state, and basing

[15] Ago, 3rd Rpt., *supra* ch. 1 n. 16, at 253. Ago continues: '[O]f course, there are organs which, by the nature of their functions, will in practice have more opportunity of doing so than others; but the great variety of international obligations precludes any prior distinction between organs which can commit internationally wrongful acts and those which can not.' *Id.*

[16] The Sohn and Baxter draft describes two basic categories of persons through which the state acts: (*a*) 'organs' and 'agencies' (including heads of state and 'any legislative, deliberative, executive, administrative, or judicial organ or agency'), and (*b*) 'officials' and 'employees' (including 'both a civilian official or employee of a State and any member of the armed forces or of a para-military organization'). Sohn and Baxter, *supra* ch. 1 n. 11, at 249.

[17] *Case Concerning Certain German Interests in Polish Upper Silesia*, (*Germ.* v. *Pol.*), [1926] PCIJ Ser. A., no. 7 (Merits).

[18] *Id.*, at 19.

[19] Eagleton, *supra* ch. 1 n. 4, at 66. See Ago, 3rd Rpt., *supra* ch. 1 n. 16., at 246; Christenson, 'The Doctrine of Attribution in State Responsibility', in *Injuries to Aliens*, ed Lillich, *supra* ch. 1 n. 2, at 321, 330; Jiménez de Arechaga, *supra* ch. 1 n. 11, at 545; Borchard, *supra* ch. 1 n. 19, at 181; Brownlie, *System*, *supra* ch. 1 n. 2 at 142–3; Garcia-Amador, Draft, *supra* ch. 1 n. 3, at 22; Hoijer, 'La Responsabilité internationale des états, en matière d'actes législatifs', 4 RGDIP 577 (1929).

[20] See generally Ago, 3rd Rpt., *supra* ch. 1 n. 16, at 246; Amerasinghe, *supra* ch. 1 n. 11, at 53; Brownlie, System, *supra* ch. 1 n. 2, at 144; Eustathiades, *La Responsabilité internationale de l'état pour les actes des organes judiciaires et le problème du déni de justice en droit international* (1936); Sohn and Baxter, *supra* ch. 1 n. 11, at 249.

[21] The *SS Lotus* Case (*Fr.* v. *Turk.*), [1927] PCIJ Ser. a., no. 10, at 24.

responsibility upon, the judiciary's 'denials of justice', i.e. breaches of international standards of judicial procedural or substantive behaviour.[22]

It would seem safe to conclude that most cases of international responsibility have arisen out of the attribution to the state of the acts of individuals vested with the third element of public power: executive or administrative authority.[23] The examples are extremely diverse: responsibility has been found with respect to acts of the police,[24] the armed forces,[25] consular officials,[26] heads of state,[27] and, generally, administrative officials of every description.[28] Certain scholars, most notably Borchard, have suggested that conduct of 'minor' officials may not be so attributed; state responsibility may only arise for a failure to punish such officials.[29] Cases which appear to support this conclusion are, however, properly viewed as resting on the requirement that the claimant exhaust available local remedies.[30] Eagleton is most articulate on this point:

> [I]f damages were denied in these cases, it was not because the injury was caused by a minor official, for whom the government was not responsible, but because local remedies had not been exhausted; and if damages were awarded, in the case of such inferior authorities, it was usually because of the insufficiency, or failure in operation, of these local remedies . . . Practice does not justify the conclusion that no responsibility exists for injurious acts by inferior officials of the state: it merely reveals the fact

22 See e.g. the *Chattin* Case (1927) (*US* v. *Mex.*), 4 R. Int'l Arb. Awards 282; the *De Galvan* Case (1927) (*Mex.* v. *US*), 4 R. Int'l Arb. Awards 273; cases collected in Digest of the Decisions of International Tribunals Relating To State Responsibility, ii *Yb. Int'l L. Comm'n* 132, UN Doc. A/CN 4/169 (1964) (hereinafter cited as Case Digest), at 143 ff. See also Eagleton, 'Denial of Justice In International Law', 22 *Am. J. Int'l L.* 538 (1928); Fitzmaurice, 'The Meaning of Denial of Justice', 13 *Brit. Yb. Int'l L.* 93 (1932), Freeman, *The International Responsibility of States for Denial of Justice* (1938).

23 The tripartite division is only used to illustrate the point that any species of authority delegated may trigger responsibility. The division is not universally apparent in the organization of states. A rigid adherence to this structure in the process of determining the propriety of attribution is, therefore, not appropriate.

24 See e.g. the *Mallen* Case (1927) (*Mex.* v. *US*), 4 R. Int'l Arb. Awards 173; the *Roper* Case (1927) (*US* v. *Mex.*), 4 R. Int'l Arb. Awards 145; *Filartiga* v. *Pẽna-Irala*, 577 F. Supp. 860 (ED NY 1984).

25 See e.g. the *Caire* Case (1929) (*Fr.* v. *Mex.*), 5 R. Int'l Arb. Awards 516; *Earnshaw and Others*: *The Zafiro* Case (1925) (*UK* v. *US*), 6 R. Int'l Arb. Awards 160; the *Youmans* Case (1926) (*US* v. *Mex.*), 4 R. Int'l Arb. Awards 110.

26 See e.g. the *Hemming* Case (1920) (*UK* v. *US*), 6 R Int'l Arb. Awards 51.

27 See e.g. the *Aguilar-Amory & Royal Bank of Canada* Claims (1923) (UK v. Costa Rica), 1 R. Int'l Arb. Awards 369.

28 The *Jessie, the Thomas F. Bayard and the Pescawha* (1921) (*UK* V. *US.*), 6 R. Int'l Arb. Awards 57 (revenue officers); the *Deutz* Case (1929) (*US* v. *Mex.*), 4 R. Int'l Arb. Awards 472 (textile contracting agents); the *Landlear* Claim (1922) (*US* v. *Peru*), 1 R. Int'l Arb. Awards 347 (government agency working guano deposits); the *Rudloff* Case (1903) (*US* v. *Venez.*), 9 R. Int'l Arb. Awards 244 (minister of works and provincial governor).

29 Borchard, *supra* ch. 1 n. 19, at 189 ff. See Harvard Research Draft Convention on Responsibility of States, 23 *Am. J. Int'l L.* 133, at 165–6 (Supp. 1929).

30 See Brownlie, *supra* ch. 2 n. 52, at 447; Cheng, *supra* ch. 1 n. 6 at 195; Eagleton, *supra* ch. 1 n. 4, at 48–51.

that, due to domestic legislation, local remedies may more often be found against the acts of minor officials, and less frequently against those of superior officials.[31]

Freed from the exhaustion requirement by agreement of the States, the Mexico–United States General Claims Commission clearly rejected any general distinction based on the status of the representative of the state.[32] The relevance of status is, moreover, denied by almost all contemporary publicists; there is current consensus that the conduct of any administrative or executive official may generate state responsibility.[33] Article 6 of the ILC draft provides a concise summary with respect to 'organs', denoting individuals and collective entities, defined by internal law as state representatives:

> The conduct of an organ of the State shall be considered as an act of that state under international law, whether that organ belongs to the constituent, legislative, executive, judicial or other power, whether its functions are of an international or an internal character and whether it holds a superior or a subordinate position in the organization of the State.[34]

ii. Objective or International Definition

Identification of the individuals within the state whose conduct may be attributed to the state may not be completed simply by reference to municipal law.[35] Contrary to certain earlier opinion, it now seems quite clear that, even if an individual or group is not designated in the internal legal order as a representative of the state, international law may operate independently to treat it as such and attribute its actions to the state.[36] Two points, however, are to be emphasized: (*a*) the converse process will not occur, i.e. the designation of an 'organ' by the state will be respected; and (*b*) the independent definition operates solely to fix responsibility on the international plane—the state's definition of its 'organs' is not disturbed for any other internal or external purpose.[37] The rationale of imposing an 'objective' determination at all relates, once again, to the principle of the essential unity of the state *vis-à-vis* the international community. As noted above, the fashion in which the state elects to organize to achieve its objectives is not a matter with which international law is concerned.[38] The international order imposes

[31] Eagleton, *supra* ch. 1 n. 4, at 48–9.

[32] The *Quintanilla* Case (1926) (*Mex.* v. *US*), 4 R. Int'l Arb. Awards 101; the *Roper* Case (1927) (*US* v. *Mex.*), 4 R. Int'l Arb. Awards 145; the *Massey* Case (1927) (*US* v. *Mex.*), 4 R. Int'l Arb. Awards 155.

[33] See Christenson, *supra* n. 19, at 333; de Arechaga, *supra* ch. 1 n. 11, at 547; Ago, 3rd Rpt., *supra* ch. 1 n. 16, at 213; Brownlie, *System*, *supra* ch. 1, n. 2 at 134–5; Brownlie, *supra* ch. 2 n. 52, at 447; Garcia-Amador, Draft *supra* ch. 1 n. 3, at 23; ILC, Summary Records of the 25th Session, 1 *Yb. Int'l L. Comm'n*, at 53, UN Doc. A/CN/Ser. A (1973). (Comments of Kearney); Meron, *supra* ch. 2 n. 71, at 98.

[34] ILC 1973 Rpt., *supra* ch. 2 n. 2, at 193.

[35] See Comments of Kearney, ILC 1974 Sum. Rec., *supra* n. 11, at 25.

[36] See Ago, 3rd Rpt., *supra* ch. 1 n. 16, at 234.

[37] *Id.*, at 237.

[38] See text at nn. 14–16 *supra*.

no impediments either to decentralization through the delegation of authority to individuals outside the formal machinery of the state or to extreme centralization. The degree of such centralization, however, ought not to reduce the international responsibility of the state for activities conducted for the state's public purposes. International law, therefore, seeks objectively to identify those individuals or collectives that in specific or general circumstances, ought to be treated as representatives of the state.[39]

Several distinct sets of cases illustrate the character of this objective process. In a number of such cases the formal organs of one state are, with respect to specific conduct, treated as the agents of another state.[40] In the *Chevreau* Case, for example, the negligent loss of certain documents by the British Consul in Persia, while temporarily in charge of the French consulate, could only be attributed to France, as the state on whose behalf the conduct occurred.[41] Similarly, a French court concluded, considering international law on the subject of a claim against France for negligent failure of its police to prevent the assassination of the heir to the throne of Tunisia:

> At the time in question police powers were exercised by the French authorities, but notwithstanding that they were so exercised, such exercise of power was undertaken for and on behalf of the Tunisian State. It follows in the present case only responsibility of that State can be taken into account . . . .[42]

Ago describes the governing principle in such cases as follows: '[A]n act or omission committed by the organ of one State in the performance of functions on behalf of another State, in whose interests it has been requested to act, must be considered at the international level as an act of that other State.'[43] In a technical sense, then, the organ is objectively defined as the organ of that state whose public function it performs with the conduct in question—regardless of the fact that municipal law would not concur in this designation.

Further illustrations of the objective determination involve collective institutions performing 'public' functions yet maintaining a legal identity separate from the state.[44] Perhaps the clearest example of such institutions are

[39] See ch. 10 for a discussion of this objective analysis with respect to flag vessels.

[40] See generally Ago, 3rd Rpt., *supra* ch. 1 n. 16, at 267 ff.

[41] The *Chevreau* Case (1931) (*Fr.* v. *UK*), 2 R. Int'l Arb. Awards, 1113.

[42] *Prince Sliman Bey* v. *Minister for Foreign Affairs*, [1959] D. Jur. 357, trans. in 28 *Int'l L. Rep.* (1963), at 79.

[43] Ago, 3rd Rpt., *supra* ch. 1 n. 16, at 269.

[44] 'The emergence and proliferation of public institutions is a phenomenon of our time, which is marked today by a tendency towards progressive differentiation and a wider separation between the organization of these institutions and the administration, structures, and methods of the State. The diversity of the tasks of common interest which the community itself has to perform in a modern society, the ever-increasing number of services which only the community is able to provide, the gradual extension of these services to the most widely different sectors of economic, social and cultural life, the fact that they are often of a technical nature and thus require autonomy of decision and action and the possession of special qualifications, the need to make procedures more flexible and simplify controls in order to increase the efficiency of the service—these, in short, are the main causes of the phenomenon.' *Id.*, at 254. See Amerasinghe, *supra* ch. 1 n. 11, at 102; Lenoble, 'Responsabilité internationale des états et controle territorial', 16 *Rev. belge droit int'l* 95, at 101–3 (1981–2).

the subsidiary governments within the state—local, district, or federal—whose conduct is uniformly attributed to the state under international law.[45] Rather less clear authority exists for the attribution to the state of conduct of a political movement or party which is deemed the effective 'repository of public power'.[46] Although precedents are few, the ILC has concluded that an 'established rule' exists which extends such attribution to conduct of any entity within the state 'empowered, if only exceptionally and to a limited extent, to exercise specified functions which are akin to those normally exercised by organs of the State'.[47] The problem, of course, is in the delimitation of this principle. Different approaches, focusing on either the 'public' nature of the function or the authority of the entity, were evident in the ILC discussions.[48] Ushakov, for example, advocated a strict definition in terms of delegated legislative, judicial, and executive authority.[49] Kearney articulated a broader view, referring to institutions which, 'in a public capacity, provided specific services for the community or performed functions considered to concern the community.'[50] A number of participants seem to have favoured such a focus on the 'public character' of the function performed.[51] The final formulation, however, refers only to entities 'empowered by the internal law of that State to exercise elements of governmental authority.'[52]

A subsidiary issue, of great significance in the environmental context given the industrial or commercial source of most pollution, is the application of the concepts of 'public' authority and function to commercial activity.[53] Nowhere does the ILC appear to have dealt directly with the problem of how to treat commercial entities with which the state is intimately involved but

[45] See e.g. the *Pellat* Case (1929) (*Fr.* v. *Mex.*), 5 R. Int'l Arb. Awards, at 536. See Ago, 3rd Rpt., supra ch. 1 n. 16, at 257–62; Ago, Fourth Report on State Responsibility, ii *Yb. Int'l L. Comm'n*, 71, UN Doc. A/CN 4/264 and Add 1 (1972); Queneudec, *La Responsabilité internationale de l'état pour les fautes personnelles de ses agents* 69 (1966).

[46] See the *Dame Mosse* Case (1953) (*Fr.* v. *Italy*), 13 R. Int'l Arb. Awards 486; Lenoble, *supra* n. 44, at 102; Queneudec, *supra* n. 45, at 520; Bouvé, 'The National Boycott as an International Delinquency', 28 *Am. J. Int'l L.* 19 (1934). *Contra* Lauterpacht, 'Boycott in International Relations', 14 *Brit. Yb. Int'l L.* 125 (1933).

[47] ILC, 1974 Rpt., *supra* ch. 1 n. 18, at 282; Sohn and Baxter, *supra* ch. 1 n. 11, at 250.

[48] See ILC, 1974 Sum. Rec., *supra* n. 11, at 8–30, 32–53. The delimitation issue is in many ways analogous to the issue of 'state action' in US constitutional law. A material element of state involvement in an enterprise is required to support the intervention of federal law through the 14th Amendment. Hence, issues such as the 'public function' of apparently private activities have been considered at length—without any definition, as yet, of a clear rule of decision. See e.g. *Evans* v. *Newton*, 382 US 296 (1966) (park was public function); *Jackson* v. *Metropolitan Edison Co.*, 419 US 345 (1974) (electric company was not). See generally Tribe, *American Constitutional Law* 1147–74 (1978); Christenson, *supra* n. 19, at 341–5.

[49] ILC, 1974 Sum. Rec., *supra* n. 11, at 14–20 (Comments of Ushakov).

[50] *Id.*, at 14 (Comments of Kearney). Kearney later expressed a view more supportive of the delegated authority approach. *Id.*, at 25.

[51] See *id.*, at 8 (Comments of Ago) and 11 (Comments of Calle y Calle).

[52] ILC, 1974 Rpt., *supra* ch. 1 n. 18, at 277, 282–3.

[53] See extensive discussion with respect to flag vessels in ch. 10.

which possess a legal identity distinct from the state.[54] Ushakov's advocacy of a formulation focusing on the delegation of traditional aspects of authority arose out of his argument that state 'ownership' of an enterprise was not a relevant issue, since all property is 'owned' by the state in certain political systems.[55] Yet, even this position only obliquely touches the point. Should legally independent commercial entities with a relationship to the state ever be viewed as exercising aspects of 'public' authority?

One of the few efforts to consider the issue directly suggests a linkage to the issue of state jurisdictional immunity: Sohn and Baxter concluded that responsibility for the conduct of a commercial entity with a juristic identity separate from the centralized state, regardless of state ownership or other involvement, will only attach if the entity enjoys state jurisdictional immunity.[56] Several observations are in order. It is, appropriately, implicit in this formulation that even clearly commercial conduct of organs with a legal identity as part of the state is attributed to the state. Moreover, as to distinct legal entities, the positive side of the immunity linkage is quite persuasive. A claim or rule of immunity constitutes an acknowledgement that the entity is in fact, from an internal perspective, a state organ.[57] It must be submitted, however, that the converse linkage, the denial of responsibility in the absence of immunity, seems inappropriate. 'The rationale [of state immunity] rests equally on the dignity of the foreign nation, its organs and representatives, and on the functional need to leave them unencumbered in the pursuit of their mission.'[58] These concerns, which may justify the non-application of 'intrusive' local jurisdiction, do not appear relevant to the issue of state responsibility.[59] If the state is indeed the actor, it should be deemed responsible for its actions regardless of the position it may take, for any of a host of political or economic reasons, on the issue of state immunity.

The question remains in what circumstances, if any, should the conduct of a legally distinct commercial entity be attributed to the state? Any categorical denial that commercial activity may be a public function or a manifestation of state authority subject to delegation

> does not rest on any sound logical basis; it involves making assumptions as to what are the proper functions of government which might be justifiable assumptions according

[54] The only reference to the matter is a footnote citation, without substantive comment, to Sohn and Baxter. See ILC, 1974 Rpt., *supra* ch. 1 n. 18, at 282 n. 583.

[55] ILC, 1974 Sum. Rec., *supra* n. 11, at 19–20.

[56] Sohn and Baxter, *supra* ch. 1 n. 11, at 256–7. This is true if immunity is afforded internally or claimed internationally. *Id.*, at 257. See discussion in Christenson, *supra* n. 19, at 330, 332–3.

[57] See text at n. 11 *supra*.

[58] Brownlie, *supra* ch. 2 n. 52, at 326.

[59] Friedmann implicitly reaches this conclusion in arguing that state responsibility may expand, given the 'gradual intrusion of the state into spheres which constituted formerly a reserve of the individual', without a corresponding expansion of state jurisdictional immunities. Friedmann, 'The Growth of State Control over the Individual and Its Effect upon the Rules of International State Responsibility', 19 *Brit. Yb. Int'l L.* 118 (1938).

to the laissez-faire theories of the nineteenth century but may seem arbitrary today in a world community which contains socialist and communist as well as capitalist states.[60]

The Supreme Court of the United States has observed that there is 'no international usage which regards the maintenance and advancement of the economic welfare of a people in time of peace as any less a public purpose than the maintenance and training of a naval force.'[61] The state, of course, ought not to be deemed the actor with respect to all commercial activity in the state, however important the advancement of commerce to the society. It would seem that the most appropriate key to attribution with respect to commercial entities would be the state's own perspective of the 'public' character or function of the entity. As noted in the ILC discussions, if the state itself views a matter as sufficiently important to treat it as a matter of public concern, it should be respected as public by the rest of the world.[62] The state's own conduct provides the best evidence of the state's definition of public versus private commercial conduct. The actions of the centralized state are, by definition, taken pursuant to public authority and in pursuit of public objectives. When the state elects to act in a central role in a commercial enterprise, through organization, ownership, capitalization, receipt of profits, administration and similar involvements, that action dictates that the entity be treated, at least for purposes of international attribution, as a 'public' representative of the state.[63]

To return from this brief but important excursion, the final category of cases in which the objective determination of state representatives is illustrated relates to individuals deemed private in the internal legal order.[64] The most frequently cited example remains *Earnshaw and Others*: The *Zafiro* Case in which the United States was required to pay compensation for damage caused by a civilian crew on shore leave.[65] The interpretation of the case which suggests the objective analysis is that the conduct of the crew was an act of the state since the vessel was commanded by a naval officer and was operating in support of the naval fleet.[66] Given the language of the award, however, the negligent failure of the naval officer to provide adequate supervision appears to have been the state conduct to which responsibility attached.[67] A better

[60] Brierly, *supra* ch. 2 n. 41, at 250. See Brownlie, *supra* ch. 2 n. 52 at 330–1.

[61] *Berizzi Bros.* v. *SS Pesaro*, 271 US 562, at 574 (1926).

[62] Comments of Bilge, ILC, 1974 Sum. Rec., *supra* n. 11, at 19.

[63] See Amerasinghe, *supra* n. 3, at 102–3; Christenson, *supra* n. 19, at 338–9.

[64] See generally Ago, 3rd Rpt., *supra* ch. 1 n. 16, at 262–7; Cheng, *supra* ch. 1 n. 6, at 193.

[65] *Earnshaw and Others: The Zafiro Case* (1925) (*UK* v. *US*), 6 R. Int'l Arb. Awards 160, *repr. in* 20 *Am. J. Int'l L.* 385 (1926).

[66] See Ago, 3rd Rpt., *supra* ch. 1 n. 16, at 264.

[67] At the heart of the Tribunal's reasoning lay its conclusion that it was *not* true that 'letting this Chinese crew go ashore uncontrolled at the time and place in question was like allowing shore leave to sailors in a policed port where social order is maintained by the ordinary agencies of government.' 20 *Am. J. Int'l L.* 385, at 390 (1926). See de Arechaga, *supra* ch. 1 n. 11, at 549; Meron, *supra* ch. 2 n. 71, at 105; Comments of Sette Camara, ILC, 1974 Sum. Rec., *supra* n. 11, at 39.

example is provided by the *Stephens* Case in which the conduct of a civilian member of an 'unofficial but tacitly recognized guards organization' operating on behalf of the government was attributed to the Mexican state.[68] The ICJ has, in fact, rather explicitly engaged an objective analysis in the recent *Case Concerning United States Diplomatic and Consular Staff in Tehran.*[69] In concluding that private individuals were not state representatives when they originally took over the US embassy, the Court stated: 'Their conduct might be considered directly imputable to the Iranian State only if it were established that, in fact, on the occasion in question the militants acted on behalf of the State, having been charged by some competent organ of the Iranian State to carry out a specific operation.'[70] It was held, however, that the state did later place its imprimatur on the holding of the hostages by failing to seek a release and eventually by imposing conditions to the release.[71] This subsequent conduct translated the acts of the militants in maintaining the hostage situation into public acts on behalf of the state. In short, the key to attribution to the state of private conduct is the 'public character of the function or mission in the performance of which the act or omission contrary to international law was committed, rather than the formal link between the State organization and the person whose conduct is in question.'[72]

iii. Ultra Vires *Conduct*

A conclusion (based on municipal law or objective analysis) that an individual or group should be designated a state organ does not exhaust the inquiry regarding attribution. The mantle of 'state organ' does not deprive the person or collective of persons constituting the organ of the capacity to assume a private posture and act in a fashion unrelated to any public function. The point at which the conduct of an organ is sufficiently remote to its role as state representative to escape the logic and role of attribution has been highly controversial.[73] Early authorities, notably Grotius, maintained that the line was simply coextensive with the scope of the organ's authority defined by municipal law.[74] The position that *ultra vires* conduct could not be attributed to the state found expression in a number of cases and classical theoretical works well into the nineteenth century.[75] By 1928, however, Eagleton was

[68] The *Stephens* Case (1927) (*US* v. *Mex.*), 4 R. Int'l Arb. Awards 265. The quoted characterization is from de Beus, *supra* ch. 1 n. 13, at 102.

[69] [1980] ICJ 3, (*US* v. *Iran*) (Judgment of 24 May 1980).

[70] *Id.*, at 29.

[71] *Id.*, at 35.

[72] Ago, 3rd Rpt., *supra* ch 1 n. 16, at 264.

[73] On this issue generally, see Ago, 4th Rpt. *supra* n. 45, at 79–95; Amerasinghe, *supra* n. 3, at 104–14; Brownlie, *System*, *supra* ch. 1 n. 2, at 145–50; Borchard, *supra* ch. 1 n. 19, at 184 ff; Eagleton, *supra* ch. 1 n. 4, at 54–9; Meron, *supra* ch. 2 n. 71, *passim*.

[74] Grotius, *supra* ch. 2 n. 26, at 437.

[75] See e.g. Calvo, iii *Le Droit international théoretique et pratique* 120 (5th edn., 1896); Hall, *Treatise on International Law* 323 (8th edn., 1924); Opin. of US Attn. Gen. in the *Tunstall* Case, [1885] US *For. Rel. Papers* 450.

able to conclude that '[m]odern writers upon the subject of responsibility are in practically complete agreement that the state is responsible for the acts of its agents, even in excess of their powers.'[76] It is not surprising, therefore, that the classical position, proposed by its last significant advocate, Guerrero, was categorically rejected in the draft articles adopted at the 1930 Hague Conference.[77] Writers today certainly exhibit no hesitation in concluding that *ultra vires* conduct may be attributed to the state.[78] Decisions in this century are equally unanimous in such a conclusion.[79] In the *Youmans* Case, one of the leading examples, in which Mexican troops dispatched to protect a group of Americans from a riot shot and killed one and participated in the killing of the others, the arbitral tribunal expressed the logic of the position:

> Soldiers inflicting personal injuries or committing wanton destruction or looting always act in disobedience of some rules laid down by superior authority. There could be no liability whatever for such misdeeds if the view were taken that any acts committed by soldiers in contravention of instructions must always be considered as personal acts.[80]

The only dispute remaining, then, appears to be the proper limits of attributable *ultra vires* conduct, i.e. when is conduct inconsistent with authority simply too remote to deem the state responsible? Several criteria have emerged in the literature. The award in the *Caire* Case recites the two tests most frequently propounded: 'il faut qu'il aient agi au moins apparement comme des fonctionnaires ou organes competent, ou que, en agissant, ils aient usé de pouvoirs ou de moyens propres à leur qualité officielle.'[81] The former of

[76] Eagleton, *supra* ch. 1 n. 4, at 55 n. 41.

[77] 'International responsibility is likewise incurred by a State if damage is sustained by a foreigner as a result of unauthorized acts of its officials performing under cover of their official character, if the acts contravene the international obligations of the State.' Acts of the Conference for the Codification of International Law, Minutes of the Third Committee, League of Nat. Doc. C. 351(*c*). M. 145(*c*). 193. OV., at 237–8. See also Guerrero, Report, *supra* ch. 1 n. 8, at 244–6.

[78] See e.g. Accioly, *supra* ch. 2 n. 29, at 359–63; Amerasinghe, *supra* n. 3, at 114; Jiménez de Arechaga, *supra* ch. 1 n. 11, at 548; Brownlie, *System*, *supra* ch. 1 n. 2, at 145–50; Brownlie, *supra* ch. 2 n. 52, at 449; Cheng, *supra* ch. 1 n. 6, at 203; Christenson, *supra* n. 19, at 329–30; Eagleton, *supra* ch. 1 n. 4, at 54; Garcia-Amador, Draft, *supra* ch. 1 n. 3, at 23; Meron, *supra* ch. 2 n. 71, *passim*; Sohn and Baxter, *supra* ch. 1 n. 11, at 248; Starke, *supra* ch. 2 n. 52, at 110.

[79] See e.g. the *Caire* Case (1929) (*Fr.* v. *Mex.*), 5 R. Int'l Arb. Awards 516, at 530; the *Massey* Case (1927) (*US* v. *Mex.*), 4 R. Int'l Arb. Awards 155, at 159. See also Cheng, *supra* ch. 1 n. 6, at 204.

[80] The *Youmans* Case (1926) (*US* v. *Mex.*), 4 R. Int'l Arb Awards 110, at 116. See de Beus, *supra* ch. 1 n. 13, at 101. Cheng notes that indeed most cases of international violation by police organs arise out of breaches of domestic law. Cheng, *supra* ch. 1 n. 6, at 202 n. 33. The extreme of this logic is articulated by Sohn and Baxter: 'If responsibility were to arise only when the act or omission was expressly or apparently directed or authorized by the State, it would always rest with the State to avoid responsibility altogether by directing all persons acting for the Government not to violate international law as regards aliens.' Sohn and Baxter, *supra* ch. 1 n. 11, at 248.

[81] The *Caire* Case (1929) (*Fr.* v. *Mex.*), 5 R. Int'l Arb. Awards 516, at 530. Supporters of these two as alternatives include: Amerasinghe, *supra* ch. 1 n. 11, at 106; Meron, *supra* ch. 2 n. 71, at 94 and 111; Queneudec, *supra* n. 45, at 120.

these requirements, variously stated in terms of the actor's 'apparent', 'manifest', or 'purported' authority or 'colour of authority', is a product of the literature on the treatment of aliens.[82] It seems to be conceived in two quite distinct fashions. On the one hand, it is often used in a subjective sense to exclude conduct so obviously *ultra vires* that the alien should have known it, and presumably, therefore, have avoided injury.[83] The limited utility of this approach was duly noted by the ILC.[84] Other authors, however, have used the language of 'apparent' authority, without this subjective meaning, simply to describe the scope of the public function of the actor.[85] This approach is closely related to the requirement advocated by a number of commentators that the conduct must be within the 'general competence' or 'scope of function' of the state agent.[86] The second of the *Caire* Case criteria, that the powers or means utilized have an official character, also finds a great deal of support in the literature.[87] Meron describes this test as satisfied when there is an 'abuse of means which the State put at the official's disposal and which made the occurrence of the act possible.'[88] Finally, the draft articles prepared recently by the ILC seem to embrace yet a third formulation of the *ultra vires* limitation:

> The conduct of an organ of a State, of a territorial governmental entity or of an entity empowered to exercise elements of the governmental authority, such organ having acted in that capacity, shall be considered as an act of the State under international law even if, in the particular case, the organ exceeded its competence according to internal law or contravened instructions concerning its activity.[89]

It is not clear from either text or commentary precisely how one determines if conduct is in the 'capacity' of a state organ. Does, for example, an officer who arrests, jails, and beats an alien for utterly personal reasons act in an 'official capacity'? The answer, no doubt, is yes.[90] To arrive at this conclusion,

[82] Acts of the Conference, *supra* n. 77, at 238; Sohn and Baxter, *supra* ch. 1 n. 11, at 248.

[83] See e.g. Acts of the Conference, *supra* n. 77, at 238; Garcia-Amador, Draft, *supra* ch. 1 n. 3, at 23. See discussion at ILC, Report to the General Assembly, ii *Yb. Int'l L. Comm'n* 47, at 69, UN Doc. A/CN. 4/Ser. A/1975/Add. 1 (1975).

[84] ILC, 1975 Rpt., *supra* n. 83, at 69. The ILC here points out that it is extremely rare that knowledge makes any difference whatsoever in the avoidance of injury.

[85] See e.g. Ago, 4th Rpt., *supra* n. 45, at 94–5 (couched in negative terms as 'manifestly not' within authority); Amerasinghe, *supra* ch. 1 n. 11, at 104–5; Meron, *supra* ch. 2 n. 71, at 94–6.

[86] See Sohn and Baxter, *supra* ch. 1 n. 11, at 248; Starke, *supra* ch. 2 n. 52, at 110; the *Union Bridge Co.* Case (1924) (*US* v. *UK*), 6 R. Int'l Arb. Awards 138. Ago criticizes this approach based on the absence of any international concept of 'generic' or 'objective' authority. Yet, he seems to accept the notion of an objective determination of lack of competence in the formulation of the rule excluding conduct when the 'lack of competence was manifest.' Ago, 4th Rpt. *supra* n. 45, at 94–5.

[87] See ILC, Amerasinghe, *supra* ch. 1 n. 11, at 53; Cheng, *supra* ch. 1 n. 6, at 207; Meron, *supra* ch. 2 n. 71, at 107 ff.; ILC, Summary Records of the 27th Session, 1 *Yb. Int'l L. Comm'n* 8, at 19 UN Doc. A/CN 4/Ser. A (1975) (Comments of Kearney).

[88] Meron, *supra* ch. 2 n. 71, at 107.

[89] ILC, 1975 Rpt., *supra* n. 83, at 61 (emphasis added). See Christenson, *supra* n. 19, at 330.

[90] See the *Mallén* Case (1927) (*Mex.* v. *US*), 4 R. Int'l Arb. Awards 173; the *Magee* Case (1874)

however, i.e. to interpret 'capacity', reference is made to the slightly less abstract criteria articulated in the *Caire* Case. It would seem that a workable rule of decision must clearly contemplate the blending and balancing of such customary factors. Although the reference to official 'capacity' seems to do so, it is submitted that a far more direct and instructive statement of the principle of limitation is suggested by Quentin-Baxter: the key is the '*substantial connexion* between the role of the agent as an organ of the State and the misuse of authority.'[91]

B. PRIVATE INDIVIDUALS

i. Attribution to State

Private individuals, in the context of state responsibility, are simply those persons who do not possess a relationship to the state that places them within the set of state organs or representatives defined pursuant to the foregoing analysis. The distinction between public and private is not, of course, absolute. Even a municipally designated state organ enjoys a private sphere of activity.[92] Conversely, private individuals may act as representatives of the state with respect to but a single act.[93] The issue to be considered in this section is therefore properly formulated: to what extent does state responsibility arise with respect to conduct of individuals who, as to such specific conduct, may not be deemed state organs or representatives? As most individual actors, in environmental and other contexts, fall within the 'private' category, the answer is critical.

In the words of Jiménez de Arechaga, '[t]he initial, almost primitive reply to such acts is based on the notion of group solidarity: a collectivity is responsible for the crimes committed by any of its members against another group or the individuals composing it.'[94] Prior to the development of the concept of the modern state, this was indeed the governing doctrine.[95] Among modern authorities, however, attribution based simply on the 'solidarity' of the societal group finds no real support.[96] On the other hand, several authors

(*UK* v. *Guat.*), [1873–4] *Brit. & For. State Papers* 875; *Filartiga* v. *Pēna-Irala*, 577 F. Supp 860 (EDNY 1984).

[91] Comments of Quentin-Baxter, ILC, 1975 Sum. Rec., *supra* n. 87, at 13 (emphasis added). See also similar language focusing on the 'relationship' between authority and breach in de Arechaga, *supra* ch. 1 n. 11, at 548., Note the issue of *ultra vires* treated in the US jurisprudence on the constitutional problem of 'state action'. See n. 48 *supra*. The question examined is whether a state is to be deemed the actor when an officer of the state acts *ultra vires*. Similar formulations of 'means', 'colour of authority', relationship to function etc., have been described. See e.g. *Home Tel. & Tel. Co.* v. *Los Angeles*, 227 US 278 (1913).

[92] See the *Mallen* Case (1927) (*Mex.* v. *US*), 4 R. Int'l Arb. Awards 173.

[93] See cases discussed in text at nn. 64–70 *supra*.

[94] De Arechaga, *supra* ch. 1 n. 11, at 558.

[95] See Ago, 4th Rpt. *supra* n. 45, at 121; Eagleton, *supra* ch. 1 n. 4, at 76.

[96] See Ago, 4th Rpt., *supra* n. 45, at n. 254 for discussion of several possible supporters of solidarity.

have advocated a similar conclusion, i.e. attribution of private conduct without consideration of the position of the state *vis-à-vis* such conduct, on somewhat different grounds. Fauchille, for example, argued that it is the state which benefits from the presence of aliens in state territory; the state should therefore bear responsibility even for private conduct injuring aliens.[97] Another rationale is reflected in Garcia-Mora's conclusion that 'present day governmental control over the movement and actions of persons is so pervasive and complete that any harmful action of a person against a foreign state is almost certain to be carried out under the moral approval and acquiescence of the state.'[98] Such views, however, stand in doctrinal isolation. Indeed, a number of theorists reject such automatic attribution precisely because the state lacks the capacity to control private individuals to the degree agents may be controlled.[99] In any event, it is now a 'postulate' of international law that private conduct is not attributed to the state; only the conduct of the state itself may trigger state responsibility.[100]

This should not suggest, however, that an event of private conduct may not lead to a conclusion of state responsibility. The first theorist to reject the automatic, all-embracing attribution of the 'solidarity' approach, Grotius, argued that the state could be responsible for 'complicity' in private conduct through acts such as *patientia* (failure to prevent) and *receptus* (failure to punish).[101] Private conduct standing alone could not be attributed to the state; the original private act would be so attributed, however, if the conduct of the state merited a conclusion of complicity.[102] As explained by Vattel, one of the principal exponents of 'complicity' theory: 'If the nation, or its ruler, approve and ratify the act of the citizen, it takes upon itself the act, and may then be regarded by the injured party as the real author of the affront of which the citizen was perhaps only the instrument.'[103] The watershed of this 'attribution through complicity' doctrine was reached at the beginning of this century.[104] Criticism culminated in the direct and influential rejection of the

[97] Comments of Fauchille, 'Étude responsabilité des états à raison des dommages soufferts par des estrangers en cas d'émeute ou de guerre civile', 18 *Annuaire inst. droit int'l* 234 (1900). Support may found in Dupuy, *La Responsabilité internationale des états pour les dommages d'origine technologique et industrielle* 15–25 (1976).

[98] Garcia-Mora, *supra* ch. 2 n. 37, at 29. His conclusion does seem limited to hostile expeditions and similar threats to peace.

[99] See Eagleton, *supra* ch. 1 n. 4, at 79; Guerrero, Report, *supra* ch. 1 n. 8, at 247; Lenoble, *supra* n. 44, at 104.

[100] Guerrero, Report, *supra* ch. 1 n. 8, at 246. 'All the authorities on international law are a unit as regards the principle that an injury done by one of the subjects of a nation is not to be considered as done by the nation itself.' The *Lovett* Case (1892) (*US* v. *Chile*), Moore, iii *Arbitrations* 2991 (1898).

[101] Grotius, *supra* ch. 2 n. 26, at c. xvii, c. xviii s. 21, c. xxi s. 1–4. See Ago, 4th Rpt., *supra* n. 45, at 121; Jiménez de Arechaga, *supra* ch. 1 n. 11, at 558–9; Eagleton, *supra* ch. 1 n. 4, at 76.

[102] *Id.*

[103] Vattel, *Le Droit des gens ou principes de la loi naturelle* (trans. Fenwick, 1758 edn. 1916), at 136.

[104] Ago, 4th Rpt., *supra* n. 45, at 121–2.

doctrine of complicity in the *Janes* case decided by the Mexico–United States General Claims Commission in 1925.[105] Mexican police were found to have been negligent in their efforts to apprehend the murderer of an American citizen. The Commission rested Mexico's responsibility not on the 'indirect' basis of complicity, but on the state's direct violation of an obligation to punish. 'The culprit is liable for having killed or murdered an American national; the Government is liable for not having measured up to its duty of diligently prosecuting and properly punishing the offender.'[106] There was, therefore, no attribution of private conduct, only responsibility for the state's breach of a duty relating to such conduct.[107] There seems little question that the contemporary rule is consistent with the independent basis of state responsibility identified by the *Janes* Tribunal.[108] Jiménez de Arechaga summarizes:

There is no reason to speak of State complicity or 'vicarious' or 'indirect' responsibility, since the state is internationally responsible not for the acts of any private individual, but for its own omission, for the lack of 'due diligence' of its organs. The delinquency of private individuals is no longer taken as a basis of state responsibility but as merely the occasion for calling into operation certain duties for the state.[109]

ii. State 'Due Diligence'

What, then, are the obligations of the state which arise with respect to private conduct? The state must first exercise 'due diligence' to *prevent* conduct which, if the state were the actor, would breach its international obligations.[110] If such conduct nevertheless occurs, the apprehension and punishment of the offenders must be 'diligently' pursued.[111] Ago perceptively notes, in the context of attacks on aliens:

Prevention and punishment are simply two aspects of the same obligation to provide protection and both have a common aim, namely to discourage potential attackers of protected persons from carrying out such attacks. The system of protection that the

[105] The *Janes* Case (1925) (*US* v. *Mex.*), 4 R. Int'l Arb. Awards 82. Similar logic was evident in the *Menebhi* Case in the *Spanish Zone of Morocco* Claims (1925) (*UK* v. *Spain*), 2 R. Int'l Arb. Awards 615, at 707.

[106] The *Janes* Case (1925) (*US* v. *Mex.*), 4 R. Int'l Arb. Awards 82, at 87.

[107] Following the case there was a substantial discussion on the issue of damages appropriate when the injury to the alien is not attributed to the state. See discussion in n. 115 *infra.*

[108] See Amerasinghe, *supra* ch. 1 n. 11, at 51; Ago, 4th Rpt., *supra* n. 45, at 100; Cheng, *supra* ch. 1 n. 6, 175–6; Christenson, *supra* n. 19, at 329. Eagleton, *supra* ch. 1 n. 4, at 215; Garcia-Amador, *supra* ch. 1 n. 1, at 404; Sohn and Baxter, *supra* ch. 1 n. 11, at 337.

[109] Jiménez de Arechaga, *supra* ch. 1 n. 11, at 560.

[110] See the *Alabama* Claims (1872) (*US* v. *UK*), Moore, i. *Arbitrations* 495; the *St Albans* Raid Case (1873) (*US* v. *UK*), Moore, iv *Arbitrations,* at 4042; the *Home Frontier and Foreign Missionary Society* (1920) (*US* v. *UK*), 6 R. Int'l Arb. Awards 42. For the purposes of this work, conduct which would violate international obligations if the state were the actor will be referred to as 'violative' or 'wrongful' conduct.

[111] See the *Chase* Case (1928) (*US* v. *Mex.*), 4 R. Int'l Arb. Awards 337; the *De Galvan* Case (1927) (*Mex.* v. *US*), 4 R. Int'l Arb. Awards 273; the *Janes* Case (1925) (*US* v. *Mex.*), 4 R. Int'l Arb. Awards 82; the *Massey* Case (1927) (US v. *Mex.*). 4 R. Int'l Arb. Awards 155.

State must provide therefore includes not only the adoption of measures to avoid certain acts being committed but also provision for, and application of, sanctions against the authors of acts which the implementation of preventive measures has failed to avert.[112]

His observation is equally valid with respect to all species of international duty. As the *Janes* Tribunal concluded: 'If the nonprosecution and non-punishment of crimes (or of specific crimes) in a certain period and place occurs with regularity, such nonrepression may even assume the character of nonprevention and be treated as such.'[113] The obligation to apprehend and punish wrongdoers, then, is but an expression of the general obligation to prevent private individuals from engaging in conduct in which the state is prohibited to engage.

One distinction between the obligations of prevention and punishment should be underscored. When responsibility and a consequential duty to compensate follow a breach of the duty to exercise due diligence to prevent, a casual relationship generally exists between the state's omission and the private conduct, i.e. but for the failure of the state, the conduct might have been prevented.[114] An *ex post facto* failure to punish, on the other hand, cannot logically have any direct causal connection with the private conduct. Even if punishment is, appropriately, conceived as a means of contributing to prevention through enhancing respect for legal processes, a causal relationship between a specific failure to punish and the prior conduct of the offender is difficult to draw. The issue of the appropriate measure of compensation, given the absense of a causal connection to the consequences of the violative conduct, therefore remains in dispute.[115]

[112] Ago, 4th Rpt, *supra* n. 45, at 98.

[113] The *Janes* Case (1925) (*US* v. *Mex.*), 4 R. Int'l Arb. Awards 82, at 118.

[114] See cases cited at n. 119 *infra*.

[115] Certain authorities do seek to limit reparation for failure to punish to damages caused directly. Hence, Sohn and Baxter's extreme perspective, logical but without support in the cases, that compensation should reflect only the lost opportunity to recover damages from the wrongdoer. A pauper offender, therefore, means *no* damages. Sohn and Baxter, *supra* ch. 1 n. 11, at 338. The *Janes* case itself represents a centrist approach, assessing damages on the victim's relatives' 'indignity' and the general 'mistrust and lack of safety' caused by the failure to punish. The *Janes* Case (1925) (*US* v. *Mex.*), 4 R. Int'l Arb. Awards 82, at 89. See also the *Spanish Zone of Morocco* Claims (1925) (*UK* v. *Spain*) 2 R. Int'l Arb. Awards 615, at 709–10. See criticism in Whiteman. i *supra* ch. 1 n. 6, at 40–6. Most publicists, however, reject the search for an independent basis for damages, concluding that the consequences of the private conduct which has gone unpunished (or insufficiently punished) should provide, at least, the basic guideline for the measure of reparation. See Ago, 4th Rpt., *supra* n. 45, at 98 (non-punishment treated as a failure to prevent); Brierly, 'The Theory of Implied State Complicity in International Claims', 9 *Brit. Yb. Int'l L.* 42 (1928) (state assessed as a party to conduct by 'condonation'); Eagleton, 'Measure of Damages in International Law', 39 *Yale L.J.* 52, at 54–61 (1929) (all 'due diligence' damages measured by private conduct consequences); Whiteman, at 38–69 (empirical conclusion based on cases). Freeman persuasively argues that the search for 'casual' logic in the cases in this area is futile: the real force that animates the decisions regarding the measure of damages, regardless of the stated basis, is the desire to penalize the state to deter future repetition of the failure to punish. Freeman, *supra* n. 22, at 604–23. See also Dunn, *The Protection of Nationals* 186 (1932).

In any event, as noted above, these obligations are not generally absolute.[116] State responsibility will arise only for the failure to perform with 'due diligence' the tasks of prevention and punishment. These two obligations with respect to private conduct are often referred to collectively as the 'obligation of due diligence'.[117] As to the content of the duty, Garcia-Amador was quite correct in reporting to the ILC that 'the rule of "due diligence" cannot be reduced to a clear and accurate definition which might serve as an objective and automatic standard for deciding, regardless of the circumstances, whether a state was "diligent" in discharging its duty of vigilance and protection.'[118] It is, however, possible to identify certain relevant factors. Analysis of the feasibility of effective state action is, for example, evident in cases concerning responsibility for insufficient diligence in the prevention of injury. Findings that no reasonable degree of diligence could have prevented the event have thus contributed to denials of responsiblity.[119] Conversely, states have been deemed responsible following a conclusion that effective action could have been taken.[120] Foreseeability of private conduct is a related factor frequently playing a principal and explicit role in the decisions of arbitral tribunals as to whether states have acted with diligence.[121]

The factor perhaps most disputed is whether such questions of diligence should be assessed in light of the capabilities and practices of the particular state or subjected to an international standard. The positions taken in the leading case of the *Alabama Claims* illustrate the conflict.[122] The United States asserted a claim against Great Britain for violation of a neutral's obligation of due diligence to prevent conduct supportive of a belligerent,

[116] See text at n. 139 *infra* regarding the merger of the regime of due diligence with that of strict liability.

[117] See e.g. Accioly, *supra* ch. 2 n. 29, at 560 ('la diligence convenable'); Borchard, *supra* ch. 1 n. 19, at 279; Garcia-Amador, Draft, *supra* ch. 1 n. 3, at 27.

[118] Garcia-Amador, Draft, *supra* ch. 1 n. 3, at 27.

[119] See e.g. the *Salvador Prats* Case (1868) (*Mex.* v. *US*), Moore, iii *Arbitrations* 2886, at 2893; The *St Albans Raid* Case (1873) (*US* v. *UK*), Moore, iv *Arbitrations* 4042, at 4054; the *Kummerow, Redler & Co., Fulda, Fischbach, and Friedericky* Cases (1903) (*Germ.* v. *Venez.*), 10 R. Int'l Arb. Awards 369, at 400. In fact, it may be argued that impossibility and the existence of a causal connection to the injury should be factors determining whether an obligation to compensate arises as a consequence of responsibility. If the state made no effort to prevent when in a position to do so, it should still be deemed responsible—not for the material injury, but for the 'moral' injury attendant to every breach of an international obligation. The cases cited may not conflict with this conclusion; the language used may only reflect a determination that in each case the state did what it reasonably could have done in the circumstances. See discussion at ch. 4 n. 10 *infra*.

[120] See e.g. the *Corfu Channel* Case (*UK* v. *Albania*), [1949] ICJ 4, at 23 (Albania could have given warning of mines); *Case concerning United States Diplomatic and Consular Staff in Tehran* (*US* v. *Iran*), [1980] ICJ 3, at 31–3 (Iran could have prevented attack on embassy).

[121] See e.g. the *Alabama* Claims (1872) (*US* v. *UK*), *Moore*, i *Arbitrations* 495, at 655 (US warned UK of ship construction in violation of neutrality); the *Home Insurance Co.* Case (1926) (*US* v. *Mex.*), 4 R. Int'l Arb. Awards 48, at 52 (suddeness of revolt made protection impossible).

[122] The *Alabama* Claims (1872) (*US* v. *UK*), Moore, i *Arbitrations*, at 495. Eagleton in fact views the *Alabama* matter as establishing 'due diligence' in the international legal vocabulary. Eagleton, *supra* ch. 1 n. 4, at 89 n. 38.

based on the construction and equipping of a Confederate vessel within British jurisdiction.[123] Britain responded that it had indeed exercised the required level of diligence, i.e. *diligentia quam in suis* or that which 'a nation is in the habit of employing in the conduct of its own affairs.'[124] The Tribunal, finding Britain responsible, implicitly accepted the American perspective of an objective test of due diligence.[125] Support for such an international definition may be found in a number of arbitral awards: the *Neer* case specifically subjected a state's conduct in punishing the killer of an alien to 'the test of international standards';[126] a failure of due diligence to prevent injury to aliens was found in the *Montijo* Case regardless of the incapacity of the particular state to perform adequately.[127] Eagleton's position is representative of that of a number of publicists: 'the regular or even the utmost activity of the state may here, as elsewhere, be regarded as insufficient because of the failure of the State to measure up to the international standard.'[128]

The contrary position remains that the circumstances of the particular state define the standard of 'due diligence'. In its extreme form, arising in the jurisprudence of the treatment of aliens, this view has been expressed in terms of the obligation to afford aliens only the same measure of protection from private conduct provided citizens, without any reference to international minima.[129] This purely subjective approach has encountered substantial contemporary opposition.[130] Even recent literature, however, is replete with evidence of the relevance of the specific circumstances of the state. Garcia-Amador, for example, speaks of diligence in light of the 'resources available to the state'.[131] Friedmann argues that the degree of control over private activity exercised in totalitarian regimes implies a higher standard of due diligence.[132]

[123] The parties agreed prior to the arbitration that the central obligation of neutrality to be tested was the exercise of 'due diligence' to prevent conduct in aid of a belligerent. Art. 6 of the Treaty of Washington (United States Great Britain) done 8 May 1871, reproduced in Moore, i *Arbitrations*, at 549–50.

[124] Moore, i *Arbitrations*, at 600.

[125] *Id.*, at 654. See Eagleton, *supra* ch. 1 n. 4, at 89.

[126] The *Neer* Case (1926) (*US* v. *Mex.*), 4 R. Int'l Arb. Awards 60, at 61. See also the *Mecham* Case (1929) (*US* v. *Mex.*), 4 R. Int'l Arb. Awards 440, at 443. See de Beus, *supra* ch. 1, n. 13, at 134 5.

[127] The *Montijo* Case (1874) (*US* v. *Colombia*), Moore, ii *Arbitrations* 1421, at 1444.

[128] Eagleton, *supra* ch. 1 n. 4, at 89–90. See also Borchard, *supra* ch. 1 n. 19, at 39, 179; Dupuy, 'Due Diligence in the International Law of Liability', in OECD, *Legal Aspects of Transfrontier Pollution* 369, at 374 (1977); Roth, Das volkerrechtliche Delikt vor und in den Verhandlungen auf der Haagar Kodifications Konferenz 1930 177–8 (1932) trans. in Ago, 1st Rpt., *supra* ch. 1 n. 2, at 152; Sohn and Baxter, *supra* ch. 1 n. 11, at 167–8.

[129] See Guerrero, Report, *supra* ch. 1 n. 8, at 239; cases cited at Brownlie, *supra* ch. 2 n. 52, at 524 nn. 3–5.

[130] See Brownlie, *supra* ch. 2 n. 52, at 524 n. 6; Eagleton, *supra* ch. 1 n. 4, at 83–6; Freeman, *supra* n. 22, at 504; Yates, 'State Responsibility for Nonwealth Injuries to Aliens in the Postwar Era', in *Injuries to Aliens*, Lillich ed., *supra* ch. 1 n. 2, at 215.

[131] Garcia-Amador, Draft, *supra* ch. 1 n. 3, at 130. See also de Visscher, *Theory and Reality in International Law* 307 (trans. Corbett 1957).

[132] 'The range of injurious acts is infinitely great, and the most totalitarian state cannot fully

Numerous authorities, including, most notably, the ICJ in the recent *Iran Hostages* Decision, have analysed due diligence in terms of the 'means at the disposal' of the specific state.[133] Yet, one need not conclude that such views are inconsistent with an objective standard. Rather, the contemporary view would seem to be a hybrid of the two approaches: the diligence of the state will be considered in light of its particular capacities and practices; if, however, its conduct falls below an international minimum standard, responsibility will nevertheless lie.[134]

The interests at stake in the particular case constitute another recognized factor central to decisions regarding state due diligence. A number of significant cases have spoken in terms of a response proportional to the nature of the threatened or actual injury.[135] In fact, there appear to be certain specific categories of interests, or conduct affecting interests, which demand a stricter level of diligence by the state. The most traditional of these relates to the protection of the person and property of diplomats.[136] Following the dispute between Italy and Greece regarding the assassination of members of the *Tellini* diplomatic mission resident in Greece, the League of Nations Committee of Jurists defined state obligations with respect to such matters as follows:

> The responsibility of the State is only involved by the commission in its territory of a political crime against the persons of foreigners if the State has neglected to take all reasonable measures for the prevention of the crime and the pursuit, arrest and bringing to justice of the criminal.
> The recognized public character of a foreigner and the circumstances in which he is present in its territory entail upon the State a corresponding duty of special vigilance on his behalf.[137]

The other principal category for which an elevated due diligence requirement is imposed consists of matters for which the State is held to a strict standard of responsibility. As discussed above, the presence of strict

control the movements of many millions of individuals. On the other hand, the "due diligence" required of every state in the supervision of its citizens may, on the circumstances of the case, make the proof of guilt easier against totalitarian states than against others.' Friedmann, *supra* n. 59, at 143.

[133] *Case Concerning United States Diplomatic and Consular Staff in Tehran* (*US* v. *Iran*), [1980] ICJ 3, at 33. See Borchard, *supra* ch. 1 n. 19, at 214; Eagleton, *supra* ch. 1, n. 4, at 89 and 89 n. 42; ILC, 1975 Sum. Rec., *supra* n. 87, at 37 (Comments of Ramangasoavina).

[134] See Dupuy, *supra* n. 128, at 375–6. The content of such standards remains ill-defined and the subject of robust debate. See discussions Brownlie, *supra* ch. 2 n. 52, at 524–8; Dupuy, *supra* n. 97, at 261–74; Freeman, *supra* n. 22, at 497–570.

[135] See e.g. the *Alabama* Claims (1872) (*US* v. *UK*), Moore, i *Arbitrations* 495, at 654; the *Spanish Zone of Morocco* Claims (1925) (*UK* v. *Spain*), 2 R. Int'l Arb. Awards 615, at 644. See Cheng, *supra* ch. 1 n. 6, at 220–1.

[136] See discussions in Ago, 4th Rpt. *supra* n. 45, at 117–20; Brownlie, *supra* ch. 2 n. 52, at 453; Dupuy, *supra* n. 128, at 376–7; Eagleton, *supra* ch. 1 n. 6, at 80; Garcia-Amador, Draft, *supra* ch. 1 n. 3, at 27; Yates, *supra* n. 130, at 233, Eagleton also notes that there is some authority for a higher standard of due diligence imposed with respect to the private acts of state officials. Eagleton, at 59.

[137] 5 *League of Nations* OJ 524 (1924).

responsibility as a regime of customary law is rather controversial.[138] The merits of this dispute regarding environmental norms will be discussed in detail in Part II. It is important to note at this point, however, during the discussion of general principles, that an assertion of strict responsibility for private conduct does not demand deviation from the rules of attribution. Rather, as to such conduct, due diligence merges into a strict regime.[139] The diligence required of the state is simply that necessary to prevent the private conduct. A failure to prevent is a failure of due diligence. If one were to assume, for example, a regime of strict responsibility for the consequences of 'ultrahazardous' activity within the state, the integrity of the general principles of attribution need not be disturbed in order to find the state strictly responsible when private ultrahazardous conduct causes injury to a neighbour. The responsibility of the state arises not out of the conduct itself but the state's failure to achieve the required standard of diligence, i.e. that necessary to prevent injury.[140]

The final point to be made concerning due diligence is simply that the emphasis on the territorial character of the obligation evident throughout the literature ought not to suggest that the state may not, depending on the character of the primary obligation, be required to exercise due diligence with respect to conduct *outside* the state. A brief look at the issue dictates a significant and contrary conclusion: in certain circumstances, the state must exercise territorial or extraterritorial legal authority, or both, to satisfy the demands of due diligence. Language linking due diligence to territory is, of course, exceedingly common in the traditional literature of State responsibility: 'La responsabilité au titre de prévention d'actes contraires au droit des gens est . . . restreinte, en rapport étroit avec la surveillance que l'État exerce sur le territoire qu'il domine et dans lequel il exerce son pouvoir législatif et exécutif.'[141] Similarly, Guerrero concludes that protection of foreign interests 'must be afforded in all territories over which the State exercises its sovereignty, though it cannot be afforded outside these limits.'[142] Eagleton summarizes the logic of the linkage:

> Since international law must prevail within each state, all states in consequence thereof are burdened with the obligation of respecting the rights, within their own territories, of other states or their members. The responsibility of the state for the acts of individuals is therefore based upon the territorial control which it enjoys, and which

[138] See text commencing at ch. 2 n. 76 *supra*.

[139] See Handl, *supra* ch. 2 n. 82, at 553–60.

[140] Hence, arguments to the effect that 'due diligence' is 'obsolete' with respect to certain obligations (e.g. hostile expeditions) are somewhat less disruptive conceptually when viewed as assertions of strict liability rather than solidarity. See e.g. the position of Garcia-Mora, *supra* ch. 2 n. 37, at 61–5.

[141] Opinion of the Legal Division, Political Department of the Swiss Federal Council, 28 Feb. 1955, 16 *Ann. suisse droit int'l* 222, at 225 (1959).

[142] Guerrero, Report, *supra* ch. 1 n. 8, at 241.

enables it, and it alone, to restrain and punish individuals, whether nationals or not, within its limits.[143]

Such comments, however, reflect the particular character of the subject which dominated and shaped the traditional jurisprudence of state responsibility: treatment of aliens. The conduct with which this specific subject is concerned is, by definition, territorial; to assert the territorial limits to due diligence with respect to the treatment of aliens is to state a truism.[144] Not all of the state's primary obligations, however, are so limited. In many areas (e.g. neutrality and aggression), international law operates to prohibit conduct which may occur beyond the borders of the state. It must be submitted that the obligation of due diligence attaches even to distinctly extraterritorial conduct. Logically, the state must exercise all available means to prevent and punish conduct anywhere which, if committed by the state, would violate international obligations.[145]

The state's legal authority, of course, constitutes the means available to it for action either within or outside its territory. Due diligence in the context of certain primary obligations, then, is, properly viewed as an obligation to act to the extent of such legal authority.[146] The language of Judge Ammoun in the 1971 *Namibia* Case is instructive:

> [States] must show due diligence in preventing any individual or collective act contrary to neutrality. This obligation relates to nationals and subjects, and to foreign residents . . . For a State which undertakes an obligation commits its own subjects and those who live under its law, and must employ every kind of means, legislative, administrative and judicial, by which it governs.[147]

When, therefore, the state possesses legal authority to prevent or punish

[143] Eagleton, *supra* ch. 1 n. 4, at 78. Consider the language of Max Huber in the *Island of Palmas (or Miangas)* Arbitral Award: 'Territorial sovereignty . . . involves the exclusive right to display the activites of a state. This right has as corollary a duty: The obligation to protect within the territory the rights of other states, in particular their right to integrity and inviolability in peace and in war, together with the rights which each state may claim for its nationals in foreign territory.' (1928) (*US* v. *Neth.*), 2 R. Int'l Arb. Awards 829, reprinted in 22 *Am J. Int'l L.* 867, at 876 (1928).

[144] It should be pointed out that a number of cases have established that when the state exercises authority in foreign territory which is the effective equivalent of sovereign territorial authority, the due diligence regime applies with full force. See the *Spanish Zone of Morocco* claims (1925) (*UK* v. *Spain*), 2 R. Int'l Arb. Awards 615, at 649; *Cyprus* v. *Turkey* (Applic. No. 8007/77), 2 *Yb. Europ. Comm. Hum. Rights* 100 (1978). On the other hand, when less than territorial authority is exercised, responsibility has been denied. See the *Brown* Case (1923) (*US* v. *UK*), 6. R. Int'l Arb. Awards 120.

[145] Consider Grotius' asertion: 'Kings and public officials are liable for neglect if they do not employ the remedies which they can and ought to employ for the prevention of robbery and piracy.' Grotius, *supra* ch. 2 n. 26, at c. xvii s. 20.

[146] See Hyde, ii *International Law* 872 (2nd edn. 1945), which speaks of the obligation as a 'duty of jurisdiction'.

[147] *The Legal Consequences for States of the Continued Presence of South Africa in Namibia (South West Africa) Notwithstanding Security Council Resolution 276 (1970)*, [1971] ICJ 16, at 95 (Advisory Opin. 21 June 1971) (Sep. Opin. of J. Ammoun).

violative conduct, wherever it may occur, 'due diligence' should require the exercise of such authority. The simplest illustrations of this principle in action are cases in which territorial legal authority may be exercised to prevent external conduct. The obligation to exercise legal authority within state territory to prevent hostile expeditions into neighbouring states provides an excellent example.[148] The legal authority of the state does not, however, end at its borders; each state possesses a measure of extraterritorial prescriptive legal authority, most clearly, for example, over its own nationals.[149] A state performing with due diligence should logically be required to exercise such jurisdiction to proscribe for its nationals extraterritorial conduct which, if the state were the actor, would violate international law. Two points support this conclusion. First, the prescription itself may prevent such conduct. Thus, if a causal connection can be established, state responsibility and a consequential obligation to compensate should arise for a failure to exercise such authority.[150] Moreover, it is only through the enforcement of such extraterritorial prescriptions that the state may fulfill the complementary due diligence obligation of punishment.[151] The *Menebhi* Case in the *Spanish Zone of Morocco Claims* is illustrative.[152] Spain was there deemed responsible for a failure to punish residents for violative conduct, thefts, committed outside the Spanish Zone. Thus, territorial enforcement authority must be exercised in pursuit of due diligence to punish violations of prescriptions applicable to extraterritorial conduct. In short, one may conclude that due diligence relates both to territorial and extraterritorial private conduct. The outer boundary of a state's responsibility with respect to the latter is coextensive with that of its legal authority. Evidence of the validity and illustrations of the application of this theoretical conclusion in the specific context of marine environmental duties are set forth in Chapter 5 Section C below.

[148] See e.g. the *St Albans Raid* Case (1873) (*US* v. *UK*), Moore, iv *Arbitrations* 4042. See generally Brownlie, International Law and the Activities of Armed Bands, 7 *Int'l & Comp L.Q.* 712 (1958); Lillich and Paxman, 'State Responsibility for Injury to Aliens Occasioned by Terrorists', 26 *Am. U.L. Rev.* 219, at 275 (1977). See also Brownlie, *System*, *supra* ch. 1 n. 2, at 165.

[149] See ch. 9 at n. 27.

[150] Such a causal connection could perhaps be based upon a showing that property of the national could have been seized, serving in the circumstances as a deterrent likely to have been effective. See generally Christenson, *supra* n. 19, at 338–9.

[151] As noted in Part III, it is a truism that an exercise of enforcement authority, such as punishment, must logically relate to a prescription which has been violated. See discussion ch. 9, at n. 62.

[152] The *Spanish Zone of Morocco* Claims (1925) (*UK* v. *Spain*), 2 R. Int'l Arb. Awards 615, at 707–10. See also the *Alabama* Case, where failure of the British to apprehend and punish was considered as a component of the overall failure of due diligence. The *Alabama Claims (1872) (US* v. *UK*), Moore, i *Arbitrations* 495, at 654–6.

4

Multiple State Responsibility

A. CIRCUMSTANCES

State responsibility arises, as discussed above, when the rights of one state are disturbed by the breach of another state's correlative duties.[1] The traditional characterization of state responsibility as a bilateral relationship between the state in breach and the injured state is, then, quite appropriate. Yet, the emphasis on 'bilateral' ought not to suggest that a single event or set of facts may not give rise to multiple relationships; logically, the conduct of several states with respect to one event may place each in a position of responsibility *vis-à-vis* the injured state.

The circumstances in which such 'multiple state responsibility' may arise fall into two categories. The simpler of the two consists of those situations in which states engage in *concerted* conduct in breach of an international obligation. To borrow from municipal legal parlance, this is the circumstance of 'joint tort-feasors' participating in a common breach of obligation. The second category, predictably, consists of those situations in which states engage in *independent* or several breaches of obligation with respect to a single event.[2] To illustrate, consider the phenomenon of responsibility for complicity based upon the rendering of aid in another state's breach of obligation.[3] Ago notes that complicity is properly characterized as a breach independent of that of the recipient state, thus falling squarely in the category of a distinct breach relating to a single event.[4] A second example arises in the environmental context. Several states may engage in polluting conduct which, in the aggregate, seriously damages another state. The specific issue of the wrongfulness of conduct causing such environmental injury will be treated in Part II.[5] For present purposes, it need only be noted, assuming wrongfulness, that the conduct of each state is appropriately defined as an independent (as opposed to part of a concerted) breach of obligation. Final illustrations arise in circumstances of overlapping state jurisdiction and consequent responsibility, circumstances which, as subsequent chapters will demonstrate, are of

[1] See ch. 1 at nn. 16–17 *supra*.

[2] For discussion of the distinction between joint and independent tort-feasors, see generally James and Brown, *General Principles of the Law of Torts* 349 (4th edn. 1978); W. Prosser, *The Law of Torts* 293–99 (4th edn. 1971); Williams, *Joint Torts and Contributory Negligence* 1–6 (1951); *Winfield and Jolowicz on Tort* 555–6 (9th edn. Jolowicz, Lewis, and Harris eds. 1971).

[3] See ch. 2 at nn. 18–24 *supra*.

[4] See Ago, 7th Rpt., *supra* ch. 2 n. 11, at 59–60; discussion in ch. 2 n. 22 *supra*.

[5] See particularly ch. 5.

particular significance in the context of the law of the sea. Consider, for an onshore example, a case in which military agents of state *A* enter the territory of state *B* and, pursuant to orders, attack the diplomatic mission of state *C*.[6] Responsibility for the attack certainly lies with state *A*. If, however, state *B* has failed to exercise due diligence to prevent such conduct, it too may stand responsible to state *C*.[7] A similar result may follow a breach of the punishment component of the due diligence obligation. Take the same facts outlined above, except (*a*) alter the attackers to private citizens of state *A* acting without governmental knowledge or approval who return home following the attack, and (*b*) assume state *A* has made no effort to apprehend or punish the individuals. In this case, state *B* may still be responsible for a failure of due diligence. The conduct of the private attackers, however, can no longer be attributed to state *A*. On the other hand, state *A* now may bear responsibility for a breach of its independent obligation to punish.[8]

This final example raises an important point. In each of the preceding illustrations of independent breaches, the injury experienced was unitary. 'The *damnum* was single, but each commits a separate *injuria*.'[9] As noted above, however, it is difficult to establish a link between a specific failure to punish and the material injury occasioned by the prior conduct; however defined, the injury caused by non-punishment is distinct from the original damage.[10] Hence, in the example out of a single set of facts, states *A* and *B* stand responsible to state *C* for two quite different species of injury caused. This may also occur, of course, with respect to obligations other than that of due diligence to punish. It is to be recalled from Chapter 1 that material injury is not a requisite element of all breaches of international obligation. There is no reason, therefore, why a state whose conduct bears an insufficient causal connection to material damage present in a given case might not still be responsible for breach of an obligation, and have certain consequential duties unrelated to the material damage. To illustrate, consider a state which fails to exercise due diligence to prevent a material injury. If due diligence would have prevented the injury, a causal connection between the breach and the injury exists. If, on the other hand, such exercise would not have prevented the material injury, the state is not responsible for such injury; it should, however, nevertheless stand responsible for the 'moral' and 'political' injury attendant

6 For an example of an assertion of multiple responsibility against the actor organ's state and the territorial state, consider the Soviet Union's protests to the United States, Turkey, and West Germany regarding the launching of alleged reconnaisance balloons by the US from the territories of the latter two states. See ILC, 1975 Rpt., *supra* ch. 3 n. 83, at 84.

7 See the discussion in text preceding n. 11 *infra*. Article 12 of the ILC draft text reflects the fact of potential dual responsibility in stating that the acts of organs of one state in the territory of another state are not attributed to the latter—without prejudice, however, to the possible breach by the latter of due diligence obligations. See ILC, 1975 Rpt., *supra* ch. 3 n. 83, at 83.

8 See ch. 3 at nn. 151–2 *supra*.

9 Williams, *supra* n. 1, at 16.

10 See text at and discussion in ch. 3 n. 115 *supra*.

to the breach of its obligation of due diligence.[11] Even when the injury caused is single or undifferentiated, material distinctions may exist in the character of the causal connection or blameworthiness of the conduct of the several responsible states.[12] In summary, distinctions in the results or the gravity of violative conduct of several states ought not to obscure the fact of multiple responsibility arising out of an event. Based on such distinctions the *consequences* of responsibility may vary among the states, but each state should nonetheless be deemed in a position of responsibility.

The scholarly literature is, strikingly, almost devoid of reference to the circumstances or consequences of multiple state responsibility.[13] State assertions of multiple responsibility are exceedingly rare; judicial or arbitral decisions addressing such assertions are essentially unknown. One may surmise that several factors have contributed to this situation. Certainly, the most important is the fact that the majority of cases do involve the responsibility of only a single state. Significantly, circumstances of multiple responsibility are particularly rare in the area of 'treatment of aliens' which has so dominated and influenced the jurisprudence of state responsibility. The fact that assertions of responsibility generally commence with a diplomatic initiative before proceeding to more formal methods of dispute settlement may also have had an effect on the nature of state assertions themselves. Such diplomatic efforts are most often and effectively conducted on a bilateral basis. Even in situations of possible multiple state responsibility, the tendency would be to make a single assertion of responsibility against the most blatant, or perhaps politically accessible or responsive, wrongdoer. In fact, the procedures of available formal mechanisms of dispute settlement reflect and reinforce the practice of such assertions of 'single' responsibility. The provisions governing the Permanent Court of Arbitration and the terms of the ILC's Model Rules on Arbitral Procedure both assume single claims; the procedures do not contemplate disputes among multiple parties.[14] The

[11] As to non-material injury see ch. 1 nn. 13–21 *supra*. As to distinctions in consequences, see text commencing at n. 19 *infra*.

[12] This is not to suggest, of course, that an insufficient causal connection may not preclude responsibility for specific harm. To the contrary, if required causation is not present, there is no consequential responsibility as to such harm. There may, however, be several causes to a single injury, each contributing in equal or different degrees. If the casual contribution of more than one state may be defined as proximate or material, a situation of multiple responsibility obtains with respect to the injury.

[13] Among the numerous general and specific treatises surveyed on the subject of state responsibility, only Brownlie, *System*, *supra* ch. 1 n. 2, at 189–92 and Brownlie, *supra* ch. 2 n. 52, at 456 even identify the specific issue of multiple state responsibility, stating, absolutely correctly, that the principles of joint responsibility are 'as yet indistinct'. See also a notation of the issue, without analysis or conclusion, in Magraw, 'Transboundary Harm: The International Law Commission's Study of "International Liability",' 80 *Am. J. Int'l L.* 305, at 329 (1986).

[14] As to the Permanent Court of Arbitration, see Hague Conventions On Pacific Settlement of International Disputes of 1899 and 1907 done 29 July 1899, entry into force 4 Sept. 1900, and done 18 Oct. 1907, entry into force 27 Nov. 1909; Hudson, *Permanent Court of International Justice 1920–1942* 3–35 (1943); Rosenne, *The World Court* 14–19 (1973). The ILC Rules are set forth in ii

Statute of the International Court of Justice reflects the same assumption in expressing procedures relating to provisional measures, document production, and non-appearance all in terms of a two-party dispute.[15] Judicial practices born out of the inherent constraints of bilateral claims have further reinforced exclusively single assertions even in circumstances of possible multiple responsibility. When the breach of the defending party is, in any event, of lesser gravity than that of a non-party state, fairness would dictate a denial of any responsibility rather than the imposition of the entire burden of responsibility on the party state.[16] The doctrines of responsibility developed in cases relating to 'transferred servants' and 'dependent states', which exonerate without even acknowledging the possibility of multiple responsibility, seem to reflect this tactic.[17] The final factor is the effect of inertia in international practice. The pattern of state assertions of single, even in circumstances suggesting multiple, responsibility is so well-established to challenge deviation. The fact that practice has generally reflected a rudimentary approach to state responsibility does not deny, however, the propriety of, or the capacity of the current international system to manage, more complex claims consistent with established principles of responsibility. As the ICJ has observed: 'There is no obligation upon the possessors of rights to exercise them. Sometimes no remedy is sought, though rights are infringed. To equate this with the creation of a vacuum would be to equate a right with an obligation.'[18] If more than one state breaches its international obligations in the course of an event, each breaching state is in a position of responsibility *vis-à-vis* the injured state. The difficult questions, to which the balance of this

Yb. Int'l L. Comm'n 81 (1958). Consider, for example, the choice of arbitrator provisions. In a recent case, the Court of Arbitration of the International Chamber of Commerce noted both the absence of any specific multiple respondent procedures in the ICC rules and the practical logic of such provisions: 'It is indeed in the interest of good administration of justice to deliver a single decision applicable to all, so as to avoid either contradictions or conflict between decisions.' *Westland Helicopters Ltd.* v. *The Arab Org. For Indus., United Arab Emirates, Saudia Arabia, Qatar, Egypt, Arab-Brit. Helicopter Co.* (Interim Award on Jurisd. 5 Mar. 1985), reprinted in 23 *Int'l Legal Materials* 1087 (1984).

[15] Statute of the International Court of Justice, arts 441 ('either party'), 43 (the 'other party'), and 53 (the other party'), reprinted in Brownlie, *Basic Documents in International Law*, 2nd edn. (1972), at 267. Intervention by other parties is permitted pursuant to Art. 62. This is not likely in view of the fact that the decision of the Court can only affect the parties. See *Monetary Gold Removed from Rome* Case (*Italy* v. *US*), [1954] ICJ 19, at 33.

[16] See discussion in n. 62 *infra*.

[17] In such circumstances it is always possible that both states possess sufficient authority to suggest dual attribution or exercise of due diligence, and thus multiple responsibility. See the *Chevreau* Case (1931) (*Fr.* v. *UK*), 2 R. Int'l Arb. Awards 1113; the *Brown* Case (1923) (*US* v. *UK*), 6 R. Int'l Arb. Awards 120; *Prince Sliman Bey* v *Minister for Foreign Affairs*, [1959] D. Jur. 357, *trans.* reprinted in 28 *Int'l L. Rep.* 79 (1963). See also *Restitution of Household Effects Belonging to Jews Deported from Hungary* (Germany) Case (1965), (Crt. of App. of Berlin), trans. reprinted in 44 *Int'l L. Rep.* 301 (1972), in which Germany was exonerated though clearly a co-participant and catalyst to Hungarian conduct because Hungary was *more* responsible. See Brownlie, *System*, *supra* ch. 1 n. 2, at 188.

[18] *Barcelona Traction Light & Power Co. Ltd.* Case (*Belg.* v. *Spain*), [1970] ICJ (Second Phase) 4, at 45.

section will be addressed, arise with respect to the consequences of responsibility in such circumstances.

B. CONSEQUENCES

To reiterate, the juridical consequence of the breach of *any* international obligation is the creation of a duty to make reparation.[19] The language of the Permanent Court of Justice in the *Chorzów Factory* Case represents the classic articulation of the content of this duty:

> The essential principle contained in the notion of an illegal act—a principle which seems to be established by international practice and in particular by the decisions of arbitral tribunals— is that reparation must, as far as possible, wipe out all the consequences of the illegal act and re-establish the situation which would, in all probability, have existed if that act had not been committed.[20]

'Reparation', then, may be understood in a broad sense to refer to all measures which a breaching state may be required to take to accomplish the defined objective.[21] The forms of reparation appear to fall into three categories, the boundaries of which are rather blurred by inconsistent terminology in the literature: restitution, compensation, and satisfaction.[22]

Restitution, in the broad sense of *restitutio in integrum*, represents the obligation to eliminate the effects of the breach, i.e. to restore the situation to its pre-breach state.[23] Restitution 'in kind', the return of persons or property wrongfully taken, constitutes a specific subset of the general *restitutio* obligation.[24] The specific performance of restitution may, of course, in certain cases either be inapplicable or impossible given the nature of the breach and its consequences: '*restitutio in integrum* should be discarded when there is

[19] See ch. 1 at nn. 4–7 *supra*.

[20] The *Chorzów Factory* Case (Merits), [1928] PCIJ Ser. A, no. 17, at 47.

[21] See generally as to reparation: Jiménez de Arechaga, *supra* ch. 1 n. 11, at 564–72; Borchard, *supra* ch. 1 n. 19, at 413–30; Brownlie *System, supra* ch. 1 n. 2, at 199–240; Brownlie, *supra* ch. 2 n. 52, at 457–64; Cheng, *supra* ch. 1 n. 6, at 233–40; Eagleton, *supra* ch. 3 n. 115, at 52; Mann, 'The Consequences of an International Wrong in International and National Law', 48 *Brit. Yb. Int'l L.* 1 (1976–7), Personnaz, *supra* ch. 2 n. 52; Riphagen, *supra* ch. 1 n. 4; Schwarzenberger, *International Law* 653–81 (3rd edn. 1957); Whiteman, *Damages in International Law* (1937–43).

[22] As to the terminological confusion see Brownlie, *supra* ch. 2 n. 52, at 450; Riphagen, *supra* ch. 1 n. 4, at 16. For example, certain authorities define satisfaction and compensation for moral injury as alternatives to reparation (*stricto senso*). See Garcia-Amador, Draft, *supra* ch. 1 n. 3, at 96.

[23] Riphagen argues that when the injury to the state is through an injury to a national, the state responsible should have the option of restitution or compensation. Riphagen, *supra* ch. 1 n. 4, at 43. Obviously, this is of particular relevance to wrongful expropriation.

[24] See Brownlie, *supra* ch. 2 n. 52, at 461–3; Mann, *supra* n. 21, at 2–5; Riphagen, *supra* ch. 1 n. 4, at 17 and 43. See particularly Brownlie, *System, supra* ch. 1 n. 2, at 210–22, for discussion of the uncertainty in the literature as to whether *restitution* is indeed available by right in the nationalization context.

absolute impossibility of envisaging specific performance or when an irreversible situation has been created.'[25]

Pecuniary compensation arises where restitution does not occur or is insufficient. *Chorzów Factory* again provides an instructive summary:

> Restitution in kind, or, if this is not possible, payment of a sum corresponding to the value which a restitution in kind would bear; the award if need be, of damages for loss sustained which would not be covered by restitution in kind or payment in place of it—such are the principles which should serve to determine the amount of compensation due for an act contrary to international law.[26]

Issues of causation, remoteness and foreseeability, of course, play a key role—analogous to their municipal role in tort—in the delimitation of damages attributable to the breach and, thus, compensable by the breaching state.[27] Particular problems are encountered in the assessment of the measure of the award when the 'injury' experienced is non-material or only the 'moral' or 'political' injury attendant to every breach of an obligation.[28] Thus, there are few guidelines to quantification of loss when the breach consists, for example, of a violation of territory or, perhaps, a failure to punish, when no economic loss is occasioned.[29]

The third form of reparation, 'satisfaction', is, in fact often associated with such non-material injury breaches.[30] Measures of satisfaction, however, are neither limited in application to 'moral' or 'political' injury cases, nor used to the exclusion of other forms of reparation in such cases.[31] Brownlie does logically suggest that pecuniary awards predominantly designed to express apology are properly viewed as cases of satisfaction, rather than compensation in the strict sense.[32] In any event, the forms of satisfaction may include formal apology or declaration of responsibility, guarantees against repetition, punishment of individual actors, and other measures fashioned appropriately to the facts.[33]

[25] The *Topco/CalAsiatic* v. *Libya* (Award of 19 Jan. 1977), 17 *Int'l Legal Materials* 1, at 112 (1978).

[26] The *Chorzów Factory* Case (Merits), [1928] PCIJ, Ser. A, no. 17, at 47.

[27] As to the basic requirement that the harm for which the state is deemed responsible must bear a material causal relationship to the state's conduct see *Bollecker-Stern*, *supra* ch. 1 n. 16, at 185–359; Cheng, *supra* ch. 1 n. 6, at 241–53; Whiteman, *supra* n. 21, vol iii at 1767–1832.

[28] See ch. 1 at nn. 13–17 *supra*.

[29] See discussion *re* punishment at ch. 3 n. 115 *supra*.

[30] See e.g. Garcia-Amador, Draft, *supra* ch. 1 n. 3, at 96.

[31] See Brownlie, *supra* ch. 2 n. 52, at 460–1. Note the *I'm Alone* Case (1933 and 1935) (*Can.* v. *US*), 3 R. Int'l Arb. Awards 1609, in which both an apology and a cash award were recommended as material amends for the wrongful sinking of a vessel. But see n. 32 *infra*.

[32] Brownlie, *supra* ch. 2 n. 52, at 459; Brownlie, *System*, *supra* ch. 1 n. 2, at 223. Thus an affront to territory, with no further material consequences, might yield an apology payment properly denominated 'satisfaction'. Payments arising out of a failure to punish present a more difficult case, given the various perspectives on the character of the 'injury' caused. See discussion at ch. 3 n. 115 *supra*.

[33] As to satisfaction generally see Brownlie, *System*, *supra* ch. 1 n. 2, at 208–9; Brownlie, *supra* ch. 2 n. 52, at 459–61; Riphagen, *supra* ch. 1 n. 4, at 16 and 23; Schwarzenberger, *supra* n. 21, vol. i, at 658–9; Whiteman, *supra* n. 21, vol. ii, at 1211.

One further, and perhaps too obvious, obligation related to the occurrence of responsibility rarely receives specific mention in the literature: the duty to stop the conduct constituting a breach of obligation. As Riphagen, writing as a Special Rapporteur to the ILC, submits: 'It does not seem relevant whether one considers this duty as a consequence of the continuing "validity" or "force" of the primary obligation, or as a duty which arises as a consequence of the breach.'[34] Nor, if defined as a consequential obligation, does it matter whether the duty is viewed as subsumed in the notion of *restitutio in integrum* or as an independent form of restitution. There is no question that a state in a position of responsibility must cease its violative conduct.[35]

The selection of the appropriate form of reparation in a particular case, of course, depends on the facts, i.e. the specific nature of the breach and its consequences. It is not intended here to consider generally the fashion in which the suitable measure or type of reparation is determined.[36] Rather, the concern is simply how this process of determination is affected by circumstances of multiple state responsibility. With respect to all forms of reparation other than pecuniary compensation, it is submitted that there is *no* effect. Consider the example of an attack by representatives of state *A* on the diplomatic mission of state *B* in the territory of state *C*. Assume that official documents are stolen, hostages are taken, and state *C* has failed to exercise due diligence to prevent the attack. The analysis of the appropriate forms of reparation, other than compensation, due to state *B* from states *A* and *C* is the same whether the assertion is of single or multiple responsibility. As to state *A*, in either procedural posture the initial duty is to cease the wrongful conduct—the retention of hostages and documents. This duty of restoration could, of course, also be imposed in application of the principle of restitution. Appropriate measures of satisfaction, including perhaps formal apology and a token payment to support such apology, could also be required. The analysis with respect to state *C* is similar. If one views the breach of obligation as a general failure to provide adequate protection to diplomats, state *C* must cease such violative conduct by providing due protection. In any event, satisfaction might be demanded in the form of apology, token payment, and perhaps a guarantee of future protection. The key to these conclusions is that the measures of non-compensatory reparation required of each breaching state may be determined *independently* in a multiple responsibility situation.

Compensation, e.g. for damage to the diplomatic premises in the example presented, demands, on the other hand, a dependent analysis. By definition, a principal objective of compensation is to make whole the loss experienced by the injured state, The aggregate compensation received by the injured state

[34] Riphagen, *supra* ch. 1 n. 4, at 15.

[35] See *id.* See also Comments of Pinto, ILC, Summary Records of the 33rd Session UN Doc. A/CN 4/Ser. A/1981, i *Yb. Int'l L. Comm'n* 137 (1981).

[36] See generally materials cited at n. 21 *supra*.

ought not to exceed the measure of that loss, even when the conduct of more than one state bears a causal connection to the injury. How then is the burden of compensation to be borne? It is to this rather unexplored (in an international context) territory that the discussion now turns.

C. COMPENSATION

i. Municipal Practice

For several reasons, it is appropriate to begin this discussion with a brief look at the fashion in which municipal legal systems, in their relatively sophisticated state of development, respond to the problem of multiple party responsibility for harm occasioned by wrongful conduct. First, the structures adopted at a municipal level simply provide a useful framework for considering the international problem. Moreover, to the extent municipal rules exhibit the characteristics of 'general principles of law recognized by civilized nations', they may serve as a source in the determination of international law.[37] In any event, as Lauterpacht observed, municipal private law belongs to the same 'genus' as international public law: each 'regulates relations of legal entities in a state of coordination', as distinct from that of subordination.[38] Thus, substantive analogies present in municipal practice may, at the very least, assist in the progressive formulation of an international regime.[39]

The treatment of the circumstance of multiple responsibility in municipal systems is, fact, remarkably consistent. At the most basic level, all systems approach multiple party responsibility as a juridical fact, and possess substantive and procedural regimes designed specifically to manage such situations.[40] Consider, for example, the rules developed with respect to the category of wrongdoers engaged in concerted conduct. Such 'joint tortfeasors' are, in both the common and civil law traditions, uniformly held to be jointly and severally liable; a claim may be made for the entire amount of compensation due to the injured party against all or any of the joint participants in an injurious act.[41] Under common law, a joint tort-feasor burdened with the full claim possessed no right to seek contribution from its

[37] See Statute of the International Court of Justice, art. 38(1)(c), reprinted in Brownlie, *supra* n. 15, at 267. See also Parry, *The Sources and Evidence of International Law* (1965).

[38] Lauterpacht, *Private Law Sources and Analogies of International Law* 81 (1927).

[39] See Váli, *Servitudes of International Law: A Study of Rights in Foreign Territory* 51 (2nd edn. 1958). But see Brownlie, *supra* ch. 2 n. 52, at 456, who is of the view that municipal analogies are 'unhelpful' in the context of multiple responsibility.

[40] See James and Brown, *supra* n. 2, at 23–4 and 349 ff.; Prosser, *supra* n. 2, at 291–323; Williams, *supra* n. 2, *passim*.

[41] See Lawson and Markesinis, i *Tortious Liability for Unintentional Harm in the Common Law and the Civil Law* 126, at 129–30 (1982); Prosser, *supra* n. 2 at 291; Williams, *supra* n. 2, at 3.

fellow wrongdoers.[42] Pursuant to decision or legislation, the right of contribution among joint tort-feasors is now well established in almost all systems.[43] The basis of the apportionment among wrongoders in the contribution context is, however, the subject of some dispute. The debate arising out of the text of British legislation is illustrative: 'In any proceedings for contribution under this section the amount of the contribution recoverable from any person shall be such as may be found by the court to be just and equitable having regard to the extent of that person's responsibility for the damage . . . '.[44] Two interpretations of this directive have been advocated. The share of responsibility will be determined on the basis of relative causation or 'blameworthiness' (i.e. fault in its broadest sense).[45] Glanville Williams has championed the 'blame' approach, arguing that a determination of relative causation is simply not feasible.[46] Other authorities now appear to advocate a hybrid approach, factoring both causation and blame in the apportionment decision.[47]

The category of wrongdoers acting independently with respect to a single event presents certain of the same, and certain rather different, issues. If the harm occasioned by the conduct of an independent wrongdoer may be separately identified, the solution to the problem is easy and uniform. In such cases, the measure of each wrongdoer's responsibility will be limited to compensation for the specific harm caused.[48] If, on the other hand, the injury is not so divisible, both common and civil law systems deem the contributing independent tort-feasors severally liable to the injured party for the entire amount of compensation due.[49] Prosser summarizes:

Where a logical basis can be found for some rough practical apportionment, which limits a defendant's liability to that part of the harm which he has in fact caused, it may be expected that the division will be made. Where no such basis can be found, and any division must be purely arbitrary, there is no practical course except to hold the

[42] See *Merryweather* v. *Nixan*, 8 Term Rep. 186 (1799).

[43] See Prosser, *supra* n. 2, at 306–7 (US); Lawson and Markesinis, *supra* n. 41, at 130 (Civil law states); Williams, *supra* n. 2, at 86–7 (Commonwealth states); *Winfield and Jolowicz on Tort* 557–61 (9th edn. Jolowicz, Lewis, and Harris eds. 1971) (hereinafter cited as *Winfield and Jolowicz*). In the United Kingdom the first legislation to accomplish this result was the Law Reform (Married Women and Tortfeasors) Act of 1935, s. 6 (1) (*c*). This was eventually replaced by the Civil Liability (Contribution) Act of 1978, s. 3.

[44] The Law Reform (Married Women and Tortfeasors) Act of 1935, s. 6(2).

[45] As to the dispute generally, see James and Brown, *supra* n. 2, at 353 n. 3; *Salmond and Heuston on the Law of Torts* 422 (18th edn. Heuston and Chambers eds. 1981) hereinafter cited as *Salmond and Heuston*; Williams, *supra* n. 2, at 156–60; *Winfield and Jolowicz on Tort*, *supra* n. 43, at 558.

[46] Williams, *supra* n. 2, at 157–58.

[47] See e.g. *Winfield and Jolowicz*, *supra* n. 43, at 118 and 558 n. 36.

[48] Williams, *supra* n. 2 at 1–3, defines 'concurrent tort-feasors' at joint tort-feasors and independent tort-feasors when the latters' 'torts concur (run together) to produce the same damage'.

[49] See *id.*; Lawson and Markesinis, *supra* n. 41, at 129–30. But see the special case of admiralty described at n. 54 *infra*.

defendant liable for the entire loss, notwithstanding the fact that the other causes have contributed to it.[50]

As with joint tort-feasors, independent tort-feasors may demand contribution, with apportionment of the aggregate compensation premised on the same basis of relative causation, blame or both.[51] It should be underscored, of course, that such a regime does reflect a policy choice. Apportionment could precede compensation, i.e. each wrongdoer could be deemed liable to the injured party only to the extent of its ultimate, post-contribution liability under the existing system.[52] The logic dictating the full several liability approach present in municipal law is, however, patent: '[T]he real explanation behind this widely accepted rule is the desire to afford the victim of the harm the maximum possible chance of having his harm properly and fully compensated.'[53]

In fact, in the limited context of admiralty practice the approach of several liability for the entire harm is not generally followed. The United Kngdom's Maritime Conventions Act of 1911 is representative:

> Where, by the fault of two or more vessels, damage or loss is caused to one or more of those vessels, to their cargoes or freight, or to any property on board, the liability to make good the damage or loss shall be in proportion to the degree in which each vessel was in fault: Provided that if, having regard to all the circumstances of the case, it is not possible to establish different degrees of fault, the liability shall be apportioned equally.[54]

Following the lead suggested by the Brussels Unification Convention, almost all leading maritime states so apportion the original liability to an injured third party on the basis of comparative fault.[55]

The issue of independent wrongdoer responsibility for a single event arises in one further context—when the injury is in part related to the conduct of the injured party. In civil law jurisprudence, 'the rule of apportionment of liability on the basis of the gravity of the respective faults has prevailed since the very early days of the Code Napoleon. . . '.[56] In common law, the first break from

[50] Prosser, *supra* n. 2, at 313–14, 465.

[51] See *Croston* v. *Vaughan*, [1938] KB 540, [1937] iv All E.R. 249; *Pride of Derby and Derbyshire Angling Assoc. Ltd.* v. *British Celanese Ltd.*, [1952] i All E.R. 1326; James and Brown *supra* n. 2 at 352.

[52] See text at n. 54 immediately below regarding admiralty practice.

[53] Lawson and Markesinis, *supra* n. 41, at 126.

[54] Maritime Conventions Act of 1911, 1 § 2 Geo. V., c. 57, s. 1.

[55] See Prosser, *supra* n. 2, at 435; Williams, *supra* n. 2, at 23–32 (who notes a lacuna in the UK legislation which applies the apportionment to third party claims for cargo damage but not for ship damage). See the Brussels International Convention for the Unification of Certain Rules of Law With Respect to Collisions Between Vessels; done 23 Sept. 1910, art 4, reprinted in *International Conventions of Merchant Shipping* 1337 (2nd edn. Singh ed. 1973).

[56] Lawson and Markesinis, *supra* n. 41, at 132–3. See also Prosser, 'Comparative Negligence', 51 *Mich. L. Rev.* 465, at 467 (1953); Prosser, *supra* n. 2, at 435; *Salmond and Heuston, supra* n. 45, at 483–4; Williams, *supra* n. 2, at 257.

the traditional doctrine, which barred recovery in the presence of any claimant negligence or fault, occurred in British admiralty practice with the apportionment regime described in the quoted text of the Maritime Conventions Act.[57] This principle was eventually extended generally to situations of contributory negligence by legislative action in the United Kingdom.[58] Such a 'comparative' approach now also represents the dominant trend in United States' practice.[59] As in the context of *inter se* contribution among wrongdoers, municipal practice as to the basis upon which comparative fault is to be determined, i.e. causation versus blameworthiness, remains inconsistent.[60]

ii. International Practice

Relative to such highly developed and distinct municipal rules, the position of international law on the subject of compensation in a multiple responsibility context is quite obscure. Yet, one does not encounter a total vacuum of relevant material. An examination of an albeit limited body of decisions and state practice does at least yield a fragmented picture and a sense of direction. On the basis of such materials, municipal analogies, and certain first principles of the international system, a progressive regime may be identified.

In the *Anglo-Chinese Shipping Co.* Case a claim was asserted against the United States by a Hong Kong corporation for the use of a vessel seized by Japan during World War II and retained until 1950 by order of the allied forces occupying Japan.[61] The US Court of Claims denied the claim, holding that Japan retained 'possession' of the vessel at all times—notwithstanding the fact of the ultimate authority of the allies over the use and disposition of the vessel.[62] Prior to expressing this conclusion, the Court noted in an *obiter dictum* that the United States could not, in any event, be deemed solely responsible for allied conduct:

> The occupation of Japan was a joint venture participated in by the United States of America, the United Kingdom, China, and Russia; and whatever benefit the occupying powers derived from the use of plaintiff's vessel in the laying and repairing of submarine cables was derived by all of them in common and not by any one more than another.[63]

[57] See text at n. 54 *supra*.

[58] See *Salmond and Hueston*, *supra* n. 45, at 492; Williams, *supra* n. 2, at 258.

[59] See Prosser, *supra* n. 2, at 480–503.

[60] Williams, *supra* n. 2, at 390, does argue that 'blame' is uniformly accepted as the criterion in the context of contributory negligence. But see *Winfield and Jolowicz*, *supra* n. 43, at 115–18. Among civil law systems, the trend is to the 'comparative causation' approach. Lawson and Markesinis, *supra* n. 41, at 134.

[61] *Anglo-Chinese Shipping Co. Ltd.* v. *United States*, 130 Ct. Cl. 361, 127 F. Supp. 553, *cert. den.* 349 US 938 (1955).

[62] One may make a credible argument that this is a fine example of a case in which responsibility was denied because a more 'blameworthy' party was not before the court—when, in fact, both the defendant and the third party might properly have been deemed responsible.

[63] *Anglo-Chinese Shipping Co. Ltd.* v. *United States*, *supra* n. 61, at 985.

Hence, implicitly, responsibility for the conduct of the several states acting in concert would necessarily be multiple and shared. As to the procedural impact of this conclusion, the Court first noted the uniform municipal rule of joint and several liability, and then reserved judgment: 'Whether this rule should be applied to sovereign nations engaged in a joint enterprise has never been decided, and we do not decide it . . .'.[64]

The general conclusion that joint enterprises yield shared responsibility for compensation finds additional support in the instance of the lump-sum payment made to Germany by the United States and United Kingdom, following an arbitral decision assigning responsibility to the two states, in settlement of claims for the consequences of joint military activities in Samoa at the turn of the century.[65] The United States directly asserted such joint and several responsibility in its separate pleadings against Hungary and the USSR before the ICJ in the *Case of the Treatment in Hungary of Aircraft of United States of America.*[66] Demand was made from each state for the full measure of damages arising out the alleged co-operation of Hungary and the Soviet Union in the interception and detention of a US military plane and its crew. As to the compensatory obligations of one member of such an enterprise in action against only that member, Brownlie notes that the *Corfu Channel* Court was 'untroubled by the possibility that another State [Yugoslavia, acting in concert with Albania, according to British submissions] had laid the mines in Albanian waters.'[67] In fact, given the Court's conclusions that (*a*) the authors of the minelaying were unknown and (*b*) Albania's breach was in knowingly allowing its territory to be used to harm other states, the decision may point to several liability among *independent* wrongdoers for the entire amount of compensation.[68]

[64] *Id.*, at 986. Fawcett has noted that the responsibility of constituent member-states for the wrongful conduct of international organizations depends on the specific 'constitutive instrument'. Fawcett, *International Law and the Uses of Outer Space* 46 (1968). The International Court specifically refused to examine the meaning of 'shall be borne' in Art 17(2) of the UN Charter to determine the sharing of expenses among UN members in the *Certain Expenses of the United Nations (Art. 17, parag. 2 of the Charter)*, Advisory Opin. of 20 July 1962, [1962] ICJ 151, 158. The specific issue of the possibility of several liability among members of organizations party to the Space Objects Convention is discussed in Comment, 'The Participation of International Organizations in the Proposed International Agreement on Liability for Damage Caused by Objects Launched into Outer Space,' 3 *Can Yb. Int'l L.* 265 (1965). As to the responsibility of international organizations as international persons, see generally Bowett, *The Law of International Institutions* (4th edn. 1982); Schermers, *International Institutional Law* 937–8 (1982).

[65] See the *Samoan Claims* Arbitration (1899) (*Germ.* v. *US & UK*), 9 R. Int'l Arb. Awards 21; i Whiteman, *supra* ch. 1 n. 6, at 1778–81. Brownlie notes as evidence of the absence of a rule of joint and several liability that claims versus Axis powers have been singular, disregarding the common purpose of their war efforts. Brownlie, *supra* ch. 2 n. 52, at 456. On the other hand, these 'single' claims might be viewed as expressing only a conclusion as to the nature of the alliance—as to the specific subjects of the claims, the conduct was not deemed concerted.

[66] *Case of the Treatment in Hungary of Aircraft of United States of America* (*US* v. *Hungary*) (*US* v. *USSR*), [1954] ICJ 99 (Order of 12 July 1954) and [1954] ICJ Pleadings 38, at 58–9.

[67] Brownlie, *supra* ch. 2 n. 52, at 456.

[68] The fact that the Court accepted that Albania lacked the technical capacity to lay the mines alone contributes to this interpretation.

In any event, the most fertile area of state practice on the subject of multiple party compensation clearly relates to activities in outer space. Specifically, the 1972 Convention on International Liability for Damage Caused by Space Objects sets forth certain concrete provisions regarding the circumstance of multiple responsibility. Article V of the Convention provides that states jointly participating in the launch of a space object 'shall be jointly severally liable for any damage caused.'[69] A right of contribution among the wrongdoers is then established: 'A launching State which has paid compensation for damage shall have the right to present a claim for indemnification to other participants in the joint launching.'[70] 'Launching states' deemed to be jointly participating in a launch include states which launch or procure the launch and states from whose territory or facility the launch occurs.[71] Prior to the Convention itself, there was substantial discourse in the literature as to whether the state of the territory or the facility ought to share the full burden of joint and several responsibility.[72] Debate on the subject continued in the course of the Convention proceedings, with several states proposing variations on the theme of subsidiary or secondary liability.[73] The final text of the Convention, however, reflects the view that although participating states may choose unevenly to apportion liability by *inter se* agreement, joint and several liability is appropriate for the protection of the injured state.[74] Article V(2) thus reads:

> The participants in a joint launching may conclude agreements regarding apportionment among themselves of the financial obligation in respect of which they are jointly and severally liable. Such agreements shall be without prejudice to the right of a State

[69] Space Object Convention, *supra* ch. 2 n. 83, art. v(1). For a parallel regime see art. 4 of the IMO's recent Draft Convention on Liability and Compensation in Connexion with the Carriage of Noxious and Hazardous Substances by Sea, IMO Doc. LEG. CONF, G/3, 13 Jan. 1984, reprinted in 23 *Int'l Legal Materials* 148 (1984).

[70] *Id.*, at art. V(2).

[71] *Id.*, at art. I(c). See also Art. 8 of the Declaration of Legal Principles governing the activities of States in the Exploration and Use of Outer Space, Gen. Ass. Res. 1962 (XVIII), 13 Dec. 1963; Art. 7 of the Treaty on Principles Governing the Activities of States in the Exploration and use of Outer Space, including the Moon and Other Celestial Bodies, entry into force 10 Oct. 1967, reprinted in Brownlie, *supra* n. 15, at 117.

[72] See e.g. Jenks, *Space Law* 284 (1965); Malik; *supra* ch. 3 n. 83, at 348–5; McDougal, Laswell, and Vlasic, *Law and Public Order in Outer Space* 350 (1964); Theraulaz, *supra* ch. 3 n. 83, at 264–9. Much of the discussion focused on Art. 7 of the Moon Treaty, cited in the preceding note, which imposed liability on all four categories of state, but failed to refer to the nature of the 'shared' liability.

[73] As to the debate generally, see Cheng, *supra* ch. 2 n. 83, at 120; Foster, *supra* ch. 2 n. 83, at 163–8. A majority of such proposals suggested that the territorial state should be liable only in the event that the states launching or procuring the launch are not identified or not parties to the treaty. See e.g. France: Proposal concerning the State Responsible and Joint and Several Responsibility, UN Doc. A/AC. 105/C. 2/L. 36, 10 June 1968; Australia: Proposal, UN Doc. A/AC. 105/C. 2/L. 39, 12 June 1968. In the IMO's recent Hazardous Substances Carriage Convention a regime of subsidiary liability is proposed for shippers; a shipper would be liable only if the shipowner is unable or not required to pay full compensation. See art. 7, Draft Conv. *supra* n. 69.

[74] See Wiewiorowska, *supra* ch. 3 n. 83, at 29–30.

sustaining damage to seek the entire compensation due under this Convention from any or all of the launching States which are jointly and severally liable.[75]

In summary, the adopted approach of joint and several liability with a right of *inter se* contribution tracks precisely the municipal model of compensation obligations in the context of such concerted activities.

The Space Objects Convention further embraces, with an interesting variation, the approach of municipal systems with respect to compensation by *independent* wrongdoers. Article IV provides that a third party injured as a consequence of the collision of two space objects may claim compensation for the total injury from any or all of the 'launching states' of *either* space object.[76] The distinctive characteristic of this regime is that, *vis-à-vis* an injured third party, the launching states of space objects are categorically deemed responsible. Even if the state of one object is patently and exclusively at fault, the state of the other object stands liable to the injured third state for the entire amount of any compensation due.[77] As between the two launching states, an orthodox regime of contribution based on comparative fault is adopted: '[t]he burden of compensation for the damage shall be apportioned between the first two States in accordance with the extent to which they were at fault; if the extent of the fault of each of these States cannot be established, the burden of compensation shall be apportioned equally between them.'[78]

Although not directly touching on the circumstance of such multiple state compensation to an injured state, a substantial number of decisions evidence the capacity of international tribunals to apportion or adjust the measure of damages on a similar comparative basis. As noted by Judge Azevedo in the *Corfu Channel* Case, for example, when the injured state contributes to the occurrence of its injury 'the conduct of the victim can be taken into account by reducing the degree of responsibility and consequently apportioning the damages.'[79] Certain earlier decisions reflected an older common law view and denied any responsibility in the event of a contribution by the injured party.[80] As on the municipal plane, comparative apportionment of compensation in circumstances of contributory conduct now appears the dominant rule in

[75] Space Objects Convention, *supra* ch. 2 n. 83, art. V(2).

[76] See Cheng, *supra* ch. 2 n. 83, at 121–2; Foster, *supra* ch. n. 83, at 167–8.

[77] Compensation is due based on absolute (no-fault) liability for damage on the earth's surface or to aircraft. Space Objects Convention, *supra* ch. 2 n. 83, art. IV(1) (*a*). Fault on the part of at least one of the colliding objects is a prerequisite to liability for damage to other space objects. *Id.*, at art. IV(*b*).

[78] *Id.*, at art. IV(2). See Wiewiorowska, *supra* ch. 3 n. 83, at 30.

[79] The *Corfu Channel* Case (*UK* v. *Albania*), [1949] ICJ 4, (Merits) (Dissenting Opin. of Judge Azevedo) at 78, 95. See also the *Alabama* Claims Arbitration (1872) (*US* v. *UK*), Moore, i *Arbitrations* 495, at 623 (1898).

[80] See i Whiteman, *supra* ch. 1 n. 6, at 216; the *Davis* Case (1903) (*UK* v. *Venez.*), 9 R. Int'l Arb Awards 460; the *Andresen* Case (1930) (*Germ.* v. *Mex.*), Whiteman, *supra* 21, at 217. But see Bollecker-Stern, *supra* ch. 1 n. 16, at 341–2, who argues that if injury is caused by the *combination* of the conduct of the injured state and another state, there is no liability.

international judicial practice.[81] The apportionment, and, in earlier cases, the denial, process engaged in these situations generally reflects an analysis of relative causation.[82] There are cases, however, in which the compensation appears to be apportioned on the basis of relative 'blameworthiness', in a broad, moral sense.[83] In the *Garcia and Garza* Case, for example, the measure of compensation awarded for the unjustified shooting by US officials of a Mexican national illegally crossing the border was expressly reduced due to the knowingly wrongful character of the victim's conduct.[84] Similarly, the 'imprudent' conduct of Americans firing into the air for fun led the *Kling* Case tribunal to mitigate the damages otherwise payable for the wrongful shooting of one of the Americans by Mexican troops.[85] Such recourse to the abstraction of relative 'blame' appears consistent with the undisputed submission of Great Britain in the *Alabama* Claims that compensation should be proportional 'not only to the loss incurred as a consequence of a wrong (act or omission), but also to the gravity of the wrong itself.'[86]

The final illustrations of the comparative apportionment of compensation in international practice arise in cases in which independent causes have contributed to an undifferentiated total damage.[87] Interest was disallowed in the *Zafiro* Case, for example, based on a finding that a portion of claimed looting damage was caused by unidentified wrongdoers.[88] In the *Alliance* Case, the principal amount of compensation was similarly reduced in a holding that damages claimed as the consequence of the wrongful detention of a vessel were in some part attributable to an earlier accident.[89] Compensation in the *Martini* Case was reduced to two-thirds of the total damages experienced by a foreign company during the Venezuelan civil war; the state's wrongs combined with two independent causes, the acts of revolutionaries and the fact of a condition of war, to produce the injury.[90] Such cases of apportionment among causes illustrate well the existence of the 'wide

[81] See Garcia-Amador, Draft, *supra* ch. 1 n. 3, at 35–6; Personnaz, *supra* ch. 2 n. 52, at 107; Schwarzenberger, *supra* n. 21, at 662–3.

[82] See e.g. Bollecker-Stern, *supra* ch. 1 n. 16, at 326–44; i. Whiteman, *supra* ch 1 n. 6, at 216–22.

[83] Whiteman notes that compensation in arrest, detention, and imprisonment cases is 'influenced considerably by the conduct of the claimants.' i Whiteman, *supra* ch. 1 n. 6, at 375.

[84] The *Garcia and Garza Case* (1926) (*Mex.* v. *US*), 4 R. Int'l Arb. Awards 119, at 123.

[85] The *Kling* Case (1930) (*US* v. *Mex.*), 4 R. Int'l Arb. Awards 575, at 585.

[86] The *Alabama* Claims Abitration (1872) (*US* v. *UK*), De Lapradelle and Politis, ii *Recueil des arbitrages internationaux* 713, 825 (1932); Moore, i. *Arbitrations* 495, at 623 (1898).

[87] As to such 'complementary' or concurrent causes, each of which causes a part of the damage, see generally Bollecker-Stern, *supra* ch. 1 n. 16, at 281–5.

[88] *Earnshaw and Others: The Zafiro* Case (1925) (*UK* v. *US*), 6 R. Int'l Arb. Awards 160, at 163–4.

[89] The *Alliance* Case (1903) (*US* v. *Venez.*), 9 R. Int'l Arb. Awards 140.

[90] The *Martini* Case (1930) (*Italy* v. *Venez.*), 10 R. Int'l Arb. Awards 644. See also the *Petrocelli* Case (1903) (*Italy* v. *Venez.*), 10 R. Int'l Arb. Awards 477, at 592, in which undifferentiated total harm to a residence during a revolution was divided to reflect the fact that part was due to the wrongful conduct of the state and part was simply an incident of war not subject to compensation.

discretionary powers' of international tribunals in the determination of appropriate compensation.[91] As Schwarzenberger concludes: 'In establishing the amount of compensation, international judicial institutions admit more freely than in discharging other functions of a similar kind the equitable character of their jurisdiction.'[92] There would seem to be little question, then, of the capacity or relevant experience of such institutions to engage in apportionment of compensation among multiple wrongdoers.

iii. A Progressive Regime

The sum of the foregoing international judicial and state practice does not, unfortunately, equal a whole. The rules of compensation in the circumstance of multiple state responsibility are clearly not yet mature. Yet, based on the existing international practice and municipal analogies, it does seem possible to suggest (or, perhaps, anticipate) the logical direction of such rules. The objectives of the allocation of obligations to compensate on the international and municipal planes do, after all, appear identical: make the injured party whole though pecuniary compensation for loss; and channel the cost or burden of the injury to its author to deter repetition.[93] There are, however, two distinctive characteristics of the international system, each a corollary of the principles of equality and independence, which do qualify the utility of municipal analogies.

First, dispute settlement in the international system depends on the will of the states involved. There is no truly compulsory method to obtain a resolution or judgment regarding a claim of responsibility.[94] Even the putative 'compulsory jurisdiction' of the ICJ only operates when states have affirmatively expressed their consent to the Court's jurisdiction, often coupling such consent with reservations and conditions which severely limit the effective scope of the compulsory jurisdiction.[95] The absence of a mandatory process of dispute settlement potentially affects both injured and breaching states in a multiple responsibility context. The former may find no state or only one state (due either to prior consent to judicial process or simply moral, political or economic susceptibility) responsive to the settlement of a claim for compensation. A wrongdoer similarly may find no fellow wrongdoer willing or obligated to entertain a claim for contribution. These disabilities unique to the international plane must temper the instinct to adopt municipal principles in wholesale fashion.

91 Borchard, *supra* ch. 1 n. 19, at 413.

92 Schwarzenberger, *supra* n. 21, at 661.

93 For an interesting discussion of the theory of allocation of the costs of torts, in terms particularly relevant to the context of pollution, see Calabresi, 'Some Thoughts on Risk Distribution and the Law of Torts', 70 *Yale L.J.* 499 (1961).

94 See Brownlie, *supra* ch. 2 n. 52, at 705.

95 See Brierly, *supra* ch. 2 n. 41, at 355–61; Rosenne, *The Law and Practice of the International Court* 364–421 (1961). But see n. 99 *infra* regarding prior agreements.

The second characteristic is somewhat more abstract. As noted above, the municipal approach of joint and several liability reflects a policy decision to protect the injured party by imposing upon each wrongdoer an original obligation to pay compensation for the entire injury, even for that share of the harm ultimately defined as the responsbility of another party. There is nothing inherent in international society which would preclude a parallel system. The international community, however, lacks a legislative authority to make such policy decisions or to dictate rules designed for the collective good. International law remains the product of common perceptions of private good.[96] It is a principal impediment to the development of effective international law that states continue to identify any qualification of the prerogatives of 'independence' with private detriment.[97] An international rule of joint and several liability, imposing on one state a measure of liability conceptually attributable to another state, certainly would establish a relationship encroaching on such independence. This denies, of course, neither the logic nor the propriety of the relationship, for all of international law encroaches on independence. In advocating such a rule, one must simply respect the force and justify the qualification of the tenet of state independence.[98]

Having stated the foregoing cautions, it is nevertheless submitted that, as to states engaged in a wrongful common enterprise, joint and several liability coupled with a right of contribution, as evident in municipal systems and reflected in international convention, represents an appropriate general principle for the international system. The noted objections to burdening one state with the entire measure of due compensation are not sufficiently telling in the context of a concerted action to outweigh the objective of providing injured states with the greatest opportunity to achieve compensation. States participating in a common activity have the opportunity to establish a mechanism for 'compulsory' dispute settlement through prior *inter se* agreement.[99] By means of such agreements, states acting pursuant to a common plan in fact have the benefit of an opportunity to establish specific indemnity obligations representing their own view of the appropriate allocation of risk.[100] Considerations of state 'independence' are similarly

[96] Harold Lasswell argues that the privatism which dominates the international community will give way to a collective orientation as states more and more perceive shared values, risks, and characteristics. See Lasswell, 'Future Systems of Identity in the World Community', in iv *The Future of the International Legal Order* 26 (Black and Falk eds. 1972).

[97] For excellent discussions of the role of the principle of sovereign independence see de Visscher, *supra* ch. 3 n. 131, at 89; Larson and Jenks, *Sovereignty within the Law* 1–28 (1965).

[98] 'The vices of a system are not remedied by abstract conceptions that denature the forces animating it; doctrinal anticipations cannot triumph over the age-old propensity of nations to make the State the guardian of their supreme interests.' De Visscher, *supra* ch. 3 n. 131, at 105.

[99] As to jurisdiction of a judicial institution based upon an agreement preceding the particular dispute see Rosenne, *supra* n. 95, at 332–5; the *Ambatielos* Case (*Greece* v. *UK*), [1952] ICJ 28 (Prelim. Objections).

[100] This fact provided the basis for the ultimate agreement to accept joint and several liability

mitigated in this circumstance. It may be argued cogently that participation in an enterprise to achieve a common benefit renders the correlative costs or consequences of the enterprise equally common to all participants, *vis-à-vis* the rest of the community and particularly an injured state. Moreover, if such a regime were indeed established, states would expect and independently consent to the attendant risks and burdens by entry into the concerted activity. If the notion of independence has any effect, it is merely to suggest the propriety of the right of contribution; each state should ultimately bear only the consequences of its share of the common enterprise. The contribution process finds support, in any event, in the underlying policy objective of deterrence through channelling costs to all responsible states and, perhaps, simply in general considerations of fairness.[101]

The factors cited in support of joint and several liability for participants in common enterprises do not apply in the circumstance of independent actors producing a single harm. By definition, such wrongdoers have neither the prior opportunity to establish substantive or procedural rights with respect to the sharing of liability nor the communal benefits and expectations present in the concerted conduct situation.[102] The relationship of independent wrongdoers is established only by and upon the event of the injury; there is no pre-existing or even expected linkage between the states' conduct.[103] An exception, of course, exists when states may anticipate injury arising out of the conjunction of certain independent acts (for example, the placement and operation of space objects), and reach agreement as to the sharing of liability and rights of indemnity.[104] In such cases, the imposition of joint and several liability is supported by the same logic applicable to concerted conduct. To impose such liability as the general rule applicable to independent wrongdoers (as it is on the municipal plane), however, requires a policy decision that the problems of states in breach, i.e. uncertainty of contribution and qualified independence, are outweighed by the objective of securing adequate compensation for injured states. Fixing each state with the entire original compensation obligation to the injured state seems to present little difficulty in situations in which the acts of any one of the independent wrongdoers would have been sufficient to cause the harm.[105] Problems of policy are far greater

for all 'launching states' in the Space Objects Convention. See text at nn. 71–5 *supra*. For an example see Agreement of 6 May 1964 among Australia, United Kingdom and the European Organization for the Development and Construction of Space Vehicle Launchers, in Jenks, *supra* n. 72, at 368–74.

[101] At least one author appears to regard joint and several liability as the established rule with respect to joint enterprises. See Handl, *supra* ch. 2 n. 82, at 535 n. 47. For further support see Goldie, *supra* ch. 2 n. 92, at 1254.

[102] The situation of complicity would seem to represent a possible exception, suggesting perhaps that for these purposes complicity should be treated as a circumstance of 'concerted' activity. See discussion in text at ch. 2 nn. 19–24 and ch. 3 nn. 3–4 *supra*.

[103] To the extent this is not the case, the 'independent' character of the actor's conduct must be questioned.

[104] See text at nn. 76–8 *supra*.

[105] See Prosser, *supra* n. 2, at 316.

when harm is the consequence only of the combination of conduct essentially equivalent in terms of causation and blameworthiness.[106] Most troubling are situations in which joint and several liability might result in a state with a relatively minor degree of responsibility standing entirely liable without any effective means to achieve contribution.[107]

If one is persuaded that such results are unacceptable, the alternative to joint and several liability is suggested by municipal admiralty practice.[108] Following that model, the obligations of each state to compensate the injured state would be limited to a proportional share based on fault. This approach has two obvious merits: it avoids the perils of the contribution process; and it satisfies even aggressive notions of independence by limiting each state's liability to a share of the harm for which it alone is deemed responsible. Yet, there would seem to be a serious inequity in the adoption of such an 'apportioned liability' approach to protect the interests of breaching states. The central question is who is to bear the risk of loss arising out of injury: the injured state (though a failure of compensation) or the members of the set of wrongdoers (though a failure of contribution)? Such risks are certainly exacerbated by the procedural limitations in dispute settlement among states. On both the municipal and the international plans, however, as the injured party and *any* wrongdoer, it seems the burden of loss should fall upon the latter. Hence, it is submitted that a regime of joint and several liability with a right of contribution is also appropriately applied to independent wrongdoers producing a single harm.

Existing international judicial practice in apportioning damages in other contexts provides an adequate pattern for the division of compensation among wrongdoers through the contribution process.[109] As in municipal practice, of course, such apportionment may rarely be determined with mathematical precision.[110] The jurisprudence amply demonstrates, however, that international tribunals, in the exercise of vested discretion, are both equipped and willing to make such approximate and often intuitive judgments as to comparative fault. Decisions have focused on the same two criteria of relative fault evident in municipal practice: causation and blameworthiness.

[106] Consider the case of two acts of pollution harmless in themselves which combine through predictable chemical processes to cause damage. See *id.*, at 322–3. One author views apportionment of liability to the extent of contributory fault appropriate in this situation—*unless* the states were aware of each others' contributions or the activities were ultrahazardous, in which case joint and several liability is proper. See Rest, 'Convention On Compensation for Transfrontier Environmental Injuries', Project of the Institute of International and Comparative Law of the University of Cologne (1976), at 47–50.

[107] This situation might arise, for example, in the scenario described above in which one state attacks an embassy in the territory of another state which fails to exercise due diligence.

[108] See text at nn. 54–5 *supra*.

[109] See text at nn. 79–92 *supra*.

[110] See Williams, *supra* n. 2, at 158, who notes this fact but concludes '[w]e have to act more or less arbitrarily because the alternative is not to act at all.'

The choice between the two seems to reflect the facts in each specific case. In certain situations different degrees of causation may be identified; in others, the facts support only a comparative distinction in 'moral' blame.[111] Facts presenting elements of both perceptibly unequal causation and blameworthiness would likely merit and receive an analysis comprehending both factors.

In any event, the principal categories of facts relevant to a determination of comparative fault, whether denominated criteria of causation, blame or both, may be identified. In all cases, for example, it would seem that the character of each state's intent in committing a breach of its international obligations is relevant to the degree of fault attributed to it. Thus, a wrong of specific intent ought to be treated more harshly than one of simple negligence. Among states engaging in concerted wrongful conduct, the apportionment decision would logically reflect the character of each state's participation in the enterprise. Factors such as the source of financing, equipment, and personnel, the direction of benefits, and the vesting of decision-making authority should enter into a determination of the participating states' respective shares of the compensation burden.[112]

Among independent wrongdoers producing a single harm, the facts relevant to the apportionment of fault will vary even more with the specific circumstances. To illustrate, as between two states wrongfully depositing toxic waste in a third state's territory, the share of compensation for the undivided harm would logically reflect the relative measure and potency of the contributions of the states. Quite different factors, a comparison of the states' relative capacities and efforts to prevent, would apply in a situation in which two states fail to exercise due diligence to prevent an event. In most cases, the measure of each state's jurisdiction over the injury-producing conduct will represent a factor of paramount importance in distinguishing degrees of fault. The character of a state's legal authority over an event represents a shorthand definition of its effective control of that event. The inquiry into legal authority and control is perhaps best viewed as an expression of the criterion of causality; the state with the greater measure of jurisdiction to control conduct is appropriately defined as possessing a greater casual connection to the consequences of such conduct.[113] In any event, apportionment on the basis of authority to control directly furthers the objective of deterrence by imposing

[111] Admittedly, the cited decisions based on abstract blame have been limited to the context of apportionment between the injured party and the wrongdoer. There is every reason to assume, however, that the same analysis would apply to apportionment among wrongdoers. Decisions based on causation, of course, appear both in contexts of such injured party contributory causation and external causation. See text at nn. 89–90 *supra*.

[112] See Goldie, *supra* ch. 2 n. 92, at 1253–4. As to the criterion of benefit, see language of the *Anglo-Chinese Shipping Co.* Case quoted at n. 63 *supra*.

[113] See generally, Eagleton, *supra* ch. 1 n. 4, at 7 and 27; Friedmann, *supra* ch. 3 n. 59, *passim*. Garcia-Mora, *supra* ch. 2 n. 37, at 29; Hyde, *supra* ch. 3 n. 146, at 922; Handl, *supra* ch. 2 n. 92, at 531–4; Lenoble, *supra* ch. 3 n. 44, *passim*.

the burden of compensation in proportion to the relative capacities of the states to prevent repetition of the injurious event.

A state possesses maximum legal authority over conduct, of course, when it is the actor. When an organ of the state is the author of the conduct which directly inflicts injury, a mere exercise of self-control would suffice to prevent the injury. Hence, it would seem appropriate to view a state actor more at fault than a state whose responsibility arises out of its failure to prevent the state actor from inflicting the injury. The clearest illustration is, again, the circumstance of an attack by state *A* on a diplomatic mission in state *B* accomplished due to a failure of state *B* to exercise due diligence. Based on the foregoing logic, as between the two responsible states, state *A* would be assigned the greater degree of fault.

This same analysis logically extends to apportionment between states which are each responsible for other than the primary injuring conduct. In the event more than one state fails to exercise required due diligence to prevent an event, the nature of each state's legal authority over the injurious event should be a threshold concern. The greater the measure of such authority, the greater the relative degree of fault. Hence, the fault of a state with only extraterritorial prescriptive authority over conduct is likely less than that of a state vested with authority to prescribe and take immediate enforcement measures to prevent the conduct.[114] If two states in breach possess the same general order of authority, recourse may be made to distinctions such as the specific capacities of each state to exercise authority with respect to the injurious conduct.[115] In short, the scales of fault should tip in the direction of the state in a position to exercise jurisdiction more effecively to control the wrongful conduct.

[114] As to the possibility of responsibility arising out of a failure to exercise prescriptive authority over conduct see text at ch. 3, nn. 145–52 *supra*. In all but extraordinary circumstances, of course, such a failure would bear an insufficient causal connection to the harm to give rise to *any* obligation to compensate for the harm. The breach of obligation should, however, give rise to other consequences of responsibility. See text at n. 11 and following n. 36 *supra*.

[115] Capacity may, of course, be interpreted in either an objective or subjective sense. The hybrid approach now advocated with respect to due diligence generally would assume a minimum standard of administrative capacity and hold states which in fact possess a greater degree of administrative prowess to a high standard. See text at ch. 3 nn. 122–34 *supra*. Factors such as relative foreknowledge and opportunity are of similar relevance.

PART II

Marine Environmental Obligations of the State

5

Harm Within Another State's Territory

A. A PREFATORY NOTE

Part I of the present work has been devoted to an analysis of the general rules relating to the circumstances and consequences of state responsibility. As often noted, the principles treated thus far are 'secondary' in the sense that they apply to breaches of all 'primary' international obligations. The next appropriate step is to define the specific category of obligations germane to the present inquiry: the obligations of the state with respect to the marine environment. The question to be addressed, in essence, is in what circumstances the 'objective' condition to state responsibility is satisfied. What constitutes a breach of international duty with respect to the marine environment? Two brief comments are in order regarding the fashion in which Part II will proceed to this task.

First, the objective of this part, and indeed of this work, is to consider the status and direction of customary international law on the subject of marine environmental responsibility. It is not intended, therefore, to detail the numerous, specific, and often technical obligations which states contractually have assumed in bilateral or multilateral conventions.[1] Rather, such contractual duties will be discussed only to the admittedly significant extent that they provide declarative evidence of customary *lex lata* or, perhaps, *lex ferenda*.[2]

Second, as to organization, the analysis in Part II is subdivided into four segments, the first three based on the *locus* of environmental injury. The obligation to prevent environmental harm within the territory of another state

[1] For particularly worthy efforts accomplishing this task see de Yturriaga, 'Regional Conventions on the Protection of the Marine Environment', i *Recueil des cours* 244 (1979); Timagenis, *International Control of Marine Pollution* (1980).

[2] As to the relationship between treaties and custom, Judge Lachs has noted: 'It is generally recognized that provisions of international instruments may acquire the status of general rules of international law. Even unratified treaties may constitute a point of departure for a legal practice. Treaties binding many States are, *a fortiori*, capable of producing this effect, a phenomenon not unknown in international relations.' *North Sea Continental Shelf* Case (*Germ.* v. *Denm.*), [1969] ICJ 219, at 225 (Diss. Opinion of Judge Lachs). For interesting discussions of the relationship between the Law of the Sea Convention and customary law, see Lee, 'The Law of the Sea Convention and Third States', 77 *Am J. Int'l L.* 541 (1983), Jennings, 'What Is International Law and How Do We Tell It When We See It?' 37 *Swiss Yb. Int'l L.* (1981). Jennings argues generally that reference to the traditional language of 'custom' is inapposite with respect to those areas of contemporary international law in which change is extremely rapid or contentious: '[M]uch of this new law is not custom at all, and does not even resemble custom. It is recent, it is innovatory, it involves topical policy decisions, and it is often the focus of contention. Anything less like custom in the ordinary meaning of that term it would be difficult to imagine.' *Id.*, at 67.

will receive initial and principal attention in this chapter, reflecting the relatively advanced state of jurisprudence and doctrine concerning such 'transboundary' pollution. The following two chapters will consider, respectively, the less chartered environmental obligations of states with respect to harm experienced beyond the territory of any state and within the territory of the polluting state itself. The concluding chapter will then be devoted to the particularly vexing issue of whether, or to what extent, fault is a requisite element of the breach of these specific environmental obligations.

B. SOVEREIGN INDEPENDENCE

The appropriate point to begin a discussion of the international rules circumscribing state prerogative with respect to environmental matters is the concept of the state itself. The character of these rules of obligation follows from the position of the state as a participant in international society, i.e. its relationship to other states and to international law. 'Sovereignty' is the concept most frequently engaged to describe that position. It is, therefore, to the import of the notion of the 'sovereign state' that the discussion first turns.

The concepts of 'sovereignty' and the 'state' did not, of course, spring from an effort to describe the position of societal groups in an intersocietal context. On the contrary, these notions were 'evolved in a municipal framework by political and legal thinkers who . . . framed theories of the State in isolation from its international relations . . .'[3] In essence, the 'sovereign state' was a response to the need for a political theory which would lend stability and cohesion to the social organization emerging from the process of the reformation.[4] This was accomplished by the definition of a 'state' consisting of a community of individuals under one 'sovereign' law-giving authority, that is, the monarch. The individual members of the state were to heed absolutely the commands of the sovereign ruler; the ruler, on the other hand, was by definition subject neither to the ruler's own laws nor those promulgated by any external authority. The nature of this internal political theory carried certain inevitable implications with respect to the development of an inter-state system. The authority of each sovereign within its state was supreme and independent. No state, therefore, could be deemed subordinate to external authority, including the rule of a body of international law. As to those matters subject to a state's sovereignty, then, the prerogatives of the state were theoretically not subject to qualification.[5]

[3] *Sovereignty Within the Law* 11 (Larson and Jenks eds. 1965). *See* Brierly, *The Law of Nations* 45–9 (6th edn., Waldock ed. 1963).

[4] Indeed, Charles Rousseau argues that the concept of sovereignty 'must be regarded first and foremost as a technical instrument devised by the French Crown for the purposes of its struggle against the Emperor and the Pope abroad and against the nobles at home.' See Larson and Jenks, *supra* n. 3, at 45.

[5] The only restrictions to the sovereign's otherwise absolute prerogative were (*a*) the

The first step in the erosion of this 'absolutist' perspective of sovereignty was the conceptual recognition that subordination to the external authority of international law could occur if it proceeded from the will of the state itself. This 'consent theory', introduced in the mid-eighteenth century and matured through the nineteenth century, simply asserted that only consent, express or implied by acquiescence, could subordinate sovereign prerogative to international rules of order. Representative of the reasoning of the consent approach is the often quoted language of Chief Justice Marshall in *The Schooner Exchange* v. *McFaddon:*

> The jurisdiction of the nation within its own territory is necessarily exclusive and absolute. It is susceptible of no limitation not imposed by itself. Any restriction upon it, deriving validity from an external source, would imply a diminution of its own sovereignty to the extent of the restriction, and an investment of that sovereignty to the same extent in that power which could impose such restrictions.[6]

With the consent theory, then, there existed at least a theoretical foundation for the development of international laws applicable, albeit by self-imposition, to sovereign states.[7]

The profound change in the perspective of states regarding the character of sovereignty did not occur until the early years of this century with the emergence of the doctrine of 'relative sovereignty'. An early decision succinctly summarized the then incipient relativist view:

> The function of sovereignty in a state is neither unrestricted nor unlimited. It extends as far as the sovereign rights of other states . . . a state may not claim more than such independence and liberty as is compatible with the necessary organization of humanity, with the independence of other states, and with the ties that bind states together.[8]

In the language of more recent commentators:

> [N]o State is entitled to invoke the plenitude of its internal sovereignty . . . as the basis for freedom of action, unrestrained by law, in the international arena. By the very nature of international society, by the mere fact that no State is entire of itself, by the

'constitutional' rules of the state, e.g. the principles of succession, and (*b*) divine or natural law. Brierly, *supra* n. 3, at 45. With the decline of natural law theory and the advent of positivism, there remained no external authority to which a sovereign would be subject.

[6] The *Schooner Exchange* v. *McFaddon,* 11 US (7 Cranch) 116, at 156 (1812). One of the earliest expressions of the consent theory is in Vattel, *Droit des gens ou principes de la loi naturelle* (Fenwick trans. 1758, 1916 edn.). The basic principle is echoed throughout the theoretical literature of the 19th century.

[7] The criticisms of consent theory as sufficient explanation of the source of state subordination to law are numerous and persuasive. In summary, they submit (*a*) affirmative consent to the minutia of modern international rules is simply not plausible, (*b*) consent theory fails to explain the consensus as to the incapacity of states to withdraw consent, and (*c*) states, in practice, adhere to law not out of a specific will to do so but out of a preception of its inherently obligatory character. See Larson and Jenks, *supra* n. 3, at 336.

[8] *El Salvador* v. *Nicaragua* (Central American Court of Justice), 11 *Am. J. Int'l L.* 674, at 718 (1917).

interdependence which is as inherent in the coexistence of States as it is in the social nature of man, every State is bound by the law of nations . . .[9]

It is international law, then, which defines the points of intersection, and therefore the limits of states' sovereignty. The consent of a state is not required to subordinate state prerogative to a rule which has risen to the dignity of international law. By definition, such rules describe the reciprocal limits to sovereign rights in a society of sovereigns.[10]

This contemporary view of sovereignty does not, of course, deny the existence of a region of state independence or freedom. To the contrary, subject to the boundaries delimited by international law, each sovereign state is acknowledged to exercise an equal measure of discretionary authority. Indeed, the Permanent Court in the *Lotus* Case identified state liberty of action as the starting point for an inquiry into the existence of a restrictive international rule.[11] One may perhaps dispute whether the liberty so enjoyed by states is an original or inherent condition, subject to limits imposed by international law, or simply an abstraction of the set of freedoms bestowed by international law.[12] Viewed from either perspective, the principle of state independence subordinate only to the strictures of international law undeniably remains valid and active.[13]

The influence of the principle is, moreover, manifest in several subsidiary legal principles particularly germane to the present inquiry into environmental obligations. The *Right of Passage* Case, for example, is evidence of the general legal presumption, albeit rebuttable, that a state's conduct within its own territory is unrestricted by international legal rules.[14] More concretely, the specific right of states to render independent decisions with respect to their natural resources has been identified in a series of statements from the UN General Assembly:

[9] Larson and Jenks, *supra* n. 3, at 11.

[10] Note, however, that the remnants of absolutism are still to be detected. Consider the suggestion in the *Anglo-Norwegian Fisheries* Case that consistent opposition to a rule of customary international law may excuse a state from adherence to such a rule. *Anglo-Norwegian Fisheries* Case (*UK* v. *Nor.*), [1951] ICJ 116, at 131 (Merits). See Fitzmaurice, 'The General Principles of International Law', ii *Recueil des Cours* 1, at 99–101 (1957); Brownlie, *Principles of Public International Law* 291–3 (3rd edn. 1979). A second, yet somewhat more subtle, example of the continuing effect of the concept of absolute sovereignty is the principle that states must consent to the jurisdiction of an international body—administrative or judicial. See the *Eastern Carelia* Case (*Fin.* v. *USSR*), [1923] PCIJ, Ser. B, no. 5 (Judgment of 23 July 1923), at 27. An approach free of the influence of absolute sovereignty might acknowledge that the authority of an international body may, in theory and dependent on the requisite *opinio juris*, rise to the level of international law and thus become universally binding.

[11] The *SS Lotus* Case (*Fr.* v. *Turk*), [1927] PCIJ Ser. A, no. 10, at 19.

[12] See Verzijl, i *The Jurisprudence of the World Court* 85 (1965).

[13] See de Visscher, *Theory and Reality in Public International Law* 104–5 (1957); O'Connell, i *International Law* 318–20 (1965); Waldock, 'General Course on Public International Law', i *Recueil des cours* 157 (1962).

[14] The *Right of Passage over Indian Territory* Case (*Port.* v. *India*), [1960] ICJ 6. See Delupis, *International Law and the Independent State* 23–4 (1974); O'Connell, *supra* n. 13, at 320.

The right of peoples freely to use and exploit their natural wealth and resources is inherent in their sovereignty and is in accordance with Purposes and Principles of the Charter of the United Nations.[15]

The right of peoples and nations to permanent sovereignty over their natural wealth and resources must be exercised in the interest of their national development and of the well-being of the people of the State concerned;

The exploration, development and disposition of such resources . . . should be in conformity with the rules and conditions which the peoples and nations freely consider to be necessary or desirable with regard to the authorization, restriction or prohibition of such activities.[16]

Among the rights logically subsumed in this general freedom of action with respect to natural resources is the right to render decisions, based on the state's private political, economic, and social objectives, which are prohibitive, permissive, or even conducive to the degradation of environmental resources. As recited in the 1972 Declaration of the UN Conference on The Human Environment, 'States have, in accordance with the Charter of the United Nations and the principle of international law, the sovereign right to exploit their own resources pursuant to their own environmental policies . . .'[17]

A principle of independent environmental decision-making is not inconsistent, however, with the imposition of international legal constraints. In a system of equal states, order and the logic of relative sovereignty demand that the freedom or independence enjoyed by each state be restrained at the point at which it interferes with the exercise of the correlative freedom of other states.[18] No state may be vested with exclusive competence or unfettered

[15] General Assembly Res. 626 (VII), 21 Dec. 1952, 7 UN GAOR Supp. (no. 20) at 18, UN Doc. A/2361 (1953). See generally Brownlie, 'Legal Status of Natural Resources in International Law (Some Aspects)', i *Recueil des cours* 244 (1979). See particularly the discussion regarding the role of UN Resolutions in the formulation of customary law. *Id.*, at 260–1.

[16] General Assembly Res. 1803 (XVII), 14 Dec, 1962, 17 UN GAOR Supp. (no. 17) at 15. UN Doc. A/5217 (1963).

[17] Principle 21, Declaration of the United Nations Conference on the Human Environment, adopted 16 June 1972, UN Doc. A/Conf.48/14 and Corr. 1 (hereinafter cited as the Stockholm Declaration). See also Art, 193, United Nations Convention on the Law of the Sea, done 10 Dec. 1982, UN Doc. A/CONF.62/122 of 7 Oct. 1982, reprinted in 21 *Int'l Legal Materials* 1261 (1982) (hereinafter cited as the LOS Convention). Each of these statements is coupled with an affirmative statement of the obligation to prevent environmental injury. See text at nn. 41, 43 *infra*. Many developing states perceive environmental degradation as a legitimate trade-off for increased industry and investment. See Pinto, 'Problems of Developing States and Their Effects on Decisions on Law of the Sea', in *LOS Needs and Interests of the Developing Countries*, Proceedings of the 7th Annual Conf. Law of the Sea Institute 3, at 12 (1972). See generally Shinn, *The International Politics of Marine Pollution Control* (1979).

[18] Max Huber made the classic expression of this point with respect to state prerogative over territorial matters: 'Territorial sovereignty . . . involves the exclusive right to display the activities of a state. This right has a corollary duty: the obligation to protect within the territory the rights of other states, in particular their right to integrity and inviolability in peace and in war, together with the rights which each state may claim for its nationals in foreign territory.' The *Island of Palmas (or Miangas)* Arbitral Award (1928) (*US* v. *Neth.*), 2 R. Int'l Arb. Awards 829, reprinted in 22 *Am. J. Int'l L.* 867, at 876 (1928). Consider too the language of the *Lac Lanoux* Tribunal: 'La souveraineté territoriale joué à la manière d'une présomption. Elle doit fléchir devant routes les

liberty even as to its own resources when the interests of other states are implicated. International law has defined certain reciprocal limits to state freedom and independence in the environmental context for precisely this reason.

C. THE OBLIGATION TO PREVENT

It is quite clear that conduct within the territory of one state may materially and adversely affect the resources and environmental interests of other states. The environment is not conveniently divided into discrete units corresponding to the juridical zones of state territory; rather, it constitutes a 'single indivisible system' encompassing the entire planet.[19] Within that system there exist myriad effective mechanisms for the transport and dispersal of pollution to regions quite remote from the site of the introduction of the pollution into the environment.[20] Absolute freedom with respect to decisions and conduct affecting the environment within the bounds of state territory would, therefore, permit interference with and injury to the interests of other states. In one early and notable instance, that was precisely the prerogative claimed. In 1898, US Attorney General Harmon, responding to Mexican protests regarding the adverse impact of the diversion of the waters of the Rio Grande, categorically denied the existence of any international rule restricting a state's conduct within its own territory, regardless of transboundary effects.[21] The so-called 'Harmon doctrine', as an expression of the then ebbing view of absolute sovereignty, was never reflected in subsequent practice and is currently discredited.[22] International decisions, practice, and opinion now clearly evidence the emergence of an international obligation designated to check the potentially intrusive liberty of states with respect to environmental matters: *sic utere tuo alienum non laedas* (one must use his own so as not to damage that of another).

obligations internationales, quelle qu'en soit la source, mais elle ne fléchit que devant elles.' The *Lac Lanoux* Case (1957) (*Spain* v. *Fr.*), 12 R. Int'l Arb. Awards 281, at 301.

[19] Handl, 'Territorial Sovereignty and the Problem of Transnational Pollution', 69 *Am. J. Int'l L.* 50, at 53 (1976). See also Caldwell, 'Concepts in Development of International Environmental Policies', in *International Environmental Law* 19 Teclaff and Utton eds. 1974).

[20] See Coppoc, 'The Environment: No Respecter of National Boundaries', 43 *Albany L. Rev.* 520, at 521–4 (1979); Goldberg, 'The Chemical Invasion of the Oceans by Man', in *Global Effects of Environmental Pollution*, 178, at 184 (Singer ed. 1968); Gustafson, 'PCBs: Prevalent and Persistent', [1970] *Envt'L Sci. & Tech.* 814; Nelson-Smith, *Oil Pollution and Marine Ecology* 82 (1972); Council On Environmental Quality, 'Ocean Dumping, a National Policy: A Report to the President' (1970), reprinted in *Pollution Crisis: Official Documents* (Rabin and Schwartz eds. 1972) at 107; Wetstone, 'Air Pollution Control Laws in North America and the Problem of Acid Rain and Snow', 10 *Envt'l L. Rep.* 50001 (1980).

[21] Opinion of Attn. Gen. Judson Harmon, 21 *Op. US Att'y Gen.* 274 (1898).

[22] See Quentin-Baxter, Preliminary Report on International Liability for Injurious Consequences Arising out of Acts Not Prohibited by International Law, ii *Yb. Int'l L. Comm'n* 24 UN Doc. A/CN4/Ser A/1980/Add. 1 (Pt. 1) (1980), at 257 (hereinafter cited as Q-B, Prelim. Rpt.); Larson and Jenks, *supra* n. 3, at 349; Springer, 'Towards a Meaningful Concept of Pollution in International Law', 26 *Int'l & Comp. L.Q.* 531, at 536 (1977).

The introduction to international jurisprudence of the *sic utere tuo* principle is invariably traced to the decision of the arbitral tribunal in the *Trail Smelter* dispute between the United States and Canada.[23] The arbitration concerned the obligations of Canada with respect to certain undisputed damage experienced in US territory from sulphur dioxide fumes drifting from a private smelting operation in Trail, British Columbia. The charge to the Tribunal was to determine the measure of Canada's duty to compensate for past injury and the character of any obligation to prevent future injury.[24] The *compromis* permitted the application of 'the law and practice followed in dealing with cognate questions in the United States of America as well as international law and practice.'[25] On this basis, the Tribunal concluded:

> [u]nder the principles of international law, as well as of the law of the Unted States, no State has the right to use or permit the use of its territory in such a manner as to cause injury by fumes in or to the territory of another or the properties or persons therein, when the case is of serious consequence and the injury is established by clear and convincing evidence.[26]

Although unable to locate sufficient international materials to support this conclusion, the Tribunal was careful to assert that 'the law followed in the United States in dealing with the quasi-sovereign rights of the states of the Union, in the matter of air pollution, whilst more definite, is in conformity with the general rules of international law.'[27] Hence, from the Tribunal's perspective, the award represented a statement of a governing principle of general international applicability.[28]

Recent critics have questioned the 'mythologized' significance of *Trail Smelter* as an exposition of customary international law.[29] Criticism has centred on the facts that (*a*) the conclusions of the Tribunal rested principally upon the municipal practice of a single state and (*b*) the basic issue of Canadian responsibility was assumed by the terms of the *compromis* and never

[23] Decision of the *Trail Smelter* Arbitral Tribunal (1941), (*US* v. *Can.*), 3 R. Int'l Arb. Awards 1905. For useful general discussions on the case, see Harris, 'The Law on Air Pollution: International Aspects', in *Environmental Pollution Control* 77 (McKnight, Marstrand, and Sinclair eds. 1974); Hoffman, 'State Responsibility in International Law and Transboundary Pollution Inquiries', 25 *Int'l & Comp. L.Q.* 509 (1976); Quentin-Baxter, Second Report on International Liability for Injurious Consequences Arising out of Acts Not Prohibited by International Law, UN Gen. Ass. Doc. A/CN4/346 (12 June 1981), at 12–21 (hereinafter cited as Q-B, 2nd Rpt); Read, 'The Trail Smelter Dispute', 1 *Can. Yb. Int'l L.* 213 (1963); Rubin, 'Pollution by Analogy: The Trail Smelter Arbitration', 50 *Oreg. L. Rev.* 259 (1971).

[24] Art. 3, 'Convention for the Settlement of Differences Arising From Operation of Smelter at Trail, BC', 3 R. Int'l Arb. Awards 1907 (1941).

[25] Art 4, *id.*, at 1908.

[26] *Trail Smelter*, *supra* n. 23, at 1965.

[27] *Id.*, at 1963.

[28] See Rubin, *supra* n. 23, at 268–9.

[29] The quoted adjective is from Munton, 'Dependence and Interdependence in Transboundary Pollution', 36 *Int'l J.* 139, at 140 (1980–1). Quentin-Baxter notes that *Trail Smelter* 'appears to be undergoing the same kind of eclipse that attends the work of some artists of good reputation in the period after their death.' Q-B, 2nd Rpt, *supra* n. 23, at 12.

addressed in the decisions[30] Despite its awkward entrance, however, the obligation to prevent significant transboundary injury identified by the *Trail Smelter* Tribunal has found a secure place in international jurisprudence. The International Court in the *Corfu Channel* Case endorsed a quite general variation on the *sic utere tuo* theme (not limited to harm to state territory), referring to 'every State's obligation not to allow knowingly its territory to be used for acts contrary to the rights of other States.'[31] The opinion of Judge de Castro in the 1974 *Nuclear Tests* Cases directly confirmed the status of the obligation to prevent transboundary harm as an operative principle of international law.[32] The obligation was further acknowledged, in an unequivocal *dictum*, in the decision in the *Lac Lanoux* arbitration between Spain and France.[33] The award denied a Spanish claim regarding French diversion of water from a French lake into a hydroelectric system; since water was to be returned to the river which normally drained the lake to Spanish territory, no injury to Spanish water use was established.[34] The Tribunal emphasized, however, that if injury had been alleged, through, for example, chemical or thermal pollution, Spanish rights might indeed have been violated.[35]

Instances of state practice provide further evidence of the existence of the obligation to prevent material transboundary environmental harm.[36] The submissions of both Australia and New Zealand in the *Nuclear Tests* Cases, for example, alleged injury in and to state territory through the dispersion of radioactive materials as an alternative basis of French responsibility.[37] The

[30] See e.g. Dupuy, *supra* ch. 3 n. 97, at 186; Handl, 'Balancing of Interests and International Liability for the Pollution of International Watercourses: Customary Principles of Law Revisited', 13 *Can. Yb. Int'l L.* 156, at 167–8 (1975).

[31] The *Corfu Channel* Case (*UK* v. *Albania*), [1949] ICJ 4, at 22.

[32] The *Nuclear Tests* Cases (*Australia* v. *Fr*), [1974] ICJ 253 (Judgment) (Dissenting Opin. Judge de Castro), at 388–9. The issue was never addressed by the majority.

[33] The *Lac Lanoux* Arbitration (1957) (*Spain* v. *Fr.*), 12 R. Int'l Arb. Awards 281.

[34] *Id.*, at 303–5.

[35] *Id.*, at 303. Brownlie does note that the specific concern of the Tribunal was the interpretation of *treaty* obligations requiring the parties to reach agreement regarding any activity which would interfere with either state's use of the lake or the river Carol. Brownlie, *supra* n. 10, at 271–2.

[36] The *Gut Dam* Arbitration, in which Canada agreed to a settlement to compensate the US for flood damage caused by Canadian construction of a dam, has been cited as a prime example of the obligation. See Schneider, 'World Public Order of the Environment', Ph.D diss., Yale (1975), published in 1979 under same title, at 89, 270. Gunther Handl persuasively argues that the basis of the responsibility was an indemnification agreement which Canada granted at the time of construction as the *quid pro quo* for US consent to construction of the dam between Canada and US territory. Handl, *supra* ch. 2 n. 82, at 538–9. The case is then only helpful if Canadian willingness to enter the indemnification agreement is viewed, at least in part, as based on the expectation or assumption of the preventive obligation.

[37] [1978] ICJ Pleadings, *Nuclear Tests* (*Australia* v. *Fr.*) vol. i at 14; (*New Zealand* v. *Fr.*) vol. ii at 8. It is also noteworthy that the criterion of 'substantiality' for wrongful transboundary pollution was acknowledged by each claimant in response to Judge Waldock's question as to whether some measure of pollution must be 'tolerated as merely an incident of the industrialization or technological development of modern society'. *Id.* i. at 524–6 (Australia); ii at 429–31 (New Zealand).

tactit agreement of the United States, in response to Mexican protests, to control stockyard fumes in El Paso, Texas, causing injury in Ciudad, Mexico, constitutes further evidence of the obligation to prevent environment injury.[38] Similar acknowledgements of the preventive obligation may be detected in the pattern of claims and responses involving industrial emissions across the French-German and Swiss-German borders.[39] State declarations and participation in environmental conventions provide extensive evidence of the acceptance of an obligation to prevent transboundary harm. A most persuasive example is the consensus evident in the negotiations at the Third UN Conference on the Law of the Sea (LOS III); the host of proposals submitted by states with respect to the proper expression of marine environmental obligations uniformly acknowledged a duty to prevent harm to the territory of other states.[40]

Article 194(2) of the Convention reflects this consensus:

> States shall take all measures necessary to ensure that activities under their jurisdiction or control are so conducted as not to cause damage by pollution to other States and their environment, and that pollution arising from incidents or activities under their jurisdiction or control does not spread beyond the areas where they exercise sovereign rights in accordance with this Convention.[41]

Similar unequivocal expressions of the obligation to prevent transboundary harm may be found in such authoritative multilateral statements as the UN Charter of Economic Rights and Duties of States,[42] the Stockholm Declaration on the Human Environment[43] and the 1972 London Dumping Convention.[44]

[38] See Whiteman, 6 *Dig. Int'l L.* 256–7 (1908). Without addressing the issue of compensation, the US responded by outlining the preventive steps taken. See also Harris, *supra* n. 23, at 79.

[39] See International Law Association, 'Report of the 58th Conference (1978)' (hereinafter cited as ILA 58th), at 398–9; International Law Association, 'Report of the 59th Conference (1980)' (hereinafter cited as ILA 59th), at 537. See also the *River Mur* incident, in which Austria compensated Yugoslavia for damage attendant to release of sludge downstream. See du Pontavice, 'Compensation For Transfrontier Pollution Damage', in OECD, *Legal Aspects of Transfrontier Pollution* 409, at 434 (1977).

[40] See e.g. US: Draft Articles on the Protection of the Marine Environment and the Prevention of Marine Pollution, art. 9 UN Doc. A/AC.138/SC.iii/L.40; Canada: Draft Articles for a Comprehensive Marine Pollution Convention, arts. 1 and 2, UN Doc. A/AC.138/SC.iii/L.28; Canada, Fiji, Ghana *et al.*: Draft Articles on a Zonal Approach to the Preservation of the Marine Environment, art. 1, UN Doc. A/CONF.62/C.3/L.6; USSR: Additional Draft Articles on Prevention of Pollution of the Marine Environment, art. 1, UN. Doc. A/CONF.62/C3/L.25.; Kenya: Draft Articles for the Preservation and the Protection of the Marine Environment for Inclusion in the Convention of the Law of the Sea, art 3, UN Doc. A/CONF.62/C/L.25.

[41] LOS Convention, *supra* n. 17, art. 194(2).

[42] Art. 30, Charter of Economic Rights and Duties of States, Gen. Ass. Res. 3281 (xxix), UN GAOR Supp. (no. 31), UN Doc. A/RES/3281, reprinted in 14 *Int'l Legal Materials* 251 (1975).

[43] Stockholm Declaration, *supra* n. 17, at Principle 21. See also Gen. Ass. Res. 2996 (xxvii), 15 Dec. 1972, UN GAOR Supp. (no. 30), at 42–3, which confirms Principle 21 as a 'basic rule' governing international environmental responsibility.

[44] Convention on the Prevention of Marine Pollution by Dumping of Wastes and Other Matter, done at London, Mexico City, Moscow, and Washington 29 Dec. 1972, entered into force 30 Aug. 1975, TIAS no. 8165, 26 UST 2403, TS no. 43 (1976).

In the light of the foregoing, essentially all publicists' writing on the subject conclude that the obligation to prevent conduct in state territory from causing material environmental harm in the territory of another state has risen to the dignity of a rule of customary international law.[45] The ILA in its 1982 'Montreal Rules of International Law Applicable to Transfrontier Pollution', recently defined the principle of *sic utere tuo* as the customary foundation of the existing rules of international environmental law.[46]

It is particularly important for present purposes to recognize that the formulation originally articulated in *Trail Smelter*, limited by its terms to harm arising out of territorial conduct, represents only a partial, inadequate expression of the preventive obligation. In fact, the obligation to prevent harm to the environment of other states is now rarely expressed in purely 'transboundary' terms referring only to the prevention of damage arising out of territorial conduct. Article 192 of the LOS Convention, for example, speaks in the broadest terms: 'States have the obligation to protect and preserve the marine environment.'[47] No suggestion of a territorial limitation to the conduct to which the preventive obligation applies is present. Rather, the import of such general language is that the state's duty extends to conduct in any location with respect to which the state is in a position to take preventive measures. This perspective is supported in the language of Principle 7 of the Stockholm Declaration: 'States shall take all possible steps to prevent pollution of the seas by substances that are liable to create hazards to human health, to harm living resources and marine life, to damage amenities or to interfere with other legitimate uses of the sea.'[48] Similar general undertakings to take all 'practicable', 'appropriate', or 'possible' measures to prevent environmental harm, without reference to the territorial *locus* of the injury-producing conduct, may be found in the principal multilateral anti-pollution conventions.[49] In summary, it would seem that the boundaries of the state's

[45] See Beesley, 'The Canadian Approach to International Environmental Law', 13 *Can Yb. Int'l L.* 3 (1973); Caflisch, 'International Law and Ocean Pollution: The Present and the Future', 8 *Revue belge droit int'l* 7, at 15 (1972); Dupuy, *supra* ch. 3 n. 97, at 31; Goldie, *supra* ch. 2 n. 92, at 1226; Handl, *supra* n. 19, *passim;* Legault, 'The Freedom of the Seas: A Licence to Pollute?', 31 *U. Tor.* L.J. 211, at 217 (1971); Schneider, *supra* n. 36, at 84 ff.; Sohn, 'The Stockholm Declaration on the Human Environment', 14 *Harv. Int'l L.J.* 423, at 493 (1973); Stein, 'Responsibility and Liability for Harm to the Marine Environment', 6 *Ga J. Int'l & Comp. L.* 41, at 48 (1976). See also ILA 58th, *supra* n. 39; ILA 59th, *supra* n. 39; Académie de Droit International de La Haye, Colloque 1973: 'The Protection of the Environment and International Law' (1975).

[46] Art. 3(1) and Comments of 'The Montreal Rules of International Law Applicable to Transfrontier Pollution,' Resolution No. 2/1982 on Legal Aspects of the Conservation of the Environment, International Law Association, Report on the 60th Conference (1982) (hereinafter cited as the Montreal Rules).

[47] LOS Convention, *supra* n. 17, art. 192. This language is also general as to the *locus* of the harm. This will be treated in chs. 6 and 7 below.

[48] Stockholm Declaration, *supra* n. 17, Principle 7 (emphasis added).

[49] See, respectively, 1972 London Dumping Convention, *supra* n. 44, art. 1; Convention for the Protection of the Mediterranean Sea against Pollution, done at Barcelona 16 Feb. 1976, reprinted

capacity to take measures to prevent environmental injury to another state will define the ambit of the obligation to take such measures.[50]

When the activities of an organ or agent of the state produce damage to the territory of another state, there is no spatial or other juridical limit to the state's capacity to act to prevent the injury: prevention is merely an exercise in self-control. Each state would seem, therefore, to be obligated to prevent environmental harm to another arising out of the conduct of state organs or representatives in *any* location.[51] Supportive of this conclusion is the settlement of Canada's claim for damages following the deposit of the radioactive remnants of Cosmos 954 on Canadian territory; the Soviet Union paid $3 million to compensate for injuries to Canada (principally, the costs of environmental clean-up) arising out of the extraterritorial activities of an organ of the Soviet government.[52] A similar illustration may be found in the United States' tacit acceptance of the obligation to locate, remove, and dispose of the radioactive materials deposited in Spanish territory following the crash of a US bomber equipped with nuclear weapons.[53]

The issue, predictably, becomes somewhat more complex when the actors causing environmental injury to another state are private individuals, i.e. other than state organs or representatives as determined by muncipal or international law. Chapter 3 defined the 'secondary' obligation of the state with respect to all territorial or extraterritorial private conduct. Each state must exercise 'due diligence' to prevent and punish conduct which, if the state were the actor, would violate its 'primary' international obligations.[54] Due diligence demands the exercise of the full extent of the legal authority possessed by the state over the private actor to prevent such conduct.[55] In the environmental context, this translates into a duty to prevent environmental

in 15 *Int'l Legal Materials* 285 (1976). Convention for the Prevention of Marine Pollution by Dumping from Ships and Aircraft, done at Oslo 15 Feb. 1972, reprinted in 11 *Int'l Legal Materials* 262 (1972).

[50] Quentin-Baxter has noted consensus as to the linkage between the state's obligation and its authority over private conduct: '[T]here was a very wide measure of agreement among legal writers of all persuasions that activities of which a State had knowledge, or which fell within its *regulatory capacity*, could properly be attributed to that State, There was virtually no tendency, either in literature or in State practice, to seek escape from obligations of that kind, merely because the cause of harm lay within private hands.' ILC, Summary Records of the 33rd Session, i *Yb. Int'l L. Comm'n* 222, UN Doc. A/CN.4/Ser. A (1981) (emphasis added).

[51] See Declaration of Santo Domingo: The Specialized Conference of the Caribbean Countries on Problems of the Sea, reprinted in UN Doc. ST/LEG/SER, B/16, at 599; Jenks. 'Liability for Ultrahazardous Activities in International Law', i *Recueil des cours* 100, at 178 (1966); Stein, *supra* n. 45, at 48; ILC 1981 Sum. Rec., *supra* n. 50, at 219.

[52] See Letter from the Canadian Dept. External Affairs to the Ambassador of the USSR reprinted in 18 *Int'l Legal Materials* 899 (1979); Protocol Between the Government of Canada and the Government of the USSR, done at Moscow 2 Apr. 1981, reprinted in 20 *Int'l Legal Materials* 689 (1981) See also Christol, 'International Liability for Damage Caused by Space Objects', 74 *Am. J. Int'l L.* 346, at 347–50 (1980).

[53] See Szuk, *The Bombs of Palomares* (1967); du Pontavice, *supra* n. 39, at 435.

[54] See ch. 3 nn. 110–11.

[55] See ch. 3 commencing at n. 141.

harm to other states arising out of private conduct subject to the jurisdiction of the state. In fact, this is precisely the environmental obligation identified in the LOS Convention, the Stockholm Declaration, and the Charter of Economic Rights and Duties of States; each recites the duty to ensure that conduct within the 'jurisdiction or control' of the state does not injure the environment of any other state.[56] A substantial number of commentators have adopted this same language to express the scope of state obligation with respect to injurious private conduct.[57]

Properly understood, the expression 'jurisdiction and control' would seem to refer to two dimensions of state legal authority. The first is simply the geographic ambit of jurisdiction. Due diligence clearly requires the exercise of legal authority with respect to private conduct within the zone of state territory.[58] Part III will demonstrate, however, that international law recognizes the jurisdiction of the state over regions of the ocean well beyond the territorial boundary. The logic of due diligence dictates that the state must exercise authority possessed over private activities in areas such as the contiguous zone, the continental shelf, and the exclusive economic zone to prevent environmental harm to another state.[59] Specific discussion of the evidence and consequences of this obligation with respect to each such juridical zone must await definition of the applicable regimes of authority in Part III.[60] For present purposes it is sufficient to identify, in principle, the state's obligation to exercise any jurisdiction possessed in an extraterritorial zone to prevent injury to another state arising out of private conduct.

The second aspect of state legal authority to which 'jurisdiction and control' refers is extraterritorial authority over subject matter not so geographically defined. As discussed in Chapter 3, the due diligence obligation operates generally to require states to exercise such jurisdiction, including that possessed over nationals, to endeavour to prevent private parties in any *locus* from engaging in prohibited conduct.[61] The evidence of the validity of this principle in the specific context of the environmental preventive obligation is substantial. The set of customary and conventional obligations of states with respect to flag vessels represents a significant expression of the general principle. Chapter 10 will be devoted to an inquiry into the precise legal

[56] LOS Convention, *supra* n. 17, art. 194(2); Stockholm Declaration, *supra* n. 17, Principle 21; Economic Charter, *supra* n. 42, art. 30.

[57] See e.g. Hakapaa, *Marine Pollution in International Law: Material Obligations and Jurisdiction* 33 (1981); R. Hallman, *Towards an Environmentally Sound Law of the Sea* 15, at 30 (1974); Handl, *supra* n. 36, at 526; Stein, *supra* no. 45, at 48. See also Draft Principles: Protection and Preservation of the Atmosphere prepared by the Australian Branch of the ILA, in ILA 59th, *supra* n. 39, Appendix.

[58] Note that the Trail Smelter factory was a private activity. See Comments of Blix in 1973 Colloque, *supra* n. 45, at 506.

[59] See text at ch. 13, nn. 69–136 *re* authority.

[60] See ch. 13 at nn. 153–208 *re* responsibility.

[61] See ch. 3 at nn. 146–52.

authority, environmental obligations, and consequential responsibility of the state with respect to vessels flying its flag. For present purposes, however, it is important to anticipate a central conclusion: each state has a duty to take steps to prevent any vessel flying its flag from engaging in conduct harmful to the environment of another state.[62] There is no spatial limit to the operation of this obligation.

The evidence is by no means limited to the singular species of legal authority possessed over flag vessels. Article 6 of the 1967 Outer Space Treaty, for example, provides that states are responsible for the consequences of 'national activities in outer space, including the Moon and other celestial bodies, whether such activities are carried on by governmental or non-governmental entities . . .'[63] Although the language 'national activities' suffers from ambiguity, a suggested interpretation applies the rule of responsibility to activites of nationals even when commenced with an extraterritorial launching.[64] The Action Plan for the Human Environment adopted at the UN Stockholm Conference recommends that states 'ensure that ocean dumping by their nationals anywhere . . . is controlled'.[65] As noted above, the introductory general statement of obligation in the 1982 LOS Convention implies a duty to take all possible steps, including the exercise of extraterritorial authority, to prevent marine pollution.[66] Article 139, set forth in that part of the Convention which defines the rights and obligations of states with respect to the resources of the sea-bed beyond national jurisdiction, the 'Area', is rather more explicit:

> States Parties shall have the responsibility to ensure that activities in the Area, whether carried out by States Parties, or State enterprises or natural or juridical persons which possess the nationality of States Parties or are effectively controlled by them or their nationals, shall be carried out in conformity with this Part.[67]

Certain of the major proposals submitted in the course of, or in preparation for, the negotiation of the provisions of the Convention devoted to the problems of marine environmental protection stated the obligation *vis-à-vis* nationals in even broader terms. Draft articles proposed by Kenya in 1974, for example, provided: 'States shall be responsible for damage caused by their activities, those of their nationals, physical or juridical, and others under their control or registration to any part of the marine environment.'[68] Similarly, a United States' draft of 1975 required states to implement marine pollution

[62] See ch. 10 at nn. 60–6.

[63] Treaty on Principles governing the Activities of States in the Exploration and Use of Outer Space, including the Moon and Other Celestial Bodies, *supra* ch. 4 n. 71, art 6.

[64] See generally Fawcett, *supra* ch. 4 n. 64, at 44–5; Jenks, *supra* ch. 4 n. 72, at 210; Wiewiorowska, *supra* ch. 2 n. 82, at 25–8 (1979).

[65] Stockholm Declaration, *supra* n. 17, Recommendation 86.

[66] LOS Convention, *supra* n. 17, art. 192.

[67] *Id.*, art. 139.

[68] Kenya: Draft Articles, *supra* n. 40, art 29. See also USSR: Draft Articles, *supra* n. 40, art. 3.

laws to international standards or higher with respect to any spatial areas over which they possess jurisdiction, flag vessels, and nationals.[69]

The comments of a number of publicists are in accord with this broad formulation of the obligation to prevent nationals from engaging in conduct harmful to other states.[70] Particularly illustrative are the ILC materials regarding 'International Liability for Injurious Consequences Arising out of Acts Not Prohibited by International Law.'[71] Mr Sucharitkul, for example, commented repeatedly that developed states must bear responsibility for the activities of nationals controlling environmentally injurious technologies situated in developing states.[72] Of more general significance is the meaning attributed by the Special Rapporteur Quentin-Baxter to the phrase 'territory or control', used to define the scope of state liability for injurious conduct.[73] Both during oral proceedings and in his written report to the Commission, the Special Rapporteur emphasized that, with reference to the regions beyond state territory, the phrase referred to activities (*a*) within the substantial control of the state, (*b*) on ships or aircraft of the state, or (*c*) of nationals of the state.[74]

On the basis of the foregoing, it seems that the theoretical conclusions of Chapter 3 as to the requirements of due diligence over private extraterritorial conduct is borne out in the literature of international environmental law. The state's obligation to prevent environmental harm to other states applies both to its own acts and private conduct in any *locus* over which it possesses a measure of legal authority. Chapter 8 will consider the standard of performance applicable to this duty, i.e. whether, or in what circumstances, the 'fault' of the state is a condition to breach.

D. PROCEDURAL OBLIGATIONS

Mention should be made of two specific procedural duties, products of the general obligation to prevent environmental harm to other states, which

[69] US: Draft Articles, *supra* n. 40, art. 4 (emphasis added).

[70] See generally discussions in Hallman, *supra* n. 57, at 30; Treves, 'Les Tendances récentes du droit conventionnel de la responsabilité et le nouveau droit de la mer', 21 *Ann. Français droit int'l* 767, at 782–3 (1975).

[71] See ch. 8 for general discussion of these materials.

[72] See ILC, Summary Records of the 32nd Session, i. *Yb. Int'l L. Comm'n* 241, UN Doc. A/CN4/SER.A (1980), at 246; ILC, 1981 Sum. Rec., *supra* n. 50, at 224; Quentin-Baxter, Third Report on International Liability for Injurious Consequences Arising out of Acts Not Prohibited by International Law, UN Gen. Ass. Doc. A/CN.4/360, 23 June 1982, at 20 (hereinafter cited as Q-B, 3rd Rpt).

[73] *Id.*, at 19 and 20.

[74] See Q-B, 3rd Rpt., *supra* n. 72, at 24; ILC, 1981 Sum. Rec. *supra* n. 50, at 253. Note that items 2 and 3 are qualified. They do not apply if the conduct is in the 'territory or control' of another state. This, it is submitted, is an improper avoidance of the possibility of multiple responsibility. The fact that nationals or vessels are also subject to another state's authority does not eliminate the state's own authority or obligation to exercise such authority to the extent possible to prevent environmental injury.

appear to have emerged as customary legal rules. The obligations to *inform* and to *consult and negotiate* regarding activities presenting a risk of environmental injury may now be found in both doctrine and practice. The treaty between France and Spain which was the subject of the *Lac Lanoux* Arbitration discussed above, for example, required procedures of information and consultation before commencement of any activity interfering with the resource rights of the other state.[75] The Charter of Economic Rights and Duties of States provides specifically: 'In the exploitation of natural resources shared by two or more countries, each State must cooperate on the basis of a system of information and prior consultation in order to achieve optimum use of such resources without causing damage to the legitimate interest of others.'[76] Similar statements appear in the ILA's Helsinki Rules on the Uses of Waters of International Rivers,[77] and its Montreal Rules regarding 'Transfrontier Pollution'.[78] The duty to consult and negotiate when activities are likely to prejudice the environmental interests of other states is specifically noted in the Paris Convention for the Prevention of Marine Pollution from Land-based Sources.[79] The obligation to provide notice to any potentially affected state is variously expressed in the UNEP 'Draft Principles of Conduct in the Field of the Environment for the Guidance of States in the Conservation and Harmonious Utilization of Natural Resources Shared By Two or More States',[80] the UN General Assembly Resolution on 'Cooperation Between States in the Field of the Environment',[81] the OECD's 'Recommendation of the Council for the Implementation of a Regime of Equal Right of Access and Non-discrimination in Relation to Transfrontier Pollution', and 'Decision and Recommendation of the Council on Transfrontier Movements of Hazardous Waste',[82] and the LOS Convention.[83]

[75] Additional Act to the Treaty of Bayonne, 26 May 1866. The *Lac Lanoux* Case (1957) (*Spain* v. *France*), 12 R. Int'l Arb. Awards 281.

[76] Economic Charter, *supra* no. 42, art. 3.

[77] International Law Association, 'Report of the 52nd Conference' 477–533 (1967). See Bourne, 'International Law and Pollution of International River and Lakes', 21 *U. Tor. L.J.* 182 (1971).

[78] The Montreal Rules, *supra* n. 46, arts. 5 and 6. See also ILA 59th, *supra* n. 39, 543–50 (1980). Note that these rules are intended to express *lex lata. Id.*, at 532.

[79] Done at Paris, 21 Feb, 1974, reprinted in 13 *Int'l Legal Materials* 352 (1974).

[80] United Nations Environment Programme, Report of the Governing Council on the Work of its 6th Session, 33 UN GAOR Supp. (no. 25), at 154, UN Doc. A/33/25 (1978). See Adede, 'United Nations Efforts toward the Development of an Environmental Code of Conduct for States Concerning Harmonious Utilization of Shared Natural Resources', 43 *Albany L. Rev.* 485 (1979).

[81] Gen. Ass. Res 2995 (xxvii), 15 Dec. 1972, UN GAOR Supp. (no. 30), at 42.

[82] OECD Doc. C (77) 28, reprinted in 16 *Int'l Legal Materials* 977 (1977). See also OECD Envronment Committee, 'Application of Information and Consultation Practices for Preventing Transfrontier Pollution', in OECD, *Transfrontier Pollution and the Role of States* 8 (1981); OECD Decision and Recommendation of the Council on Transfrontier Movements of Hazardous Waste, OECD Doc. C (83) 180, 23 *Int'l Legal Materials* 214 (1984). As to an earlier and similar effort see Stein, 'The OECD Guiding Principles on Transfrontier Pollution', 6 *Ga. J. Int'l & Comp. L.* 245 (1976).

[83] LOS Convention, *supra* n. 17, art, 198 (notice if a state is aware of imminent danger) and arts. 204–6 (publication of anticipated adverse effects of activities within jurisdiction and control).

It is not surprising, in light of the foregoing, that Handl has concluded that there exists 'overwhelming evidence to the effect that states are subject to a duty of prior information and consultation when they plan activities which carry or may carry a significant risk of transnational environmental harm.'[84] As to the obligation to notify, the ILA is in accord: 'a rule of international customary law has emerged that in principle a state is obliged to render information on new or increasing pollution to a potential victim state.'[85] The view of the ILA with respect to consultation and negotiation, on the other hand, is that the obligation is well-established law regarding shared resources, but only inchoate as to general environmental matters.[86] The suggested distinction appears open to criticism; the environment is, precisely, a shared resource. In any event, the ILA's further caveat that agreement following the steps of notice and consultation is not an additional procedural obligation, i.e. not a condition to engaging in the subject activity, seems undisputed.[87]

Several issues arise with respect to the consequences of the failure to notify or consult. The question of whether injunctive relief would be available to enjoin an activity prior to injury based on a breach of these procedural obligations is both unanswered and beyond the scope of the present inquiry.[88] Quentin-Baxter has proposed that the only sanctions for failure either to take such procedural steps or to reach agreement are 'a continuation of the conflict of interest, and the possibility that a State which has failed to cooperate may be at some disadvantage, if a loss or injury entailing questions of reparation subsequently occurs.'[89] The latter point is quite persuasive: failure to take the requisite procedural steps or to co-operate in the pursuit of agreement might well suggest 'blameworthiness' affecting the measure of apportionment of reparation.[90] To conclude, however, that a breach of the procedural obligations is without any immediate consequence does not seem justified.

[84] Handl, 'The Environment: International Rights and Responsibilities', in [1980] *Proc. Am. Soc. Int'l L.* 223, at 224. This conclusion is presumably intended to extend to both activities of the state itself *and* activities within the state's 'jurisdiction and control'.

[85] ILA 58th, *supra* n. 39, at 405–7. See also Van Lier, *Acid Rain and International Law* (1981). See *contra* as to the present state of the law, Kiss, 'Survey of Current Developments in International Environmental Law', IUCN Policy Paper no. 10 (1976), at 31; Springer, *The International Law of Pollution* 146–8 (1983).

[86] ILA 58th, *supra* n. 39, at 407–8. See also Springer, *supra* n. 35, at 148–50; Van Lier *supra* n. 85, at 122–4. See contra Bothe, 'International Legal Problems of Industrial Siting in Border Areas and National Environmental Policies', in OECD, *Transfrontier Pollution and the Role of States* 79 (1981).

[87] See ILA 59th *supra* n. 39, at 549–50. Of course, if the activity then causes material damage, the responsibility of the state may be engaged.

[88] Indeed, the general issue of the availability of injunctive relief in circumstances of a 'threat' of injury is unresolved. See the *Nuclear Tests* Cases (*Australia* v. *Fr.*), [1973] ICJ 99, at 131 (Dissenting Opin. Judge Ignacio-Pinto); Commentary to Australian Rpt., ILA 59th, *supra* n. 39, at 558. As to injunctive relief see Mann, *supra* ch. 4 n. 21, at 1.

[89] Q-B, 3rd Rpt., *supra* n. 72, at 16. See Magraw, *supra* ch. 4 n. 13, at 312. Although the subject is activities not prohibited, this conclusion appears generally applicable to conduct prior to injury, i.e. prior to wrong.

[90] See text at ch. 4 nn. 69–72.

Although material injury may only be potential, the acting state has wrongfully omitted to perform an international obligation. The general principles discussed in Part I suggest two consequential obligations: (*a*) cessation of the breach (i.e. commence to inform and consult); and (*b*) provision of appropriate reparation (likely in the form of satisfaction).[91]

E. GOOD NEIGHBOURLINESS AND ABUSE OF RIGHTS

Prior to turning from the issue of responsibility for the breach of the obligation to prevent territorial environmental harm, it is important to note two principles often defined either as the sources of the obligation or as alternative rules of limitation—good neighbourliness and abuse of rights. The former is generally regarded as an abstraction reflecting the specific principles set forth in the UN Declaration on Principles of International Law Concerning Friendly Relations and Cooperation Among States[92] and the admonition of Article 74 of the UN Charter to take 'due account' of 'the interests and well-being of the rest of the world, in social, economic, and commercial matters.'[93] 'It obligates states, enterprises and individuals to respect the rights of others to participate in the enjoyment of community rights and in the social process.'[94] In these terms, the relevance of the principle to the problem of environmental pollution is patent. Indeed, the notion of *sic utere tuo* may constitute an expression of the tenet of good neighbourliness.[95] It does not appear, however, that the principle has crystallized into the sort of concrete rule which may serve independently to define wrongfulness in the context of dispute.[96] In Goldie's words, the principle of good neighbourliness 'may be seen as providing the general guidelines and directions of an emerging body of law. They have not been adumbrated as specific rules providing the major premises governing decisions in international and domestic courts alike.'[97]

[91] See text at ch. 4 nn. 30–35.

[92] UN Doc. A/RES 2625 (xxv), 24 Oct. 1970. See generally Bramsen, 'Transnational Pollution and International Law', 42 *Nordisk Tidsskrift* 153, at 154–5 (1972); Sorensen, 'Principes de droit international public', iii *Recueil des cours,* 198 (1960).

[93] UN Charter, art. 74. See generally Andrassy, 'Les Relations Internationales de Voisinage', ii *Recueil des cours* 88 (1951); Dupuy, *supra* n. 30, at 30–6; Hakapaa, *supra* n. 57, at 141–5; ILA 58th, *supra* n. 39, at 390; Popp, *Voisinage et bon voisinage en droit international* (1980).

[94] Goldie, 'A General View of International Environmental Law', in 1973 Colloque, *supra* n. 45, at 68.

[95] See Dupuy, *supra* n. 30, at 31; Dupuy, 'International Liability of States for Damages Caused by Transfrontier Pollution', in OECD, *Legal Aspects of Transfrontier Pollution* 345, at 350 (1977).

[96] As noted by the ILA: '[T]he direct application of these principles would not be of great help in taking a concrete legal decision,' ILA 58th, *supra* n. 39, at 390.

[97] Goldie, *supra* n. 94, at 68. A related abstraction is the notion of 'good faith' in state relations. One recent study has defined the notion as another policy principle without concrete utility. Zoller, *La Bonne foi en droit international public* (1977). Virally's review argues that although the concept is not an autonomous source of law, it has a role in the interpretation of other rules of conduct. Virally, 'Good Faith in Public International Law', 77 *Am. J. Int'l L.* 130 (1983).

The relationship between the abstraction of good neighbourliness and the principle of abuse of rights is indistinct. Handl views the former as an expression of the latter.[98] It might be argued that the converse is the case. In either event, it is quite clear that abuse of rights has secured the greater measure of doctrinal support as a concrete rule of decision. Commentators on the abuse of rights tend to fall into three categories, representing quite different perspectives of the meaning and role of the doctrine.

In its broadest formulation, abuse of rights is conceived as a general principle of the international law of torts.[99] Kiss, in an influential work on the subject, asserted that the doctrine imposes limits on the exercise of rights when (*a*) interference with the correlative rights of other states results, (*b*) the exercise is for a reason other than that for which the right was conferred, or (*c*) the exercise is otherwise arbitrary.[100] Friedmann described it as the substantive rule that states may not use rights 'in such a manner that its anti-social effects outweigh the legitimate interests of the owner of the right'.[101] In effect, these advocates view abuse of rights as a 'jural postulate' which will determine wrongfulness in the interstices between developed prohibitory rules.[102]

A second group of publicists accepts abuse of rights as a viable rule of decision, but rejects this expansive perspective in favour of a narrow interpretation focusing on the purpose of the exercise of the right. In the words of Taylor, the doctrine operates only to prohibit the exercise of a 'power for a reason, actual or inferred, which is contrary to the purpose or purposes for which international law contemplates the power will be used.'[103] The ILA has expressed an even more restrictive version of this formulation, basing wrongfulness on an intent to injure: 'No one may exercise his rights in such a manner as to damage another when causing this damage is the purpose of exercising such rights.'[104]

A significant number of commentators deny entirely the function of abuse of rights as a rule of decision. Schwarzenberger speaks simply of the absence of such a rule in international law.[105] Brownlie advocates the more common perspective that 'the doctrine is a useful agent in the progressive development

[98] Handl, *supra* n. 19, at 57.

[99] See Lauterpacht, *The Function of Law in the International Community* 298 (1933). See also Cheng, *supra* ch. 1 n. 6, at 121–36.

[100] Kiss, *L'Abus de droit en droit international* (1953). See Taylor, 'The Content of the Rule against Abuse of Rights in International Law', 46 *Brit. Yb. Int'l L.* 323, at 341 (1972–3).

[101] Friedmann, 'The Uses of General Principles in the Development of International Law', 57 *Am. J. Int'l L.* 279, at 288 (1963). See also Handl, *supra* n. 30, at 57–8.

[102] See Garcia-Amador, *supra* ch. 1 n. 1, at 380; Garcia-Amador, *supra* ch. 1 n. 3, at 12. Judge Ammoun in the *Barcelona Traction* Case described abuse of rights as an 'international tort' like denial of justice. *Barcelona Traction* Case (*Belg.* v. *Spain*), [1970] ICJ 324 (Sep. Opin. J. Ammoun).

[103] Taylor, *supra* n. 100, at 352. See also Akehurst 'Jurisdiction in International Law', 46 *Brit. Yb. Int'l L.* 145, at 189–90 (1972–3).

[104] ILA 58th, *supra* n. 39, at 404.

[105] Schwarzenberger and Brown, *A Manual of International Law* 86 (6th edn. 1976).

of the law, but that, as a general principle, it does not exist in positive law.'[106] The logic of this position is quite compelling. When international law defines conduct as wrongful it is by reference to rules, such as the obligation to prevent environmental harm, which may reflect the logic of abuse of rights; it is not, however, by recourse to the abstraction of abuse of rights itself.[107] This is precisely the view taken by the ILC in their study of state responsibility. No separate examination of the doctrine of abuse of rights was deemed necessary:

> for if there were situations in international law in which the exercise of a right was subject to limits, that was because there was a rule which imposed the obligation not to exceed those limits. In other words, the abusive exercise of a right then constituted failure to fulfill an obligation.[108]

In summary, the principles of good neighbourliness and abuse of rights provide the underlying or animating logic of the preventive obligation defined in the preceding section. They do not, however, appear to have advanced from policy abstractions to concrete rules of decision which limit state prerogatives with respect to the environment.

[106] Brownlie, ch. 1 n. 2, at 52; Brownlie, *supra* n. 10, at 445. See also Bowett, *The Law of the Sea* 44 (1967), who states that the specific rules of the law of the sea are designed to prevent abuse of rights.

[107] Dupuy writes: 'Dire qu'il y a abus de droit, c'est simplement dire que le droit a été exercé de manière telle qu'il s'est traduit par la méconnaissance d'une obligation préexistante mais, éventuellement, encore mal formulée'. Dupuy, *supra* n. 30, at 29–30.

[108] Comments of Ago, ILC, Summary Records of the 25th Session, i *Yb. Int'l L. Comm'n* 19 (1973), UN Doc. A/CN.4/Ser.A/1973. See also Comments of Bartoś, *id.*, at 13; Comments of Ago, ILC, Summary Records of the 28th Session, i *Yb. Int'l L. Comm'n* 7 (1976), UN Doc. A/CN.4/Ser.A/1976.

6

Harm Occurring Beyond Any State's Territory

A. DEFINITION OF THE PROBLEM

The entire preceding discussion in Part II has focused on the obligation of states to prevent material environmental harm within the *territory* of other states. Indeed, part of the central logic of the defined reciprocal obligation is that it is necessary to ensure that each state may render independent decisions with respect to the environmental integrity of state territory.[1] Obligations pertaining to harm to the environment outside the territory of any state, i.e. in terms of the traditional law of the sea, the 'high seas', have not yet been considered.[2] The starting point for an analysis of this issue must be the *laissez-faire* tradition of international law with respect to conduct on the high seas. Article 2 of the 1958 Convention on the High Seas codified customary law in expressing the freedoms of navigation, fishing, laying of submarine cables, overflight, and 'others which are recognized by the general principles of international law.'[3] The enumerated list was in no sense intended to be exhaustive of the permissible uses of the common high seas; rather the premise was one of liberty of action.[4] The principal constraint to such liberty identified in the Convention was simply the obligation to act 'with reasonable regard to the interests of other States in their exercise of the freedom of the seas.'[5] Liberty checked only by the reciprocal liberty of other states is, then, the orthodoxy of high seas doctrine. The tasks of this chapter will be to consider the extent to which an obligation to prevent harm to the high seas environment may be identified, either in this traditional regime of relative freedom or in more specific environmental rules pertaining to the high seas.

B. HARM TO EXCLUSIVE INTERESTS

The first step must be to distinguish harm to the high seas environment from harm to the particular interests of individual states which happen to be

[1] See ch. 5 at n. 18 *supra*.

[2] Article 1 of the Geneva Convention on the High Seas, done 29 Apr. 1958, entry into force 30 Sept. 1962, 450 UNTS 82, TIAS. no. 5200, 13 UST 2312, defines the 'high seas' as: 'all parts of the sea that are not included in the territorial seas or in the internal waters of a State.'

[3] *Id.*, art. 2. Note that the preamble of the High Seas Convention declares the purpose to be the codification of *lex lata*.

[4] See McDougal and Burke, *The Public Order of the Oceans* 758–9 (1962).

[5] High Seas Convention, *supra* n. 2, art. 2.

situated in or relate to that environment.[6] The former constitutes injury to an interest shared by *all* states in the integrity of the high seas environment; the latter constitutes injury to the exclusive interests of a single state. This distinction, it is submitted, has significant juridical consequences. Even if no obligation to prevent harm to the high seas environment is identifiable, an extension of the *sic utere tuo* principle would require states to endeavour to prevent injury to the individual interests of other states through conduct affecting that environment. This point may be demonstrated by reference to the two categories of exclusive interests which may be so injured.

The first consists of those users of the high seas juridically related to the state, i.e. state organs and representatives, private flag vessels, and nationals. It is quite beyond dispute that conduct on the high seas which injures such users will trigger the responsibility of the state to which such conduct is attributed. Witness such well-known cases as the *I'm Alone*,[7] the *Jessie*, the *Thomas F. Bayard*, and the *Pescawha*,[8] the *Cape Horn Pigeon*,[9] and the *Lusitania*.[10] Further, the *Corfu Channel* Case, although concerned with harm to foreign vessels within the territory of the state in breach, demonstrates adequately that *sic utere tuo* is not limited to the obligation to prevent harm to the private interests of another state within *its* territory. Similarly, it has been noted that when conduct within state territory harmful to the high seas environment injures users of the high seas, *sic utere tuo* operates:

> [I]f the injury from land-based pollution of the high seas was to ships or persons engaged in legitimate activities (such as navigation or fishing), the situs of harm (State territory or the high seas) would make little difference because it is clear that international law entitles States to protect their vessels and nationals from injury caused by other States on the high seas.[11]

This conclusion finds support in a number of instances of state practice relating to nuclear weapons tests conducted in the South Pacific. In the *Daigo Fukuryu Maru* incident, for example, Japan claimed and received from the United States $2 million compensation for injuries sustained by nationals on board a fishing vessel on the high seas during the 1954 Eniwitok tests.[12] In

[6] Note well that the phrase 'individual interests' is used here in an exclusively international sense. It refers to interests held individually by states—as distinct from interests held only by the personified international community. It does not refer to the domestic distinction between 'public' interests held by the government of the state and the 'private' interests of individual members of the state. From an international perspective, interests designated public or private pursuant to the internal legal order of the state constitute 'individual interests' of the state.

[7] (*Canada* v. *US*), 3 R. Int'l Arb. Awards 1609 (1933–5).

[8] (*UK* v. *US*), 6 R. Int'l Arb. Awards 57 (1921).

[9] (*US* v. *Russia*), 9 R. Int'l Arb. Awards 51 (1902).

[10] (*US* v. *Germ.*), 7 R. Int'l Arb. Awards 32 (1923).

[11] See Hickey, 'Custom and Land-based Pollution of the High Seas', 15 *San Diego L. Rev.* 409, at 426, 428, 431 (1978).

[12] The payments were specifically characterized as *ex gratia* by the US, without reference to legal liability. Japan, on the other hand, asserted precisely such liability. Whiteman, 4 *Dig. Int'l L.*

response to Japanese protests regarding further testing in the Marshall Islands, the United States agreed 'to give consideration to the question of compensation' if 'substantial economic losses' were experienced by Japan or its nationals.[13] Finally, the obligation to prevent injury to users of the high seas arising out of the environmental consequences of territorial conduct is implied in the positions of Australia and New Zealand in the *Nuclear Tests* Cases regarding French weapons tests.[14] In summary, there is certainly adequate authority for the conclusion of Quentin-Baxter to the ILC that injury to one state's users of the high seas caused by environmental conduct of another state's users is juridically tantamount to 'transboundary' injury.[15]

The second type of exclusive interest subject to injury from activities affecting the marine environment beyond the territorial sea is the spatially defined exclusive resource zone. One of the principal developments in the law of the sea since World War II has been the acknowledgment of certain zones carved out of the high seas over which coastal states enjoy exclusive rights to resource exploitation. These specific regimes of authority will be identified in Part III.[16] It is important at present to recognize that environmental injury affecting the resources in these zones constitutes harm to the *exclusive* interests of a particular state.[17] Such injury, it would seem, should be viewed as equivalent to, and subject to the same preventive obligation as, harm to state territory itself.

The conclusion finds support in the language chosen by the ILA to define actionable harm: 'substantial injury in the territory of another state or to *any of its rights under international law* or to the marine environment.'[18] Indeed, in an earlier set of 'Draft Rules on Sea Pollution' the ILA specifically identified the obligation to prevent injury 'in the territory, territorial sea and *contiguous zone* of another State.'[19] Similarly, the London Convention on Civil Liability

563–6 (1965) United States' Note, 237 UNTS 198. See discussion Quentin-Baxter, 'Fourth Report on International Liability for Injurious Consequences Arising out of Acts Not Prohibited by International Law', UN Doc. A/CN.4/372 (27 June 1983), at 25, 28 and 30 (hereinafter cited as Q-B, 4th Rpt); Yates, 'State Responsibility for Nonwealth Injuries to Aliens in the Postwar Era', in *International Law of State Responsibility for Injuries to Aliens* 213, at 220 (Lillich ed., 1983).

13 Whiteman, *supra* n. 12, at 485–6.

14 [1978] ICJ Pleadings, the *Nuclear Tests* Cases, (*Australia* v. *France*) vol. i at 14; (*New Zealand* v. *France*) vol. ii at 8.

15 Q-B, 3rd Rpt., *supra* ch. 5 n. 72, at 20.

16 See ch. 13 *infra*.

17 Note that the exclusive interests of more than one state may be implicated. See ch. 13 at nn. 153–4.

18 International Law Association, Report of the 55th Conference (1972), Rpt. of the Comm. on International Water Resources: Marine Pollution of Continental Origin (hereinafter cited as ILA 55th Pollution), at 97 (emphasis added). This language also supports the conclusion reached in the preceding section regarding harm to the exclusive interests of the state in its 'users'.

19 International Law Association, Report of the 53rd Conference (1968) (hereinafter cited as ILA 53rd), art. 3 (emphasis added). The Report does note that the 'continguous zone' is intended to refer to the Territorial Sea Convention's 12-mile maximum zone. It is the fact of the linkage of extraterritorial rights and injury which is significant, however, not the extent or present status of those rights.

for Oil Pollution Damage Resulting from Exploration for and Exploitation of Sea-bed Mineral Resources establishes uniform private law liability with respect to pollution damage to any party's territory 'or in the areas in which, in accordance with international law, it has sovereign rights over natural resources.'[20] Finally, as noted above, the reports submitted to the ILC by the Special Rapporteur Quentin-Baxter attached state responsibility to conduct within the 'territory or control' of the state. Significantly, the definition of injury reflects the same perspective: 'any loss or injury, whether to the property of a State, or to any person or thing within the territory or control of a State.'[21] Resources within the juridical zones over which the state exercises exclusive rights may be defined either as property of the state or as within state 'control' for these purposes.[22] In summary, then, one may conclude that the obligation to prevent environmental harm to other states defined in Chapter 5 applies equally to injury to the individual, exclusive interests of the state in its extraterritorial resource zones or users.

C. HARM TO COMMON INTERESTS

i. Obligation to Prevent

Injury to the common interests in the high seas environment presents quite distinct juridical problems. The orthodox *sic utere tuo* preventive obligation relates to injury to the interests of another state; here the interests of all states are at stake. Doctrine and practice, however, now evidence the existence of a parallel obligation to prevent harm to the shared resource of the high seas environment.

Section A above noted that the High Seas Convention itself imposes on states exercising 'freedoms' of the high seas the obligation to act with 'reasonable regard' for the corresponding rights of others.[23] This restriction is reiterated in the 1982 LOS Convention as the obligation to exercise freedom with 'due regard' for other states.[24] A number of authorities have assumed that pollution of the high seas environment is among the recognized 'freedoms' subject to this constraint.[25] The US Council On Environmental

[20] Opened for signature, 1 May 1977. The Convention is to apply to the North Sea, Baltic, and North Baltic, and North Atlantic above 36 degrees latitude.

[21] Q-B, 3rd Rpt., *supra* ch. 5 n. 72, at 24. See text at ch. 5 nn. 71–4 *supra*.

[22] Note that Canada's Supreme Court has denied that the international rights of the state over the continental shelf are properly characterized as property rights. Newfoundland Continental Shelf Reference 1984, 5 DLR 4th 385, at 395–6 (1984).

[23] High Seas Convention, *supra* n. 2, art. 2.

[24] LOS Convention, *supra* ch. 5 n. 17, art. 87(2).

[25] Goldie provides an excellent description of the advantages to a polluting state of the freedom to injure a common resource: 'The tragedy of a common zone and of its open-access resources is that any of wastage, pollution or over-production which may, on balance, be disadvantageous to the actor when property is private, or access is controlled, will balance a private gain against a shared detriment (shared by all the other users). Hence, in the case of the

Quality, for example, reports that '[t]he right to dispose of waste materials in the high seas is a traditional freedom of the seas' tempered only by the 'reasonable regard' standard.[26] From the Council's perspective, that standard operates to prohibit pollution which 'threatens life or directly damages property.'[27] Other publicists have engaged a somewhat broader view of the 'reasonableness' requirement, focusing on factors such as the measure and quality of the environmental harm, alternatives, and the relative importance of competing uses.[28] The problem, of course, is to define a rule of decision when each of the asserted rights—to pollute and to enjoy resources free of environmental harm—is based on the same parent right, the freedom of the seas.[29]

An opposing doctrinal perspective denies that environmental pollution is a freedom at all. In other words, advocates of this view maintain that harm to the high seas environment is *per se* unreasonable:[30]

> Indeed, it would appear contrary to the very principle of freedom of the seas to permit actions which could interfere with the undisturbed and safe use of the sea by the community of nations and to destroy the living resources whose common enjoyment has always been one of the principal objects of the freedom of the high seas.[31]

Whether or not one views this argument alone as sufficient to define any significant harm to the high seas environment as wrongful is not essential.[32] The community appears to have acknowledged the logic of the position in rejecting the permissive approach suggested in the 'reasonable user' rule and recognizing an affirmative obligation to prevent such injury.

Initial evidence of the requisite *opinio juris* with respect to this obligation is the magnitude of the pattern of multilateral conventions in which states have defined and accepted specific obligations to prevent harm to the high seas environment. Multilateral efforts establishing such preventive obligations

high seas, for example, not only is pollution permitted, but it becomes more advantageous than it could be in a private or closed-access environment, since the polluter is, at best, required to suffer an infinitesimally small share of the disutility arising from his polluting act, and can enjoy, alone, all the economics which he can derive from it.' Goldie, 'The Management of Ocean Resources: Regimes for Structuring the Maritime Environment', in iv *The Future of the International Legal Order* 172 (Black and Falk eds. 1972).

[26] Council on Environmental Quality, *supra* ch. 5 n. 20, at 143.

[27] *Id.*, at 144.

[28] See *e.g.* McDougal and Burke, *supra* n. 4, at 863; Moore, 'Legal Aspects of Marine Pollution Control', in *Marine Pollution* 589, at 594–5 (Johnston eds. 1976); Commentary to art. 27, ILC, Report to the Gen. Ass., ii *Yb. Int'l L. Comm'n* 253, at 278, UN Doc.A/CN. 4/Ser.A Add 1 (1956).

[29] See O'Connell, *supra* Introd. n. 1, at 710.

[30] See Legault, *supra* ch. 5 n. 45, at 217–18; Livingston, 'Marine Pollution Articles in the Law of the Sea Single Informal Negotiating Text,' Occasional Paper no. 31 of the Law of the Sea Institute 4 (1976).

[31] Legault, *supra* ch. 5, n. 45, at 217–18.

[32] It might be argued, of course, that all uses of the seas, from spatially exclusive navigation to consumptive fishing, involve a measure of interference. Yet, injury to the environment interferes in a far broader sense—denying other States the opportunity to exercise resource rights by harming or degrading the entire resource.

date back to the 1926 Conference on Oil Pollution of Navigable Waters.[33] The Final Act of the Conference, never ratified in treaty form, provided for zones extending from 50 to 100 miles from the coast within which oil discharge was to be prohibited.[34] The 1954 International Convention for Prevention of Pollution of the Sea by Oil, representing the first major and productive multilateral effort on the subject, adopted the same basic zonal approach to vessel-source oil pollution.[35] By subsequent amendments, the zonal structure was eventually discarded in favour of a prohibition of discharge in *any* region of the seas over limits defined by cargo, capacity, and vessel speed.[36] The obligation to prevent vessel-source pollution in any part of the high seas was then reflected in the 1973 Convention for the Prevention of Pollution by Ships, designed to strengthen and expand the 1954 effort by applying prescriptions to substances in addition to oil and adding standards of construction, design, and equipment.[37] Article 211 of the Law of the Sea Convention again articulates the high seas duty in requiring preventive measures with respect to vessel-source pollution of the 'marine environment' generally.[38]

Conventional obligations to prevent harm to the high seas environment are by no means limited to pollution from vessels. The intentional dumping of radioactive wastes was, for example, specifically subjected to a preventive obligation by Article 25 of the High Seas Convention.[39] Obligations to prevent dumping of *any* substance harmful to the high seas environment are now present both in general multilateral efforts, such as the 1972 London Dumping Convention[40] and the LOS Convention,[41] and specific regional initiatives governing such conduct in local zones of the high seas.[42] Similar

[33] The Conference of seventy-two nations was called by the United States pursuant to a Resolution Noting Damage Done by Oil Pollution and Calling for an International Conference to deal with the Problem, Whiteman, *supra* n. 12, at 696. See Teclaff, 'International Law and the Protection of the Oceans from Pollution', in *International Environmental Law* 107 (Teclaff and Utton eds. 1974).

[34] Final Act of the Preliminary Conference in Oil Pollution of Navigable Waters, done 16 June 1926, 1 *For. Rel. US* 238, at 245 (1926), Annex art. 1. This same approach was reflected in the Draft Convention and Draft Final Act prepared by the League of Nations Committee of Experts, 11 *League of Nations* OJ 1391 (1935).

[35] Done at London 12 May 1954, entry into force 26 July 1958, 327 UNTS 3, TIAS no. 4900, Annex A.

[36] The 1962 amendments entered into force 18 May and 28 June 1967, TIAS no. 6109; the 1967 amendments entered into force 20 Jan. 1978, TIAS no. 8505. For a composite text see 9 *Int'l Legal Materials* 1 (1970). A third set of amendments imposing construction standards is not yet in force. See 11 *Int'l Legal Materials* 267 (1972).

[37] Done at London 2 Nov. 1973, entry into force 2 Oct. 1983 with and subject to exclusions of 1978 Protocol.

[38] LOS Convention, *supra* ch. 5 n. 17, art. 211.

[39] High Seas Convention, *supra* n. 2, art. 25. Brown concludes that the language of Art. 25 applies to dumping of all species of harmful waste. Brown, *The Legal Regime of Hydrospace* 195 (1971). For a contrary view see Hickey, *supra* n. 11, at 436–7.

[40] London Dumping Convention, *supra* ch. 5 n. 44, art. 4 and Annex 3. See Timagenis, *supra* ch. 5 n. 1, at 171–287.

[41] LOS Convention, *supra* ch. 5 n. 17, art. 210.

[42] See e.g. Convention for the Protection and Development of the Marine Environment of the

sets of obligations designed to prevent injury to the high seas environment may be found with respect to each of the other two sources of marine pollution: land-based activity[43] and the exploitation of sea-bed resources.[44]

In addition to such examples of specific contractual obligations to prevent environmental injury to the high seas, there exist a host of multilateral statements evidencing or reciting the existence of a customary preventive obligation. The Stockholm Declaration refers, for example, to the obligation to ensure that activities within a state's 'jurisdiction and control do not cause damage to the environment of other States *or of areas beyond the limits of national jurisdiction*.'[45] Precisely the same language is found in the Charter of Economic Rights and Duties of States[46] and the preamble to the London Dumping Convention.[47] A similar statement of the obligation to prevent harm to the 'marine environment', including 'areas beyond national jurisdiction', is set forth in General Assembly Resolution 2749 (xxv) of 17 December 1970.[48] The Caribbean states' Santo Domingo Declaration further identified every state's duty to prevent pollution 'either inside or outside its respective jurisdictions.'[49] Finally, the drafts submitted in preparation for and during

Wider Caribbean Region, done 24 Mar. 1983, reprinted in 22 *Int'l Legal Materials* 227 (1983) art. 6; Oslo Dumping Convention, *supra* ch. 5 n. 49, art 2; Barcelona Mediterranean Convention, *supra* ch. 5 n. 49; Kuwait Regional Convention for Co-operation on the Pollution of the Marine Environment from Pollution, done 24 April 1978, reprinted in 19 *International Protection of Environment* 9551 (ed. Ruster and Simma 1974), art 5; Council of European Communities Proposed Directive on Dumping Wastes at Sea, 12 Jan. 1976, 40 *J.O. Comm. Eur.* 20 Feb. 1976, art. 2. See also Boczek, 'International Protection of the Baltic Sea Environment Against Pollution: A Study in Marine Environment', 72 *Am. J. Int'l L.* 782 (1978); Timagenis, *supra* ch. 5 n. 1, at 124–70, 294–303.

[43] See e.g. Barcelona Mediterranean Convention, *supra* ch. 5 n. 49, art. 8, and Protocol for the Protection of the Mediterranean Sea against Pollution from Land-based Sources, done at Athens 17 May 1980, entered into force 17 July 1983; reprinted in 19 *Int'l Legal Materials* 869 (1980); Caribbean Convention, *supra* n. 42, art. 7; Kuwait Convention, *supra* n. 42, art. 6; LOS Convention, *supra* ch. 5 n. 17, art. 207; Convention for the Prevention of Marine Pollution from Land-based Sources, done at Paris 21 Feb. 1974, entered into force 6 May 1978, UN TS 64 (1978), reprinted in 13 *Int'l Legal Materials* 352 (1974). For discussions of this obligation see Hickey, *supra* n. 11, *passim*; Comment, 'The Convention for the Prevention of Marine Pollution from Land-based Sources: An Effective Method for Arbitrating International Effluent Pollution Disputes', 5 *Cal. West. Int'l L.J.* 350 (1975).

[44] See e.g. Barcelona Mediterranean Convention, *supra* ch. 5 n. 49, art. 7; Caribbean Convention, *supra* n. 42, art. 8; Kuwait Convention, *supra* n. 42, art. 7; High Seas Convention, *supra* n. 2, art. 24; LOS Convention, *supra* ch. 5 n. 17, arts, 208, 209; Belgium, France; Federal Republic of Germany, Italy, Japan, Netherlands, United Kingdom, and United States: Memorandum on the Implementation of the Provisional Understanding Regarding Deep Sea-bed Matters, art. 3, done at Geneva, 3 Aug. 1984, entered into force 2 Sept. 1984, reprinted in 23 *Int'l Legal Materials* 1358 (1984).

[45] Stockholm Dclaration, *supra* ch. 5 n. 17, Principle 21 (emphasis added). Note again that UN Gen. Ass. Res. 2996 (xxvii), 15 Dec. 1972, UN GAOR Supp. (no. 30), at 42–3 confirmed the validity of this principle. See generally McDougal and Schneider, 'The Protection of the Environment and World Public Order: Some Recent Developments', 45 *Miss. L.J.* 1085, at 197 (1974); Sohn *supra* ch. 5 n. 45, at 464.

[46] Economic Charter, *supra* ch. 5 n. 42, art. 30.

[47] London Dumping Convention, *supra* ch. 5 n. 44, Preamble.

[48] Gen. Ass. Res. 2749 (xxv), 17 Dec. 1970, UN GAOR Supp. (no. 28) at 24–5.

[49] Declaration of Santo Domingo, *supra* ch. 5 n. 51, at 599.

the LOS III Conference were quite uniform in expressing the preventive obligation either in terms of (*a*) harm to the general 'marine environment' or (*b*) harm to another state's territory or regions beyond state territory.[50] This consensus is reflected in Articles 192 and 194 of the LOS Convention, which describe the obligation to prevent harm to the 'marine environment' as a whole.[51]

Two instances of state practice regarding the dumping of toxic wastes seem further to evidence states' recognition of the obligation to prevent harm to the high seas. In 1971 a Dutch privately owned vessel planning to deposit 600 tons of vinyl chloride waste in the North Atlantic was refused entry to Irish and British ports for refuelling.[52] Following international protests to the Netherlands government and the consequent official 'urging' of recall, the vessel abandoned the disposal scheme.[53] A similar pattern of events in 1975 concluded in the recall of a Finnish state vessel following diplomatic protests with respect to the planned dumping of 690 barrels of arsenic waste on the South Atlantic high seas.[54]

Final support for the obligation may be found in the opinion of publicists. Certain writers, admittedly, have identified the obligation to prevent harm to the high seas environment as only a trend in international law.[55] The ILA, in a commentary to its draft articles on 'Marine Pollution of Continental Origin', recited the obligation but characterized it as a necessary 'innovation'.[56] On the other hand, most commentators presently view the preventive obligation relating to the 'marine environment', including the high seas, as an established

[50] See e.g. Canada, Fiji, Ghana *et al.*, Draft Articles *supra* ch. 5 n. 40, art. 1; USSR Draft Articles, *supra* ch. 5 n. 40, art. 2; Kenya Draft Articles, *supra* ch. 5 n. 40, art. 3. See also Statement by Maurice Strong, exec. director of UNEP at LOS III Caracas Session, reprinted in Papers Presented at a Conference at Bellagio organized by the Amer. Soc. Int'l Law, July 1974. (Squire Law Library, Univ. of Cambridge); Livingston, *supra* n. 30, at 4.

[51] LOS Convention, *supra* ch. 5 n. 17, art. 1. See Boyle, 'Marine Pollution under the Law of the Sea Convention', 79 *Am. J. Int'l L.* 347, at 367 (1985). Note the draft US Restatement position with respect to the *lex lata* character of the Convention (with one exception—the deep sea-bed): 'The United States and other states generally regard the provisions of the Draft Convention, with the exception of Part XI relating to sea-bed mining, as authoritative statements of existing international law', *US Rest. For. Rel. L.* 56 (Tent. Draft no. 3, 1982).

[52] See 2 *Mar. Poll. Bull.* 115 (1971).

[53] *Id.*

[54] See 5 *Mar. Poll. Bull.* 68 (1975). Note certain states do continue limited dumping of hazardous wastes. See Boehmer-Christiansen, 'Dumping Nuclear Waste into the Sea', 7 *Mar. Policy* 25 (1983). Plans in the UK in 1983 to dump nuclear waste were foiled by trade union action. Plans for future dumping continue to be the subject of dispute. See the *Guardian*, 2 Sept. 1983, at 22, col. 7. As to US practice—no current but possible future dumping; see *Int'l Env. Rep., BNA Current Reports*, 10 Feb. 1982, at 81–2; Anderson, 'A Return to Ocean Dumping', *City of New York* v. *US Environmental Protection Agency*, 14 *Nat. Res. L. Newsl.* 3 (1982).

[55] See Kwiatkowska-Czechowska, 'States' Responsibility for Pollution Damage Resulting from the Exploration for and Exploitation of Sea-bed Mineral Resources', 10 *Polish Yb. Int'l. L.* 157, at 162–3 (1980); Rubin, *supra* ch. 5 n. 23, at 279. These views may perhaps be explained as a response to the realities of the procedural problem described in section (ii) below.

[56] ILA 55th Pollution, *supra* n. 18, at 101. In terms of formal expression in conventions at the time, it was perhaps properly so characterized.

customary rule. Consider, for example, de Visscher's observation of 'l'accord sur l'obligation, consacrée par le droit existant, pour tous les États de prendre des mesures afin de prévenir la pollution des espace martimes par des navires ou des personnes relevant de leur jurisdiction.'[57] Tunkin has expressed the same conclusion: 'Le principe que tout État est obligé d'exercer une diligence suffisante pour prévenir la pollution de la mer est un principe du droit international en vigeur qui est accepté par tout les États . . .'[58] The ILC has gone so far as to identify as an 'international crime', i.e. a breach of obligations of fundamental significance to the community, any 'serious breach' of the obligation 'prohibiting massive pollution of the atmosphere or the areas.'[59] Commission discussions evidence the opinion that the preventive obligation with respect to material injury of the high seas already exists; when the violation is particularly heinous, it is to be treated as a 'criminal' breach.[60] The overwhelming opinion of contemporary authors appears in accord with the view that the obligation to prevent material injury to the high seas environment has achieved customary legal status.[61]

ii. Consequences of Breach

Although each state is thus obligated to take steps to prevent harm to the high seas, the consequences of the breach of this obligation are anything but clear; international law is obscure on the issue of the procedural right of any one state to invoke the responsibility of another state for wrongful injury to the common interests of all states in the high seas. In the *South West Africa* (Second Phase) Case, the ICJ observed that '[i]n the international field, the existence of obligations that cannot in the last resort be enforced by any legal process, has always been the rule rather than the exception . . .'[62] The Court was then untroubled to conclude that no individual state possessed a right to assert the responsibility of South Africa for violation of its obligations to the community as a UN Mandatory. To argue that states ought to be vested with such a right:

[57] 53 *Ann. inst. droit int'l* 286 (1969).

[58] *Id.*, at 282.

[59] Art. 19, ILC, Report to the General Assembly, ii *Yb. Int'l Comm'n* 74, UN Doc A/CN.4/Ser.A/1976/A. 1 (Pt. 2) (1976). Accord Australian Branch Report, ILA 59th, *supra* n. 39, art. 11.

[60] See e.g. Comments of Ago and Ushakov, ILC, Summary Records of the 28th Session, i *Yb. Int'l L. Comm'n*, 71–3, UN Doc. A/CN.4/Ser.A (1976). See also Ago, 5th Rpt., *supra* ch. 2 n. 4, at 109; Dupuy, 'Le Droit à la santé et la protection de l'environnement', in *The Right to Health as a Human Right*, Acad. Droit Int'l. Colloq. 340, at 406 (Dupuy ed. 1978).

[61] See Beesley, 'Rights and Responsibilities of Arctic Coastal States: The Canadian View', 3 *J. Marit. L. & Comm.* 1, at 9–10 (1971–2); Bramsen, *supra* ch. 5 n. 92, at 159–60; Hickey, *supra* n. 11, *passim*; Kiss, 'La Notion de patrimoine common de l'humanité', ii *Recueil des cours* 109, at 227–8 (1982); Legault, *supra* ch. 5 n. 45, at 217–18; Sohn, *supra* ch. 5 n. 45, at 493; Stein, *supra* ch. 5 n. 45, at 48.

[62] The *South West Africa* Case (Second Phase) (*Ethiopia and Liberia* v. *South Africa*), [1966] ICJ 6, at 46, See generally for an interesting discussion of the import of the decision, Falk, 'The South West Africa Cases: An Appraisal', 21 *Int'l Org.* 1 (1967).

amounts to a plea that the Court should allow the equivalent of an '*actio popularis*', or right resident in any member of a community to take legal action in vindication of a public interest. But although a right of this kind may be known to certain municipal systems of law, it is not known to international law as it stands at present . . .[63]

It is this unequivocal denial of the existence of a customary right to an *actio popularis* which presumptively stands in the way of the invocation by any one member of the community of the responsibility of another for breach of the obligation to prevent harm to the common resource of the high seas environment.[64] There is, however, emerging evidence and certain persuasive logic that this rejection does not constitute an insurmountable impediment to actions based upon threatened or actual harm to the high seas.

The ICJ in the *South West Africa* decision, itself suggested that standing to pursue such a claim might exist if vested expressly by a legal rule or instrument.[65] Judge Jessup, in dissent, specifically explored and confirmed this conclusion, arguing that there may be no 'generally established *actio popularis* in international law. But intentional law has accepted and established situations in which states are given a right of action without any showing of individual substantive interest as distinguished from the general interest.'[66] The 1970 Judgment in the *Barcelona Traction* Case was in certain respects supportive of this conclusion.[67] The decision first unequivocally confirmed the existence of certain obligations which are owed to the entire community of states: 'In view of the importance of the rights involved, all States can be held to have a legal interest in their protection; they are obligations *erga omnes*.'[68] As to standing to protect the community interest in human rights protection, however, the Court concluded that the instruments setting forth human rights obligations *erga omnes* conferred standing to invoke responsibility for breach only on the state of the victim's nationality.[69]

The *Nuclear Tests* Cases (Judgment) presented the ICJ with the next opportunity to consider the issue of standing to act in the common interest.[70]

[63] The *South West Africa* Case, *supra* n. 62, at 47. See generally Bollecker-Stern, *supra* ch. 1 n. 16, at 68–82.

[64] See Goldie, *supra* ch. 5 n. 94, at 103–8.

[65] The *South West Africa* Case, *supra* n. 62, at 32–4.

[66] *Id.*, at 388 (Dissenting Opin. Judge Jessup). In accord, Dissenting Opins. Judge Koo and Judge Tanaka at 223 and 252, respectively. Brownlie argues persuasively that an 'interim approach' to actions in the public interest might be to seek acknowledgement or vesting of such rights in the context of the enforcement of multilateral environmental conventions. Brownlie, 'A Survey of International Customary Rules of Environmental Protection', in *International Environmental Law* 1, at 5 (Teclaff and Utton ed. 1974).

[67] The *Barcelona Traction Light & Power Co. Ltd.* Case (*Belg.* v. *Spain*), [1970] ICJ 4.

[68] *Id.*, at 32. See authorities noted at Ago, 5th Rpt., *supra* ch. 2 n. 4, at n. 277, See also Bollecker-Stern, *supra* ch. 1 n. 16, at 83–90; Tunkin, *Theory of International Law* 419 (trans. Butler 1974).

[69] *Barcelona Traction*, *supra* n. 67, at 47.

[70] The *Nuclear Tests* Cases (Judgment) (*Australia* v. *France*), [1974] ICJ 253 and (*New Zealand* v. *France*), [1974] ICJ 457.

Among the alternative grounds of complaint asserted by both Australia and New Zealand were charges that French weapons' tests would violate the shared rights of states to be free from fall-out from nuclear testing and to exercise the freedoms of the high seas.[71] Judge Gros expressed the view that *Barcelona Traction*'s recognition of *erga omnes* obligations must be read in light of its subsequent denial of the existence of any vested, customary right to respond to violations of such obligations.[72] The dissent of Judge de Castro endorsed a similar interpretation of *Barcelona Traction*, denied the place of *actio popularis* in international law, and concluded: 'The Applicant has not legal title authorizing it to act as spokesman for the international community and ask the Court to condemn France's conduct.'[73] Judge Petren, on the other hand, reiterated the *Barcelona Traction* conclusion relating to the existence of *erga omnes* obligations and described the absence of appropriate jurisdictional causes for bringing disputes regarding such obligations to adjudication as a 'self-contradiction.'[74] The joint dissent of Judges Onyeama, Dillard, Jiménez de Arechaga, and Waldock expressed the view that *actio popularis* represented, at least, a disputed and credible doctrine deserving consideration:

> Although we recognize that the existence of a so-called *actio popularis* in international law is a matter of controversy, the observations of this Court in the *Barcelona Traction, Light and Power Company, Limited* case suffice to show that the question is one that may be considered as capable of rational legal argument and a proper subject of litigation before this Court.[75]

The merits of the issue were, of course, never squarely addressed by the Court; a French undertaking to cease testing was deemed to render the case moot.[76]

The positions of Australia and New Zealand with respect to the standing issue were, not surprisingly, supportive of an *actio popularis*. Australia, citing *Barcelona Traction*, argued that the Court had already acknowledged the existence of 'general' or 'collective' legal interests, created by customary or treaty law, which are entitled to protection by all states.[77] New Zealand's pleadings echoed the conclusion that all states possess standing to enforce *erga omnes* obligations such as the preservation of the environment and the prevention of fall-out from nuclear testing.[78] In oral argument, New Zealand identified a distinction between two types of *erga omnes* obligations: 'certain

[71] [1978] ICJ Pleadings, *Nuclear Tests* Cases, (*Australia* v. *France*) vol. i, at 14; (*New Zealand* v. *France*) vol. ii, at 8. Each state also alleged private, exclusive territorial injury. *Id.*

[72] [1974] ICJ 253, at 290 (Sep. Opin. J. Gross).

[73] *Id.*, at 390 (Dissenting Opin. J. De Castro).

[74] *Id.*, at 224–5 (Dissenting Opin. J. Petren).

[75] *Id.*, at 370 (Joint Dissenting Opin. Judges Onyeama, Dillard, de Arechaga, and Waldock).

[76] *Id.*, at 267–70 (*Australia* v. *France*); 472–5 (*New Zealand* v. *France*).

[77] Australian Memorial on Jurisdiction and Admissibility, [1978] ICJ Pleadings, *Nuclear Tests* Cases, vol. i, at 329, 332–5.

[78] New Zealand Memorial on Jurisdiction and Admissibility, [1978] ICJ Pleadings, *Nuclear Tests* Cases, vol. ii, at 204–11.

obligations, by their very nature, are owed to the whole of the international community, and it makes no sense to conceive of them as sets of obligations owed, on a bilateral basis, to each member of that community. In other cases this is not true.'[79] Human rights obligations as to the breaching state's own nationals provide an example of 'indivisible' obligations to the community which 'cannot be regarded as the sum of a series of discrete bilateral duties.'[80] Non-aggression duties, on the other hand, illustrate *erga omnes* obligations which are also 'bilaterally' owed to all states.[81] One implication of this distinction is that the standing of a state to invoke the responsibility of another for violating its specific 'bilateral' obligations rests on a quite orthodox perspective of private 'legal interests,' even if the conduct is violative of an obligation *erga omnes*. The standing of states not so directly affected to respond to the breach in vindication of the public interest would, however, depend on an *actio popularis*.

This point is both significant and persuasive. When an obligation logically may be defined as directed only to the 'community,' it is patent that only an *actio popularis* will support an action by any member state based on a breach of such obligation. On the other hand, standing to assert a violation of an obligation directly owed to the state should not require recourse to an *actio popularis* even if the interests of the community are also implicated. For present purposes, the key is to recognize that two types of *erga omnes* obligations with such 'bilateral' characteristics exist; in certain cases the breach may violate the bilateral or individual rights of *all* states. Critically, the obligation of states to prevent harm to the high seas environment is properly characterized as lying within this subset of duties owed to each state, and not just to the personified community. New Zealand's representative expressed a contrary view, noting that the duty to prevent harm to the environment lacks any bilateral aspect.[82] This conclusion, at least referring to the high seas environment, does not seem analytically correct. Each state possesses individual substantive rights with respect to the use of the high seas. The interest of each state in the resource of the high seas environment is certainly not exclusive. Nor, however, is it only the collective or community interest which is affected when that resource is injured, for the individual rights of each state are infringed. This is quite distinct from an obligation directed only to the community such as human rights obligations *vis-à-vis* the state's own nationals. No individual state has a right or interest in such cases other than as a member of the community. It also differs, of course, from the example of aggression in which the exclusive interest of each state in its own security is

[79] Argument of Dr Finlay, [1978] ICJ Pleadings, *Nuclear Tests* Cases, vol. ii, at 265–6.

[80] *Id.*, at 266.

[81] *Id.*, at 266–7.

[82] *Id.*, at 266. Dr Finlay then argued that obligations without a bilateral aspect owed to the community might be deserving of even greater protection than those bilateral obligations which have been elevated to *erga omnes* status.

protected by an obligation *erga omnes*.[83] The legal interest of each state protected by the obligation to prevent injury to the high seas environment is non-exclusive; it is nevertheless 'individual'. The preventive obligation as to the high seas is properly characterized as 'bilateral', obligating each state to protect the non-exclusive individual rights of each other state. When that obligation is breached, the individual interests of all states are injured. It follows, then, that standing to invoke responsiblity for a violation of such obligation should be viewed as resting on the right to protect the legal interests of the state, not the community.[84]

This theoretical argument, of course, is yet to be articulated in authoritative doctrine or practice. It is certainly the present expectation that an *actio popularis* is required to establish the standing of a single state to invoke the responsibility of another for injuring the high seas environment. The progression of ICJ opinion on the subject does suggest an emerging recognition of the place of such a doctrine. Moreover, a variety of commentators have advocated adoption of the procedure of an *actio popularis* as a technique to ensure protection of common environmental interests.[85] Finally, the 1982 Draft Restatement of US Foreign Relations Law recites, quite unequivocally, that *any* state may pursue remedies for the violation by any other state of customary human rights obligations *erga omnes*.[86] Weighing current evidence, however, one can only conclude that the *actio popularis* now enjoys no more than inchoate status as a functional principle of customary law.[87]

As a final note on the subject of the invocation of responsibility by means of an *actio popularis*, two possible objections to the doctrine should be specifically identified and rebutted in the context of environmental violations, Riphagen, in a report to the ILC on the consequences of state responsibility, has suggested that the UN Charter 'collective decision-making' provisions preclude any single state from 'responding' to the breach of an international obligation constituting an international crime, including 'massive pollution' of the seas.[88] In terms of responses which threaten international peace and security, e.g. reprisals, this is a laudable restriction. The requirement of collective action ought not logically to apply, however, when the response is

[83] Which, of course, also protects general community interests in peace and security.

[84] Language in the *Nuclear Tests* Joint Dissent supports this distinction: 'That States have individual as well as common rights with respect to the freedoms of the high seas is implicit in the very concept of such freedoms which involve rights of user possessed by every State, as is implicit in numerous provisions of the Geneva Convention of 1958 on The High Seas'. *Id.*, at 370.

[85] See e.g. Bollecker-Stern, *supra* ch. 1 n. 16, at 83; Brownlie, *supra* n. 66, at 5; Kwiatkowska-Czechowska, *supra* n. 55, at 172–3.

[86] *US Rest. For. Rel. L.* § 703(2) (Tent. Draft no. 3 1982).

[87] See Caflisch, supra ch. 5 n. 45, at 16–17; Goldie, *supra* ch. 5 n. 94, at 103–9; Kwiatkowska-Czechowska, *supra* n. 55, at 172–3; Legault, *supra* ch. 5 n. 45, at 217–18.

[88] Riphagen, Third Report on the Content, Forms and Degrees of State Responsibility, UN Doc. A/CN.4/354/Add 2 (5 May 1982), at 6–7.

simply an assertion, and submittal to international dispute settlement, of a claim of responsibility.[89]

The second concern to be dismissed relates to the determination of appropriate reparation when common rights are violated. It should first be recognized that only the fixing of compensation or monetary tokens of satisfaction are problem issues. Other forms of reparation, e.g. cessation of violative conduct, repair, acknowledgment of wrong, and apology, would not bestow upon the state acting pursuant to an *actio popularis* any benefits inconsistent with the nature of a claim presented to protect the public interest. It would certainly not seem appropriate, on the other hand, for the 'representative' state to be enriched by compensation for injury experienced by the entire community. It might be suggested, therefore, that monetary tokens of satisfaction would not be proper in an *actio popularis* claim. Compensation, similarly, might be limited to the particular injury, if any, suffered by the claiming state or states, perhaps based on historical exploitation of the damaged high seas resource.[90] If no individual harm is demonstrable, compensation too may be inappropriate. The absence of a compensable, material injury to the plaintiff state should not, however, constitute an impediment to an action to vindicate an international obligation.[91]

[89] Riphagen grants that when a state is 'specially affected' by an international crime, collective action may not be necessary. Thus, if private (perhaps even non-exclusive) interests are harmed, a single, direct response may be justified even under the suggested rule.

[90] This would be true either in an *actio popularis* or a claim based on private, non-exclusive rights in the high seas environment. See generally the Japanese claims regarding prospective harm to fishing industries caused by loss of access to high seas fisheries cited at n. 13 *supra*.

[91] See generally the *South West Africa* Case (Second Phase) (*Ethiopia and Liberia* v. *South Africa*), [1966] ICJ 6, at 32; the *Barcelona Traction Light & Power Co. Ltd.* Case (*Belgium* v. *Spain*), [1970] ICJ 3, at 326 (Sep. Opin. Judge Ammoun).

7

Harm Within the State's Own Territory

THE preceding two chapters have considered, in turn, the obligations of the state to prevent environmental harm occurring within the territory of another state and beyond the territory of any state. The subject of this chapter is the final possible *locus* of environmental injury—the territory of the state itself. As discussed above, the tenet of state 'sovereignty' or independence as to matters within its own borders is well-established in customary law.[1] Moreover, it has been specifically expressed in terms of the right of each state to render independent decisions with respect to its natural resources, including the environment.[2] When the exercise of such territorial prerogative interferes with the rights or interests of other states, however, international law may operate to impose obligations limiting the scope of state independent conduct. Hence, as to each of the regions treated above, a customary preventive obligation has developed to protect the clearly defined interests of other states, i.e. the exclusive interest in each state's territory and the common and exclusive interests in the high seas. The interests of other states in matters which affect the environment within a state's own territory are, however, not so readily defined. If no such juridically cognizable interest may be discerned, the inquiry is at an end; international law will only restrict the liberty of the state *vis-à-vis* its own territory when the interests of other states are implicated. The initial section of this chapter will, therefore, be dedicated to the question of whether any international interest with respect to environmental injury occurring within a state's own territory may be defined to serve as the *raison d'être* of a restrictive international obligation.

A. THE INTERNATIONAL INTEREST

As a prefatory matter, it should be noted that the central concern here is not harm to the territorial environment which involves consequential injury to the individual, exclusive or non-exclusive, rights or interests of other states situated in such territory. The *Corfu Channel* decision established, quite unequivocally, that the basic *sic utere tuo* obligation described in Chapter 5 applies with equal vigour to harm to other states taking place in the breaching state's own territorial waters.[3] Thus, one must conclude that *sic utere tuo* itself

[1] See ch. 5 at n. 13 *supra*.
[2] See ch. 5 at nn. 15–17 *supra*.
[3] The *Corfu Channel* Case (*UK* v *Albania*), [1949] ICJ 4.

would obligate a coastal state to prevent harm from environmental sources to, for example, foreign vessels in innocent passage through the territorial sea.[4] Moreover, environmental conduct which interferes generally with the non-exclusive right of all states to navigate in innocent passage should be viewed as prohibited by a variation on the *sic utere tuo* obligation conceptually the same as that discussed in Chapter 6 with respect to similarly common rights in the high seas.[5] The issue at hand, then, is whether other states or the personified community might possess a legal interest in harm to the territorial environment, from which a preventive obligation may proceed, when no such particularized interest of another state is involved. Two distinct approaches to the definition of such an interest may be identified.

i. Human Rights

Prior to World War II, the fashion in which a state elected to treat its own nationals was generally regarded as a matter beyond the reach of international law since the recognized interests of no other state were implicated.[6] Since that time, however, consensus has emerged that 'how a State treats individual human beings, including its own citizens, in respect of their human rights, is not the State's own business alone and therefore exclusively within its "domestic jurisdiction," but is a matter of international concern and a proper subject for regulation by international law.'[7] The international legal obligation to protect the human rights of all individuals subject to the state's authority was first authoritatively defined in the 1948 Universal Declaration of Human Rights.[8] It has since found expression in a number of significant multilateral agreements designed to safeguard the rights of the individual.[9] The protective obligation appears now to have matured, at least with respect to certain 'fundamental' human rights, into customary international law.[10]

[4] It should be noted, however, that the question of whether *sic utere tuo* operates equally to protect state nationals (including vessels) in another state's territory only by the leave of such state, i.e. not present by right such as innocent passage, is rather more difficult. In such circumstances, it would seem that these interests may only be entitled to the greater of (*a*) the protection afforded the host State's own nationals, or (*b*) any applicable international minimum standard. See ch. 3 at nn. 129–34 *supra*.

[5] See text at nn. 82–4 *supra*.

[6] The *Nuclear Tests* Case (*Australia* v. *France*), [1974] ICJ 324 (Dissenting Opin. Judge Petren).

[7] Intro. Note: Protection of Persons, *US Rest. For. Rel. L.* 138 (Tent. Draft no. 3 1982).

[8] Gen. Ass. Res. 217, 10 Dec. 1948, 3 UN GAOR (A/810) 71.

[9] E.g. International Covenant on Civil and Political Rights and International Covenant on Economic, Social and Cultural Rights, Annex, Gen. Ass. Res. 2200, 16 Dec. 1966, 21 UN GAOR Supp. (no. 16), UN Doc. A/6316, at 49 and 52, respectively; European Convention for the Protection of Human Rights and Fundamental Freedoms, done 4 Nov. 1950, entry into force 3 Sept. 1953, 213 UNTS 211. See generally Brownlie, *Basic Documents on Human Rights* (1971); Sohn and Buergenthal, *Basic Documents on International Protection of Human Rights* (1973); *US Rest. For. Rel. L.* 142 ff., 209 (Tent. Draft no. 3 1982).

[10] See generally Delupis, *International Law and the Independent State* (1974); Lauterpacht, *International Law and Human Rights* (1950); Moskowitz, *The Politics and Dynamics of Human Rights* (1968); McDougal, Laswell and Chen, *Human Rights and World Public Order* (1980); *US Rest. For. Rel. L.* 137–78 (Tent. Draft no. 3 1983)

For present purposes, the significant point is that freedom from environmental degradation and injury has been identified by certain commentators as a protected human right.[11] The source of this conclusion is the 'right to health' propounded in a number of the basic human rights instruments, including the Universal Declaration.[12] It may be argued persuasively that the right to environmental protection is implicit in the right to health; the relationship between the well-being of the individual and the quality of the natural environment is patent.[13] In any event, this linkage was expressly acknowledged in Article 12 of the International Covenant on Economic, Social and Cultural Rights which defines improvement of environmental hygiene as one of the essential steps to secure the individual's right to 'the highest attainable standard of physical and mental health.'[14] The Stockholm Declaration took the final step with the specific identification of a primary human right to environmental protection: 'Man has the fundamental right to freedom, equality and adequate conditions of life, in an environment of a quality which permits a life of dignity and well-being . . .'.[15] This right, then, provides a plausible theoretical base for an obligation to prevent material injury to the state's own environment. The requisite international interest is the community's concern for the protection of the human right, possessed by all persons within the state's territory, to be free from the adverse effects of environmental degradation.[16]

ii. Environmental Unity

The second approach to defining an international interest in matters affecting the territorial environment proceeds from the premise of the 'unity' of the global environment. In a physical sense, this simply refers to the fact of the 'systemic' character of the environment, including the oceans.[17] Handl

[11] See Ho, 'UN Recognition of the Human Right to Environmental Protection', 2 *Earth L.J.* 225 (1976); Dupuy, *supra* ch. 6 n. 60. See also Heine, *The Attitudes of the Asian-African States toward the Laws of State Responsibility* 294–4 (1976). For the view that the right remains inchoate see Van Lier, *supra* ch. 5 n. 85, at 134–7; OECD Secretariat, 'Observations on the Concept of International Responsibility of States in Relation to the Protection of the Environment', in OECD, *Legal Aspects of Transfrontier Pollution* 388, at 389–90 (1977).

[12] Universal Declaration, *supra* n. 8, art. 25. See also art. 8(iv), Draft Declaration on the Human Rights of Individuals Who Are Not Citizens of the Country in which They Live, Annex I, in Elles, International Provisions Protecting the Human Rights of Non-Citizens, UN Doc. E/CN 4/Sub. 2/392/Rev. 1 (1980); International Covenant on Economic, Social and Cultural Rights, *supra* n. 9, art. 12. See generally van Boven, 'The Right to Health', in *The Right To Health as a Human Right*, Dupuy ed., Acad. Droit Int'l Colloq. 54 (1978); Dupuy, *supra* ch. 6 n. 60, at 403.

[13] Consider, for example, the dramatic mercury poisoning experienced in Japan from industrial effluent. See W. Smith and A. Smith, *Minamata* (1975).

[14] International Covenant on Economic, Social and Cultural Rights, *supra* n. 9, art. 12(2) (*b*).

[15] Stockholm Declaration, *supra* ch. 5 n. 17, Principle 1. See also *id.*, at Procl. 1; Australian Branch Report, ILA 59th, *supra* ch. 5 n. 39, art 3.

[16] Notably, an obligation protecting such a right would constitute a 'public' duty owed the community; standing to vindicate its violation would require a right *actio popularis*.

[17] The principal definition of 'system' serves well in this ecological context: 'A set or

summarizes: 'It is nowadays accepted as an undeniable fact that the earth's biosphere represents a single indivisible system characterized by the interrelation of its various functional and ecological subsystems, the disruption of any one of which promotes the breakdown and destabilization of another.'[18] Pursuant to this conception, injury to any part of the ocean environment, even within an exclusive juridical zone, constitutes, by definition, injury to the whole, i.e. to a resource in which the international interest is patent.

In less abstract terms, the realities of physical ecological unity dictate that the preservation of the protected environments of other states and the high seas may only effectively be accomplished if injury to those portions of the integrated environment within a states' own borders is prevented. Moreover, it is clear that pollution of the territorial environment, even if it did not inevitably threaten direct injury to another state or the high seas, does have diverse systemic repercussions. Every act of pollution, for example, contributes to the total level of the pollutant absorbed in the system, reducing incrementally the amount which may be introduced by any other actor before the assimilative capacity of that system is exceeded and injury occurs.[19] Pollution not physically spreading beyond territorial limits may, in addition, directly and adversely affect system-wide resources, such as migratory species of fish; the overall biological stock of such species may be reduced or degraded by exposure to a significantly damaged environment in any juridical zone.[20] Any state may exploit such resources situated in a zone of exclusive authority

assemblage of things connected, associated, or interdependent, so as to form a complex unity . . .' ii *Oxford Dictionary* comp. edit. 3213 (1971).

[18] Handl, *supra* ch. 5 n. 19, at 53. The intellectual history of this 'systemic' perception of the environment has been described in Caldwell, *supra* ch. 5 n. 19, at 19. 'Although its philosophical origins are ancient, the biosphere as an operational concept has had much less than a century of practical usage. This concept, basic to global environmental policy, is multi-national in origin. Its beginnings have been traced to the French naturalist, Lamarck. It was first applied in the descriptive geographical writings of the Australian geologist Suess, and . . . was elaborated by the Russian mineralogist, U.I. Vernadsky, into a comprehensive biophysical theory. The dissemination of the theory was assisted by the published writings of the French Jesuit paleontologist, Pierre Teilhard de Chardin.'

[19] The precise assimilative capacity of the total system of the oceans remains the subject of conjecture—the only established point appears to be that it is finite. See Ray, 'Ecology, Law and the Marine Revolution', in *Pacem in Maribus* 6, at 11 (Borghese ed. 1972); Report of the Intergovernmental Working Group on Marine Pollution, Second Session, UN. Doc. A/Conf. 48/IWGMP, 22 Nov. 1971. In certain subsystems, however, that capacity has been exceeded with consequential harm. See Boczek, 'International Protection of the Baltic Sea Environment against Pollution: A Study in Marine Environment', 72 *Am. J. Int'l L.* 782 (1978): Lundholm, 'The Oceans: their Production and Pollution—The Baltic as a Case Study', in *Pacem in Maribus* 25 (Borghese ed. 1972).

[20] See e.g. Topping, 'Sewage and the Sea', in *Marine Pollution* 303, at 322–33 (Johnston ed. 1976): 'Estuaries act as nursery grounds for a considerable number of migratory fish species that spend their adult life in the open ocean. Pollution of coastal areas is possibly affecting and ultimately might well damage important offshore fisheries by the insidious deterioration of relatively small inshore spawning and nursery areas.' See also Council on Environmental Quality, *supra* ch. 5 n. 20, at 120; Ballschmiter, 'Pollutants in the Environment: A Global Experiment', 22 *Universitas* 131 (1981).

or the high seas. Each state, therefore, possesses an interest in their protection from harm in any region.

A final and distinct variation on this premise of environmental unity takes the logic a step further to assert not only a physical but a proprietary unity, positing that natural resources in any juridical zone may be conceived, in part, as the common resources of mankind.[21] Pursuant to this thesis, it is not only the state with authority to exploit territorial resources which possesses an interest in their protection; all states have a concern that the 'heritage' of *global* natural resources does not suffer injury. Excerpts from the Stockholm Declaration well illustrate this perspective:

Principle 1

Man . . . bears a solemn responsibility to protect and improve the environment for present and future generations.

Principle 2

The natural resources of the earth including the air, water, land, flora and fauna and especially representative samples of natural ecosystems must be safeguarded for the benefit of present and future generations . . .

Principle 5

The non-renewable resources of the earth must be employed in such a way as to guard against the danger of their future exhaustion and to ensure that benefits from such employment are shared by all mankind.[22]

The same approach to unity is reflected in the identification in the 1972 Convention Concerning the Protection of the World Cultural and Natural Heritage of the 'universal value' of resources of outstanding character.[23] Finally, the recent UN General Assembly Resolution on 'A World Charter for Nature' reiterates this notion of 'mankind's' interest in natural systems in all juridical zones of the earth.[24]

Based on such physical or metaphysical conceptions of the unity of the environment, it may be argued cogently that the resources of the environment are in some sense 'international' even within zones of exclusive, territorial authority. Kiss, for example, has recently specifically written that the 'natural solidarity' of the sea renders all regions part of an indivisible 'public domain': 'Ainsi, l'homogeneité naturelle des mers impose une unité globale du regime.'[25] This conclusion is an expression of Scelle's thesis that there exist regions or matters within state territory of sufficient social importance to the

[21] See e.g., Djordjevic, 'The Social Property Of Mankind' in *Pacem in Maribus*, Borghese ed. 178–9 (1972); Ginsburgs, 'The Soviet Union and the Biosphere', 28 *Int'l J.* 50, at 60–1 (1972–3), Hakapaa, *supra* ch. 5 n.57, at 145–6; Livingston, 'Science, Technology, and International Law: Present Trends and Future Developments', in iv *The Future of the International Legal Order* 110 (Black and Falk eds. 1972).

[22] Stockholm Declaration, *supra* ch. 5 n. 17, Principles 1, 2, 5.

[23] Convention for the Protection of the World Cultural and Natural Heritage, done at Paris, 23 Nov. 1972, entry into force 17 Dec. 1975, TIAS no. 8228, 27 UST 39.

[24] UN Gen. Ass. Res. 37/7, 9 Nov. 1982, reprinted in 22 *Int'l Legal Materials* 455 (1983).

[25] Kiss, *supra* ch. 6 n. 61, at 125.

community to constitute part of the 'public international domain'.[26] With respect to the domain of international concerns, state territorial authority is subject to 'dédoublement fonctionnel'; in addition to acting in the state's private interest, the state must perform the public task of protecting international interests.[27] Critically, based on notions of ecological unity, the quality of the territorial marine environment has been treated by a variety of publicists as part of the 'public international domain', i.e. a subject of material and juridically cognizable international interest. Most frequently, this opinion is articulated in terms of the need for international machinery and standards to govern activities affecting the environment in any region.[28] Variant expressions of this same basic perspective are found in the recent assertions of the existence of 'custodial' or 'public trust' obligations with respect to those portions of the environment subject to a state's exclusive authority.[29]

On the basis of the foregoing, then, there would appear to be alternative conceptual foundations upon which an international obligation to prevent material harm to the territorial environment might rest. A recognized international interest in either the protection of the human right to a healthy environment or the prevention of injury to the common and indivisible ocean environment would suffice to support and explain the imposition of an international duty restricting a state's prerogatives with respect to its marine territory.[30] It remains only to consider whether or not these theoretical interests have found legal expression. In other words, has a concrete preventive obligation emerged in customary law?

[26] Scelle, *Droit International Public* 21 (1922).

[27] For an excellent discussion see Kiss, *supra* ch. 6. n. 61, at 123–8.

[28] See e.g. vii and viii *The Future of the International Legal Order,* (Black and Falk ed. 1972); Brown *et al.*, *Regimes for the Ocean, Outer Space, and Weather* 239–41 (1977); Hallman, *supra* ch. 5 n. 57, at 15; Johnston, 'Law, Technology and the Sea', 55 *Cal L. Rev.* 449, at 459 n. 35 (1967).

[29] Most of the assertions of notions of 'custodianship' have related to extraterritorial authority over environmental matters. See discussion of these views in ch. 13 at n. 62. Certain scholars have noted the relevance of the concept to state authority over the territorial environment. See Hakapaa, *supra* ch. 5 n. 57, at 146; Jennings, 'A Changing International Law of the Sea', 31 *Camb. L.J.* 32: 45 (1972); Comments of de Visscher, 53 *Ann. inst. droit int'l* 284 (1969). As to the public trust concept, see Nanda, 'The Establishment of International Standards for Transnational Environmental Injury', 60 *Iowa L. Rev.* 1089, at 1116–19 (1975); Kiss, *supra* n. 25, at 229–32; Sohn, *supra* ch. 5 n. 45, at 492. See also Sax, 'The Public Trust Doctrine in Natural Resources Law', 68 *Mich. L. Rev.* 471 (1969).

[30] Note that the preceding description of an international interest based on environmental unity has assumed a 'public' character—a protective obligation would be directed to the personified community. A violation of such an obligation would require a claim on behalf of the community, i.e., *actio popularis.* It should be noted, however, that the interests protected also have a private character. When the system is affected, the private, exclusive and non-exclusive, rights of all states are affected. Hence, a protective obligation would have a distinct 'bilateral' aspect. As noted above with respect to breach of the 'bilateral' *erga omnes* obligations relating to the high seas, it might be argued cogently that a claim for breach of an obligation to prevent harm to the international interest in environmental unity might proceed even without *actio popularis.*

B. THE PREVENTIVE OBLIGATION

The short answer to this question is no. In 1982 the ILC reported to the General Assembly that one issue on the subject of state liability for injury caused by lawful activites was 'beyond question': no liability attaches when both the activity causing injury and the injury itself occur in the territory of the same state.[31] There can be little dispute that this assertion represents the orthodox and dominant perspective on the state's international obligations with respect to environmental injury. Notably, even progressive formulations such as the London Dumping Convention and the Charter of Economic Rights and Duties mentioned in Chapter 6 refer only to the obligation to prevent damage 'to the environment of other States or of areas beyond the limits of national jurisdiction'.[32] Academic opinion, generally prone to robust debate, appears similarly uniform in the conclusion that there is no preventive obligation *vis-à-vis* harm to the state's own territory in customary law to support an assertion of international responsibility.[33]

There are, however, a number of instances of practice in which an international interest in the preservation of each state's territorial environment has been recognized and specific preventive obligations accepted. The London Dumping Convention and the several regional treaties on the same model, for example, require states-party to prevent the dumping of specified wastes outside and within territorial waters.[34] The major multilateral vessel-source pollution conventions of 1954 and 1973 appear, similarly, to apply discharge restrictions generally to regions including the responsible state's own territory.[35] Finally, the several recent regional agreements which have imposed restrictions on land-based marine pollution limit, by definition, pollution of the territorial environment.[36]

[31] ILC, Report to the General Assembly, UN GAOR Suppl. (no. 10) (A/37/10) (1982), at 186. See Magraw, *supra* ch. 4 n. 13, at 311. Two caveats should be noted. First, the ILC itself has noted the exception of conceptual 'transboundary' injury in cases such as harm to vessels in innocent passage. Second, the subject of the Report is 'liability'. It is arguable that *liability* (or the obligation to compensate) might be absent even in circumstances in which responsibility exists.

[32] See text at ch. 5 nn. 44, 42 *supra*.

[33] See e.g. Handl, *supra* ch. 5 n. 30, at 175, for a specific recitation of the requirement of extraterritorial harm. See also de Mestral, 'The Prevention of Pollution of the Marine Environment Arising from Offshore Mining and Drilling', 20 *Harv. Int'l L.J.* 469, at 513 (1979).

[34] London Dumping Convention, *supra* ch. 5 n. 44, art. 7; Protocol for the Prevention of Pollution of the Mediterranean Sea by Dumping from Ships and Aircraft, done 16 Feb. 1976, entry into force 12 Feb. 1978, reprinted in 15 *Int'l Legal Materials* 300 (1976); Oslo Dumping Convention, *supra* ch. 5 n. 49, art. 2; Convention on the Protection of the Marine Environment of the Baltic Sea Area, done at Helsinki, 22 Mar. 1974, reprinted in 13 *Int'l Legal Materials* 546 (1974), art. 9. See generally de Ytturriga, *supra* ch. 5 n. 1, at 370–2.

[35] 1954 Convention, *supra* ch. 6 n. 35, art. 3; 1973 Convention, *supra* ch. 6 n. 37, arts. 4(1) and (2).

[36] Paris Convention and Protocol, *supra* ch. 6 n. 43, *passim*; Kuwait Convention, *supra* ch. 6 n. 42, art. 6; Helsinki Convention, *supra* n. 34, art. 6; Barcelona Revised Draft Protocol for the Protection of the Mediterranean Sea Against Pollution from Land-based Sources, UNEP

Although such practice may evidence the growing recognition of the international importance of environmental protection in any region, it does not suffice to demonstrate present acceptance of a customary obligation to prevent injury to each state's territorial environment, a breach of which would involve international responsibility.[37] Indeed, even in those few instances when such a preventive obligation has been articulated, it has been seriously qualified by the influence and language of state 'sovereignty'. At the Stockholm Conference, for example, the expression of an international interest in the preservation of the entirety of the environment, including regions subject to exclusive territorial authority, could not have been clearer. The reference to a universal human right to environmental quality and the several allusions to the international character of the resources of the integrated environment, in both physical and a proprietary sense, have already been noted.[38] As Sohn has observed, the Declaration produced by the Conference:

> emphasizes the fact that no part of the global environment can be separated from the rest and that it has to be preserved and improved for the benefit of all the people of both the present and future generations . . . Destruction and depletion of irreplaceable resources are clearly condemned by the Declaration, even when there is no effect abroad, and a state cannot engage in such activities behind the shield of misconceived sovereignty.[39]

Consistent with such convictions, Principle 7 asserts the obligation to prevent harm in terms of the whole of the marine environment: 'States shall take all possible steps to prevent pollution of the seas by substances that are liable to create hazards to human health, to harm living resources and marine life, to damage amenities or to interfere with other legitimate uses of the sea.'[40]

The linkage of this obligation to concrete principles of responsibility, and thus the legal protection of the identified international interests, did not occur in Stockholm. In fact, any suggestion that the ultimate prerogatives of the state with respect to its territorial resources were to be qualified encountered substantial opposition.[41] Principle 21, the negotiated conclusion as to legal responsibility, reflected this conflict:

Report, UNEP/W6. 17/6/Annex IV and W.6.18/4 Annex IV (1979). See generally de Yturriaga, *supra* ch. 5 n. 1, at 384; Hickey, *supra* ch. 6 n. 11, at 447–54.

[37] Consider the language of the ILA regarding their inclusion of a preventive obligation with respect to the entire 'marine environment' in their draft articles on 'Marine Pollution of Continental Origin': 'There is now more and more support for the philosophy according to which maritime waters need general protection, as they constitute—*apart from narrow lanes near the coasts*—a sort of global resource, and the flora and fauna living in these massive quantities of waters must be protected in the interest of all. It was therefore decided to introduce an innovation, consisting of the establishment of the obligation to protect the 'Marine Environment'. ILA 55th Pollution, *supra* ch. 6 n. 18, at 101 (emphasis added).

[38] See text at ch. 7 nn. 17–30 *supra*.

[39] Sohn, *supra* ch. 5, n. 45, at 492.

[40] Stockholm Declaration, *supra* ch. 5 n. 17, Principle 7.

[41] See Sohn, *supra* ch. 5 n. 45, at 486–91.

States have, in accordance with the Charter of the United Nations and the principle of international law, the sovereign right to exploit their own resources pursuant to their own environmental policies, and the responsibility to ensure that activites within their jurisdiction or control do not cause damage to the environment of other States or of areas beyond the limits of national jurisdiction.[42]

In short, no legal responsibility for injury to environmental resources within state territory is identified. To the contrary, the independence of the state with respect to such resources is affirmed, qualified only in the event of external injury.

The same tension between the concerns of sovereignty and environmental integrity greatly influenced the negotiations at the LOS III Conference.[43] Consensus as to the existence of an international interest in the protection of the whole of the integrated marine environment was apparent at the Conference.[44] On the other hand, as in Stockholm, there was great resistance to any effort to protect this interest with an effective preventive obligation applicable to regions of the environment within each state's zone of exclusive authority.[45] The principal defenders of the right of independent decision-making with respect to each state's own resources were the representatives of developing states.[46] The basic argument presented was one of economic equity. The developed states achieved their current level of development and created the pollution problem in a *laissez-faire* legal environment; it is unfair for such states now to seek to impose costly environmental restrictions which may impede developing states' industrialization and progress towards economic parity.[47] The persuasive character of this argument, and the negotiating and voting strength of the developing states, are reflected in the delicate balance of the Convention text.

Article 192 commences the marine pollution provisions with an assertion of the same all-inclusive 'obligation to protect and preserve the marine environment' articulated in Stockholm.[48] Articles 210 and 211 proceed from

[42] Stockholm Declaration, *supra* ch. 5 n. 17, Principle 21.

[43] See Frank, 'Protection of the Marine Environment from Pollution', 6 *Ga. J. Int'l & Comp. L.* 73, at 82 (1976); Kindt, 'The Effect of Claims by Developing Countries on LOS International Marine Pollution Negotiations', 20 *Va. J. Int'l L.* (1980) 313, *passim*; Livingston, *supra* ch. 6 n. 30, at 10–11.

[44] This is true even with respect to the submissions of developing states generally advocating the rights of sovereign discretion. See e.g. Art. 8, Ecuador, El Salvador, Peru, and Uruguay: Preservation of the Marine Environment, 24 July 1973, UN Doc. A/AC.138/SC III/L.47.

[45] See materials cited at n. 43 *supra*.

[46] See generally as to the North–South debate regarding environmental matters. Borghese, 'The New International Economic Order and the Law of the Sea', 14 *San Diego L. Rev.* 584 (1977); Hardy, 'The United Nations Environment Programme', 13 *Nat. Res. J.* 235 (1973); Juda, 'UNCLOS III and the New Economic Order', 7 *Ocean Dev. & Int'l L.* 221 (1974); Kindt, *supra* n. 43; Pinto, supra ch. 5 n. 17; Train 'Perspective: Environment, Energy, Economic Equity—Can We Balance These Vital Elements?', 6 *Envt'l Aff.* 1 (1977).

[47] See particularly Pinto, *supra* ch. 5 n. 17, at 12.

[48] LOS Convention, *supra* ch. 5 n. 17, art. 192. See De Mestral and Legault, 'Multilateral

this general obligation with recitations of the duty to prevent pollution of the 'marine environment' from dumping and vessels, respectively.[49] Article 207 imposes the preventive obligation as to the whole environment with respect to land-based marine pollution.[50] As to this specific undertaking, however, the concern for state independence with respect to territorial matters produced two significant qualifications: (*a*) international standards applied to developing states are to reflect the need for economic development; and (*b*) states are required to act only 'taking into account' established international standards.[51]

The basic relationship between state territorial independence and environmental obligation is defined in Article 193: 'States have the sovereign right to exploit their natural resources pursuant to their environmental policies and in accordance with their duty to protect and preserve the marine environment.'[52] Interpretation of the significance of this provision is difficult. In certain respects, it appears to represent a progression from the formulation of Stockholm's Principle 21. Most noticeably, the environmental duty juxtaposed to sovereign resource independence refers to the protection of the entire 'marine environment', not just to the prevention of extraterritorial harm. Further, the provision might be read to imply subjection of resource rights to this environmental duty; one interpretation is that exploitation may be conducted pursuant to discretionary policies only if such policies prevent material harm to any part of the marine environment. The narrow scope of the responsibility provision, Article 194(2), however, suggests a more plausible construction.

> States shall take all measures necessary to ensure that activities under their jurisdiction or control are so conducted as not to cause damage by pollution to other States and their environment, and that pollution arising from incidents or activities under their jurisdiction or control does not spread beyond the areas where they exercise sovereign rights in accordance with this Convention.[53]

This language, of course, expresses the orthodoxy of state environmental responsibility described in Chapters 5 and 6: material extraterritorial harm to the environment of other states and the high seas must be prevented.

Negotiation: Canada and the Law of the Sea Conference', 35 *Int'l J.* 46, at 66 (1979–80), who note that this general obligation was easily secured.

[49] LOS Convention, *supra* ch. 5 n. 17, arts. 210, 211.

[50] *Id.*, art. 207.

[51] *Id.* For commentary on the retention of sovereign discretion in this area, see Frank, *supra* n. 43, at 82; Livingston, *supra* ch. 6, n. 30, at 10–11; Timagenis, *supra* ch. 5 n. 1, at 604.

[52] LOS Convention, *supra* ch. 5 n. 17, art. 193. See also Canada, Fiji, Ghana, Guyana, Iceland, India, Iran, New Zealand, Phillipines, and Spain: Draft Articles on a Zonal Approach to the Preservation of the Marine Environment, arts. 2 and 5, UN Doc. A/CONF.62/C.3/L.6 (31 July 1974); Kenya: Draft Articles for the Preservation and the Protection of the Marine Environment for Inclusion in the Convention on the Law of the Sea, UN Doc. A/CONF.62/C.3/L.2 (23 July 1974).

[53] LOS Convention, *supra* ch. 5 n. 17, art. 194(2).

Significantly, there is no complementary provision which directly confronts the tenet of sovereignty and identifies an obligation to prevent harm limited to the environment within regions of exclusive state authority. The expression of the general preventive obligation in terms of the 'marine environment' in Articles 192 and 193 does not, therefore, represent a juridical innovation. Applied to regions beyond the exclusive jurisdiction of the state, it merely reiterates the customary preventive obligation using a convenient shorthand reference to the integrated environment. If the reference is in fact intended to apply to internal regions at all, it seems to be limited to a hortatory effect, for harm external to the state remains a condition to responsibility. Under the LOS Convention, then, custom is not disturbed. The right to pursue independent policies as to the state's own environment is constrained only by (*a*) any specific contractual duties undertaken by the state and (*b*) the customary duty to prevent 'transboundary' harm.[54]

Two conclusions may be drawn from the foregoing analysis. First, recognition of the international interest in the preservation of the environment in all regions of the sea is manifest in certain doctrinal opinions, the growing body of specific conventional undertakings to prevent pollution within state territory, and perhaps even the juridically ambiguous references to harm to the undivided 'marine environment' at Stockholm and the LOS III Conference. Second, no customary rule has yet emerged to protect this interest by requiring the prevention of injury to the resources of that part of the environment which is subject to exclusive state authority. To the contrary, there continues to be firm resistance to any principle derogating from state discretion with respect to such resources. In sum, a state may, in recognition of an international interest, consent to limit its prerogatives by undertaking to adopt specific protective environmental policies as to its resources; under *lex lata*, however, the only general and mandatory limit to state independence remains the prohibition of material external harm.

Judge Tanaka of the ICJ has observed: 'The historical development of law demonstrates the continual process of the cultural enrichment of the legal order by taking into consideration of values or interests which had previously been excluded from the sphere of law.'[55] The initial step in this process is consensus recognition of the existence of an international interest deserving of such legal protection. The preventive obligation with respect to injury to a state's own environmental resources is in precisely this early stage of development. At present, there is simply not sufficient agreement as to the character or importance of the international interest, *vis-à-vis* exclusive state interests, in such resources to advance it to a legally protected status.

[54] See ch. 5 and ch. 6.

[55] *South West Africa* (Second Phase) Case, [1966] ICJ 250, 252 (Diss. Opin. Judge Tanaka).

8

Standard of Performance

A. THE ISSUE: A STRICT OR FAULT STANDARD

The preceding chapters of this Part II have demonstrated the presence in customary law of an obligation to exercise the full extent of state legal authority to prevent material injury to other states, in exclusive or common zones, from marine environmental pollution. The standard to which states are to be held in pursuit of the performance of this obligation has not yet been discussed. One of the conclusions set forth in Part I was that the general rules of state responsibility do not supply such a standard. There is no *generic* requirement, for example, that failure to perform an obligation must be linked to the state's 'fault' in the sense of intent or negligence.[1] Rather, to satisfy the objective element of responsibility there need only occur a violation of an international obligation; the content of the specific obligation will determine the prerequisites to such violation.[2] The task of this chapter, therefore, is to consider the standard applicable to violation of the identified preventive obligations with respect to marine environmental injury.

The principal question to be considered is whether or not the requirement of malicious intent or culpable negligence traditionally associated with the breach of *any* international obligation operates in the context of the specific marine environmental obligations. The doctrinal foil to the orthodoxy of subjective 'fault' is, of course, the notion of 'strict' responsibility, i.e. responsibility determined without reference to the intent or diligence of the state.[3] The policy underlying the strict approach is simply that the state which acts or controls an activity, and not the victim-state, ought to bear the burden

[1] See ch. 2 at nn. 47–94 *supra*.

[2] Riphagen has recently confirmed the view that issues of fault 'seem to turn on the interior and application of the primary rule rather than on any supposed general rule relating to the content of state responsibility irrespective of the content of the primary rule.' Riphagen, Second Report on the Content, Forms and Degrees of State Responsibility, UN Doc. A/CN.4/344, (1 May 1981), at 26–7.

[3] The choice of the term 'responsibility', rather than 'liability', is purposeful. The latter constitutes only one of the consequences of the former: the obligation to compensate following a wrongful act. See the discussion below regarding the ILC for the view that liability is perhaps the only appropriate consequence when injury is not serious enough to justify the consequential obligation to cease violative conduct. Goldie, in an interesting discussion of the distinction between the two terms, takes a broader view of liability, embracing all of the consequences of responsibility: 'liability connotes exposure to legal redress once responsibility has been established.' Goldie, 'Responsibility and Liability in the Common Law', in OECD, *Legal Aspects of Transfrontier Pollution* 306, at 307 and 344 (1977).

of the injurious consequences of the activity. Social utility, in addition to equity, may suggest the propriety of the strict regime, for the total costs of conduct to international society ought to be taken into account when each state makes a decision to proceed with or permit that conduct. Only if the burden of injury is directed to the decision-maker will this occur.[4] This chapter will consider the available evidence to determine whether or not (and in what form) the principle of strict responsibility has secured a place in customary international law with respect to the environment. A final section will consider briefly the distinctions which must be drawn with respect to the imposition of strict responsibility for injuries arising out of state versus private activity and territorial versus extraterritorial private activity.

B. THE ROLE OF STRICT RESPONSIBILITY

i. International Decisions

As one might expect, there are very few cases germane to an inquiry into the standard of performance for customary environmental duties. In fact, reference to judicial opinion in the doctrinal debate on the subject has been limited to the same series of decisions noted above as evidence of the *sic utere tuo* obligation: the *Corfu Channel* Case; and the *Trail Smelter*, *Gut Dam* and *Lac Lanoux* Arbitrations.[5] Unfortunately, the interpretative problems encountered with respect to each of these cases make it difficult to extract conclusive evidence of judicial opinion one way or the other.

The *Corfu Channel* Case, for example, has been cited by proponents of a strict approach to environmental duties as evincing a general principle that the state is strictly responsible (i.e. without reference to intent or negligence) for injury to another state arising out of activities within its territorial jurisdiction.[6] Yet, the ICJ's inquiry into Albania's knowledge of the presence of mines within its territorial waters suggests certain problems with this view.[7] By implication, it was the Court's opinion that without knowledge and the attendant opportunity to warn Britain of the damage, no responsibility would have arisen. It is true that the fact of territorial authority was viewed as important circumstantial evidence of such knowledge; however, both *prima*

[4] See Jenks, *supra* ch. 5 n. 51, at 152, 179–80; Goldie, *supra* ch. 5 n. 45, at 1200–7. See also Calabresi, 'Some Thoughts on Risk Distribution and the Law of Torts', 70 *Yale L.J.* 499 (1961); Calabresi, 'The Decision for Accidents: An Approach to Non-fault Allocation of Costs', 78 *Harv. L. Rev.* 713 (1965).

[5] See ch. 5 nn. 23–30, 31, 33–5, 36 *supra*.

[6] See e.g. Goldie, 'International Principles Of Responsibility for Pollution', 9 *Colum. J. Transnat'l L.* 283, at 306–7 (1970); Kelson, 'State Responsibility and the Abnormally Dangerous Activity', 13 *Harv. J. Int'l L* 197, at 236–7 (1972); Schneider, *supra* ch. 5 n. 36, at 272–3.

[7] See Ago, 4th Rpt., *supra* ch. 3 n. 45, at 106; de Arechaga *supra* ch. 1 n. 11, at 537–8; Dupuy, *supra* ch. 5 n. 30, at 187–90; Handl, *supra* ch. 5 n. 30, at 167; Handl, *supra* ch. 2 n. 82, at 537; Hardy, 'Nuclear Liability: The General Principles Of Law and Further Proposals', 36 *Brit. Yb. Int'l L.* 223, at 229 (1960).

facie responsibility and the presumption of *res ipsa loquitur* were expressly rejected.[8] It might be argued that once knowledge was established, breach of the duty to warn was strict. Yet, there is no language in the opinion to suggest that proof of reasonable efforts to warn might not have operated as a defense. Albania's responsibility, then, flowed from its knowledge of a dangerous situation and failure to take steps to prevent injury, not simply from the existence of the injury. In short, the decision, although perhaps not falling squarely into either camp, appears more comfortably construed as a variation on the negligence approach.[9]

The arbitral award in the *Trail Smelter* Case is even more frequently noted in support of the principle of strict environmental responsibility.[10] The net result of the arbitration was Canadian responsibility for the injury to US interests caused by the flight of sulphur fumes from a private plant situated in British Columbia.[11] It is certainly true that the language of the award appears strictly to attribute responsibility as a consequence of transboundary environmental injury—without any reference to intent or a failure to act with due care.[12] Yet, the evidentiary value of the decision is severely undercut by the fact that the tribunal was not charged to consider, and did not consider, the *basis* of Canadian responsibility for breach of the preventive obligation. The *compromis* presented to the Tribunal assumed that Canada was responsible for the injuries experienced in the US.[13] It is, then, perhaps as an instance of state practice, rather than authoritative judicial decision, that *Trail Smelter* is best cited as evidence of strict responsibility for environmental injury.

A similar conclusion must be reached with respect to the arbitral proceedings and eventual settlement between Canada and the United States pertaining to flood damage caused by Canada's construction of the Gut Dam across the St Lawrence boundary waters.[14] It has been argued that the Tribunal's preliminary decision that causation and the measure of damages were the only questions requiring consideration constituted a judicial recognition of the strict responsibility principle.[15] The Tribunal's lack of concern with the issue of Canadian negligence did not, however, necessarily express its view of the basis of responsibility. Rather, the dispute was governed

[8] The *Corfu Channel* Case (*UK* v. *Albania*), [1949] ICJ 4, at 18. See Brownlie, *supra* ch. 2 n. 52, at 439.

[9] Judges Ečer and Krylov in dissent affirmed the *culpa* requirement and argued it had not been satisfied. [1949] ICJ 4, at 127–8 and 71–2. As noted above, a number of respected authorities have in fact viewed the case as an affirmation of the general rule of *culpa*. See text at ch. 2 n. 37.

[10] See e.g.Goldie, *supra* n. 6, at 306–7; Jenks, *supra* ch. 5 n. 51, at 121–2; Kelson, *supra* n. 6, at 235–6; Schneider, *supra* ch. 5 n. 36, at 269; Sohn, *supra* ch. 5 n. 45, at 171.

[11] See ch. 5 commencing at n. 23 *supra*.

[12] See language quoted at ch. 5 n. 26 *supra*.

[13] See Dupuy, *supra* ch. 3 n. 97, at 185–6; Handl, *supra* ch. 5 n. 30, at 167–8; Hardy, *supra* n. 7, at 229.

[14] See discussion in ch. 5 n. 36 *supra*.

[15] Schneider, *supra* ch. 5 n. 35, at 270–1.

by an indemnification agreement with respect to any injuries arising out of the construction of the Gut Dam secured by the United States as the *quid pro quo* for permission to build.[16] Hence, the issue of responsibility for damages caused never reached the Tribunal. Again, therefore, the case seems to represent, at best, an example of state, and not judicial, practice supportive of strict responsibility.[17]

The expression of the principle of strict responsibility for external environmental injury in the final case, the *Lac Lanoux* Arbitration, presents fewer interpretative problems.[18] As noted above, the award denied Spain's attempt to enjoin construction of a French hydroelectric project designed to utilize waters governed by a treaty between the two states.[19] The tribunal did observe, however, that a Spanish allegation of environmental injury would have altered the result since downstream injury would ellicit responsibility.[20] The significance of this statement is diminished, of course, by its status as *dictum*.[21]

ii. State Practice

Substantially more persuasive evidence of the emergence of a doctrine of strict responsibility for environmental injury may be found in instances of international practice. As noted in Part I, a regime of strict responsibility has been incoporated in several significant multilateral conventions treating issues of environmental harm.[22] Four of these efforts relate to civil liability for injuries arising out of nuclear activities: the 1963 Vienna Convention on Civil Liability for Nuclear Damage;[23] the 1962 Brussels Convention on the Liability of Operators of Nuclear Ships;[24] the 1960 Paris Convention on Third Party Liability in the Field of Nuclear Energy;[25] and the 1963 Convention Supplementary to the Paris Convention of 1960.[26] Each of these treaties is designed to unify municipal law on the subject of nuclear liability by conforming both substantive and procedural rules, particularly regarding compensation limits and guarantees.[27] Critically, liability is established in

[16] See Handl, *supra* ch. 5 n. 36, at 538–9.

[17] Handl argues that the fact that the indemnification agreement was bargained for makes the case a bad example even of state practice. *Id.* On the other hand, one might argue that the agreement was designed to secure the United States' customary rights against an argument that consent to the dam constituted a waiver of strict responsibility.

[18] See ch. 5 at nn. 33–5.

[19] *Id.*

[20] But see Handl, *supra* ch. 5 n. 30, at 170.

[21] See Brownlie, *supra* ch. 2 n. 52, at 271.

[22] See ch. 2 commencing at n. 79.

[23] Done 21 May 1963, 2 *Int'l Legal Materials* 727 (1963).

[24] Done 25 May 1962, 37 *Am. J. Int'l L.* 268 (1963).

[25] Done 29 July 1960, OEEC Doc. no. C(66)93 (1960), 8 *Eur. Yb.* 202.

[26] Done 31 Jan. 1963, 2 *Int'l Legal Materials* 685 (1963).

[27] See generally Dupuy, *supra* ch. 3 n. 97, at 98–140; Jenks, *supra* ch. 5 n. 51, 127–92.

each case based simply on the fact of causation of injury; there need be no showing of intent or negligence.[28]

The same pattern of strict civil liability provisions appears in two conventions directed at the problem of the pollution of the sea by oil. The 1969 Brussels Convention on Civil Liability for Oil Pollution Damage establishes a regime of limited, but guaranteed, civil liability for any damage from the discharge or escape of oil from privately owned or state commercial vessels.[29] Again, liability exists without reference to fault. Indeed, fault is specifically identified as only an aggravating factor which disposes of otherwise applicable maxima and shields insurers from certain direct exposure to claimants.[30] Essentially the same structure of strict civil liability is incorporated in the 1976 London Convention on Civil Liability for Oil Pollution Damage Resulting from Exploration for and Exploitation of Sea-bed Mineral Resources.[31]

Participation in these conventions is not, of course, a direct declaration of state attitudes towards the issue of strict responsibility in public international law. The states party to these initiatives have agreed only to establish uniform rules of municipal law governing liability for environmental injury. Yet, it is quite clear that the participant states have subjected themselves, and not only private individuals subject to their uniform laws, to the consequences of the regime of a strict standard of responsibility. A state may find itself in a position of civil liability either as the 'person' or 'operator' engaged in the injurious activity[32] or as surety for any deficiency in the compensation paid by a private individual.[33] More importantly, the consequences of strict liability under the conventions may lead to responsibility on a international plane. As noted in Part I, Handl has observed that if a state is liable to the national of another state and fails to pay, that liability may be converted into international responsibility *vis-à-vis* the state of the victim's nationality.[34] In addition, one may assume that state responsibility for payment of sums due

[28] In each case, certain *force majeure* exceptions are allowed. Thus the liability is strict, not absolute.

[29] Done 29 Nov. 1969, entry into force 19 June 1975, 9 *Int'l Legal Materials* 45 (1970). See also 1976 Protocol to the 1969 Convention on Civil Liability for Oil Pollution Damage, done 19 Nov. 1976, entry into force 8 Apr. 1981, TS no. 26 (1981), reprinted in 21 *Int'l Env. L. Rep.* 521 (1978). To supplement the Liability Convention a fund has been established which will compensate when damages exceed the maxima of the Convention and defray the burden of compensation. See 1971 Convention of an International Fund for Compensation for Oil Pollution Damage, done 17 Dec. 1971, entry into force 16 Oct. 1978, TS no. 95 (1978), 11 *Int'l Legal Materials* 284 (1972) and Protocol done 19 Nov. 1976, reprinted in 21 *Int'l Env. Rep.* 71 (1978). See generally Abecassis, 'The Law and Practice relating to Oil Pollution from Ships', Ph.D. diss., Cambridge Univ. (1978), at 243–331; Dupuy, *supra* ch. 3 n. 97, at 140–6.

[30] Arts. 5(2), 7(8).

[31] Opened for signature 1 May 1977, reprinted in 121 *Int'l Env. Rep.* 0601 (1978).

[32] See e.g. Brussels Civil Liability Conv., *supra* n. 29, art, 1(2); London Civil Liability Conv., *supra* n. 29, art. 1(5).

[33] See e.g. Brussels Civil Liability Conv., *supra* n. 29, art. 11; Vienna Civil Liability Conv., *supra* n. 23, art. 8.

[34] See ch. 2 at n. 82.

pursuant to the strict test of liability would arise in any case in which compensation by a private operator was precluded due to the state's failure to perform its treaty obligations, e.g. failing to require adequate financial security or to legislate effective substantive or procedural rules. Finally, although the specific legal context of these conventions is civil, it may also be argued that the rules adopted reflect acceptance of a 'general principle of law' applicable on either the private or the international plane. Jenks, speaking in terms of 'ultrahazardous' activities makes this point succinctly:

> [T]he conventions concerning civil liability for such activities have a significance transcending the unification of the law of civil liability; they state principles no less applicable to international than to civil liability. They are not, in themselves, an authoritative formulation or acceptance of international liability, but the principles which they embody must be regarded as general principles of law relating to ultrahazardous liability which may reasonably be invoked in discussions or proceedings between States relating to such liability.[35]

In short, then, the civil liability conventions may be viewed as evidence of the acceptance of the rule of strict responsibility for the international consequences of activities affecting the environment.

The Space Objects Convention discussed in some detail in Part I presents a more direct expression of the strict responsibility principle in an international context.[36] Article 2 provides that '[a] launching State shall be absolutely liable to pay compensation for damage caused by its space object on the surface of the Earth or to aircraft in flight.'[37] Fault is only a condition to responsibility with respect to injuries to other states operating in outer space.[38] As to surface damage, including environmental injury, the Convention defines an unambiguously strict or more precisely, absolute preventive obligation.[39]

Several recent examples of state practice, in the sense of claims and responses, suggest that the principle of strict responsibility evident in these conventions is advancing to customary status, i.e. that it is *opinio juris* that explains the presence of the principle. Following the disintegration of the Soviet Union's Cosmos 954 satellite over Canadian territory, a claim was submitted for compensation for consequential injuries, consisting principally of environmental clean-up costs, based upon both the Space Objects Convention and customary law.[40] The Canadian diplomatic note stating the claim asserted:

[35] Jenks, *supra* ch. 5 n. 51, at 178. See also de Arechaga, *supra* ch. 1, n. 11, at 539.

[36] See generally ch. 4 at n. 68–78.

[37] Art. 2. See generally Foster, *supra* ch. 2 n. 83, at 137; Theraulaz, *supra* ch. 2 n. 83, at 229.

[38] Art 3.

[39] The responsibility is here appropriately designated as 'absolute' since the only exoneration is gross negligence or intent on the part of the victim. Art 6.

[40] Letter From Dept. of External Affairs to the USSR Ambassador, Plus Annexes, reprinted in 18 *Int'l Legal Materials* 899 (1979).

The principle of absolute liability applies to fields of activities having in common a high degree of risk. It is repeated in numerous international agreements and is one of 'the general principles of law recognized by civilized nations' (Article 38 of the Statute of the International Court of Justice). Accordingly this principle has been accepted as a general principle of international law.[41]

Support for this conclusion is found in Liberia's offer to compensate Japanese interests following the *Juliana* tanker incident in the absence of any assertion of fault in the allegation of responsibility.[42] Japan's assertions of US responsibility for the consequences of nuclear testing in the South Pacific further reflect an assumption of strict responsibility for environmental injury. The formal response of the United States failed to admit or deny strict responsibility, tendering compensation for past injury 'without reference to the question of legal liability.'[43] The US payment of compensation for injury to Spanish interests following the Palomares incident, however, evinces a strict standard.[44] Mexico's refusal to accept legal responsibility for injuries to US territorial interests arising out of the prolonged oil spill from the *Ixtoc I* well, operated by the Mexican national oil company, represents, on the other hand, a denial of strict and arguably even fault responsibility.[45]

Declarations of principle constitute the final form of instructive state practice. The most recent forum for the multilateral expression of legal rules regarding the marine environment, the 1982 LOS Convention, is not particularly helpful. Article 194, for example, recites that 'States shall take all measures necessary to ensure that activities under their jurisdiction or control are so conducted as not to cause damage by pollution to other States and their environment.'[46] One might construe the term 'necessary', as opposed to 'possible' or 'reasonable', as suggesting that failure to prevent strictly

[41] *Id.*, at 907. The ultimate settlement of the claim neither conceded or denied the basis of liability. Protocol between the Government of Canada and the Government of the USSR, done 2 Apr. 1981, reprinted in 20 *Int'l Legal Materials* 689 (1981).

[42] See Handl, *supra* ch. 2 n. 82, at 547; Rousseau, 'Chronique des fait internationaux', 79 RGDIP 842 (1975). See also the Indonesian position in the *Showa Maru* incident chronicled in Rousseau, *id.*

[43] See Whiteman, *supra* ch. 6 n. 12, at 363–6, 485–6, 563–6; US Note, 237 UNTS 198. Goldie argues that the US conduct was at least the product of *opinion obligationis* (moral obligation). Goldie, *supra* ch. 5 n. 45, 1231–3. Further insight into the US attitude is gained by reference to the internal conclusion that customary law established the strict regime reflected in the Space Objects Convention. See US Senate, Staff of Comm. on Aeronautic and Space Sciences, 92 Cong. 2nd Sess., Rpt. on Convention on International Liability for Damage Caused by Space Objects 44 (Comm. Print 1972).

[44] See materials cited in ch. 5, n. 51 *supra*.

[45] See 10 *Mar. Poll. Bull.* 215–16 (1979); 11 *Mar. Poll. Bull.* 115 (1980); Rousseau *supra* n. 42, at 405–8. See also Hancock and Stone, 'Liability for Transnational Pollution Caused by Offshore Oil Rigs', 5 *Hast. Int'l & Comp. L. Rev.* 377 (1982); Handl, *supra* ch. 5 n. 84, at 223. The US recently received $2 million in settlement of civil claims against the owner of the drilling rig, Sedco, Inc. The settlement required a covenant not to proceed in civil actions against either the drilling contractor or the well-owner, the Mexican National Oil Company. *Ixtoc I* Agreement reprinted in 22 *Int'l Legal Materials* 580 (1983).

[46] LOS Convention, *supra* ch. 5 n. 17, art. 194(2).

constitutes a violation of the obligation. It is not inconsistent with this language, however, to overlay the 'fault' condition that responsibility will only arise in the event of an intentional or negligent failure to prevent. The Convention deftly avoided confronting the ambiguity as to the standard of performance by providing only that states 'shall be liable in accordance with international law.'[47]

The Stockholm Declaration on the Human Environment similarly fails specifically to address the issue of the test of responsibility for the breach of the environmental obligations it defines.[48] Principle 21's recitation of the state's 'responsibility to ensure' that environmental harm does not occur is clearly susceptible to interpretation as either a fault or a strict standard. The obligation to 'take all possible steps to prevent pollution of the seas' set forth in Principle 7 does suggest, on the other hand, a rather stringent standard of fault. It is not surprising, therefore, that the Stockholm Conference has been cited in literature by supporters of each of the doctrinal perspectives.[49]

The final instance of declarative practice provides a distinctly unequivocal statement on the subject. The 1964 session of the Asian-African Legal Consultative Committee considered at some length the issue of the legal implications of nuclear weapons tests.[50] Several delegates characterized strict responsibility for injuries arising out of nuclear testing as the proper rule for *lex ferenda*.[51] The Final Report adopted by the Committee, however, concluded: 'The principle of absolute liability for harbouring dangerous substances or carrying on dangerous activities is recognized in International Law. A State carrying out test explosions of nuclear weapons is therefore absolutely liable for the damage caused by such test explosions.'[52]

iii. Doctrinal Writings

The conflicting interpretations of judicial and state practice noted above accurately reveal the continuing debate among 'the most highly qualified publicists' concerning the status of the principle of strict environmental responsibility.[53] As noted in Part I, certain authors adhere to the traditional view that fault, in the sense of *culpa*, is a condition to the breach of *any*

[47] *Id.*, art. 234(1). At least one proposal for express adoption of a strict standard was submitted to and rejected by the Conference. *See* Informal Suggestion by Bahrain, Yemen, Egypt *et al.*, Doc. MP/18, reprinted in 10 *Off. Rec.* 111 (1978).

[48] Stockholm Declaration, *supra* ch. 5 n. 17.

[49] See Handl, *supra* ch. 5, n. 84, at 229 (fault); Comments of Tammes, ILC, 1973 Sum. Rec. *supra* ch. 3 n. 33, at 9 (strict).

[50] The Committee, established in 1958, had representatives from thirteen states at the time of the report. See Final Report of the Asian-African Legal Consultative Committee on the Legality of Nuclear Tests, Report of the 6th Session in Cairo, 1964, reprinted in Heine, *supra* ch. 7 n. 11, at 343.

[51] See Heine, *supra* ch 7 n. 50, at 286.

[52] *Id.*, at 344.

[53] The 'subsidiary' source of international law. Statute of the International Court of Justice art. 38(1) (*d*). As to the issue and the debate see generally Dupuy, *supra* ch. 3 n. 97, at 41 ff.

customary law obligation.[54] Others, more directly concerned with the question of environmental responsibility, have argued that the evidence is insufficient to conclude that a general standard of strict responsibility, admittedly utilized in convention practice, has risen to customary status.[55] On the other hand, based upon different views of the same evidence, certain commentators vigorously assert the customary status of a rule of strict responsibility for environmental injury.[56] The days of this apparent doctrinal impasse may, however, be numbered. Two significant developments suggest the contours of a prospective resolution of the conflict: the emergent consensus with respect to 'ultrahazardous' activity; and the ILC work regarding 'International Liability for Injurious Consequences Arising out of Acts Not Prohibited by International Law'.

a. Ultrahazardous Activities

In 1966 Wilfred Jenks published his influential lecture at the Hague Academy presenting evidence and asserting the logic of a regime of strict responsibility for injury arising out of 'ultrahazardous' activities.[57] Jenks proposed that an exception to the traditional requirement of fault must be recognized with respect to conduct involving risks of harm (*a*) so serious that it would be unjust to place the burden of loss on a victim even without proof of fault or (*b*) so technically complex as to preclude the victim's acquisition of evidence of fault.[58] Reflecting certain municipal formulations, he defined 'ultrahazardous' activities as 'all activities which involve a risk of serious harm on an international scale which cannot be eliminated by the exercise of the utmost care.'[59] The legal rule submitted was that '[e]very State is liable for injury to the world community or to other States or their nationals from ultrahazardous activities occurring or originating within its jurisdiction or undertaken on its behalf or with its authority. Liability for injury from ultrahazardous activities exists without proof of fault.'[60]

Jenks was guarded in his introductory appraisal of the place of the 'ultrahazardous' principle in customary law, conceding that no 'comprehen-

[54] See ch. 5 commencing at n. 51.

[55] See e.g. Handl *supra* ch. 2 n. 82, at 536–40; Handl, *supra* ch. 5 n. 30, at 158–62; Dupuy, *supra* ch. 5 n. 95, at 357.

[56] See particularly Goldie, *supra* ch. 5 n. 45; Schneider, *supra* ch. 5, n. 36, 267–80.

[57] Jenks, *supra* ch. 5 n. 51.

[58] *Id.*, at 107, The same two rationales served as the basis of the strict regime in the Space Objects Convention. See Foster, *supra* ch. 2 n. 83, at 151. See also Jenks, *supra* ch. 4 n. 72, at 283–5.

[59] Jenks, *supra* ch. 5, n. 51, at 193. The US Restatement of Torts (Second) § 529 (1977) describes these factors for determining ultrahazardous character: (*a*) existence of a high degree of risk of some harm to the person, land or chattels of others; (*b*) likelihood that the harm that results from it will be great; (*c*) inability to eliminate the risk by the exercise of reasonable care; (*d*) extent to which the activity is not a matter of common usage; (*e*) inappropriateness of the activity to the place where it is carried on; and (*f*) extent to which its value to the community is outweighed by its dangerous attributes. See Kelson, *supra* n. 6, at 285.

[60] Jenks, *supra* ch. 5, n. 51, at 194.

sive and clearly thought out' rule had achieved authoritative legal expression or general acceptance.[61] On the other hand, he variously asserted that the rules of strict responsibility were 'an anticipation . . . not yet fully realized or clearly stated, but increasingly necessary and apparent,' in 'successive stages of development,' and, finally, 'general principles of law relating to ultra-hazardous liability which may reasonably be invoked in discussions or proceedings between States relating to such liability.'[62] The more ambitious perspective does indeed now seem justified. Commentators have persuasively argued that strict liability for 'ultrahazardous' conduct is sufficiently uniform in municipal systems to render it a general principle applicable to international law.[63] Moreover, essentially all of the examples of multilateral conventions and other state practice cited above in support of the general principle of strict environmental responsibility may, in fact, be viewed as illustrations of the more limited ultrahazardous activity doctrine. Based upon such evidence, most contemporary publicists, characterizing it either as an expression of or an exception to the general rules of environmental responsibility, accept strict responsibility for the consequences of 'ultrahazardous' conduct.[64]

Predictably, however, there remain substantial unsettled issues as to the definition of the categories of 'ultrahazardous' activities.[65] Jenks and most other commentators have advocated a flexible definition embracing most of the serious risks arising out of modern technology:

> [A]ll activities which involve or may occasion a substantial change in the natural environment of the earth or another State, significant pollution of air or water, the release of nuclear or other sources of energy liable to escape from human control, disturbance of the equilibrium of geophysical forces and pressures, the modification of biological processes, the creation of automata a major error of which may be irreparable, and impact damage from such sources as aircraft in flight and spacecraft.[66]

[61] *Id.*, at 105.

[62] *Id.*, at 106, 177, 178.

[63] See Hardy, *supra* n. 7, at 237; Kelson, *supra* n. 6, at 206–9. See also Handl, 'International Liability of States for Marine Pollution', 21 *Can Yb. Int'l L.* 85, at 101 (1983).

[64] See e.g. Brownlie, *supra* ch. 2 n. 52, at 285–6, 477; Cahier, 'Le Problème de la responsabilité pour risque en droit international', in *International Relations in a Changing World* 411, at 427–8 (1977); Dupuy, *supra* ch. 2 n. 97, at 158–69, 209; Goldie, *supra* ch. 5 n. 45, at 1221; Handl, *supra* ch. 2 n. 82, at 553–60; Handl, n. 63, at 94–108; Hardy, *supra* n. 7, at 237; Kelson, *supra* n. 6, *passim*; Comments of Njenda, ILC, 1979 Sum. Rec. *supra* ch. 2 n. 91, at 203; Rest, 'Convention On Compensation For Transfrontier Environmental Injuries', Project of Inst. of Int'l and Comp. Law of U. of Cologne (1976), at 18 and 39; Schneider, *supra* ch. 5 n. 36, 274–80; Comments of Ushakov, ILC, 1974, Sum. Rec., *supra* ch. 3 n. 11, at 25.

[65] See Q-B, 3rd Rpt., *supra* ch. 5 n. 72, at 7.

[66] Jenks, *supra* ch. 5 n. 51, at 195. See Dupuy, *supra* ch. 2 n. 97, at 158–69, 209; Kelson, *supra* n. 6, at 242. In Handl's formulation the key is not the category of activity *per se* but the creation of a foreseeable risk. Although the emphasis of the reasoning is different, the types of activities categorized as capable of providing strict responsibility are the same. See Handl, *supra* n. 63, at 104. See discussion of Handl in Q-B, 4th Rpt., *supra* ch. 6 n. 12, at 54. See also Cahier, *supra* n. 64, *passim*.

A different perspective would limit the customary rule of ultrahazardous strict responsibility to matters specifically so defined in multilateral conventions, i.e. nuclear activities, operations in space and carriage or other conduct threatening pollution of the seas by oil or hazardous substances.[67] Finally, an extreme, restrictive view would apply the regime only to the extraordinary risks attendant to nuclear activities.[68] In short, opinion is too fragmented to allow a conclusion to be drawn as to the state of the law on the precise definition of ultrahazardous activities. The principle, however, appears well established.[69]

b. The ILC Perspective

The controversy regarding the subject of strict environmental responsibility emerged in the course of the ILC's consideration of the very first article regarding the general rules of state responsibility: 'Every internationally wrongful act of a State entails the international responsibility of that State.'[70] It was immediately recognized that the traditional association of 'wrongfulness' with fault presented a conflict with the emerging view of state obligations with respect to environmental injury.[71] To the extent that rules of wrongfulness were distinct, e.g. with respect to injury caused by demonstrable negligence, the general rules of responsibility were sufficient. It was the consensus view, however, that some negative consequences might attach to injury even in the absence of the traditional condition of fault.[72] Rather than confuse the already complex agenda of state responsibility issues, it was decided to consider the question separately.[73]

This topic, under active consideration by the Commission since 1980, has been denominated 'International Liability for Injurious Consequences Arising out of Acts Not Prohibited by International Law.'[74] The logic of the title was well explained by Quentin-Baxter, the Special Rapporteur:

> The wrongfulness of causing loss or injury to another State is not, in principle, doubtful; but it is equally clear in State practice that, if a State goes about its legitimate business in a reasonable manner, the causing of incidental loss or injury to another State will not necessarily engage the international responsibility of the acting State.

[67] See e.g. Comments of the General Assembly at its 37th Session of the members of the 6th Committee: Gorner (GDR), UN Doc. A/C. 6/37/5R. 38, Lukyanovich (USSR), UN Doc. A/C.6/37/SR.39, Baker (Israel), UN Doc. A/C.6/37/SR.47.

[68] Dupuy notes that the Soviet Union took this position in the negotiation of the 1969 Convention on Civil Liability for Oil Pollution Damage. Dupuy, *supra* ch. 5 n. 30, at 145.

[69] Another unsettled area of opinion relates to whether ultrahazardous responsibility is strict or absolute, i.e. without exoneration for *force majeure*. See Jenks, *supra* ch. 5, n. 51, at 1881; Goldie, *supra* ch. 5 n. 45, at 1215 and 1241–9; Schneider, *supra* ch. 5 n. 36, at 274.

[70] See e.g. discussions in ILC, 1973 Sum. Rec., *supra* ch. 3 n. 33, at 1202–5 Mtgs.

[71] *Id.* Comments of Ago, Bartos, Casteñeda, Kearney, Sette Camara, Tammes, and Yasseen at 14, 13, 10, 7, 16, 9, 16, respectively.

[72] *Id.*

[73] *Id.*, at 16; Comments Ago, Kearney, and Reuter, ILC, 1974 Sum. Rec., *supra* ch. 3 n. 11, at 6–7. See also Magraw, *supra* ch. 4 n. 13, at 306.

[74] See Q-B, Prelim. Rpt., *supra* ch. 5 n. 22.

Between these opposite poles there is a wilderness that cannot be reduced to order by prohibitory rules of general application.[75]

The key that emerges in this language is a concern for the maintenance of states' freedom of action; the problem is not that adverse consequences may attach to injury without fault, but that, since that which is 'wrongful' must not occur, among the consequences of the condition of responsibility is prohibition.[76] The use of the notion of 'liability', as distinct from 'responsibility', represents a technique to transcend the issue of wrongfulness and to establish a regime of consequences for injury that does not require prohibition.[77] Hence, the Special Rapporteur has described the liability/responsibility distinction as 'above all a scheme which, so far as possible, allowed states to pursue a diversity of rights and to reconcile those rights with a minimum resort to prohibition.'[78]

It should be underscored that the ILC materials, nevertheless, clearly assume the existence of certain rules of 'wrongfulness' with respect to injury to other states. The function of the topic is to fill the interstices where rules of wrongfulness, i.e. 'responsibility,' do not apply or are as yet indistinct.[79] The basic condition described with respect to wrongful injury is the traditional fault notion of a failure of 'due diligence' or 'reasonable care'.[80] This position is supplemented by statements to the effect that harm is 'wrongful' when it reaches particularly serious dimensions, The Special Rapporteur, for example, stated that wrongfulness must be determined by reference to harm; by implication, then, when proscribed limits of harm are exceeded, injury is wrongful regardless of fault.[81] In addition, a number of members of the Commission specifically endorsed the 'ultrahazardous' doctrine, asserting that injury arising out of particularly dangerous activities involve strict responsibility.[82] Indirect support for these views is found in the apparent consensus that the standard of care to which the state is to be held is proportionate to the risk and seriousness of injury.[83]

[75] Q-B, 3rd Rpt., *supra* ch. 5 n. 72, at 23. In June of 1985, following the death of Quentin-Baxter, Julio Barboza was appointed the Special Rapporteur. Barboza's initial report indicated his intent to review the subject anew with the Commission's work to date as the key resource. Barboza, Preliminary Report on International Liability for Injurious Consequences Arising out of Acts Not Prohibited by International Law, UN Doc. A/CN. 4/394 (1985).

[76] See *id.*, at 3; Comments of Quentin-Baxter, ILC, 1981 Sum. Rec., *supra* ch. 4 n. 35, at 218. See also Springer, *supra* ch. 5 n. 85, at 140–1.

[77] See Q-B, Prelim. Rpt., *supra* ch. 5 n. 22, at 251.

[78] Comments of Quentin-Baxter, ILC, 1980 Sum. Rec., *supra* ch. 5 n. 72, at 242.

[79] See Q-B, 3rd Rpt., *supra* ch. 5 n. 72, at 2, 5, 10; Comments of Quentin-Baxter, ILC, 1981 Sum. Rec., *supra* ch. 4 n. 35, at 218.

[80] See e.g. Comments of Thiam, ILC, 1980 Sum. Rec., *supra* ch. 5, n. 72, at 253; Q-B 2nd Rpt., *supra* ch. 5 n. 23, at 21.

[81] Comments of Quentin-Baxter, ILC, 1981 Sum. Rec., *supra* ch. 4 n. 35, at 218. See also ILA Montreal Rules Report, *supra* ch. 5 n. 46, at Comment art. 3.

[82] See e.g. Comments of Ago and Tammes, ILC, 1973 Sum. Rec., *supra* ch. 3 n. 33 n. 49, at 17 and 9, respectively; Comments of Njenga, ILC, 1979 Sum. Rec., *supra* n. 64, at 203.

[83] See Comments of Quentin-Baxter, ILC, 1981 Sum. Rec., *supra* ch. 4 n. 35, at 222.

In any case, the regime contemplated with respect to activities producing injuries which are *not* defined as wrongful is straightforward. It is suggested that states within whose 'territory or control' activities occur which harm or may harm other states should engage all affected states in a dialogue regarding the injury.[84] The objective is to cause states to balance their respective needs and expectations through a sort of preventive conciliation procedure; a regime of prevention and reparation should be agreed upon by the participants which reflects the states' respective interests. As noted above, the failure to engage in this procedure does not trigger state responsibility.[85] Rather, the only consequence of a failure to reach specific prior agreement regarding injury is recourse to the general rule of a strict obligation of reparation.[86]

At the very end of the day, when all the opportunities of regime-building have been set aside—or, alternatively, when a loss or injury has occurred that nobody foresaw—there is a commitment, in the nature of strict liability, to make good the loss. The Special Rapporteur finds it hard to see how it could be otherwise, taking into account the realities of transboundary dangers and relations between States, and the existing elements of a developing chapter of international law. Every State needs to feel that law assures it large areas of liberty and initiative in its own territory, and more controlled areas of liberty and initiative in international sea and air space; but every State also needs to feel that the law does not leave it at the mercy of developers beyond its own borders.[87]

The consensus in the ILC and support in the General Assembly Sixth Committee regarding this ultimate strict obligation to compensate seems to evidence a doctrinal shift; liability without the invariable result of prohibition is identified as a strict consequence of material injury, provided the parties have not achieved an alternative agreement.[88]

Prior to turning to the impact of the ILC perspective, it is submitted that the

[84] Summarized in Q-B, 3rd Rpt., *supra* ch. 5 n. 72, at 25–9.

[85] See ch. 5 at n. 89.

[86] See Q-B, 4th Rpt., *supra* ch. 6 n. 12, at 17. The participation or lack of participation in an effort to achieve agreement on a regime governing injurious conduct, however, will affect the measure of compensation due in the event injury occurs. See Q-B 3rd Rpt., *supra* ch. 5 n. 72, at 14–15.

[87] Q-B, 3rd Rpt., *supra* ch. 5, n. 72, at 19.

[88] As to the 6th Committee support, see citations in nn. 24 and 25 of Q-B, 4th Rpt., *supra* ch. 6 n. 12, at 7. One author questions the existence of consensus, but notes increasing approval of Commission conclusions. Magraw, *supra* ch. 4 n. 13, at 342. It should be noted that the Special Rapporteur goes to great lengths to avoid categorizing the suggested regime simply as one of 'strict liability'; such a designation still evokes almost instinctive expressions of concern among publicists. See *id.* at 4, 39. Rather, the regime is described as one of an ultimate 'duty of reparation, subject to factors.' *Id.*, at 51, Yet, if no pre-injury alternative regime is adopted, the scheme proposed is strict liability—subject only to the qualification that a failure to participate in 'regime-building' may affect the measure of compensation due. The basic distinctions between the ILC approach and earlier strict liability systems are, then, the ILC's (*a*) effort to disassociate prohibition from the reparation obligation, and (*b*) recognition that states' interests ought to be balanced in each case to fix an appropriate regime regarding environmental injury—in the absence of which the duty of reparation must control.

tactic engaged to reach this conclusion, avoidance of reference to 'wrongfulness' and 'responsibility', appears unnecessarily strained. The Special Rapporteur recently reported that there has been consistent disagreement among members of the Commission regarding the disassociation of the topic from that of responsibility for wrongfulness.[89] The rationale of the distinction is, again, that wrongfulness connotes prohibition of injury. Yet, there is understandable resistance to the notion that a state may suffer adverse consequences for conduct not defined as 'wrongful.' A perspective articulated in the 1981 Commission discussions on the issue seems, however, to provide the best solution to this essentially semantic problem. Aldrich there noted that acts may be wrongful, and require compensation, yet not have the consequence of prohibition.[90] Riphagen, as Special Rapporteur on the general topic of the consequences of state responsibility, lends support to this approach with his conclusion that the breach of particular rules of international law may have particular, tailored consequences.[91] In other words, the consequences of wrongfulness and responsibility may be defined in an environmental context to avoid an invariable rule of prohibition of wrongful injury, even when compensation is required. This seems a preferable technique in terms of the unity and integrity of existing state responsibility principles.

In any event, it is possible now to distil from the foregoing a sense of the emerging direction of doctrine on the issue of the standard of performance applicable to environmental obligations. Two basic categories of material injury have been identified which trigger international responsibility. The first consists of injury arising out of either the fault of the state, in the sense of intent or failure of due diligence, or activities defined as ultrahazardous. The former represents, of course, the orthodox perspective in which a fault of the state is required. The latter is an expression of strict responsibility for failure to prevent environmental injury, which, it is submitted, has risen to customary status. Injury from fault or ultrahazardous conduct is wrongful and, thus,

[89] ILC, 1982, Report to the General Assembly, 37 UN GAOR Supp. (no. 10) (A/37/10), at 195. See also Comments of Quentin-Baxter, ILC, 1974 Sum. Rec., *supra* ch. 3 n. 11 at 22. Consider, for example, Comments of Reuter, ILC, 1980 Sum. Rec., *supra* ch. 5 n. 72, at 253–4: 'Cases of liability for the injurious consequences of pollution were not, contrary to what might be said, cases of liability without a wrongful act. In pollution, as in other matters, it was necessary to fix thresholds which must not be exceeded and when the rule fixing them was broken there would be responsibility for a wrongful act.' See also Brownlie's similar criticism of the attempt to remove the issue from the normal rules of state responsibility in *System. supra* ch. 1 n. 2, at 50. See also Magraw, *supra* ch. 4 n. 13, at 316, 320.

[90] See e.g. Comments of Aldrich, ILC, 1981 Sum. Rec., *supra* ch. 4 n. 35, at 250–1. See also Comments of Vallat, *id.*, at 230. Vallat, however, describes the circumstances in which wrongful conduct may not be prohibited as injury from ultrahazardous (but not otherwise unlawful) activities and injury due to negligence. In terms of the categorical prohibition of the activity which produces injury, this is a valid point. On the other hand, even under the current ILC approach, *injury* from such sources is 'wrongful', i.e. prohibited. The harm must be stopped; once that has occurred, the activity may continue.

[91] Riphagen, Fourth Report on the Content, Form, and Degrees of State Responsbility, UN Gen Ass. Doc. A/CN. 4/366 (14 Apr. 1983), at 7.

prohibited, i.e. it gives rise to the full panoply of the consequences of state responsibility discussed in Chapter 4. It is most important here to recognize that the obligation to cease violative conduct refers to the failure to prevent *harm*; injury is the subject of the preventive obligation and the consequential duty to stop. Responsibility for the occurrence of prohibited injury does not carry with it a categorical prohibition of the causal activity, provided the activity no longer produces material injury and reparation has been made for past injury. There are, however, two qualifications to this conclusion. First, certain activities may be labelled by the community as unlawful (i.e. prohibited) even in the absence of or prior to proof of injury, based on inherent risks and insufficient social benefits.[92] Second, even as to activities not so prohibited, it seems logical to conclude that relief might be available to enjoin an activity prior to injury when sufficient evidence is presented that prohibited injury is likely to occur.[93]

The second category consists of all harm not caused by fault or relating to activities categorized as ultrahazardous. Here, the state of the law is substantially less distinct. The traditional and still-dominant perspective would deny state responsibility for such injury.[94] An exception, however, seems to be emerging. A common denominator in current doctrinal work is support for the notion of strict responsibility to compensate (i.e. strict *liability*) with respect to particularly serious injury, without reference to the requirement that such injury relate to an activity categorized as ultrahazardous. Both the ILC and exponents of strict liability such as Goldie and Schneider would, of course, require compensation regardless of fault for all material injury.[95] Significantly, however, even Handl, an opponent of such a general customary rule, has concluded that the obligation to compensate is a function of a balancing or reasonableness test, which incorporates as a major factor the magnitude of harm.[96] When injury reaches such a severe or

[92] See Q-B, 4th Rpt., *supra* ch. 6 n. 12, at 19. This was one of the arguments made by Australia and New Zealand in the *Nuclear Tests* Cases. See [1978] ICJ Pleadings, *Nuclear Tests* Cases, vol i, at 167, 186, and 332–5 (Australia) and vol. ii at 8 and 204 (New Zealand).

[93] But see ch. 5, n. 88 *supra*. Note that the *Trail Smelter* operation, for example, did not have to cease smelting efforts once measures were taken to reduce emissions to tolerable limits. See *Trail Smelter*, *supra* ch. 5 n. 23, at 1980.

[94] One interesting question as to the meaning of due diligence in the environmental context arises in cases where the pollution of the individual state would not have caused injury, but in combination (through cumulation or synergy) with other states pollution injury occurs. Logic and municipal analogy dictate that responsibility would arise in such cases if the state knew or should have known of the potential combination. 'The explanation of the paradox [of responsibility for an act in itself harmless] is that the standard of reasonable conduct applicable to each defendant is governed by the surrounding circumstances, including the activities of other defendants.' Prosser, *supra* ch. 4 n. 2, at 322. If the pollution arose out of an ultrahazardous activity, presumably the responsibility would be strict, without reference to reasonable care. See *id.*, at 323.

[95] See e.g. Goldie, *supra* n. 6, at 306–7; Schneider, *supra* ch. 5 n. 36, at 267–80. See also Cahier, *supra* n. 64. As to the *de minimis* question, see Comments of Quentin-Baxter, ILC, 1981 Sum. Rec., *supra* ch. 4 n. 35, at 175.

[96] See Handl, *supra* ch. 5 n. 30, at 175.

unreasonable level, then, emerging opinion seems to suggest compensation is strictly due. As to lesser injury which is nevertheless sufficiently 'material' to be legally cognizable, the fault requirement seems to remain intact.

The complementary issue of the prohibition of harm unrelated to fault or ultrahazardous conduct has received little direct attention outside the ILC. Advocates of a strict environmental regime have generally focused on the compensation or 'liability' question, leaving untouched the issue of whether or not, or in what circumstances, prohibition of harm is a consequence of responsibility.[97] The essence of the ILC approach is that freedom of action demands that certain injury-producing activities be permitted to continue; injury must be tolerated as long as compensation is forthcoming. The application of this principle ends, however, at the boundary of what the ILC presently calls 'wrongful' injury.[98] As noted, wrongfulness may be in part determined by reference to the magnitude of the injury.[99] When the specified line of seriousness is exceeded, therefore, the consequences of state responsibility for failing to prevent environmental injury would include liability *and* the obligation to end or perhaps reduce the injury.[100] Although the issue is unsettled, and indeed rarely identified, the ILC perspective, prohibiting only serious harm in the absence of fault or ultrahazard, represents a logical direction for the law.

c. Relation to State Authority

To speak of any regime of strict responsibility for breach of the obligation to prevent environmental injury arising out of ultrahazardous activity or of a particularly serious character is, in an important respect, not sufficiently precise. It is an obvious assumption underlying the imposition of a strict standard of performance that the state bearing responsibility possesses sufficient legal authority over the causal activity to prevent the harm. In the absence of such authority, the rationale of equity, i.e. burdening the author rather than the victim with the costs of injury, does not seem to apply. Nor would the companion logic of deterrence be served; strict responsibility is only a disincentive to injury-threatening conduct if imposed on the state in a position to dictate whether or not such conduct will occur. It is appropriate, therefore, briefly to consider the ambit of the defined rules in terms of the two variables of state authority, the actor's identity and the *locus* of the activity.[101]

When the state itself conducts the activity producing environmental injury,

[97] See e.g. Goldie, *supra* ch. 5 n. 45; Jenks, *supra* ch. 5 n. 51; Schneider, *supra* ch. 5 n. 36, at 267–80.

[98] See Q-B, 2nd Rpt., *supra* ch. 5 n. 23, at 5; Q-B, 3rd Rpt., *supra* ch. 5 n. 72, at 2 and 6–7.

[99] See Comments of Quentin-Baxter, Sum. Rec., *supra* ch. 5 n. 50, at 218; Q-B, 3rd Rpt., *supra* ch. 5 n. 72, at 28.

[100] See ILA Montreal Rules Report, *supra* ch. 5 n. 46, Comment on Art. 3.

[101] For notations of the juridical significance of the two variables see Dupuy, *supra* ch. 2 n. 97, at 168; Treves, *supra* ch. 5 n. 70, at 782–3.

the regime described above applies without qualification. Patently, the authority of the state over its own activities is unfettered; the performance of the preventive obligation is simply an act of self-control. Hence, as to harm attributable to the state itself, responsibility will arise in the event of fault, ultrahazardous cause or, pursuant to emerging doctrine, harm of a markedly serious nature. This conclusion applies to state conduct in any juridical zone.[102]

The question is different when the actor engaged in the harm-producing enterprise is a private individual. As discussed in Part I, the conduct of private persons subject to the jurisdiction of the state is never attributed to the state. It is, however, the obligation of the state to exercise its authority with due diligence to prevent conduct which, if the state were the actor, would trigger responsibility.[103] It has also been demonstrated that the obligation of the state to exercise due diligence to prevent environmental injury extends to all private conduct, territorial or extraterritorial, subject to the force of its legal authority.[104] In sum, one might expect that only fault arising out of a failure to exercise due diligence would conclude in state responsibility for any private activity causing environmental injury.

It is quite clear, however, that the principles of strict responsibility described above may apply to private conduct subject to the state's authority.[105] Essentially all formulations of strict responsibility in an environmental context have in common the assumption that private activity within state territory is subject to the same strict standard as state conduct.[106] As Jenks noted in his ultrahazardous activity variation: '[S]o long as States remain the basic units of international political organization, controlling territory and exercising jurisdiction, they must accept international responsibility for ultrahazardous activities occurring or originating within their jurisdiction or undertaken on their behalf or with their authority.'[107] The logic of this conclusion is quite simple. Within its own territory the state is clearly the decision-maker with respect to any conduct, possessed of plenary

[102] See ch. 5 at n. 51, *supra*; Jenks, *supra* ch. 5 n. 51, at 180; Comments of Quentin-Baxter, ILC, 1981 Sum. Rec., *supra* ch. 4 n. 35, at 219; discussion regarding the *Cosmos* incident in text at n. 40.

[103] See ch. 4 at n. 58 ff and ch. 5 at nn. 54 ff.

[104] See text at n. 2 *supra*.

[105] See Q-B, 4th Rpt., *supra* ch. 6 n. 12, at 47 and n. 120.

[106] See Comments of Quentin-Baxter, ILC, 1981 Sum. Rec., *supra* ch. 4 n. 35, at 222; Q-B, 3rd Rpt., *supra* ch. 5 n. 72, at 24; Kelson, *supra* n. 6, at 242; Space Objects Convention, *supra* ch. 4, nn. 68–78, art. 1(*c*) (ii). *Trail Smelter*, notably, was precisely a case involving state responsibility for injury from territorial private conduct. See *Trail Smelter*, *supra* ch. 5 n. 23. It should be noted, however, that concern, albeit *minority* concern, has been expressed in the General Assembly 6th Committee debates on the ILC's work regarding the propriety of establishing a regime of 'liability' for 'private' territorial conduct. See Comments of Siblesz (Netherlands), UN Doc. A/C.6/37SR.46 (1982), at 12; Comments of Schwab (US), UN Doc. A/CN.6/37/SR.52, at 8.

[107] Jenks, *supra* ch. 5 n. 51, at 180. As to ultrahazardous risks, there may be an additional underlying assumption that the sophisticated technologies which involve such risks are well within the practical competence of the state to control. See Handl, *supra* ch. 5 n. 84, at 231.

authority sufficient to prevent the injury through regulation or prohibition of the activity. Yet, the capacity to control and prevent may also exist with respect to private extraterritorial conduct over which the state possesses legal authority. For this reason, Jenks speaks of responsibility for activities within the 'jurisdiction' of the state, not just within territory. Handl similarly, focuses on the flexible elements of 'jurisdiction' and 'control' in the targeting of strict responsibility.[108] The ILC explicitly acknowledges the extraterritorial reach of the rule with the application of the strict standard to conduct within the 'territory *or* control' of the state.[109]

A distinction must be drawn, however, between extraterritorial conduct over which the authority of the state involves a degree of control which approximates that enjoyed over territorial conduct, and conduct over which materially less effective authority is possessed. The specific character and degrees of state authority over conduct in the various zones of the sea will be discussed in detail in Part III. In determining whether or not it is proper to impose a strict standard of responsibility with respect to particular conduct in any zone, the criterion will be whether the state possessed meaningful control over the conduct. Does the jurisdiction of the state bestow a capacity to prevent the injurious conduct which is comparable for such purposes to territorial authority?[110] If the answer is yes, the application of the regime of strict responsibility as described would be clearly proper. Where the state posseses a lesser order of authority and capacity to prevent, the imposition of strict responsibility in any circumstance would seem inappropriate. In such cases, only the failure to exercise with diligence whatever authority is possessed ought to elicit responsibility. The specific consequences of these conclusions *vis-à-vis* flag vessels and the several maritime zones will be discussed in Part III.

It should be underscored, in conclusion, that holding the state strictly responsible in the defined circumstances for private conduct does not contradict the principle of non-attribution.[111] As discussed in Part I, the state is still responsible only for its own conduct, i.e. its failure to exercise due diligence to prevent private individuals from causing impermissible injury.[112] The diligence due, however, is elevated in the circumstance of strict responsibility to a strict standard; the state must do that which is necessary to prevent. A failure to prevent *is* a failure of due diligence.[113]

[108] See Handl, *supra* ch. 2 n. 82, at 535; Handl, *supra* n. 63, at 104.

[109] Q-B, 3rd Rpt., *supra* ch. 5 n. 72, at 24 (*emphasis added*). See also Hallman, *supra* ch. 5 n. 57, at 30; Treves, *supra* ch. 5 n. 70, at 782.

[110] Note that state authority may be so diminished even in state territory with respect to certain matters as to render the strict standard inappropriate. See e.g. discussion of innocent passage in ch. 12.

[111] For one expression of concern with respect to this issue, see Comments of Reuter, ILC, 1980 Sum. Rec. Session, *supra* ch. 5 n. 72, at 254.

[112] See ch. 3 at n. 139 *supra*.

[113] See Handl, *supra* ch. 2 n. 82, at 553–60; Q-B, Prelim. Rpt., *supra* ch. 5 n. 22, at 255.

PART III

State Legal Authority over the Seas: The Rules of Consequential Responsibility

9

Bases of State Legal Authority

A. THE FRAMEWORK: THE RELATIONS OF AUTHORITY AND RESPONSIBILITY

Parts I and II of this work have examined in detail the general and specific principles relating to the attribution of state responsibility for environmental injury. Any decision in a specific interstate dispute regarding the marine environment will be governed by the set of identified rules. Yet, it is clear from the foregoing analysis that decisions regarding the character of state legal authority—a variable of great complexity in the marine context—will affect the outcome of any application of the rules of environmental responsibility in several respects:

1. The allocation among states of legal authority over conduct producing environmental injury dictates which state is, or states are, internationally obligated to prevent such injury.

2. The character of legal authority possessed over the injurious conduct will, in turn, affect both the standard of performance of the preventive obligation to which any obligated state is to be held and, in circumstances of multiple state responsibility, the appropriate apportionment among responsible states of the burden of compensation.

3. The definition of authority over the region of the environment or resources injured will determine whether such injury indeed implicates any recognized international obligation, which states, if any, are juridically aggrieved by the injury, and the standing of any state to present an international claim based on the injury.

In light of the foregoing, it is clear that the 'rules of decision' governing state responsibility for marine environmental injury in fact comprehend three distinct sets of rules: the general principles of state responsibility discussed in Part I; the specific principles of international environmental obligation outlined in Part II; and the rules defining state legal authority over the regions of, and actors upon, the seas. Decision in a specific case will reflect the conjunction of all three bodies of law.

Part III, therefore, will venture both to define the final set of rules governing state legal authority over the seas and to explore the consequential, synthesized rules of responsibility pertaining to the marine environment. The initial step will be to consider briefly the types of jurisdiction recognized generally in international law which, subject to certain variations in application to the seas, dictate the character of state authority over conduct by any actor in any region.

B. THE BASES OF JURISDICTION

The now dominant perspective of 'relative' state sovereignty discussed in Part II is the key to an understanding of the principles governing state legal authority.[1] To borrow from F.A. Mann, jurisdiction is simply the 'subordinate instrument' through which the state exercises its sovereignty.[2] State legal authority serves as the vehicle for the definition, limitation, and exercise of the rights of sovereignty. The rules of jurisdiction, therefore, reflect the essential characteristics of the parent concept of relative sovereignty. State legal authority is apportioned (*a*) on the basis of equality among states, (*b*) with limits consistent with the principal objective of striking a balance to avoid one state's exercise of sovereignty interfering with that of another, and (*c*) subject to state independence within the reciprocal limits imposed. Parenthetically, the use of the term 'apportioned' is, perhaps, misleading. It should be emphasized that the 'sufficiency of grounds for jurisdiction is an issue normally considered relative to the rights of other states and not as a question of basic competence.'[3] Yet, the logic and practice of relativism have yielded certain identifiable governing principles regarding jurisdictional competence. It is to those principles that the discussion now proceeds.

i. Prescription v. *Enforcement*

The jurisdiction of the state is composed of two distinct species of legal authority: prescriptive and enforcement authority. The 1982 US Draft Restatement of Foreign Relations Law distinguishes and succinctly defines (*a*) the state's 'jurisdiction to prescribe, i.e., to subject to its law the conduct, relations, or status of persons or the interests of persons in things, whether by legislation, by executive act or order, by administrative rule or regulation, or by judgment of a court' and (*b*) its 'jurisdiction to enforce, i.e., to compel or induce compliance, or to impose sanctions for non-compliance, with statutes, rules, orders, regulations, or judgments, whether through judicial proceedings or by police or other administrative or executive action.'[4] The comments to

[1] See discussion in ch. 5, section B *supra*.

[2] Mann, *supra* Intro. n. 1, at 9.

[3] Brownlie, *supra* ch. 2 n. 52, at 298. Prior to commencing the enumeration of the specific principles of state jurisdiction, a cautionary note is appropriate. In this area, it is not always possible 'to infer from the practice adopted by a State the theory upon which it bases its assumption of jurisdiction since we cannot safely argue from the fact that it assumes jurisdiction only in certain cases that it regards those cases as the only ones in which the assumption of jurisdiction would be legitimate.' Report of Mr Brierly in Report of the Subcommittee on the Criminal Competence of States in Respect to Offenses Committed Outside their Territory, League of Nations Committee of Experts for the Progressive Codification of International Law, 20 *Am. J. Int'l L.* 253 (Supp. 1926), (hereinafter cited as League Report).

[4] Restatement of the Foreign Relations Law of the United States (Revised) § 401 (Tent. Draft

the Draft Restatement explain that the text 'identifies different aspects of the exercise of authority that, because they employ different means and have different consequences, have led to different principles of limitation under international law.'[5] In fact, the distinct treatment in international law reflects directly the guiding rationale of 'relative' authority. Each of the variations on the theme of enforcement, e.g. inspection, interrogation, arrest, seizure, fine, and imprisonment, has a material or even physical character. The application of a law to persons or property through such acts constitutes a juridically significant step beyond the definition of the law. Enforcement is in a sense the realization of the potential of prescription. The interference with the rights or interests of others inherent in acts of enforcement is, therefore, of a different order than that attendant to acts of prescription. International law reflects this conclusion in its articulation of quite different principles with respect to the two aspects of legal authority.

ii. Authority to Prescribe

a. Territory

The definition of the scope of sovereign authority, from the very earliest stages in the development of the modern state, was essentially spatial. As described by Charles de Visscher:

> While national unity would be only slowly defined, territorial unification was the immediate object of the policy of the sovereigns. They had inherited from feudalism an entirely territorial conception of power; the possession of the soil seemed to them the essential basis on which to develop public power.[6]

Thus, the exercise of the authority of the state, as with the preceding structures of social order, was associated from the outset with the possession of territory. In fact, the venerable linkage of state authority with territory is still 'the point of departure in settling most questions that concern international relations.'[7]

It is not surprising then that the 'first principle' of international jurisdiction remains that states possess prescriptive legal authority with respect to conduct and matters within their respective territories.[8] The articulation of this

no. 3, 1982) (hereinafter cited as 1982 Draft Rest.) The draft in fact identifies a third component of state legal authority—'jurisdiction to adjudicate.' *Id.* In a sense, adjudication is a hybrid form since judicial decision is a prescriptive act which may constitute a step in an enforcement process. Yet, in terms of its effect upon the interests of other states and the consequent limitations imposed by international law, adjudicatory authority—the competence to render judicial decisions which may lead to enforcement action—is properly viewed as an element of prescriptive legal authority. For analogous reasoning, see Mann, *supra* Intro. n. 1, at 128–9.

[5] 1982 Draft Rest. *supra* n. 4, § 402 comment (*a*). Cheng denominates the different aspects of state legal authority 'jurisfaction' (prescriptive jurisdiction) and 'jurisaction' (enforcement jurisdiction). Cheng, 'Crimes on Board Aircraft', 12 *Current Legal Prob.* 177, 181–2 (1959).

[6] De Visscher, *supra* ch. 3 n. 131, at 5.

[7] *Island of Palmas (or Miangas)* Arbitral Award (1928) (*US* v. *Neth.*), Hague Crt. Rpt. 2nd (Scott) 83.

[8] Jennings, 'Extraterritorial Jurisdiction and the United States Antitrust Laws', 33 *Brit. Yb. Int'l L.* 146 (1957).

principle is readily traced to the profoundly influential work of Ulrich Huber in the seventeenth century.[9] Huber posited, as maxims corollary to the doctrine of state sovereignty, that (*a*) 'The laws of every sovereign authority have force within the boundaries of its State, and bind all subject to it, but not beyond'; and (*b*) 'Those are held to be subject to a sovereign authority who are found within its boundaries, whether they be there permanently or temporarily.'[10] These tenets and the territorial basis of legal authority which they describe are today universally recognized and reflected in the jurisprudence of modern states.[11]

Anglo-American jurisprudence is, indeed, replete with language to the effect that 'territoriality' is the sole legitimate source of state jurisdiction.[12] Yet, this no longer represents a necessarily conservative definition of the limits to state legal authority, for the concept of territorial jurisdiction has expanded in two dimensions to reach extraterritorial matters. The less controversial of the two is denominated 'subjective' territoriality. This approach serves as the basis of state legal authority over conduct 'commenced within the State but completed or consummated abroad,'[13] In a leading case, for example, the prescriptive authority of a territorial state over the intentional destruction of a foreign vessel on the high seas was affirmed on the basis of the loading of explosives and formation of intent within state territory.[14] The assertion of such 'subjective' territorial jurisdiction is uniformly accepted, regardless of the remoteness of the completion or consequences of the conduct commenced within state territory.[15]

The second aspect of the expansion of the territorial basis of jurisdiction, 'objective' territoriality, is somewhat more problematic. The basic principle that a state possesses prescriptive legal authority over conduct 'commenced without the State but consummated within its territory' is not in dispute.[16]

[9] See Llewelyn-Davies, 'The Influence of Huber's *De conflictu legum* on English Private International Law'. 18 *Brit. Yb. Int'l L.* 49 (1937); Mann, *supra* Introd. 1, at 16.

[10] Huber, 'De conflictu legum diversarum in diversis imperiis' in *Praelectiones juris Romani et hodierni* (1689), trans. and reprinted in Llewelyn-Davies, *supra* n. 9, at 16. These basic tenets were reflected directly in the work of Justice Story 150 years later. Story, *Conflict of Laws* §§ 18–22 (1834).

[11] Jennings rightly submits that no citation is necessary to support this fundamental rule. Jennings, *supra* n. 8, at 148. One citation is sufficiently authoritative—the leading piece of research in the field—to be worthy of note. See 'Research in International Law under the auspices of the Faculty of the Harvard Law School: Jurisdiction with respect to Crime (pt II)', 29 *Am. J. Int'l L.* 435, at 480–3 (Supp. 1935) (hereinafter cited as Harvard Research–Jurisdiction.)

[12] Brierly, 'Règles générales du droit de la paix, iv *Recueil des cours* 5, at 180 (1936); Jennings, *supra* n. 8, at 148–9. See e.g. *R.* v. *Keyn*, (1876) L.R. 2 Ex. D. 63; *Am. Banana Co.* v. *United Fruit Co.*, 213 US 347, at 357 (1909); *Croft* v. *Dunphy*, [1933] AC 156.

[13] Harvard Research–Jurisdiction, *supra* n. 11, at 484.

[14] 'The *Tennyson*,' 45 *J. droit int'l* 739 (1918).

[15] Harvard Research, Jurisdiction, *supra* n. 11, at 487.

[16] Akehurst, *supra* ch. 5 n. 103, at 153; Brierly, *supra* ch. 2 n. 41, at 300; Harvard Research–Jurisdiction, *supra* n. 11, at 488–91; Jennings, 'General Course of International Law', ii *Recueil des cours* 321, at 518 (1967).

Such assertions are now reflected in the decisional literature and practice of most states.[17] The Permanent Court has expressly affirmed and applied the 'objective' expansion of the territorial principle of jurisdiction in its judgment in the *Lotus* Case.[18]

The analytical problems with 'objective' territoriality are limited to its application when only the consequences of conduct are present within the territory of the prescribing state. As with the 'subjective' approach, 'objective' territoriality does not rely upon any fiction to establish the requisite link to territory; part of the *actus reus* must in fact occur within the state.[19] It is certainly consistent with the rationale of territorial jurisdiction itself, the maintenance of order and welfare within the territorially defined state, to treat the effects of conduct as an operative component of the *actus reus* and thereby to subject it to the prescriptive legal authority of the state affected. Yet, aggressively applied, the doctrine imposes no effective limit to the ambit of prescriptive jurisdiction. 'Effects' defined to include the remote, *de minimis* or even abstract repercussions of extraterritorial conduct could serve as the basis of assertions of prescriptive authority over matters with only the most tenuous relationship to the prescribing state.[20]

Attendant to any prescriptive exercise based on the 'objective' approach which affects conduct within the territory of another state is a measure of interference with that state; to the extent that the exercise is not justified by the rationale of territoriality, the interference ought not to be permitted. Several principles have in fact emerged appropriately to qualify 'objective' territoriality. The influential Harvard Research project first stated the now consensus view that an 'essential' constituent element of the conduct must occur within

[17] See e.g. *R.* v. *Godfrey*, [1932] 1 KB 24; *DPP* v. *Doot*, [1973] AC 807 (HL); *Ford* v. *United States*, 273 US 593 (1927); *Rivard* v. *United States*, 375 F. 2d 882, at 886 (1967); *United States* v. *Pizzarusso*, 388 F. 2d 8 (1968), *cert. den.* 392 US 936 (1968); *Imperial Chem. Indus., Ltd.* v. *Comm. of the Europ. Communities*, [1972] *Recueil de la jurisp.* 619.

[18] '[I]f an offence committed on board a ship on the high seas produces its effects on a ship of another nationality, the State under whose jurisdiction the latter vessel falls is no more debarred by international law from taking criminal proceedings against the accused than it would be in the event of the offence producing its effects on its own territory properly so-called.' The *SS Lotus* (*Fr.* v. *Turkey*), [1927] PCIJ, Ser. A., no. 10. See Brownlie, *supra* ch. 2, n. 52, at 301; Brierly, *supra* ch. 2 n. 41, at 303; Harvard Research–Jurisdiction, *supra* n. 11, at 488; Jennings, *supra* n. 16, at 518; Mann, *supra* Introd. n. 1 at 25–7; Verzijl, *supra* ch. 5 n. 12, at 73.

[19] The fiction of the 'constructive presence' of the author of the conduct contributes nothing of substance to the principle of 'objective' territoriality. See e.g. the *SS Lotus*, [1927] PCIJ, Ser. A, no. 10 (Sep. Opin. Judge Moore), at 92. As long as a component of the conduct is present, to speak of the actor's presence is simply a matter of 'legal vocabulary'. Jennings, *supra* n. 8, at 159.

[20] The 'objective' territorial principle has found its most expansive expression in practice in the extraterritorial application of antitrust and trade legislation based on the economic repercussions of remote conduct. See *United States* v. *Watchmakers of Switzerland Info. Center Inc.*, 133 F. Supp. 40 (1955), 134 F. Supp. 710 (1955); *United States* v. *Aluminum Co. of America*, 148 F. 2d 416 (1945): Akehurst, *supra* ch. 5. n. 103, at 192–212; Brownlie, *supra* 2 n. 52, at 306–8, 310–13; International Law Association Report of the 55th Conference (1972), Report of the Committee on the Extraterritorial Application of Restrictive Trade Legislation (hereinafter cited as ILA 55th–Trade); Jennings, *supra* n. 8, *passim*.

state territory.[21] In terms of the 'effects' doctrine, this would seem to translate first into a requirement that the effects upon which the jurisdictional assertion rests must be substantial.[22] It further appears to be the uniform view that such consequences must be intimately related to the extraterritorial conduct, in the sense of a 'direct', 'proximate', or 'primary relationship'.[23] Finally, there is some authority for the position that the consequences must have been 'intended'.[24] The import of this principle would very much depend on whether the intent required is subjective or merely objective (focusing on foreseeability). In any event, the requirement does not appear to be reflected in dominant opinion or practice.[25]

b. Nationality

The essentially unqualified prescriptive jurisdiction of the state over the activities of its nationals, both within and without state territory, is firmly established.[26] Indeed, even Story, following what is otherwise regarded as the classic expression of the territorial principle, acknowledged 'that every nation has a right to bind its own subjects by its own laws in every other place.'[27] The diverse theoretical premises for the assertion of nationality jurisdiction are well summarized by the authors of the Harvard Research: (*a*) given that the state consists of its member-nationals, such jurisdiction is only self-control; (*b*) criminal law prescriptions attach only to the *person* and not the locale; (*c*) the state's protection of the national abroad generates a duty to obey state prescriptions; (*d*) in an abstract sense, the act of any national affects the state's order; (*e*) nationals are most fairly tried in a familiar setting; and (*f*) some crimes might go unpunished in the absence of nationality-based jurisdiction.[28]

Perhaps explained by such different perspectives on the rationale, there are substantial variations in the character of state practice based on nationality

[21] Harvard Research, Jurisdiction, *supra* n. 11, at 495.

[22] See Restatement (Second) of the Foreign Relations Law of the United States § 18(b) (1965). The International Law Association adopted this perspective in 1972. ILA 55th–Trade, *supra* n. 20, at 138. Interestingly, this only occurred in plenary session; in committee the 'effects' doctrine—at least in the context of antitrust—was rejected entirely. *Id.* at 174–5.

[23] Respectively: Rest. For. Rel., *supra* n. 22, § 18(b); Jennings, *supra* n. 8, at 159; Akehurst, *supra* ch. 5 n. 103, at 154–5.

[24] Rest. For. Rel., *supra* n. 22, § 18(b). This view is suggested in *R.* v. *Keyn*, [1876] L.R. 2 Ex. D. 63, and the separate opnion of J. Loder in the *Lotus* Case, [1927] PCIJ, Ser. A, no. 10, at 34–9.

[25] Harvard Research–Jurisdiction, *supra* n. 11, at 501. An exception to this conclusion may be emerging in the limited context of prescriptions directed at extraterritorial business activities with economic repercussions in the prescribing state. See Brownlie, *supra* ch. 2 n. 52, at 307.

[26] Akehurst, *supra* ch. 5 n. 103, at 156; Beckett, 'The Exercise of Criminal Jurisdiction over Foreigners', 6 *Brit. Yb. Int'l L.* 44, at 57–8 [1925]: Brownlie, *supra* ch. 2 n. 52, at 303; Harvard Research–Jurisdiction, *supra* n. 11, at 519, 531–5; League Report, *supra* n. 3, at 253, 258; Mann, *supra* Introd. n. 1, at 75–7. See European Communities: Comments on the US Regulations Concerning Trade With the USSR, reprinted in 21 *Int'l L. Materials* 891, at 893 (1982).

[27] Story, *supra* n. 10, at §§ 18–22, as summarized in Mann, *supra* Introd. n. 1, at 20.

[28] Harvard Research–Jurisdiction, *supra* n. 11, at 519–20.

jurisdiction. Five species of practice have been identified with respect to the conduct of nationals subjected to the extraterritorial reach of State prescriptions:[29] (*a*) All conduct subject to prescriptions at home; (*b*) Conduct violative of *lex loci delicti*; (*c*) Conduct of a certain degree; (*d*) Conduct affecting other nationals and; (*e*) Specific categories of conduct. The first of these is the rarest form; the second is the most common.[30] Anglo-American practice, which has been generally less assertive of nationality jurisdiction than that of civil law states, falls within the final category.[31] In any event, limitations in exercise must be defined as internal state policy; international law seems to impose no present limitation on the prescriptive jurisdiction of the state of allegiance.

c. *Passive Personality*

The 'passive personality' doctrine would vest the state with prescriptive legal authority over conduct abroad which affects the person or interests of a national. 'In substance, it means that the citizen of one country, when he visits another country, takes with him for his protection the law of his own country, and subjects those with whom he comes into contact to the operation of that law.'[32] In fact, the national need never have left home. Hence, in the *Cutting* Case, Mexico asserted jurisdiction based on passive personality over an American for publication in a Texas newspaper of defamatory material regarding a Mexican citizen.[33] The protests of the United States as to the absence of jurisdiction produced no resolution to the dispute.[34] The propriety of an exercise of jurisdiction based on 'passive personality' was squarely before the Permanent Court in the *Lotus* Case.[35] Turkey had acted under a statute designed to punish extraterritorial acts injurious to Turkish nationals in trying and convicting French marines following a collision of Turkish and French vessels on the high seas. The majority of the Court, however, reserved opinion on the validity of the statute and the underlying 'passive personality' principle—relying on the assimilation of vessels to the regime of territory and

[29] *Id.*, at 523–9.

[30] *Id.*, at 523–5. For a statement of the expansive form see *Case against Buscetta*, Judgment of 9 Feb. 1979, Corte Cass., Italy, 64 *Rivista di diritto int'l* 174 (1981); 77 *Am. J. Int'l L.* 164 (1983).

[31] Harvard Research Jurisdiction, *supra* n. 11, at 520–2; Jennings, *supra* n. 8, at 153–4. For several recent examples see *R.* v. *Kelly*, [1981] 2 WLR 112, aff'd *The Times*, 29 July 1981, at 24, col. 1 (HL 28 July 1981), (1982) AC 665; *United States* v. *Lansky*, 496 F. 2d 1063 (1974), *United States* v. *Black*, 291 F.Supp. 262 (1968); *United States* v. *Daniszewski*, 380 F. Supp. 113 (1974); *United States* v. *Keller*, 451 F.Supp. 631 (1978). Statement of the UK perspective appears in an *Aide-Memoire* dated 20 Oct. 1969 to the EEC Commission reprinted in Brownlie, *supra* ch. 2 n. 52, at 313: 'The nationality principle justifies proceedings against nationals of the State claiming jurisdiction in respect of their activities abroad only provided that this does not involve interference with the legitimate affairs of other States or cause such nationals to act in a manner which is contrary to the laws of the State in which the activities in question are conducted.'

[32] The *SS Lotus* Case (*Fr.* v. *Turkey*), [1927] PCIJ, Ser. A, no. 10, (Sep. Opin. J. Moore), at 92.

[33] The *Cutting* Case, [1887] *US Dig. Foreign Rel.* 751. See Beckett, *supra* n. 26, at 46.

[34] See Beckett, *supra* n. 26, at 46; [1975] *Dig. US Practice Int'l L.* 339.

[35] The *SS Lotus* Case, [1927] PCIJ, Ser. A, no. 10; See Brierly, *supra* ch. 2 n. 41, at 302; Verzijl, *supra* ch. 5 n. 12, at 77.

the objective territorial principle.[36] Certain of the individual opinions levelled specific and harsh criticism of the 'passive personality' approach.[37]

The lack of resolution in these cases is witness to the continuing doctrinal debate. Critics of the principle have asserted that (*a*) local law should suffice to protect the interests of individuals of any nationality and (*b*) there is an insufficient state interest in acts affecting nationals to merit interference with the conduct of foreigners in a foreign state.[38] In general, 'passive personality' continues to receive criticism from French and Anglo-American commentators and plays no role in the jurisprudence of their states.[39] On the other hand, it finds support among, and expression in the prescriptions of, a number of states within the civil law tradition.[40]

d. Protection of the State

Nearly all states recognize the authority of a state to exercise prescriptive jurisdiction over extraterritorial conduct which materially affects the security of the public processes of the state.[41] The rationale is simply that the state whose governmental functions or institutions are threatened is appropriately endowed with prescriptive legal authority over the threatening conduct since local law will likely not protect the public interests of other states.[42] There is, nevertheless, disagreement in theory and practice as to the categories of conduct properly subjected to 'protective' jurisdiction. With respect to conduct affecting the concrete functions or procedures of government there appears to be consensus; counterfeiting, forgery of public documents, immigration fraud, and perjured statements to consular officials are, for example, now accepted subjects of 'protective' prescriptions.[43] Even US and UK practice, belying the states' doctrinal rejection of the principle, evidence reliance on 'protective' jurisdiction in such limited cases.[44] On the other hand,

[36] *Id.* Certain commentators have cited the case as supportive of the 'passive personality' doctrine. See Cheng, *supra* n. 5, at 206–7; Lauterpacht, 'Allegiance, Diplomatic Protection and Criminal Jurisdiction over Aliens', 9 *Camb. L.J.* 330, at 343 (1947)'; Schwarzenberger and Brown, *A Manual of International Law* 77–8 (1976).

[37] The *SS Lotus* Case (*Fr.* v. *Turkey*), [1927] PCIJ, Ser. A, no. 10, (Sep. Opins J. Moore and Finlay), at 65–94, 50–8.

[38] See Comments of de Visscher, League Report, *supra* n. 3, at 258.

[39] For criticisms see *id.*; Jennings, *supra* no. 8, at 154–5; Mann, *supra* Introd. n. 1, at 78–9.

[40] Akehurst, *supra* ch. 5 n. 103, at 162; Harvard Research–Jurisdiction, *supra* n. 11, at 578–9; Mann, *supra* Introd. n. 1, at 78.

[41] See generally Akehurst, *supra* ch. 5 n. 103, at 158; Brownlie, *supra* ch. 2 n. 52, at 303–4; Harvard Research–Jurisdiction, *supra* n. 11, at 543. For what appears to be a backhanded endorsement of the validity of the principle see European Communities: Comments on the US Regulations Concerning Trade with the USSR, *supra* n. 26, at 896.

[42] Harvard Research–Jurisdiction, *supra* n. 11, at 552–3; League Report, *supra* n. 3, at 255. Akehurst notes the interesting instance of assertions of jurisdiction based upon threats to politically and economically related states. Examples include punishment of offences against the security of the allied states during World War II and the provisions of certain Eastern European states relating to acts threatening the security of similarly situated states. See Akehurst, *supra* ch. 5 n. 103, at 159.

[43] Harvard Research–Jurisdiction, *supra* n. 11, at 561–3.

[44] Harvard Research–Jurisdiction, *supra* n. 11, at 544. See e.g. *Rocha et al.* v. *United States*, 288

certain states have asserted 'protective' legal authority over activities affecting rather more abstract aspects of state security, including political integrity and independence.[45] It is in these areas that objections have arisen, without resolution, that the exercise of such authority may constitute an intolerable interference with the prerogative of the territorial state specifically to protect and promote the very political liberties (such as assembly, speech, and press freedoms) which the extraterritorial prescription is designed to suppress.[46] The compromise proposed by the authors of the Harvard Research, then and now *lex ferenda*, would deny the assertion of 'protective' jurisdiction when the subject conduct is a guaranteed liberty under local law.[47]

e. Universality

State assertions of 'universal' prescriptive jurisdiction with respect to the purely extraterritorial conduct of aliens without impact upon state or citizens may be divided into two categories. The first relates to jurisdiction to prescribe conduct constituting *delicta juris gentium* as a domestic wrong. There is general assent as to the validity of this principle.[48] When conduct is of a character so detrimental to the common interests of states to be defined an 'international wrong' any state may exercise prescriptive authority. Disputes have centred simply on the categories of activity that may be so defined. Anglo-American jurisprudence has traditionally admitted only high seas piracy to the regime of *delicta juris gentium*.[49] Even these states now seem to accept serious war crimes as an additional category of conduct subject to universal jurisdiction.[50] Far more inclusive definitions of *delicta juris gentium*

F. 2d 545, *cert den.* 366 US 948 (1961); *United States ex rel. Majka* v. *Palmer*, 67 F.2d 146 (1933); *United States* v. *Rodriguez*, 182 F. Supp. 479 (1960); *Naim Molvan* v *Attn. Gen for Palestine*, [1948] AC 531; Brendel, 'The Marjuana on the High Seas Act and Jurisdiction over Stateless Vessels', 25 *Will. & Mary L. Rev.* 313 (1983). But see *United States* v *Baker*, 136 F. Supp. 546 (1955). Persuasive criticism of Baker may be found in Note, 'Criminal Law: Jurisdiction to Punish for Crimes Committed by an Alien outside the United States', 45 *Calif. L. Rev.* 199 (1957).

[45] Akehurst, *supra* ch. 5 n. 103, at 158; Harvard Research–Jurisdiction, *supra* n. 11, at 546–52. One recent case has broadly described the subject matter of protective jurisdiction of the state as the 'security or creditworthiness of that State or other State interests.' *Compagnie europeenne des petroles* SA v. *Sensor Nederland* BV, Dist. Crt., Hague, 1982, trans, reprinted in 22 *Int'l L. Materials* 66 (1983). The security or foreign policy interests of the United States were not, however, deemed to support an assertion of jurisdiction over the sale to the USSR of goods fabricated in the US or developed on the basis of US technology by non-nationals in Europe. *Id.* See Export Administration Act Amendments of 1981, Pub. L. 97–145, 95 Stat. 1727 (1981), reprinted in 21 *Int'l L. Materials* 164 (1982).

[46] Harvard Research–Jurisdiction, *supra* n. 11, at 553.

[47] *Id.*, at 557.

[48] Brownlie, *supra* ch. 5 n. 52 at 304; Harvard Research–Jurisdiction, *supra* n. 11, at 563.

[49] Akehurst, *supra* ch. 5 n. 103, at 160 Harvard Research–Jurisdiction, *supra* n. 11, at 572. See *In re Piracy Juris Gentium*, [1934] AC 586. The definition of 'piracy' as *delicta juris gentium* does not necessarily correspond to often more inclusive municipal definitions. It must meet the distinct criteria of international law. See Geneva Convention on the High Seas, *supra* ch. 6 n. 2, art. 15; Brierly, *supra* ch. 2 n. 41, at 313–14; Brownlie, *supra* ch. 2 n. 52, at 243–5; McDougal and Burke, *supra* ch. 6 n. 4, at 875–9; O'Connell, *supra* Introd. n. 1, at 714; Oppenheim, *supra* ch. 2 n. 37, at 608–17.

[50] Akehurst, *supra* ch. 5 n. 103, at 165; Brownlie, *supra* ch. 2 n. 52, at 305; George, *Extra-*

have been embraced by certain other states relying on the conclusion that the universal jurisdiction contractually established by multilateral conventions with respect to interference with submarine cables, counterfeiting, and traffic in slaves, narcotics, and prostitutes has become customary law.[51]

The second category of universal jurisdiction refers to prescriptive legal authority over conduct not *delicta juris gentium* without regard for the locus of the conduct or its effects or the allegiance of the actors. This far broader doctrine has a tradition of state practice based upon the rationale that the very presence of an unpunished offender of society's rules constitutes a 'menace to social order'.[52] Succinctly stated: '[i]f the disturbance of the legal order within a State's territory is considered the most persuasive reason for penal jurisdiction, such disturbance may be found in the presence of an offender who has committed a crime elsewhere.'[53] Assertions of legal authority resting on this rationale are generally limited either to specific offences of a particularly serious character or conduct violative of *lex loci* following an offer and rejection of extradition.[54] This expansive formulation of universality has found no place in Anglo-American jurisprudence.[55]

f. General Criteria

F.A. Mann has described the problem of apportionment of prescriptive jurisdiction as the 'search for the State or States whose contact with the facts is such as to make the allocation of legislative competence just and reasonable.'[56] A number of publicists, including Mann, have submitted that the rigid application of the orthodox principles of prescriptive authority outlined above may yield results inconsistent with this objective—particularly with reference to extraterritorial competence.[57] Several authors have sought to extract the logic of the traditional rules to define a set of comprehensive

territorial Application of Penal Legislation, 64 *Mich. L. Rev.* 609, at 621 (1966). See *Johnson* v. *Eisentrager*, 339 US 763 (1950); *Attn. Gen. of Israel* v. *Eichmann*, 36 *Int'l L. Rep.* 5, 26–42 (Dist. Crt. 12 Dec. 1961), 277, 289–304 (Sup. Crt. 29 May 1962). Brownlie does argue that war crimes jurisdiction, admittedly enjoyed by all states, is not properly defined as 'universal' municipal jurisdiction since the act punished is a breach of international law. Brownlie, *supra* ch. 2 n. 52, at 305. It would seem, however, that, as with piracy, the offence punished is conceptually and technically a breach of *national* law which incorporates international law.

[51] See Brownlie, *supra* ch. 2 n. 52, at 304, n. 4; Harvard Research–Jurisdiction, *supra* n. 11, at 569–71. *Contra* 1982 Draft Rest., *supra* n. 4, § 522, Rep. Notes 2 and 3.

[52] Beckett, *supra* n. 26, at 58.

[53] Harvard Research–Jurisdiction, *supra* n. 11, at 580–1.

[54] *Id.*, at 575–82.

[55] Akehurst, *supra* ch. 5 n. 103, at 164; Brownlie, *supra* ch. 2 n. 52, at 304. Note that the authors of the Harvard Research viewed universal jurisdiction as an acceptable concept provided that it was effectively limited to a 'subsidiary' function, subject to extradition and limits *lex loci* such as statutes of limitation and limits to punishment. Harvard Research–Jurisdiction, *supra* n. 11, at 584.

[56] Mann, *supra* Introd. n. 1, at 34.

[57] See e.g. Akehurst, *supra* ch. 5 n. 103 at 154, 195–6; Jennings, *supra* n. 16, at 518–25; Mann, *supra* Introd. n. 1, at 31–41.

criteria pertaining to any proper exercise of prescriptive legal authority. The results may be summarized as follows: (*a*) the state must possess a substantial and direct connection with the facts; (*b*) the exercise must not interfere in the central internal affairs of another state; and (*c*) the overall logic of relativism and interdependence must not be violated.[58]

It is important to note that authors articulating such general criteria do not necessarily perceive their conclusions in the same fashion. Mann, for example, explicitly designed a set of principles to serve as a replacement rule of decision.[59] Jennings, on the other hand, appears to regard his own contributions only as guidelines for the application of the traditional rules.[60] Brownlie has designed such conclusions as only a descriptive 'distillation' of the orthodox principles for the purpose of summary and analysis.[61] In fact, contemporary state practice exhibits no tendency towards the abandonment of the structure or vocabulary of the traditional principles in favour of such an abstract, synthesized approach. Such general critieria do accurately describe, however, the underlying factors which mould state expectations with respect to any assertion of prescriptive jurisdiction. Moreover, the articulation of such principles, whatever its motivation, represents a laudable step in the progression towards consistency in the currently somewhat fragmented jurisprudence of prescriptive legal authority.

iii. Authority to Enforce

In marked contrast to the regime of prescriptive legal authority, the principles governing state jurisdiction to enforce are few, better defined, and rather restrictive. The primary rule describes the conceptual boundary of enforcement jurisdiction in terms of the state's prescriptive jurisdiction: 'Under international law a State may not exercise authority to enforce law which it has no jurisdiction to prescribe.'[62] The logic of this principle is so compelling as to render it practically a truism. A state cannot be permitted to take steps to compel obedience or penalize disobedience to prescriptions which international law deems to be beyond the ambit of state authority.[63]

[58] See Brownlie, *supra* ch. 2 n. 52, at 309–10; Jennings, *supra* n. 16, at 525; Jennings, *supra* n. 8, at 157–60; Mann, *supra* Introd. n. 1, at 34.

[59] Mann, *supra* Introd. n. 1, at 34. Mann perceptively notes that the ICJ has designed and applied similar flexible tests in the *Anglo-Norwegian Fisheries* Case, (*UK* v. *Nor.*), [1951] ICJ 116 (Merits), and the *Nottebohm* Case (Second Phase), (*Liecht.* v. *Guat.*), [1955] ICJ 4. See Mann, *supra* Introd. n. 1, at 40, n. 1. Indeed, the latter case applied an 'effective link' test quite analogous to the first tenet.

[60] Jennings, *supra* n. 8, at 157–60; Jennings, *supra* n. 16, at 525.

[61] Brownlie, *supra* ch. 2 n. 52, at 309–10.

[62] 1982 Draft Rest., *supra* n. 4, § 431 Comment (*b*). In at least one case, based upon some rather questionable logic, a court has refused to acknowledge its prescriptive competence with respect to extraterritorial activity (fishing outside territorial limits) due to its incapacity to take extraterritorial enforcement action. *South Atlantic Islands Dev. Corp.* v. *Buchan*, [1971] 1 SA 234(*c*). See Note, 'The Protection of Maritime Environment by the Courts of Third States: Some Difficulties', 19 *McGill L.J.* 279 (1973).

[63] The point here is simply that a state may only enforce lawful prescriptions. In certain

The appropriate starting point for a positive definition of enforcement competence is, then, the first principle of prescriptive authority—territoriality. Simply stated, the state's legal authority to enforce prescriptions within state territory is plenary. Investigation, inspection, arrest, seizure, imprisonment, and other measures of enforcement within the state's arsenal may be utilized with respect to any persons or property situated within state territory, regardless of nationality and subject only to exceptions such as diplomatic and consular immunity.[64] It should be noted that such territorial enforcement actions may be directed and effective against persons outside the state. Hence, enforcement tactics such as refusal of entry documents, prevention of transfer of assets, denial or revocation of import–export licenses or permits for business activities and similar steps are properly denominated 'territorial' enforcement measures.[65]

Prescriptive legal authority, as discussed above, extends far beyond the borders of the state to penetrate the territory of other states. At this point the spatial ambit of the two aspects of state jurisdiction diverge. The intrusive character of enforcement has dictated a quite distinct rule of limitation. The enforcement authority of the state within its own jurisdiction is exclusive. No state, therefore, may take any measure to enforce its law in the territory of another state.[66] Thus, although a state may clearly possess authority to prescribe with respect to the conduct of a national in a foreign state, it is denied any right to act there to enforce the prescription.[67] In the words of Beckett, it is 'universally accepted that no state can perform acts of sovereignty inside the territory of another, nor can it send its officials on to foreign soil to arrest, try, or punish offenders there, whoever they may be and whatever they may have done.'[68] This prohibition extends both to such primary acts of enforcement as arrest, detention, and punishment, and subsidiary measures such as service of process, notarial acts, and the taking of evidence.[69] Given the notoriety of the practice, it is important further to note that the issuance of orders by American courts in anti-trust cases demanding conduct or the cessation of conduct in foreign states represents neither rejection nor transgression of this rule.[70] Mann has persuasively pointed out

contexts such as 'hot pursuit' and Fitzmaurice's conception of the contiguous zone, the right to enforce may extend beyond the spatial reach of the subject prescription. See ch. 13 at nn. 12 and 113 *infra*. In any case, enforcement, wherever accomplished, is only lawful when the subject prescription is within the competence of the state.

[64] See text at nn. 77–87 *infra re* the types of limitations to which enforcement (and prescriptive) authority is subject.

[65] 1982 Draft Rest., *supra* n. 4, § 431, Comment (*a*).

[66] See the *SS Lotus* Case, [1927] PCIJ, Ser. A., no. 10, at 18–19; Brownlie, *supra* ch. 2 n. 52, at 306–7; Cheng, *supra* n. 5 at 182–3; Jennings, *supra* n. 8 at 149; Mann, *supra* Introd. n. 1, at 111; O'Connell, *supra* Introd. n. 1, at 659; 1982 Draft Rest., *supra* n. 4, § 432(2).

[67] See 1982 Draft Rest., *supra* n. 4, § 432 Rep. Note 1; Schellenberg, 'Proceedings Against Two French Customs Officials in Switzerland', 9 *Int'l Bus. Law.* 139 (1981).

[68] Beckett, *supra* n. 26, at 44.

[69] See Mann, *supra* Introd. n. 1, at 112–26.

[70] See e.g. *United States* v. *Aluminum Co. of Amer.*, 148 F.2d 416 (1945); *United States* v.

that such judicial orders constitute *prescriptive* acts which must juridically stand or fall based upon the principles governing prescriptive jurisdiction.[71] *Enforcement* to compel obedience to such orders could only take place within the United States.[72] The principle prohibiting the exercise of enforcement authority in the territory of another state remains 'unassailable'.[73]

It should not be suggested, however, that the foregoing prohibition extends to all extraterritorial enforcement measures. Enforcement in another state's territory involves an intrusion into the internal order of the state; enforcement in regions outside the territory of any state, however, may involve only interference with the exercise of external rights, e.g. navigation, fishing, or the authority of a state over its flag vessels.[74] When a vessel has a stateless character and there is, therefore, not even such limited interference, no prohibition of enforcement authority with respect to such vessel exists.[75] When the rights of another state are implicated, the less intrusive character of enforcement outside territory has resulted in the tolerance of certain limited rights of enforcement in these extraterritorial regions. The specific character of these rights will be considered in Chapters 12 and 13 in the discussion of authority over extraterritorial zones of the marine environment. In general, the outer boundary of enforcement jurisdiction in such areas is co-extensive with the substantive and spatial reach of prescriptive competence.[76]

C. CATEGORIES OF LIMITATION

The conclusion that the general principles described above may support a state's assertion of prescriptive or enforcement jurisdiction with respect to specific persons or property does not end the inquiry. International law (or practice) may impose specific limitations on the measure or character of a state's legal authority over subject matter otherwise within its jurisdictional reach. The purpose of this section is simply to identify the types of operative limitation and to note the scope of attention to be paid to each in the course of this work.

The constraints on legal authority fall analytically into three categories. The first may be defined as specific privileges and immunities afforded to certain limited persons and property by international law. Representative are the

Watchmakers of Switz. Info. Center, 133 F. Supp. 40 (1955); *United States* v. *Gen. Elec.*, 115 F. Supp. 835 (1953); *United States* v. *Imperial Chem. Ind. Ltd.*, 105 F. Supp. 215 (1952).

[71] Mann, *supra* Introd. n. 1, at 128–9.

[72] *Id.*, at 129.

[73] Jennings, *supra* n. 8, at 149.

[74] As to the relationship between the state and its flag vessels see ch. 10. See ch. 13 with respect to the external rights of the state in extraterritorial contiguous or functional zones and the high seas.

[75] *United States* v. *Cortes*, 588 F. 2d 106, 109–10 (5th Cir. 1979); *Molvan* v. *Attn. Gen. for Palestine*, [1948] AC 351, at 369.

[76] See ch. 13. But see discussion *re* the exception of 'hot pursuit' in ch. 13.

diplomatic and consular immunities from jurisdiction well established in international custom and practice.[77] The broader immunities afforded the 'state' itself in international law are a second common illustration.[78] Finally, certain functional immunities, e.g. innocent passage, fall within this generic group.[79] It is, of course, well beyond the ambition of this work to engage in a general discussion of immunities in international law. Certain of the limitations within this category do, however, obviously represent qualifications to state legal authority quite material to the present inquiry. The import of these immunities will be considered specifically in subsequent chapters detailing the character of jurisdiction over the marine environment. As a prefatory comment, it is sufficient here to note that all such immunities function to impose varying degrees of restraint on the state's exercise of its enforcement and, albeit less frequently, prescriptive legal authority.

The principles of 'comity' or *courtoisie internationale* constitute the second category of limitations. There has been, unfortunately, substantial semantic confusion in the literature with respect to the English term 'comity': it is often used either as a synonym for international law or to describe the source of international legal obligation.[80] Here, neither of these is intended. 'Comity' and *courtoisie internationale* denote simply guidelines of conduct, without the force of law, respected by states on the basis of perceived reciprocal convenience and benefit.[81] Their influence in the area of state jurisdiction is to suggest forbearance in the exercise of authority otherwise possessed.[82] Though lacking the obligatory character of international law, such guidelines have a material impact due to the fact of state expectations and the 'sanction' of reciprocity. Again specifically relevant manifestations of comity will be identified at appropriate points in the discussion of marine environmental jurisdiction.[83]

The final set of limitations on the exercise of state jurisdiction is the broadest: the substantive obligations imposed upon the state by international law.[84] It is perhaps reciting the obvious to state that legal authority must be

[77] See Vienna Convention on Diplomatic Relations, done 18 Apr. 1961, entry into force 24 Apr. 1964, 500 UNTS 95; Vienna Convention on Consular Relations, done 24 Apr. 1963, entry into force 19 Mar. 1967, 596 UNTS 261; Brownlie, *supra* ch. 2 n. 52, at 345–63; Delupis, *supra* ch. 7 n. 9, at 115–20; 'Diplomatic and Consular Privileges and Immunities', 7 UNLS (1958) and Supp. (1963); Whiteman, 7 *Digest of International Law* 1–504 (1963).

[78] See Brierly, *supra* ch. 2 n. 41, at 245; Brownlie, *supra* ch. 2 n. 52, at 321–44; Comment, 'The Jurisdictional Immunity of Foreign Sovereigns', 63 *Yale L.J.* 1148 (1954); Harvard Research–Jurisdiction, *supra* n. 11, at 592; Lauterpacht, 'The Problem of Jurisdictional Immunities of Foreign States', 28 *Brit. Yb. Int'l L.* 220 (1951); McDougal and Burke, *supra* ch. 6 n. 4, at 137–53.

[79] See ch. 12.

[80] Akehurst, *supra* ch. 5 n. 103, at 214.

[81] See generally Brownlie, *supra* ch. 2 n. 52, at 30–1; Oppenheim, *supra* ch. 2, n. 37, at 33–5; Starke, *An Introduction to International Law* 20 (7th edn. 1972).

[82] For a classic expression, see *Lauritzen* v. *Larsen*, 345 US 571, at 582 (1953).

[83] See specifically ch. 11.

[84] Arguably, of course, the immunities described above constitute a subset of the category of international obligations. The obligation of the state with respect to immunities is simply not to

exercised in a fashion consistent with international obligations.[85] Norms in areas such as human rights, administration of justice, and expropriation clearly operate to impose limits on the exercise of prescriptive or enforcement jurisdiction.[86] It is imperative, however, to underscore the distinctive character of this process. Comity and the rules of immunity limit jurisdiction by denying only the *application* of some aspect of general legal authority. International obligations, on the other hand, limit by influencing the *content* of the exercise of state jurisdiction. An international obligation may demand a positive exercise of legal authority either by (*a*) requiring a result which the state may achieve by its own choice of prescriptive and enforcement means or (*b*) directly dictating a specific course of jurisdictional conduct.[87] Conversely, a negative constraint may be imposed by an international obligation which prohibits either certain consequences of jurisdictional exercise or a specific course of jurisdictional conduct.[88] From either positive or negative perspective, then, international legal norms work to define the substantive boundaries of the exercise of state legal authority.

The task now is to consider the application of the foregoing principles of state jurisdiction in the specific context of the law of the sea, and then to identify the consequential rules of marine environmental responsibility. Chapter 10 will proceed by examining the issues of authority and correlative responsibility with respect to vessels, the principal instrument of conduct affecting the seas. The discussion will focus on responsibility for the conduct of vessels bearing a special relationship to the state based other than on the

assert the prohibited jurisdiction. In any event, however, immunities are sufficiently distinct from other obligations analytically and in their treatment in the literature to merit separate categorization.

[85] The term 'international obligations' is in this context intended to be inclusive of obligations of both custom and convention.

[86] See generally: (*a*) as to human rights, Brownlie, *supra* ch. 7 n. 9; European Convention for the Protection of Human Rights and Fundamental Freedoms, done 4 Nov. 1950, entry into force 3 Sept. 1953, reprinted in 45 *Am. J. Int'l L.* (Suppl. 1951), at 24; Lauterpacht, *supra* ch. 7 n. 9; Moskowitz, *Human Rights and World Order* (1958); Moskowitz, *supra* ch. 7 n. 9; Sohn and Buergenthal, *supra* ch. 7 n. 9; United Nations Universal Declaration of Human Rights, adopted 10 Dec. 1948, GA Res. 217A(111), UN Doc. A/810; (hereinafter cited as Univ. Declaration); (*b*) as to administration of justice, Freeman, *supra* ch. 3 n. 22; Harvard Research–Jurisdiction, *supra* n. 11, at 596–600; and (*c*) as to expropriation, Friedman, *Expropriation in International Law* (1953); White, *Nationalization of Foreign Property* (1961); *The Valuation of Nationalized Property in International Law* (Lillich ed. 1972–5).

[87] Two of the numerous examples of the former are the obligations to protect the premises of diplomatic missions (Vienna Convention on Diplomatic Relations, *supra* n. 77, art, 22(2)) and to take measures with respect to flag vessels to ensure safety at sea (Geneva Convention on the High Seas, *supra* ch. 6 n. 2, art. 10). The more exceptional latter is illustrated by the specific legislative acts required of contracting states in several environmental conventions, e.g. London Dumping Convention, *supra* ch. 5 n. 44, arts. 4–6. See generally Ago's thoughts on the distinction between obligations of 'result' and those of 'conduct' in his Sixth Rpt. on State Responsibility, ii *Yb. Int'l L. Comm'n* 3–20, UN Doc. A/CN. 4 307 and Add. 1–2 (1977).

[88] An example of the relatively rare specific prohibition is the human rights stricture against the use of torture or cruel, inhuman, or degrading punishment as part of the enforcement process. See Univ. Declaration, *supra* n. 86, art. 5.

presence of the vessel within a zone over which the state possesses legal authority. The balance of the work will be devoted to the definition of authority over vessels and other actors in the several juridical zones of the sea and the synthesis of the rules of decision regarding responsibility for environmental injury to, or arising out of conduct within, such zones.

10

State Responsibility for Vessels[1]

A. NATURE OF INQUIRY

The conduct of vessels, including accidents, purposeful operational discharge, and dumping, constitutes one of the principal sources of marine pollution.[2] 'Vessel conduct' is, of course, something of a misnomer. Vessels do not engage in conduct; they are merely the instruments of human actors. In this context, then, the term 'vessel' is properly viewed as a short-hand expression referring to the individuals associated with a vessel, including owners, operators, masters, crews, passengers, and property shippers.[3] Every instance of 'vessel conduct' is linked directly or indirectly to the acts or omissions of one or more of these participants in the process of maritime transport. State responsibility for conduct can, of course, not arise, in light of the 'subjective' requirements discussed in Chapter 3, unless the actor is either an organ or representative of the state, or a private individual over whom the state possesses legal authority.[4] States may be attributed responsibility for vessel conduct injurious to the marine environment, therefore, only to the extent that the requisite juridical relationship exists between the state and an individual vessel-user. The purpose of this chapter is precisely to explore such relationships and their consequences in terms of state responsibility for vessel-source pollution.

It is to be reiterated that the concern here is to define the rules of responsibility for vessel conduct without reference to the juridical zone within which such conduct occurs. As subsequent chapters will explore, the rules of decision governing responsibility for a specific event clearly will reflect the factor of location. The objective here, however, is simply to consider the preliminary issue of the source and character of state responsibility for vessels in any region.

[1] The term 'vessel' here refers to 'every description of watercraft or other artificial contrivance used as a means of transportation on or through water.' See the US Deepwater Port Act of 1974, § 3(19), 88 Stat. 2126, 33 USC § 1502(19). See variations on this definition described in Reporters' Notes to Sect. 501, 1982 Draft Rest., *supra* ch. 9 n. 4, at 61.

[2] See Abecassis, 'The Law and Practice relating to Oil Pollution from Ships', Ph.D. diss., Cambridge Univ. (1978); Burmester, 'Vessel-source Pollution: The Integration of International and Domestic Responses in the Search for an Effective Legal Framework', *Oceans Policy Study* 1:6, Center for Oceans Law and Policy, Univ. of Virginia (1978); Cowell, 'Oil Pollution of the Sea', in *Marine Pollution* 353, at 354 (Johnston ed. 1976). As to the distinction between 'dumping' and other forms of vessel discharge, see Convention on the Prevention of Marine Pollution by Dumping of Wastes and Other Matters, *supra* ch. 5 n. 44.

[3] See generally Meyers, *The Nationality of Ships*, 15–23 (1967).

[4] *See* ch. 3 generally.

B. JURISDICTION OVER VESSEL CONDUCT

i. Attribution of nationality

The national identity of non-government vessels, as distinct from the nationality of the ship-users, developed only at the close of the eighteenth century.[5] Problems of definition in the contexts of neutrality and interstate commercial relations served as catalysts to the evolution of the notion of the connection or allegiance of every vessel to a single, identified flag.[6] Through much of the nineteenth century the definitions of such nationality were expressed simply in bilateral agreements between states.[7] Based on the pattern of such agreements and the increasing demands of public order, three basic customary principles eventually emerged: (*a*) ships may bear the nationality of only a single state at any time;[8] (*b*) vessels without nationality ('stateless vessels') do not enjoy the benefits or protections of any state's right to freedom of the seas, and thus may be subjected to the laws of or interference by any state;[9] and (*c*) in its discretion, '[e]ach State shall fix the conditions for the grant of its nationality to ships, for the registration of ships in its territory, and for the right to fly its flag.'[10]

State practice with respect to the prerequisites for 'flag' status tends to fall within three categories.[11] At one extreme are the few states that require exclusively national contacts, with owners, master, officers, and crew limited to the state's nationals.[12] The vast majority of states have adopted less stringent conditions, demanding that the vessel be owned or manned by specified percentages of nationals.[13] The United States, for example, requires the owners to be citizens (or a corporation controlled by citizens), and all

[5] Boczek, *Flags of Convenience* 94 (1962).

[6] *Id.*

[7] *Id.*, at 95–9; Rienow, *The Test of the Nationality of a Merchant Vessel* 19–21 (1937).

[8] Meyers, *supra* n. 3, at 171–9; 1982 Draft Rest., *supra* ch. 9 n. 4, § 501, Comment (*d*); LOS Convention, *supra* ch. 5 n. 17, art. 92(1). The view expressed in *Arakas Bros.* v. *Bulgaria* remains true today: 'L'opinion unanime des auteurs reconnait que tout vaisseau doit avoir une nationalité et une seule nationalité.' 7 *Trib. Arb. Mixtes* 42 (1926).

[9] See *Molvan* v. *Attn. Gen. for Palestine* [1948] AC 351, 369–70. See also Boczek, *supra* n. 5, at 92; Meyers, *supra* n. 3, at 309–23; Singh, ch. 4 n. 55, at 2.

[10] High Seas Convention, *supra* ch. 6 n. 2, art. 5(1). See also LOS Convention, *supra* ch. 5 n. 17, art. 91(1); the *Muscat Dhows* Case, Hague Ct. Rep. (Scott) 95 (1916); *Lauritzen* v. *Larsen*, 345 US 571, at 584 (1953); Boczek, *supra* n. 5, at 93, 100–1; Rienow, *supra* n. 7, at 17–18; Singh, *supra* ch. 4 n. 55, at 24.

[11] See generally Laws on Nationality of Ships, 5 UN Leg. Ser., ST/LEG/SER. B/5 (1955), UN Publ. 56. v. 11, and Supplement, 8 UN Leg. Ser. 113–34, UN Publ. 59. v. 2. (hereinafter cited as Nationality Laws).

[12] See description of the 'Nationality School' in Singh, *supra* ch. 4 n. 55, at 17–18 and the 'Closed Registration' approach in Tache, 'The Nationality of Ships: The Definitional Controversy and Enforcement of Genuine Link', 16 *Int'l Law* 301 (1982). See also 1982 Draft Rest., *supra* ch. 9 n. 4, at § 501, Rpt. n. 4; Myers, *supra* n. 3, at 262.

[13] 1982 Draft Rest., *supra* ch. 9 n. 4, at § 501, Rpt. n. 4; Singh, *supra* ch. 4 n. 55, at 19–21; Tache, *supra* n. 13, at 303. See e.g. Argentina, Denmark, and Germany in Nationality Laws, *supra* n. 11.

officers and 75 per cent of the crew to be citizens.[14] Ethiopia, embracing a less rigorous version of the same approach, demands only 35 per cent ownership and a principal business office in the state.[15] Finally, at the other end of the spectrum is the approach of the so-called 'flags of convenience'. Such states impose limited or no requirements of nationals' participation in ownership or manning; the principal condition to the attribution of nationality is compliance with the procedures of registration and the payment of fees.[16]

The practices of such 'open registration' or flag of convenience states, which generally commenced following World War II, have been extremely controversial.[17] The principal juridical response has been the qualification of the acknowledged right of each state to fix conditions to vessel nationality with the requirement, expressed in both the 1958 High Seas Convention and the 1982 LOS Convention, that '[t]here must exist a genuine link between the State and the ship.'[18] Although an analysis of the 'genuine link' concept is beyond the scope of this work, two points should be noted. First, McDougal and others have aggressively criticized the 'genuine link' doctrine as introducing uncertainty into an area of state relations in which certainty, which existed with the earlier rule of conclusive state attribution of nationality, is of paramount importance.[19] Second, following the 'genuine link' language in the 1958 text appears the statement that 'in particular, the state must effectively exercise its jurisdiction and control in administrative, technical and social matters over ships flying its flag.'[20] There is continuing confusion in the literature as to whether this language represents a clarification of the *meaning* of the 'genuine link' principle or simply a statement of its *purpose* or objective, which presumably can only be achieved in the presence of an (as yet undefined) 'genuine link'.[21] In any event, the duty and correlative right to

[14] 46 USC §§ 11, 802, 883–1. See Norris, i *The Law of Seamen* 160 (3rd edn. 1970).

[15] Maritime Procl. no. 137 of 25 Sept. 1953, reprinted in Nationality Laws, *supra* n. 11, at 47.

[16] See e.g. Liberian Maritime Code of 12 Dec. 1948, as amended 22 Dec. 1949, 22 *Liber. Code of Laws* 51 (1973). See 1982 Draft Rest., *supra* ch. 9 n. 4, § 501, Rpt. n. 5; Singh, ch. 4 n. 55, at 18–19; Tache, *supra* n. 13, at 305.

[17] See generally Boczek, *supra* n. 5, at 9–63; Naess, *The Great Panlibhon Controversy* (1972); Osieke, 'Flags of Convenience Vessels: Recent Developments', 73 *Am. J. Int'l L.* 604 (1979). 1982 Draft Rest., *supra* ch. 9 n. 4, § 501, Rpt. n. 5. The ICJ's IMCO case raised an opportunity to address, but did not address, the propriety of such practices. Constitution of the Maritime Safety Committee of the Inter-Governmental Maritime Consultative Organization, [1970] ICJ 159 (Advisory Opinion of 8 June 1960). See Boczek, *supra* n. 5, at 125–55; Meyers, *supra* n. 3, at 227.

[18] High Seas Convention, *supra* ch. 6 n. 2, art 5; LOS Convention, *supra* ch. 5 n. 17, art. 91(1). For a discussion of the generation of this language, see Meyers, *supra* n. 3, at 197 ff.

[19] See McDougal, Burke and Vlasic, 'The Maintenance of Public Order at Sea and the Nationality of Ships', 54 *Am J. Int'l L.* 25.

[20] High Seas Convention, *supra* ch. 6 n. 2, art 5(1). See also Meyer, *supra* n. 3, at 214 for discussion of the evolution of this language.

[21] The clearest expression of the perspective that 'genuine link' requires only performance of the duty to exercise control is in Boczek, *supra* n. 5, at 260–78. See also Tache, *supra* n. 12, at 309. The view that a genuine link does not exist in the absence of specified means to achieve this objective, focusing on criteria such as national ownership and manning and the economic relationship to the state, is apparent in UNCTAD Working Group on the Economic

exercise authority is a central consequence of a state's attribution of its nationality to a vessel. The extent of such flag state authority will now be considered. The character and consequences of the obligation to exercise such authority in an environmental context will be treated later in the chapter.

ii. Flag State Jurisdiction

The legal authority of a state with respect to its flag vessels should be considered from two perspectives, reflecting the fact that vessels have a dual nature. A ship is both a moveable chattel or instrumentality which may be the subject of a jurisdictional exercise, and a jurisdictional *locus* of human conduct. The flag state's authority over the vessel as property may be accurately described as plenary. The state may by prescription and enforcement totally control the physical condition, movement, and operations of flag vessels.[22] Hence, a flag state may prescribe construction, design, equipment, and manning standards to be met by all vessels under its registration.[23] Similarly, the state may prohibit the uses of flag vessels for navigation into proscribed regions or trade with designated states.[24] Finally, in times of national need, flag vessels, regardless of the national identity of the ownership, may be subjected to requisition by the state.[25]

Conduct within the locus defined by the physical limits of a vessel is subject to an order of jurisdiction of the flag state best described as 'quasi-territorial'. Early expressions of the character and basis of such authority sought refuge in the fictional assimilation of vessels to the regime of state territory: 'A ship which bears a nation's flag is to be treated as a part of the territory of that

Consequences of the Existence or Lack of a Genuine Link between Vessels and Flag of Registry, UNCTAD Doc. TD/B/C.4/177 Annex p. 1 (1978) and 1982 Draft Rest., *supra* ch. 9 n. 4, § 501, Rpt. n. 5. Meyers adopts something of a hybrid approach by broadening the inquiry to the general capacity of the state to accomplish the control objective: 'There exists a sufficient "genuine" link when the accessibility of the ship-users or their goods to adequately equipped officials is such that the necessary authority can exist, that the necessary control can be exercised.' Meyers, *supra* n. 3, at 252. He can conclude, therefore, that a genuine link may exist even if *no* ship-users are nationals. *Id.*, at 275. The LOS Convention further supports the independent role of the genuine link standard; unlike the High Seas Convention, the genuine link reference is separate (art. 91) from the 'effective control' language, which appears as one of the 'Duties of the Flag State' (art. 94). Further unresolved issues relate to whether non-recognition of the attribution of nationality is the consequence of an insufficient 'genuine link'. See Boczek, *supra* n. 5, at 278, 284; Brownlie, *supra* ch. 9 n. 3, at 425; Meyers, *supra* n. 3, at 292; 1982 Draft Rest., *supra* ch. 9 n. 4, at § 501, Rpt. n. 6.

[22] For examples of the breadth of such authority see Chorley and Giles, *Shipping Law* 57–303 (7th edn., Giles ed. 1979); Gilmore and Black, *The Law of Admiralty* 986–90 (2nd edn. 1975).

[23] See e.g. US, Oil Pollution Act of 1961, as amended, 33 USC § 1004(*a*); UK, The Prevention of Oil Pollution Act, 1971, c. 60, sec. 4.

[24] See generally Boczek, *supra* n. 5, at 193; McDougal, Burke, and Vlasic, *supra* n. 19, at 63; Rienow, *supra* n. 7, at 4; Singh, *supra* ch. 4 n. 55, at 46.

[25] See Boczek, *supra* n. 5, at 195; McNair, 'Problems Connected with the Position of the Merchant Vessel in Private International Law, with Particular Reference to the Power of Requisition', 31 *Trans. Grotius Soc.* 30 (1946); Rienow, *supra* n. 7, at 100–4.

nation. A ship is a kind of floating island.'[26] Assimilation as the theoretical basis for jurisdiction over conduct on board flag vessels, however, has been long discarded. Rather, the accepted supporting rationale for flag state jurisdiction over the locus of the vessel is simply the consensus among states that it is necessary to ensure public order.[27] Judge Finlay's dissent in the *Lotus* Case made the point most articulately: 'The jurisdiction over crimes committed on a ship at sea is not of a territorial nature at all. It depends upon the law which for convenience and by common consent is applied to the case of chattels of such a very special nature as ships.'[28]

Territoriality remains, on the other hand, a most apt metaphor for describing the character, not the basis, of flag state jurisdiction. The legal authority of a state with respect to persons, property, and conduct on board vessels of its nationality is indeed tantamount to that enjoyed within the borders of state territory.[29] The 1982 Draft Restatement summarizes: 'The flag State may exercise jurisdiction to prescribe, to adjudicate and to enforce with respect to any conduct that takes place on a ship or that affects the ship.'[30] The annotation to this provision explains that '[t]he flag State may thus apply its laws to such events as a birth of a child, marriage, will or contract made, or crime committed, aboard ship.'[31] This is, of course, not merely a right of prescription. The flag state, acting through the master or others wielding a measure of public authority, may take action, including confinement or other disciplinary measures, to enforce the laws of the state.[32] Moreover, as in state territory, the prescriptive and enforcement authority of the flag state extends in blanket fashion to all matters on board its vessels, without regard to the nationality of persons or the ownership of property.[33]

[26] *Q.* v. *Anderson,* LR 1 CCR 161, quoted in *Patterson* v. *The Eudora,* 190 US 169 (1903). See also the majority opinion in the *SS Lotus* Case (*France* v. *Turkey*), [1927] PCIJ ser. A., no. 10.

[27] See generally *Chung Chi Cheung* v. *King*, [1939] AC 160; *Cunard Co. Ltd.* v. *Mellon*, 262 US 100, 123 (1922); *Scharenberg* v *Dollar Steamship Co.*, 245 US 122, at 127 (1917); Harvard Research–Jurisdiction, *supra* ch. 9 n. 11, at 509, O'Connell, *supra* Introd. n. 1 vol. ii, at 660; 1982 Draft Rest., *supra* ch. 9 n. 4, § 502, Rpt. n. 4.

[28] The *SS Lotus* Case (*France* v. *Turkey*), [1927] PCIJ Ser A., no. 10, at 53.

[29] *Cunard Co. Ltd.* v. *Mellon*, *supra* n. 27, at 123; Caflisch, 'Some Aspects of Oil Pollution from Merchant Ships', 4 *Annals of Int'l Studies* 213, at 219 (1974); Harvard Research–Jurisdiction, *supra* ch. 9 n. 11, at 509; McDougal, Burke, and Vlasic, *supra* n. 19, *passim*; Oppenheim, *supra* ch. 2 n. 37, at 597; Schwarzenberger and Brown, *supra* ch. 5 n. 105, at 75; Singh, *supra* ch. 4 n. 55, at 25.

[30] 1982 Draft Rest., *supra* ch. 9 n. 4, § 502(2). Note that an exception has been carved out following the *SS Lotus* for the application of objective territoriality in the context of collisions. *Id.*, at 75; Harvard Research–Jurisdiction, *supra* ch. 9 n. 11, at 518; High Seas Convention, *supra* ch. 6 n. 2, art. 11; LOS Convention, *supra* ch. 5 n. 17, art. 97; Brussels Convention for the Unification of Certain Rules relating to Penal Jurisdiction in Matters of Collisions or Other Incidents of Navigation, 439 UNTS 233 (1952).

[31] 1982 Draft Rest., *supra* ch. 9 n. 4 § 502, Rpt. n. 4. As to births, see Singh, *supra* ch. 4 n. 55, at 26; as to marriage, see *Fisher* v. *Fisher*, 165 NE 460 (NY Ct. App. 1929).

[32] See e.g. UK Merchant Shipping Act, 1970 c. 79. See generally Chorley and Giles, *supra* n. 12, at 90; Meyers, *supra* n. 3, at 277; Norris, *supra* n. 14, at 420, 575.

[33] Clark, 'Criminal Jurisdiction over Merchant Vessels engaged in International Trade', 11 *J.*

Finally, this expansive, 'quasi-territorial' authority of the flag state is not diminished by the presence of the vessel within the juridical zone of another state; although it may be concurrent with that of the coastal state, the prescriptive and enforcement jurisdiction of the flag on board the vessel remains intact in any location.[34]

iii. Jurisdiction of Other States

Spatial authority over a vessel, considered without reference to the region in which the vessel is located at the time, is vested exclusively in the flag state.[35] Conduct on board is nevertheless subject to the same types of concurrent, non-spatial jurisdiction of other states operative with respect to conduct within the flag state's territory.[36] The basis of such jurisdiction of particular significance in the context of vessels is the national allegiance of the ship-users.[37] As noted above, most states do not require beneficial ownership of a vessel to be solely in the hands of flag state nationals, and no state limits *all* ship-users, including owners, operators, officers, crew, passengers, and shippers, to nationals. A host of persons with an interest in or acting upon a vessel may then be foreign to the flag of the vessel, and therefore subject to the reach of the prescriptions of other states of nationality. The particular significance of such personal, nationality-based jurisdiction over the owners of the vessel has been identified by the Reporters of the Draft Restatement. '[W]hen a vessel is owned, directly or indirectly, by persons not nationals of the flag State, the state of nationality of the owners has no jurisdiction over the vessel but may affect the vessel by virtue of its jurisdiction to prescribe law in respect of the owner.'[38] Each state would seem to possess the authority, then,

Marit. L. & Comm. 219 (1980); Harvard Research–Jurisdiction, *supra* ch. 9 n. 11, at 542; Singh, *supra* ch. 4 n. 55, at 39.

[34] Brownlie, *supra* ch. 2 n. 52, at 316; Harvard Research–Jurisdiction, *supra* ch. 9 n. 11, at 511–14; Sack, 'The Doctrine of Quasi-territoriality of Vessels and the Admiralty Jurisdiction over Crimes Committed on Board National Vessels in Foreign Ports, 12 *NYU* L. Q. *Rev.* 628 (1934–5), and 13 *NYU* L. Q. *Rev.* 43 (1935–6). See *United States* v. *Flores*, 289 US 137 (1933); *R.* v. *Carr and Wilson*, 10 QBD 76 (1882). Issues of concurrency will be discussed in each of the remaining chapters. Note that an important qualification to enforcement authority does apply when the vessel is within the waters of another state: no enforcement measures may be taken against the vessel or persons on board by government authorities of the flag state outside the vessel. Hence, a government vessel may not arrest a flag vessel within the juridical zone of another state. See Meyers, *supra* n. 3, at 121; text at ch. 9 n. 56 *supra*.

[35] US legislative initiatives do assert spatial authority over vessels owned by US nationals. 18 USC § 7 (1) and (5). This view, however, is inconsistent with other state practice. Rienow, *supra* n. 7, at 193–213. Moreover, the US has never asserted jurisdiction in a specific case based on this position. 1982 Draft Rest., *supra* ch. 9 n. 4, § 502, Rpt. n. 5. See also O'Connell, *supra* Introd. n. 1, at 667.

[36] See the *SS Lotus*, (*France* v. *Turkey*), [1927] PCIJ Ser. A., no. 10, at 25; Verzijl, supra ch. 5 n. 12, at 90.

[37] Although not of equal practical significance, the conclusions reached here regarding nationality-based jurisidiction over conduct on board vessels could be applied equally to assertions of jurisdiction over such conduct based on other non-spatial principles, i.e. protective, passive personality, and universality.

[38] 1982 Draft Rest., *supra* ch. 9 n. 4, § 502, Rpt. n. 7.

to direct its nationals to maintain or operate vessels in which they hold an ownership or operational interest, in a fashion consistent with standards prescribed by the state.[39] Indeed, even the most extreme exercise of authority and control, state requisition, has been identified by most commentators as within the competence of the state of the vessel's owners (albeit subject to the flag state's pre-eminent right of requisition).[40]

Notably, not only owners and operators who may administer vessels from the shore of their home state are touched by the jurisdiction of the state of personal nationality. It will be recalled that the prescriptions of a state may extend to nationals' conduct in any region, including the territory of a foreign state.[41] The conduct of individuals on board a foreign flag vessel, i.e. within only the *quasi*-territorial jurisdiction of the foreign state, is certainly no less subject to the reach of state prescriptive authority.[42] Ship-users, in summary, do not escape the ambit of their national state laws by entering the precincts of a foreign flag vessel.[43]

As noted above, the authority to prescribe with respect to matters within the borders of a foreign state does not carry with it the authority to enforce in such regions. Enforcement in the territory of another state is not permitted in international law; each state's jurisdiction to enforce is dependent upon and limited to the state's territorial and extraterritorial zones of prescriptive competence.[44] Hence, enforcement of nationality-based prescriptions by measures on board or interfering with a foreign flag vessel is only tolerated in international law when the vessel happens to enter a spatially defined region of state authority. The definition of such regions and the rules governing the interaction of flag and coastal state jurisdiction will be treated in Chapters 11 through 13.

[39] As to labour standards, see *Grivas* v. *Alianza Compania Armadora SA*, 150 F. Supp. 708 (SD NY 1957). It is noteworthy that there seems to be no question that an owner's state of nationality has a right of protection in international forums. See Boczek, *supra* n. 5, at 228; Meyers, *supra* n. 3, at 90–107; Rienow, *supra* n. 7, at 104; Watts, 'The Protection of Merchant Ships', 33 *Brit. Yb. Int'l L.* 52 (1957), Boczek and Rienow conclude that this is subordinate to the flag state's right of protection in the event of any conflict.

[40] See Boczek, *supra* n. 5, at 190–205; Naess, *supra* n. 17, at 96; Rienow, *supra* n. 7, at 101–4; 1982 Draft Rest., *supra* ch. 9 n. 4, § 501, Rpt. n. 7. See US Act of June 29, 1936, as amended, § 902, 49 Stat. 2015 (1936), as amended, 53 Stat. 1255 (1939), 46 USC § 1242.

[41] See text at ch. 9 nn. 26–31 *supra*.

[42] See e.g. *United States* v. *Keller*, 451 F. Supp. 631 (D. Puerto Rico 1978); *R.* v. *Kelly and Others*, [1981] 1 WLR 112, *aff'd The Times*, 29 July 1981, at 24, col. 1., [1982] AC 665 The right of protection of nationals on board foreign vessels also appears intact. Consider the analogous case of aircraft and the recent claims of nationals' states in the Korean airlines incident. See Diplomatic Notes to the USSR from Canada, Japan, Thailand and the United States, reprinted in 22 *Int'l Legal Materials* 1190–8 (1983).

[43] In the airliner context Cheng argues that if a conflict arises between prescriptions, 'the following hierarchical order prevails: Territorial sovereignty, quasi-territorial sovereignty and personal sovereignty. In other words, if they clash, territorial sovereignty overrides the others, while quasi-territorial sovereignty overrides personal sovereignty.' Cheng, *supra* ch. 9 n. 5, at 183.

[44] See text at ch. 9 n. 66 *supra*.

C. FLAG STATE RESPONSIBILITY

Part I of this work demonstrated that a state's responsibility bears an intimate relationship to the state's legal authority.[45] It should be no surprise, therefore, to find that international law attaches a burden of responsibility to the attribution of vessel nationality. When a state assumes legal authority over a ship by grant of its flag, the state also assumes a certain obligation to take measures to ensure that the vessel, viewed both as an instrument of navigation and a collective of ship-users, acts in a fashion consistent with international law.[46] The flag state's international responsibility will arise out of a failure adequately to exercise its authority to prevent violative conduct.[47] The 'genuine link' formulation discussed above, defined either as a condition to the attribution of nationality or an independent, affirmative flag obligation, proceeds directly from this principle. If the flag state is to perform its international duties, it must possess and exercise 'effective jurisdiction and control' over its vessels.[48]

Part II pursued the thesis of the co-extensive character of authority and responsibility in an environmental context. It was concluded generally that each state has the obligation to prevent harm to the marine environment of the exclusive zone of any other state and of the high seas beyond any of such zones.[49] Moreover, it was demonstrated that this obligation, following general precepts, translates into a duty to exercise the full measure of the state's territorial and extraterritorial legal authority to accomplish such prevention.[50] It would seem logical to conclude, therefore, that each state must exercise the extensive jurisdiction enjoyed over flag vessels in pursuit of the state's general environmental obligations. This theoretical conclusion is borne out in the law.

The 1958 High Seas Convention expressed the customary legal obligation of states to ensure safety at sea by regulation of manning, construction, equipment, and seaworthiness of flag vessels.[51] The text further provides that all states are required to take measures to prevent oil pollution from ships and dumping of radioactive waste, taking account of international agreements on the subject.[52] Each of the multitude of multilateral treaties designed to

[45] See generally ch. 3 at nn. 141 ff.

[46] See generally Boczek, *supra* n. 5, at 284; Rienow, *supra* n. 7, at 104. The existence of such obligation alone, of course, does not necessarily imply attribution of the conduct of the vessel or its users to the state. See text at nn. 61–86 *infra*. As to the dual character see Singh, *supra* ch. 4 n. 55, at 37.

[47] Whether the state's exercise is adequate will depend on the applicable standard of performance. See text at nn. 87–110 *infra*. The rules subject to such transgression may relate specifically to the condition or conduct of vessels or more generally to the activities of the state or persons over which it possesses authority. An example of the former might be the violation of another state's exclusive fishery rights; the latter is illustrated by an act of aggression.

[48] See discussion in text at n. 20 *supra*.

[49] See ch. 5 and ch. 6.

[50] See ch. 8 at nn. 101–13.

[51] High Seas Convention, *supra* ch. 6 n. 2, art. 10. As to the customary status of the codifications, see the Preamble to the Convention.

[52] *Id.*, arts. 24 and 25.

prevent vessel-source pollution in one or more of its forms (operational discharge, accidental spillage, and dumping), imposes upon the flag state similar prescribed environmental duties.[53] The LOS Convention reflects this traditional allocation of pollution prevention obligations to the state of each vessel's nationality.[54] Article 211 provides: 'States shall adopt laws and regulations for the prevention, reduction and control of pollution of the marine environment from vessels flying their flag or of their registry.'[55] In addition to prescriptive efforts, '[f]lag States shall provide for the effective enforcement of such rules, standards, laws and regulations, irrespective of where a violation occurs.'[56] This same expansive view of flag state environmental duty is reflected in the Draft Restatement's conclusion as to the state of customary law: 'The flag state is obligated . . . to exercise effective authority and control over the ship in administrative, technical and labor matters . . . to take such measures as are necessary to ensure safety at sea, [and] to prevent, reduce and control pollution of the marine environment.'[57]

The evidence seems compelling, then, as to the existence of the obligation of flag states to exercise jurisdiction over their vessels to prevent marine pollution. It remains, however, to define the standard of performance of that obligation. In other words, under what circumstances is the preventive obligation breached and international responsibility triggered? As discussed at length in Part I, responsibility will only arise when the state is the actor committing the breach.[58] This may occur, in an environmental context, in either of two ways: a failure to prevent pollution arising out of the acts of the state itself; or a failure to exercise due diligence to prevent pollution arising out of the acts of private individuals.[59] The standards of performance pertaining to these two facets of the general preventive obligation of the state may differ markedly.[60] Hence, it is necessary first to consider the intriguing question: into which of these categories is the failure to prevent flag vessel polluting conduct properly placed?

[53] See e.g. 1954 Convention, *supra* ch. 6 n. 35, art. 2; 1973 Convention, *supra* ch. 6 n. 37, art. 7(1)(*a*); London Dumping Convention, *supra* ch. 5 n. 44, art. 3; Convention on Tanker Safety and Pollution of 1978, reprinted in 17 *Int'l Legal Materials* 546 (1978). See generally Abecassis, *supra* n. 2, at 34–93; Apollis, *L'Emprise maritime de l'état côtier* 222 (1981); Burmester, *supra* n. 2; de Yturriga, *supra* ch. 5 n. 1, at 244; Teclaff, ch. 6, n. 33, at 107.

[54] See generally Bernhardt, 'A Schematic Analysis of Vessel-source Pollution: Prescriptive and Enforcement Regimes in the Law of the Sea Conference', 20 *Va. J. Int'l L.* 265 (1980); Boyle, *supra* ch. 6 n. 51, at 363–4; Livingston, *supra* ch. 6 n. 30.

[55] LOS Convention, *supra* ch. 5 n. 17, art. 211(2); see also art. 94; High Seas Convention, *supra* ch. 6 n. 2, art. 10.

[56] LOS Convention, *supra* ch. 5 n. 17, art. 217(1). Flag states are not to permit vessels to proceed to sea unless CDEM standards are met, certificates of compliance issued, and periodic inspections conducted. *Id.*, art. 217(2), (3).

[57] 1982 Draft Rest., *supra* ch. 9 n. 4, § 502.

[58] Ch. 3. at nn. 1 ff.

[59] Ch. 3 at nn. 92 ff.

[60] Ch. 8 at n. 101.

i. State or Private Actor?

As noted in Part I, the starting point for determining whether conduct is to be attributed to the state is the state's own definition of the status of the actor. The decision to designate an individual as an agent or organ of the state in the municipal order conclusively renders the state the author of and responsible for the conduct of such actors.[61] It follows, then, that vessels viewed as exercising a component of governmental authority within the legal framework of the state will be so treated in international law for the purposes of the attribution of responsibility.[62] This conclusion applies equally to government ships performing commercial and non-commercial functions.[63] A distinction between these two types of functions exists in the regime of state immunities, where there is emerging consensus that government vessels employed in commerce do not enjoy the immunities afforded other organs of the state.[64] As underscored in Part I, however, state immunity and responsibility rest on different rationales, and consequently demand distinct sets of rules.[65] In summary, the conduct of government vessels of any type constitutes the conduct of the state for the purposes of responsibility.[66]

The fact that an actor possesses a legal identity distinct from that of the state under municipal law, on the other hand, does not end the inquiry. International law independently may define the actor as a representative of the state for the sole purpose of the attribution of conduct.[67] The rationale of this process, as noted in Part I, is that international law neither inhibits decentralization nor bestows a shield to state responsibility when a private actor acts on behalf of the decentralized state.[68] The test applied has been

[61] See ch. 3 at n. 10. Excluding, of course, conduct without a substantial connection to the public function of the actor. See ch. 3 at nn. 73–91.

[62] See Caflisch, *supra* n. 29, at 216; Oppenheim, *supra* ch. 2 n. 37, at 851.

[63] '[W]hen, for the purpose of advancing the trade of its people or providing revenue for its treasury, a government acquires, mans and operates ships in the carrying trade, they are public ships in the same sense that warships are.' *Berizzi Bros.* v. *SS Pesaro*, 271 US 562, 574 (1926). But see Comments of Ushakov, ILC, 1974 Sum. Rec., *supra* ch. 3 n. 11, at 25.

[64] See Bishop, 'New US Policy Limiting Sovereign Immunity', 47 *Am. J. Int'l L.* 93 (1953); Brownlie, *supra* ch. 2 n. 52, at 330; Hydeman and Berman, *supra* ch. 2 n. 80, at 264–71; Matsunami, *Immunity of State Ships* (1924); Sucharitkul, *State Immunities and Trading Activities in International Law* (1959); Thommen. *Legal Status of Government Merchant Ships in International Law* (1962); High Seas Convention, *supra* ch. 6 n. 2, arts. 8, 9; LOS Convention, *supra* ch. 5 n. 17, arts. 95, 96; US Foreign Sovereign Immunities Act of 1976, 28 USC §§ 1330, 1602–11 (1976); UK State Immunity Act of 1978, s. 3(1), c. 33; European Conv. on State Immunity, [1972] Europ. TS 74; ILC, 1983 Report to the General Assembly, 38 UN GAOR Supp. (no. 10), UN Doc. A/38/10 (1983), at 52, 75, Generally, states with centralized economies continue to embrace an absolutist perspective of immunity.

[65] See ch. 3 at nn. 58–9.

[66] Internal definitions of 'government' vessels are not always apparent. The vessel might be owned and controlled, for example, by a legally autonomous public body, funded and controlled by and benefiting the government. As the discussion to follow notes, to the extent the body is of a 'public' character or wields public authority, it may nevertheless constitute a component of government from an international perspective.

[67] See generally ch. 3 at nn. 36 ff.

[68] *Id.*

articulated in various fashions; commentators have generally focused either on the performance of functions of a 'public character' for the public benefit or the exercise of elements of public or governmental authority.[69] For several reasons, it may be argued cogently that even private vessels bearing the flag of a state satisfy this test and therefore might be treated as representatives of the state.

Vis-à-vis other states, vessels do exercise an element of the authority of their flag state. All rights pertaining to the use of the seas, e.g. the freedoms of the high seas and innocent passage through the territorial sea, are possessed exclusively by states,[70] Each state may grant private individuals the right to operate under and benefit from these sovereign rights by conferring nationality upon the ship-users' vessel. Every activity of a vessel upon the seas is conducted under the auspices and the protective mantle of such bestowed state authority.[71] A flag vessel is in this sense the representative or agent of the state: by grant of flag status, a state designates the vessels and ship-users through which it exercises and realizes the right to participate in the use of the seas. 'State responsibility may be engendered by the acts of any organ through which the state exercises the powers inherent in sovereignty.'[72] The conduct of flag vessels, acting in exercise of the international rights of the state, might, pursuant to this logic, be attributed to the state.[73]

This same result would follow from a conclusion that the activities of flag vessels are of such a 'public character', evidenced by the intensity of states' support of and involvement with their flag fleets, to be viewed as conduct on behalf of the state. The historical reason for the fact of state participation in the expansion of flag fleets is expressed by Singh:

> It was rooted in basic economic needs of the newly developing nations. The dependence for carriage of national trade in foreign flags involved not only a drain on the foreign exchange resources of the country, but vitally affected its ability to compete

[69] See ch. 3 at nn. 51–3 (collective institutions generally treated as state organ) and 64–72 (private individuals or entities so treated in a specific incident).

[70] See, as to the high seas, the High Seas Convention, *supra* ch. 6 n. 2, art. 2, and LOS Convention, *supra* ch. 5 n. 17, arts. 87 and 90. As to innocent passage in the territorial sea see Convention on the Territorial Sea and the Contiguous Zone, done at Geneva 29 Apr. 1958, entry into force 10 Sept. 1964, 15 UST 1606, TIAS no. 5639, 516 UNTS 205, art. 14, and LOS Convention, *supra* ch. 5 n. 17, art. 17. As to the conclusion that such rights are not vested in private individuals see *US* v. *Williams*, 589 F. 2d 210, 212 (5th Cir. 1979).

[71] Absent a flag, a 'stateless' vessel possesses no right to the 'freedoms' of the seas. See Meyers, *supra* n. 3, at 309, 320; Singh, *supra* ch. 4 n. 55, 21–35.

[72] Bouvé, *supra* ch. 3 n. 46, at 37.

[73] Note the analogy to individuals exercising the rights of the state to operate in outer space pursuant to state licensing. In this context, all operators are treated as state representatives for the purposes of responsibility. See Comments of Dr Blix, Colloquium, The Protection of the Environment and International Law, 1973, *Acad. Droit Int'l* Colloq. (1975) (hereinafter cited as 1973 Colloq.), at 507; Diederiks-Verschoor and Gormley, 'The Future Legal Status of Non-governmental Entities in Outer Space: Private Individuals and Companies as Subjects and Beneficiaries of International Space Law', 5 *J. Space L.* 125 (1977); Goldie, *supra* ch. 2 n. 92, at 1189.

in trade freely with all nations of the world, the terms of trade and the costs of the country's imports and exports. This is apart from the fact that the national merchant marine was legitimately regarded as the second line of defence even in the preservation of political independence.[74]

An American author recites the same economic and defence factors: 'Early in the history of this nation the value of our merchant marine was recognized as an instrument of trade during peace and as a vital adjunct of the Navy in time of war . . .'[75] The mere fact of such public benefit is not, of course, sufficient to define an activity as one of a 'public character', and the actor a state representative. As noted in Part I, however, the greater the degree of state involvement in an activity, the stronger the position that the activity itself is conducted on behalf of the state for the purposes of international responsibility.[76] The importance of commercial shipping has in fact resulted in an intimate relationship between states and their merchant fleets. Even the perspective that merchant shipping is so 'affected with a public interest' to require complete state ownership of the fleet has a long tradition.[77] Most of the commercial vessels of Venice, one of history's pre-eminent maritime states, for example, belonged to the state.[78] The United States, concerned that American trade was threatened by the absence of dependable carriage, elected in its recent past to establish a state commercial fleet—prior to privatization in the 1920s, the US government held the 'world's largest merchant fleet'.[79] Today, states with centralized economies, including the Soviet Union, continue strictly to adhere to this approach with the maintenance of state owned and operated merchant fleets.[80] Most states employ mechanisms other than exclusive ownership by government agency to achieve the public objective of a productive national commercial fleet. The devices engaged include partial state participation in ownership, direct and indirect subsidies, cargo preference and requirements, training and administration of a merchant marine, and, generally, regulation of the registration, movement, and conduct

[74] Singh, *supra* ch. 4 n. 55, at xi. See ch. 3 at n. 61.

[75] Norris, *supra* n. 14, at 594, The Merchant Marne Act of 1920 declares US policy: 'It is necessary for the national defense and for the proper growth of its foreign and domestic commerce that the United States shall have a merchant marine . . . sufficient to carry the greater portion of its commerce and serve as a naval or military auxiliary in time of war or national emergency, ultimately to be owned and operated privately by citizens of the United States . . .' (Sect. 1 of the Merchant Marine Act of 1920, 46 USC § 861 (1970).)

[76] See ch. 3 at n. 60.

[77] Gilmore and Black, *supra* n. 22 at 958. See also Matsunami, *supra* n. 64, at 11–22.

[78] Gilmore and Black, *supra* n. 22, at 960.

[79] US Dept. of Justice, The Regulated Ocean Shipping Industry (Jan. 1977) (hereinafter cited as Regulated Shipping), at 21; Gilmore and Black, *supra* n. 22, at 980–1. See US Shipping Act of 1916, c. 541, § 5–13, 39 Stat. 730–3.

[80] Guzhenko, 'Soviet Merchant Marine and World Shipping', 1 *Mar. Pol.* 102 (1977); Kwasniewski, 'Shipping Policy of the Comecon Countries', 1 *Marine Pol.* 110 (1977); US Congress, Senate Comm. on Commerce and National Ocean Policy, *Soviet Oceans Development*, 94th Cong., 2nd Sess., at 257, 331 (Comm. Print 1976).

of flag vessels.[81] Whatever the approach used, the common catalyst may be described as the perception that merchant fleets perform an essential societal function. Certain states have responded by maintaining the fleet within the machinery of government; others pursue a less direct tactic of support and control. The intensity of state involvement even in the latter species of practice suggests that a plausible case may be made that merchant shipping is so infected with a 'public character' that flag vessels are, in concept, acting on the state's behalf.

The rationale identified above for the objective or international definition of state organs and representatives is that state responsibility should not be avoided or diminished by government decisions to delegate. Conversely, the centralization of public functions ought not to be penalized. If one accepts the public character of merchant shipping, therefore, equity supplies a subsidiary argument for the representative character of private flag vessels. A state which determines that public ownership is the best way to perform the public function of maritime trade should not be disadvantaged by the rules of vessel responsibility.[82]

Proceeding from such reasoning, one might conclude that the conduct of both government and private flag vessels is attributable to the state. This position does *not* find support, however, in current international opinion or practice.[83] The question of the 'representative' status of private flag vessels, in fact, rarely has been identified or addressed, Yet, those authors who have touched upon the issue do not hesitate to conclude that a distinction exists between government and private flag vessels for the purposes of the attribution of responsibility under customary law.[84] Moreover, as will be evident, analyses of the standard of state responsibility applicable to private flag vessels uniformily rest on the unstated assumption that such vessels are not state actors.[85] In short, international law presently defines only public flag vessels, i.e. those nominally operating on behalf of and as a part of the state government, as state organs or representatives for the purposes of respons-

[81] Gilmore and Black observe that peacetime direct participation in the US is politically, not theoretically, constrained; *supra* n. 22, at 969 n. 63. Note again the parallel to mixed public–private enterprises in outer space. See Christol, *supra* ch. 5 n. 52; Diederiks-Verschoor and Gormley, *supra* n. 73. As to subsidies see Jantscher, Bread Upon the Waters: Federal Aids to the Maritime Industries (1975); Regulated Shipping, *supra* n. 79; Gilmore and Black, *supra* n. 22, at 975. As to the Merchant Marine, see Chorley and Giles, *supra* n. 22, at 67; Gilmore and Black, *supra* n. 22, at 978.

[82] See Comments of Blix, 1973 Colloq., *supra* n. 73, at 507. NB this argument could extend to all functions performed by the state in centralized economies, but not in market economies, which meet the 'public character' test.

[83] Certain commentators advocating such responsibility have nevertheless identified it as *lex ferenda*. See Comments of Blix, 1973 Colloq., *supra* n. 73, 507; Hallman, *supra* ch. 5. n. 57, at 29.

[84] See Caflisch, *supra* n. 29, at 216–17; Comments of Blix, 1973 Colloq., *supra* n. 73, at 506–7; Meyers, *supra* n. 3, at 110. See also McNair, *supra* n. n. 25, at 50.

[85] See e.g. Handl, *supra* ch. 2 n. 82.

ibility.[86] Private vessels and their ship-users, on the other hand, constitute private actors within the jurisdiction of the flag state. The standards of environmental responsibility applicable to these two classes of actors may now be defined.

ii. Standard of Performance

The state, then, is juridically treated as the author of the environmental consequences of the conduct of public government vessels. As Part I discussed at length, the attribution to the state of a result which international law seeks to prevent does not necessarily yield responsibility. International law neither requires the additional element of fault nor denies that fault may be required for a conclusion of responsibility.[87] Rather, the existence of this condition depends on the content of the specific obligation. Chapter 8 determined that standard with respect to state environmental obligations. When a state fails to prevent its own organs or representatives from causing proscribed environmental injury, responsibility arises if the injury is the result of intent or negligence, related to 'ultrahazardous' conduct or, under the progressive formula suggested in the work of the ILC, particularly serious.[88] This general standard should govern the commission of an act of pollution by any vessel whose conduct is attributable to the state.

The test applicable to state responsibility for private flag vessels is somewhat more complex. Meyers presents the issue: 'Is the State in default with respect to its international obligations as soon as its [flag vessel] ship-users perform an act which international law wants to prevent? As far as private merchant vessels are concerned this is not the case. How far then does the said duty [to prevent] extend?'[89] The answer supplied by Meyers, together with other commentators on the subject, is 'due diligence'.[90] This conclusion is in fact required by and consistent with the general principle deduced in Part I that the state is generally obligated only to exercise due diligence to prevent private actors from engaging in violative conduct.[91] It was confirmed in Part II that this general standard operates with respect to the state's performance of its obligation to prevent marine environmental injury, provided that in certain circumstances the level of diligence due may be elevated.[92]

In terms of the minimum demands of due diligence, states will be responsible for a failure to exercise, in a reasonable and diligent fashion, their

[86] One caveat to this conclusion should be noted: even a vessel not generally defined as a state actor may be so defined for the purposes of a specific mission or for a limited purpose. See ch. 3 at nn. 64–70.

[87] See ch. 3 at n. 64.

[88] See ch. 8 at nn. 90 ff.

[89] Meyers, *supra* n. 3, at 110.

[90] See *id.*; Caflisch, *supra* n. 29, at 219.

[91] See ch. 7 at nn. 26 ff.

[92] See ch. 8 at nn. 111–12.

extensive jurisdiction over private flag vessels to prevent pollution. As noted above, both the 1958 High Seas Convention and the LOS Convention contain provisions codifying this customary requirement.[93] Each of these agreements provides further content to the abstract due diligence obligation by reference to specific anti-pollution requirements. The 1958 Convention requires regulations 'taking into account existing treaties'; the LOS Convention demands that 'laws and regulations shall at least have the same effect as that of generally accepted international rules and standards established through the competent international organization or general diplomatic conference.'[94] The precise prescriptive and enforcement measures required by the language of the two conventions are not certain.[95] Yet, it seems a safe conclusion that agreements with the breadth of participation and ratification of the 1954 Convention, the 1972 Dumping Convention, and perhaps the 1973 Convention now set forth minimum requirements of flag due diligence.[96] A failure to exercise such jurisdictional diligence over private flag vessels will constitute fault and support an assertion of flag state responsibility.

In Part I it was determined that the due diligence obligation as to private conduct may be elevated, depending on the content of the specific international obligation, to impose responsibility even in the absence of fault.[97] The discussion in Part II concluded that, with respect to private actors within state territory, a regime of strict responsibility operates to trigger responsibility for injuries from ultrahazardous sources or, in the ILC-inspired regime, of a serious character, regardless of state diligence.[98] To the extent the state enjoys extraterritorial authority over private conduct which bestows a capacity to control and prevent comparable to that enjoyed within its borders, the same regime of strict environmental responsibility applies.[99]

Does state legal authority over flag vessels satisfy this test? In general terms, flag state jurisdiction over conduct on board a vessel is indeed tantamount to territorial authority. The principal qualification to that assertion is the incapacity of the flag state to take enforcement actions against a vessel or a ship-user on board while the vessel is within the territorial waters of another state.[100] The ship-board authority of the master does remain intact in any location.[101] Moreover, once outside the zone of foreign territory a vessel is

[93] See ch. 9 at nn. 39, 41–3 *supra*.

[94] High Seas Convention, *supra* ch. 6 n. 2, art. 24; LOS Convention, *supra* ch. 5 n. 17, art. 211.

[95] As to the intent of the LOS Convention language see Kingham and McRae, 'Competent International Organizations and the Law of the Sea', 3 *Marine Pol'y* 106 (1976); Timagenis, *supra* ch. 5 n. 1, at 604–6. See also Frank, *supra* ch. 7 n. 43, at 73.

[96] See 1954 Convention, 1972 London Dumping Convention and 1973 Convention, *supra* n. 53. Teclaff argues specifically that the standards set forth in the widely accepted 1954 Convention were made universally obligatory through implicit incorporation in the 1958 Convention. See Teclaff, *supra* n. 53, at 109.

[97] See ch. 3 at nn. 136–40. See also ch. 8 at nn. 110–12.

[98] See ch. 8 at n. 106.

[99] See ch. 8 at n. 110.

[100] See text at n. 34 *supra*.

[101] See text at n. 34–6 *supra*.

subject to the plenary enforcement authority of the flag state. One might conclude, then, that the capacity of the flag state to prescribe and enforce preventive regulations does merit imposition of the strict responsibility regime. Although direct analyses in the literature are few and certain important qualifications must be noted, this theoretical conclusion is shared by most commentators.

It will be recalled that the progressive formulation of the ILC would impose strict responsibility for material injury arising out of any activity within the state's territory or control.[102] Certain members of the Commission did express reservations as to the application of the regime to such 'tenuously linked chattels' as flag vessels.[103] The Special Rapporteur, however, clearly stated the dominant perspective that 'within control' embraced any activity on board vessels of a state's nationality, and that the strict regime for serious injury did, therefore, apply.[104] A caveat was noted: when a vessel is within a zone of 'paramount' coastal state authority, the control of the flag state is sufficiently diminished no longer to merit a strict standard of responsibility.[105] The logic and application of this qualification with respect to the several zones of coastal authority will be examined below. Strong support for the general conclusion as to the applicability of the strict regime may be found in the literature of the 'ultrahazardous' activity doctrine. Several of the international conventions reflecting the principle of strict responsibility for ultrahazardous conduct are designed precisely to apply to vessels, e.g. the Convention on Liability of Operators of Nuclear Ships, the Convention on Liability for Oil Pollution Damage, and the Convention on Civil Liability for Damage Caused by the Transportation of Nuclear Materials on the High Seas.[106] Proponents of the ultrahazardous regime such as Jenks and Schneider have specifically identified its role with respect to vessel activities.[107] Even publicists generally resistant to the notion of strict liability, Ushakov and Handl, for example, have acknowledged the responsibility of

[102] See ch. 8 at n. 84.

[103] ILC, 1982 Report to the General Assembly, 37 UN GAOR Supp. (no. 10), at 196. Note that the concerns expressed related to the difficulty of maintaining the control assumed in the regime over matters on flag vessels. As subsequent chapters will demonstrate, the regime proposed for flag states in this work responds to this concern by distinguishing between types of injurious conduct on the basis of the flag's opportunity to exercise control over pre-existing, forseeable matters.

[104] Comments of Quentin-Baxter, ILC, 1981 Sum. Rec. *supra* ch. 4 n. 35; Q-B, 3rd Rpt., *supra* ch. 5 n. 72, at 19 and 24; Quentin-Baxter, Fifth Report on International Liability for Injurious Consequences Arising out of Acts Not Prohibited by International Law, UN Gen. Ass. Doc. A/CN. 4/383, 12 June 1984, at 6–7 (hereinafter cited as Q-B, 5th Rpt.).

[105] Q-B, 3rd Rpt., *supra* ch. 5 n. 72, at 19, 24.

[106] See ch. 8, at nn. 24, 29–35. The Liberian offer of compensation for the *Juliana* spill suggests an acknowledgement of such strict flag state responsibility. See Handl, *supra* ch. 2 n. 82, at 547.

[107] Jenks, *supra* ch. 5 n. 51, at 137–43; *supra* ch. 5 n. 36, at 279–80. See also Hallman, *supra* ch. 5 n. 57, at 30; Rest, 'Convention on Compensation for Transfrontier Environmental Injuries', Project of the Institute of International and Comparative Law of the Univ. of Cologne 51 (1976).

flag states for ultrahazardous vessel conduct.[108] Indeed, there is a strong theoretical basis for this conclusion. The test of adequate jurisdiction to control and prevent seems readily satisfied in this context. Ultrahazardous risks usually relate to the fundamental character and function of the vessel. To prevent injury it is not necessary that the flag state possess or exercise effective jurisdiction over the specific decisions or acts on board leading to an event of pollution arising out of such causes. Rather, the state may act originally to prevent the vessel from engaging in the ultrahazardous activity at all. The flag state may prohibit, for example, operation with nuclear power or carriage of radioactive materials or large quantities of oil. When a vessel does engage in such activities, the flag state's authorization, i.e. its decision not to use its capacity and authority to prevent by prohibition, may reasonably be inferred.

There exists one major qualification to the general conclusion that it is proper to apply the strict regime to private flag vessel conduct. As noted, Quentin-Baxter has cautioned that strict responsibility may not be appropriate in coastal zones in which flag authority is diminished. Later discussions in this work will conclude that remoteness from the state may similarly call into question the imposition of a strict standard.[109] The common concern in each case is that in certain circumstances reduced flag authority or capacity to control may deny the logic of strict responsibility for ultrahazardous or other seriously injurious conduct. The key to a decision with respect to strict responsibility, it is submitted, is the precise character of the cause of the injury. If the event arises out of pre-existing vessel conditions, characteristics or behaviour over which the flag possessed a meaningful prior opportunity to exercise control, the location of the event should not affect application of the strict test. On the other hand, responsibility for spontaneous conduct in regions of diminished flag capacity should be based on the lesser due diligence standard. This premise will be explored and applied in subsequent chapters.[110]

D. RESPONSIBILITY OF OTHER STATES

Part II above examined both the logic of and authority for the proposition that the obligation to prevent environmental injury is not merely co-extensive with the state's territorial or other spatial jurisdiction. Rather, the obligation demands that the state seek to prevent harm by exercising any species of legal authority possessed including extraterritorial authority. It was specifically concluded that each state may be responsible for failure to take measures pursuant to nationality-based jurisdiction to prevent harm to the marine

[108] See Comments of Ushakov, ILC, 1974 Sum. Rec.; Handl, *supra* ch. 2 n. 82, at 565 n. 179; Handl, *supra* ch. 8 n. 63, at 111–12. But see Caflisch, *supra* n. 29, at 217.

[109] See ch. 13 at nn. 178–81 *infra*.

[110] See ch. 11 at n. 67 and ch. 12 at nn. 131–44 *infra*.

environment.[111] The national allegiance of ship-users, as noted, frequently does not correspond to the flag of the vessel. Every state possesses certain legal authority over the conduct of its nationals as ship-users, regardless of the vessel's flag.[112] The general rules of environmental obligation dictate, therefore, that a failure to exercise jurisdiction over a state's nationals in an effort to prevent environmental injury may trigger responsibility.[113]

The legal authority of a state over its nationals acting beyond the borders of the state is not, of course, of the same order as territorial authority. Only the state's prescriptions reach out to touch a national on board a foreign flag vessel; enforcement measures may not be taken within the precincts of another state's vessel.[114] The standard of performance of the environmental obligation applicable to the extraterritorial conduct of nationals, therefore, ought not to be as stringent as that applied to flag states. The general test of 'due diligence' is applicable to both states as the standard operative in all circumstances with respect to private individuals over whom the state possesses jurisdiction. Elevation to a strict responsibility standard is not proper where, as in the case of nationals' conduct on foreign ships, the state's authority and capacity to control is far less effective than that enjoyed over territorial matters.[115] Ship-users' states thus will bear responsibility only for failure to act with due diligence, in the traditional sense, to prevent nationals from engaging in conduct injurious to the environment. A failure even to enact relevant prescriptions with respect to such conduct would seem to constitute a failure of diligence. Similarly, a failure to take any or adequate, based on the higher of international minimum standards or the state's specific capabilities, enforcement measures, including punishment, should constitute a breach of obligation.[116]

The consequences of nationality-based responsibility would depend on two factors: the causal relationship between the breach of the injury; and the character of the flag state's breach. As to the former, it has been noted that the obligation to pay reparation for material injury generally will not arise in the absence of causation.[117] The other obligations which flow from respons-

[111] See ch. 5 at nn. 63–4. See also ch. 3 at nn. 149–50.

[112] See text at nn. 37–44 *supra*.

[113] See e.g. Singh, *supra* ch. 4 n. 55, at 37; Hallman, *supra* ch. 5 n. 57, at 30. Watts in fact concludes that the state of national ownership, as distinct from the flag state, is principally responsible for vessel conduct. Watts, *supra* n. 39. But see Brownlie, *System*, supra ch. 1 n. 2, at 165.

[114] See ch. 9 nn. 67–76 and n. 34 *supra*.

[115] See ch. 8 at n. 110. Note that although the ILC refers to strict liability for nationals, it only is applicable when the national is beyond the territorial jurisdiction of any other state. Since individuals are always within some state's territorial or quasi-territorial jurisdiction, on land or at sea, the point appears to have been made to emphasize the existence of a strict regime as to private conduct.

[116] As to the meaning of the 'due diligence' standard generally see ch. 3 at n. 122.

[117] See ch. 4 at n. 11. This conclusion is complicated by the debate over the nature of the obligation to compensate in the event of a failure to punish. See ch. 3 at n. 115.

ibility, cessation of the violative conduct and provision of appropriate satisfaction for the moral or political injury attendant to every breach of duty, do not require a causal link between the failure of due diligence and the environmental injury.[118] These duties will arise in every case in which a state fails to perform the duty to exercise due diligence over ship-users of its nationality, regardless of the existence of concurrent flag state responsibility.[119]

If, on the other hand, the obligation to compensate arises based on the existence of causation, the consequential duties of the nationality state will depend on the character of the concurrent responsibility of the flag state.[120] In this circumstance, the principles of multiple state responsbility discussed in Chapter 4 would apply. The apportionment of the burden of compensation between the flag state and any other responsible state would be based upon relative causation and blameworthiness.[121] As noted, a dominant factor in such a determination is the character of the legal authority possessed by the respective states over the injurious conduct.[122] The greater capacity of the flag state to control conduct on board a vessel generally would attract to it the dominant burden of compensatory responsibility. If, however, it were demonstrated that the due diligence of another state could have controlled the causal conduct more effectively, the burden logically would shift. Nor is it difficult to envisage such a result. Assume the existence of flag state *A*, with limited resources, administrative capacity, and contacts with the vessel's ship-users,[123] and state *B*, whose nationals own and operate the vessel, within whose territory such individuals and their assets reside, and which possesses effective administrative machinery. If injury follows from the vessel's lack of reasonable equipment or design safety features, it is certainly plausible to conclude that as between states *A* and *B*, each responsible for a failure to require such features, it is state *B* that enjoyed the more effective authority and control, and, therefore, ought to bear the greater burden of compensation.[124]

[118] See ch. 3 at nn. 119 and 19–24.

[119] See ch. 3 at n. 303.

[120] The same conclusion applies, of course, if the duty to compensate arises out of a failure to punish or if other ship-users' states of nationality have contributed causally.

[121] See ch. 4 at nn. 109 ff. As to whether this apportionment determines the obligations of a breaching state (*a*) to the claimant state or (*b*) to other breaching states in a regime of joint and several liability with an attendant right of contribution, see ch. 4 at nn. 102–8.

[122] See ch. 4 at nn. 114–15.

[123] This description, of course, applies to the so-called 'flag of convenience' states. One author has asserted that such states have 'neither the power nor the administrative machinery effectively to impose any government or international regulations.' Lowe, 'The Enforcement of Marine Pollution Regulations', 12 *San Diego L. Rev*. 624, at 633 (1975). The problems associated with flag of convenience lack of will and capacity have been well chronicled. See Apollis, *supra* n. 53, at 225–8; Boczek, *supra* n. 5, at 261 ff.; Burmester, *supra* n. 2, at 3; Fleischer, 'Pollution from Seaborne Sources', iii *New Directions in the Law of the Sea* 78, at 83–4 (Churchill, Simmonds, and Welsh eds. 1973); Hallman, *supra* ch. 5 n. 85, at 57; OCED Study on Flags of Convenience in Maritime Transport, reprinted in 4 *J. Marit. L. & Comm*. 231 (1972); Osieke, *supra* n. 17, at 604.

[124] This same conclusion might be reached even if the responsibility of state *A* is based on a

Apportionment is, in summary, fact-specific: the greater the opportunity and capacity to exercise jurisdiction to prevent an injury, the greater the share of pecuniary responsibility for the injury.

An outline has now been presented of the rules governing responsibility for vessel-source environmental injury without regard to the juridical zone within which the injurious conduct occurs. It is appropriate to turn to the definition of authority and the consequential rules of responsibility with respect to the zones of coastal state authority over the seas. The relationship between the vessel rules set forth and the jurisdiction and responsibility of coastal states will be discussed in each of the remaining chapters.

strict regime—without inquiry into due diligence. Although state *A*'s responsibility is thus strictly established, the burden of compensation is logically apportioned to another state if the latter state's breach bears a closer causal link to the injury or is more blameworthy.

11

Internal Waters

A. DEFINITION

The 1958 Convention on the Territorial Sea and the Contiguous Zone and the 1982 LOS Convention recite the same definition: 'waters on the landward side of the baseline of the territorial sea form part of the internal waters of the State.'[1] The applicable baseline is defined generally by the 'low-water mark along the coast' of the state.[2] Material areas of the sea may be embraced within a state's internal waters based on certain subsidiary rules: (*a*) where a coast is deeply indented or closely fringed with islands straight enclosing baselines may be drawn; (*b*) bays of prescribed characteristics and mouths of rivers may be incorporated into internal waters within permitted straight baselines; and (*c*) ports, within lines drawn from 'outermost permanent harbour works', are defined as internal.[3] In short, internal waters constitute those regions of the sea most intimate, in a physical and functional sense, with the land territory of the state. The relationship is sufficiently intimate for international law to assimilate the zone of internal waters to the regime of land territory.[4]

B. PRESCRIPTIVE AUTHORITY

As a component of state territory, internal waters are subject to the maximum prescriptive legal authority possessed by the state. Conduct within such waters may be permitted or prohibited in the sole discretion of the coastal state.[5]

[1] Territorial Sea Convention, *supra* ch. 10 n. 70, art. 5; LOS Convention, *supra* ch. 5 n. 17.art. 8

[2] Territorial Sea Convention, *supra* ch. 10 n. 70, art. 3; LOS Convention, *supra* ch. 5 n. 17, art. 5.

[3] As to straight baselines see Territorial Sea Convention, *supra* ch. 10 n. 70, art. 4; LOS Convention, *supra* ch. 5 n. 17, art. 7; *Anglo-Norwegian Fisheries* Case (*UK* v. *Norway*), [1951] ICJ 116. The subtle technical and detailed questions relating to the effect of these is beyond the scope of this work. As to bays, see Territorial Sea Convention, *supra* ch. 10 n. 70, art. 7; LOS Convention, *supra* ch. 5 n. 17, arts 9 and 10. As to ports, Territorial Sea Convention, *supra* ch. 10 n. 70, art. 8; LOS Convention, *supra* ch. 5 n. 17, art. 11. See generally Brownlie, *supra* ch. 2 n. 52, at 186–91; McDougal and Burke, *supra* ch. 6 n. 4, at 305–437; 1982 Draft Rest., *supra* ch. 9 n. 4, § 511 Comments (*c*)–(*g*) and Rpts. n. 2.

[4] See Brierly, *supra* ch. 2 n. 41, at 194–5; Brownlie, *supra* ch. 3 n. 52, at 122; McDougal and Burke, *supra* ch. 6 n. 4, at 89.

[5] See e.g. Brierly, *supra* ch. 2 n. 41, at 225; Fitzmaurice, 'Some Results of the Geneva Conference on the Law of the Sea', 8 *Int'l & Comp. L.Q.* 72, at 105 (1959); Oppenheim, *supra* ch. 9 n. 49, at 503. Note, however, that there is consensus since the 1958 Geneva Conventions that a

Such territorial jurisdiction will specifically support legislation establishing any rules or standards the state deems appropriate to protect the environment.[6] Indeed, states have proscribed activities detrimental to the quality of internal waters for centuries.[7] There are numerous current examples of coastal state exercise of such competence to forbid discharge of pollutants or require preventive construction, design, equipment, or manning (CDEM) features for vessels in internal waters.[8] Such territorial jurisdiction also may be exercised in its 'subjective' form to regulate conduct within internal waters in order to protect the environment beyond such waters.[9] Hence, many states perform the duties set forth in international anti-dumping conventions by prohibiting ships from loading wastes in internal waters for deposit elsewhere.[10] In short, the right of the coastal state to prescribe environmental standards with respect to conduct and matters within internal waters is expansive.[11]

The majority view as to the force of coastal prescriptions *vis-à-vis* foreign vessels in internal waters is succinctly stated by the US Supreme Court:

> A merchant ship of one country, voluntarily entering the territorial limits of another, subjects herself to the jurisdiction of the latter. The jurisdiction attaches in virtue of her presence, just as with objects within those limits. During her stay she is entitled to the protection of the laws of that place, and, correlatively, is bound to yield obedience to them.[12]

right of 'innocent passage' exists in those areas which became internal waters only after the drawing of straight baselines authorized by the Territorial Sea Convention. See Territorial Sea Convention, *supra* ch. 10 n. 70, art. 5(2); McDougal and Burke, *supra* ch. 6 n. 4, at 120–5; discussion of innocent passage in context of the territorial sea *infra*.

[6] See Caflisch, *supra* ch. 10 n. 29, at 10; Goldie, 'Development of an International Environmental Law: An Appraisal in Law', in *Institutions and the Global Environment* 104, at 108 (Hargrove ed. 1972).

[7] E.g., Bill for Preservation of the Havens in Devon and Cornwall, 27 Hen. 8, c. 23 (1535). See generally Teclaff, *supra* ch. 6 n. 33, at 104 n.2.

[8] As to discharge regulations, see legislative materials collected in *International Protection of Environment* (Ruster and Simma eds. 1974) under 'Municipal Legislation', and UN, *National Legislation and Treaties relating to the Law of the Sea* (UN Legislative Series 1974), UN Doc. ST/LEG/SER.B/16 (hereinafter cited as *UN Legislation*) under 'Marine Pollution'. See e.g. (US) Clean Water Act of 1977, 33 USC § 1321 (1977); Rivers and Harbours Appropriation Act of 1899, as amended, 33 USC § 407. As to CDEM regulation, see e.g. (UK) Merchant Shipping Act, 1979, c. 39 s. 449; the Prevention of Oil Pollution Act, 1971, c. 60 s. 22; (US) Ports and Waterways Safety Act of 1972, 46 USC § 391 (Supp. IV 1974).

[9] As to 'subjective territoriality, see text at ch. 9 nn. 13–15 *supra*.

[10] See e.g. (Denmark) Notice of 18 Jan. 1972, Issued By the Ministry of Pollution Control Prohibiting the Dumping of Certain Materials from Ships, reprinted in Ruster and Simma, supra n. 8, vol. iii at 1030; (UK) Dumping at Sea Act, 1974, c. 20, 27 June 1974, at Sect. 1(*c*); (US) Marine Protection Research and Sanctuaries Act of 1972, as amended. 33 USC §§ 1401–44, at Sect. 1411–12.

[11] Note that a Liberian proposal to limit environmental regulation in ports 'open to international maritime commerce' to internationally accepted standards was rejected at LOS III. See Statement of Collins (Liberia), Committee III 4th Meeting, 15 July 1974, reprinted in 2 *Official Records of the Third United Nations Conference on the Law of the Sea* (hereinafter cited as *Official Records* 315 (1974).

[12] *Cunard Co. Ltd.* v. *Mellon*, 262 US 100, 124, (1922). See also *Benz* v. *Compania Naviera Hidalgo SA*, 353 US 138 (1957).

Two limits to the ambit of such coastal jurisdiction are recognized in this expression of the rule. The vessel first must be present voluntarily. The language used by certain authorities suggests a blanket immunity from local prescriptions for vessels entering in distress.[13] Other commentators subject such vessels totally to local law—denying the coastal state only the right to prohibit entry itself.[14] A middle view recognizes a qualified immunity which subjects vessels involuntarily present to the full force of prescriptions designed to protect the health, safety, and welfare of the coastal state.[15] Either of the last two approaches would seem to support the application of coastal environmental regulations, by definition directed to the state's welfare, even to vessels present due to *force majeure*.

The second qualification to coastal authority is the immunity from prescriptive authority enjoyed by foreign warships and other public vessels operated for non-commercial purposes.[16] Although the jurisdiction of the state is greatly tempered with respect to such vessels, 'every ship, including a warship, must comply with the laws and regulations of the coastal State relating to navigation, safety, health and port administration.'[17] Thus, one may presume the competence of states to apply prescriptions designed to protect the environment even to foreign governmental vessels. The capacity of the coastal state to exercise enforcement authority against such vessels, to be discussed below, is, on the other hand, very limited.

With respect to all other foreign vessels situated in internal waters there is continuing debate as to whether any further limitations exist to coastal prescriptive jurisdiction. The French Conseil d'État opinion with respect to the *Sally* and the *Newton* in 1806 represents the leading authority for the view that the coastal state has no authority to regulate activities on foreign vessels in internal waters unless the interests of the state are implicated.[18] The

[13] See e.g. Fauchille, i *Traite de droit international public* 1022 (1925); The *Kate A. Hoff* Claim (1929) (*US* v. *Mex.*), 4 UNRIAA 444 (1951).

[14] See e.g. Hyde, *supra* ch. 3 n. 146, at 743; Jessup, *The Law of Territorial Waters and Maritime Jurisdiction* 194–208 (1927); McDougal and Burke, *supra* ch. 6 n. 4, at 110.

[15] See Hydeman and Berman, *supra* ch. 2 n. 80, at 161–2.

[16] For discussions of the subject and authority for the general principle, see materials cited in ch. 10, n. 64 *supra*; the *Parlement belge*, (1880) LR 5 PD 197; *Chung Chi Cheung* v. *King*, [1939] AC 160; the *Philippine Admiral*, [1977] AC 373; the *Schooner Exchange* v. *McFaddon*, 11 US (7 Cranch) 116 (1812) (foreign warship); *Berizzi Bros.* v. *SS Pesaro*, 271 US 562 (1926) (govt. vessel); McDougal and Burke, *supra* ch. 6 n. 4, at 130–55; Riesenfeld, 'Sovereign Immunity of Foreign Vessels in Anglo-American Law: The Evolution of a Legal Doctrine', 25 *Minn. L. Rev.* 1 (1940).

[17] 1982 Draft Rest., *supra* ch. 9 n. 4, § 512 Rpt. n. 5. See Brownlie, *supra* ch. 2 n. 52, at 367; Hyde, *supra* ch. 3 n. 146, at 827; McDougal and Burke, *supra* ch. 6 n. 4, at 136.

[18] The *Sally* and *Newton*, [1806] *Bull. des lois* no. 126, 602 (Conseil d'etat 1806). See Brierly, *supra* ch. 2 n. 41, at 223; Brownlie, *supra* ch. 2 n. 52, at 317; Jessup, *supra* n. 14, at 145–6; Gidel, ii *Le Droit international public de la mer* 204 (1934), McDougal and Burke, *supra* ch. 6 n. 4, at 164; O'Connell, *supra* Introd. n. 1, at 680; Harvard Research–Jurisdiction, *supra* ch. 9 n. 11, at 513. A number of states have followed the French view of an immunity imposed by international law, including: Belgium, Italy, Greece, Norway, Portugal, Yugoslavia, Mexico, and Brazil. O'Connell, *supra* Introd. n. 1 at 681.

majority of states, including those within the Anglo-American tradition, have denied this partial immunity and asserted that any derogation from coastal state authority is only a function of a maxim of comity that suggests deference to the flag in matters without external impact.[19] Where no effects are produced beyond the ship, advocates of the dominant perspective affirm coastal state competence but declare that states may choose not to exercise it, while the opposition insists that in this situation the coastal state has no authority, discretionary or otherwise, to act.[20] Most commentators now conclude that this doctrinal distinction is without substance, in light of uniform state practice with respect to actual exercise of jurisdiction.[21] States on both sides of the theoretical issue have so defined external effects to extend to acts which are only 'of a character to awaken public interest', and thus 'disturb tranquility and public order on shore or in the port.'[22] Moreover, in spite of the theoretical differences, it seems patent that neither group of states would express any limit of law or comity on a state's authority to exercise competence with respect to anti-pollution regulations—which by definition implicate the interests of the prescribing state.

The final aspect of the expansive prescriptive authority of coastal states over internal waters is the right simply to deny entry to foreign vessels. One arbitral tribunal has stated that '[a]ccording to a great principle of international law, ports of every State must be open to foreign vessels and can only be closed when the vital interests of a State so require.'[23] The premise of freedom of access is not, however, widely acknowledged. To the contrary, most authorities embrace the view that each state may permit, condition, or deny

[19] See Brierly, *supra* ch. 2, n. 41, at 223–37; Charteris, 'The Legal Position of Merchantmen in Foreign Ports and National Waters', [1920–1] *Brit Yb. Int'l L.* 45; Clark, *supra* ch. 10 n. 33, at 230–4; Jessup, *supra* n. 14, at 169–91; McDougal and Burke, *supra* ch. 6 n. 4, at 155–70; Oppenheim, *supra* ch. 2 n. 37, at 503; Thommen, *supra* ch. 10 n. 64, at 49–68. The position of the UK has been clouded by its adoption in a brief in *Incres SS Co. Ltd.* v. *Int'l Maritime Workers Union et al.*, 372 US 10 (1963), of a position rather consistent with the French view. See Brownlie, *supra* ch. 2 n. 52, at 318. In any event, the rationale of the rule of comity is well articulated by the US Supreme Court in *Lauritzen* v. *Larsen*: 'But the virtue and utility of sea-borne commerce lies in its frequent and important contacts with more than one country. If, to serve some immediate interest, the courts of each were to exploit every such contact to the limits of its power, it is not difficult to see that a multiplicity of conflicting and overlapping burdens would blight international carriage by sea.' 345 US 571 (1953), at 581.

[20] McDougal and Burke, *supra* ch. 2 n. 52, at 165. These authors note that the restraint of comity is often reflected in specific consular agreement to limit jurisdiction. *Id.*, at 169. See e.g. United Kingdom–United States Consular Agreement of 6 June 1951, 165 UNTS 121, at 154.

[21] See Brierly, *supra* ch. 2 n. 41, at 235; Brownlie, *supra* ch. 2 n. 52, at 318; McDougal and Burke *supra* ch. 6 n. 4, at 164–5. Indeed, Gidel has asserted that there is only an illusory theoretical distinction. Gidel, *supra* n. 18, at 204, 246.

[22] *In Re* Wildenhaus, 120 US 1, at 18 (1887). See *United States* v. *Flores*, 289 US 137 (1933); the *Tempest*, [1859] Dalloz 88; Brierly, *supra* ch. 2 n. 41, at 214; Jessup, *supra* n. 14, at 147–8, 179–80.

[23] *Saudi Arabia* v. *Arabian American Oil Co.*, (Award of 23 Aug. 1958), 27 *Int'l L. Rev.* 117, at 212 (1963). This conclusion rested largely on the authority of the Statute on the International Regulation of Maritime Ports, 9 Dec. 1923, 58 LNTS 285, 301, ratified by fewer than thirty states. See also Colombos, *The International Law of the Sea* 176 (6th edn. 1967); Delupis, ch 7 n. 9, at 47–50; 1982 Draft Rest., *supra* ch. 9 n. 4, § 512 Rpt. n. 3.

entry into internal waters in its unfettered discretion, subject only to the general obligation to grant refuge to vessels in distress.[24] This represents an extremely important prescriptive tool in an environmental context. Each state may condition entry to its ports, i.e. participation in its maritime trade, on compliance with environmental regulations as strict as it deems appropriate.[25] The United States, among others, has adopted an aggressive set of regulations which deny entry unless rigid CDEM standards are met.[26] In fact, the right to deny entry to protect the environment appears even to constitute an exception to the duty to allow entry to distressed vessels when the threat to the coastal state exceeds that to the vessel.[27] Hence, in 1981 a Panamanian tanker was denied harbour in Bermuda when a fractured hull threatened (and ultimately did cause) an oil spill.[28] In summary, the prescriptive authority to deny entry to internal waters and to regulate vessels within such waters for environmental purposes is subject to few qualifications.

C. ENFORCEMENT AUTHORITY

i. General

As internal waters constitute state territory, states possess the authority to take any measures deemed appropriate to enforce the laws of the state.[29] Such enforcement measures may relate to both territorial and extraterritorial prescriptions within the competence of the state. Violators of rules premised

[24] See the *Anglo-Norwegian Fisheries* Case (*UK* v *Norway*), [1951] ICJ 116; *Lauritzen* v. *Larsen*, 345 US 571 (1953), at 592; *Patterson* v. *The Eudora*, 190 US 169 (1902), at 178; Burke, 'Contemporary Law of the Sea: Transportation, Communication and Flight', *Law of the Sea Institute Occasional Paper* no. 28 (1975), at 1; Burmester, *supra* ch. 10 n. 2, at 10; Livingston, *supra* ch. 6 n. 30, at 18; Hakapaa, *supra* ch. 5 n. 57, at 163–8; Hsia, 'Some Jurisdictional Problems Arising from Ship-source Marine Pollution with special refernce to Port State Jurisdiction', 30 31 (M.Litt diss., Oxford Univ. 1981), Hydeman and Berman, *supra* ch. 2 n. 80, at 161–62; Lowe, 'The Right of Entry into Maritime Ports in International Law', 14 *San Diego L. Rev.* 597, 619 (1977); McDougal and Burke, *supra* ch. 6 n. 4, at 103–14.

[25] The US effort to clarify each state's right to deny entry for non-compliance with environmental regulations achieved implicit recognition in the text. See LOS Convention, *supra* ch. 5, n. 17, art. 211(3); United States Draft Artcles on the Protection of the Marine Environment and the Prevention of Marine Pollution (13 July 1973), UN Doc. A/AC.138/SC.III/L.40, art. 9.

[26] See e.g. (Belgium) Law of 25 Aug. 1920 On the Safety of Ships, Art. I; (US) Ports and Waterways Safety Act, as amended by the Port and Tanker Safety Act of 1978, 33 USC §§ 1228–32. See generally, Akehurst, *supra* ch. 5 n. 103, at 205; Anderson, 'National and International Efforts to Prevent Traumatic Vessel-source Oil Pollution', 30 *U. Miami L. Rev.* 985 (1976); Burmester, *supra* ch. 10 n. 2, at 30. The right arbitrarily to deny entry has been utilized in several instances for environmental purposes. See e.g. the refusal of entry for refueling in Irish and British ports to *Stella Maris* and port in the Canaries to *Enskeri*, with each vessel en route to the dumping of toxic wastes. See 2 *Mar. Poll. Bull.* 115 (1971) and 6 *Mar. Poll. Bull* 68 (1975).

[27] See Ago, 8th Rpt, *supra* ch. 2 n. 89, at 61; Hydeman and Berman, *supra* ch. 2 n. 80, at 161–2; McDougal and Burke, *supra* ch. 6 n. 4, at 110.

[28] The *Eastern Mariner I* incident, 12 *Mar. Poll. Bull.* 142 (1981).

[29] See text at n. 5 *supra*.

on objective territoriality, nationality, or any other principle of extraterritorial jurisdiction may be subjected to enforcement actions upon entry into internal waters.[30] The set of enforcement tools available to the state for such use is precisely that available in all regions of territory, including inspection, arrest, judicial proceedings, seizure, fines, and imprisonment. Each of these may be utilized by the state in internal waters to compel obedience to or punish violation of environmental prescriptions. The detention of vessels in internal waters until prescribed standards of seaworthiness are met, endorsed specifically in Article 219 of the LOS Convention, represents a particularly effective environmental preventive measure reflected in the practice of most major maritime states.[31]

Enforcement measures by the state within internal waters, as within other regions of state territory, are subject to certain limitations. Article 11 of the 1958 High Seas Convention, for example, restrains states from taking enforcement against foreign persons or vessels for violations of law arising out of high seas collisions.[32] Practical concerns relating to the maintenance of uninterrupted shipping led states contractually to cede the inherent right to enforce extraterritorial prescriptions of the type previously recognized in the *Lotus* Case.[33] Far more significant are the customary law immunities of warships and similar public vessels. As discussed above, such immunities will likely not shield a ship from the prescriptive authority of the coastal state with respect to matters affecting the welfare of the state, such as conduct polluting or threatening to pollute the environment.[34] The measures which the coastal state may employ to enforce such laws against vessels cloaked with such immunity, or persons associated with such vessels, are, however, few. Indeed, the only enforcement options of the coastal state appear to be diplomatic protest and the right to compel the offending vessel immediately to depart.[35]

[30] *Id.*

[31] LOS Convention, *supra* ch. 5 n. 17, art 219. See e.g. 1973 Convention, *supra* ch. 10 n. 53, art. 5(2); (UK) Merchant Shipping Act, 1974, c. 43 s. 11–12; (US) Ports and Waterways Safety Act of 1972, 46 USC § 1223 (Supp. iv 1974). See Hsia, *supra* n. 24, at 30–4.

[32] High Seas Convention, *supra* ch. 6 n. 2; art. 11 (1–3). See Brierly, *supra* ch. 2 n. 41, at 304. This restriction had been reflected in the earlier International Convention for the Unification of Certain Rules Relating to Penal Jurisdiction in Matters of Collision and Other Incidents of Navigation, done at Brussels 10 May 1952, registered 2 Oct. 1962, 439 UNTS 233 (1963), TIAS no. 6332. These provisions were the product of maritime labour organization lobbying. See Anderson, *supra* n. 26, at 935.

[33] The *SS Lotus* Case (*Fr.* v. *Turkey*), [1927] PCIJ ser. A, no. 10. See Brownlie, *supra* ch. 2 n. 52, at 255; Fitzmaurice, *supra* n. 5, 108; O'Connell, *supra* Introd. n. 1, at 654. Note that this restriction was not imposed in a civil context in the International Convention on Certain Rules Concerning Civil Jurisdiction in Matters of Collision, done at Brussels 10 May 1952, registered 2 Oct. 1962, 439 UNTS 219 (1963), TIAS no. 6331. Rather, the state of arrest was vested with jurisdiction. *Id.*, at Art. 1. Several States did enter reservations limiting jurisdiction to the states of the flag, *locus* of collision, or allegiance of defendant. *Id.*

[34] See text at n. 16 *supra.*

[35] See Brownlie, *supra* ch. 2 n. 52, at 367; Hyde, *supra* ch. 3 n. 146, at 826–7; 'Research in International Law, Harvard Law School: Draft Convention and Comments on Territorial

ii. 'Port State' Conventions

The enforcement authority of coastal states with respect to vessels in port has long been recognized as one of the keys to the development of an effective international regime to prevent marine pollution.[36] Investigation, detention, and similar acts of enforcement are more readily accomplished and less obstructive to the trade process when a vessel is lying at anchor in port than when the vessel is at sea. From the 1954 Convention onwards, therefore, international initiatives designed to protect the marine environment have looked to coastal states to enact and enforce prescriptions in internal waters.[37] The inherent territorial authority of the coastal state is utilized, for example, to prevent loading of wastes for dumping, require maintenance and review of oil record books, and accomplish physical inspections, and, if appropriate, detention, of foreign vessels in port.[38]

In the negotiating sessions of the 1973 Convention several states sought, for the first time, to require 'port' states to do more for environmental protection than enforce internally laws pertaining to matters within their own borders.[39] It was proposed that states take enforcement actions against foreign vessels in their ports for violations of

> international environmental regulations that occurred beyond the coastal waters of the port state, on the high seas or in the waters of another state. This would allow a state to initiate proceedings against any ship stopping at one of its ports for any environmental violation that was committed anywhere in the world.[40]

After an animated debate, no such provision was included in the final text.[41]

Similar proposals were made and opposed in the same year in the UN Seabed Committee's sessions preparatory to the LOS Conference.[42] In the

Waters', 23 *Am. J. Int'l L.* 243, at 328 (Suppl. 1929) (hereinafter cited as Harv. Res. Territorial Waters); 1982 Draft Rest., *supra* ch. 9 n. 4, § 512 Rpt. n. 5.

[36] As to the evolution of the 'port state' tactic generally, see Hsia, *supra* n. 24, at 113 ff, 1982 Draft Rest., *supra* ch. 9 n. 4, § 516 Rpt. n. 6; International Law Association Report of the 56th Conference, New Dehli (1974) (hereinafter cited as ILA 56th), Report on the British Branch Committee on the Law of the Sea on 'The Concept of Port State Jurisdiction', at 400.

[37] See e.g. 1954 Conv., *supra* ch. 10 n. 53, art. 9(5); 1973 Conv., *supra* ch. 10 n. 53, arts 6(2) and 6(5).

[38] See e.g. 1954 Conv., *supra* ch. 10 n. 53, art. 9(5); London Dumping Conv., *supra* ch. 5 n. 44, art. 7; 1973 Conv., *supra* ch. 10 n. 53, arts. 6(2) and 6(5). See Note, 'No Dumping in this Ocean: Nearing the End of Ship-generated Pollution', 7 *NYU J. Int'l L. & Pol'y* 545, at 149 (1974); Sweeney, 'Environmental Protection by Coastal States: The Paradigm from Marine Transport of Petroleum', 4 *Ga. J. Int'l & Comp. L.* 278, at 300–1, (1974);: Timagenis, *supra* ch. 5 n. 1, at 510–14.

[39] See IMCO Doc. MP/CONF. C. 1/WP. 25 (Canada); IMCO Doc. MP/CONF. 1. 1/WP. 34 (Canada, New Zealand, Australia); Timagenis, *supra* ch. 5 n. 1, at 515.

[40] 1982 Draft Rest., *supra* ch. 9 n. 4, § 512 Rpt. n. 6.

[41] See Timagenis, *supra* ch. 5 n. 1, at 515.

[42] See USA Draft Articles, *supra* ch. 5 n. 40; Netherlands: Draft Articles on the Enforcement of International Provisions for the Prevention of Marine Pollution from Vessels, UN Doc. A/AC.138/SC.III/L.148, 10 Aug. 1973. See *contra* Federal Republic of Germany: Draft Articles: Enforcement of Regulations concerning the Protection of the Marine Environment against Vessel-source Pollution, UN Doc. A/Conf.62/C.3/L.7, 1 Aug. 1974, at Art. II; Greece: Draft

1974 Geneva session of the Conference, the United Kingdom *et al.* submitted draft articles, which formed the basis of the Conference's preliminary texts, calling for port states to institute proceedings for discharges in violation of international rules which harm the state itself or any other state requesting such proceedings.[43] The principal criticism of this approach related to the linkage between the jurisdiction of the coastal state and coastal damage: 'That idea was inconsistent with [the] view that the port State should be free to act not only in defence of its own interests and those of other States, but also in the interest of the international community, in preserving the marine environment.'[44] Article 218 of the LOS Convention concluded with a far broader approach:

> When a vessel is voluntarily within a port or at an off-shore terminal of a State, that State may undertake investigations and, where the evidence so warrants, institute proceedings in respect of any discharge from that vessel outside the internal waters, territorial sea or exclusive economic zone of that State in violation of applicable international rules and standards established through the competent international organization or general diplomatic conference.[45]

The Convention's general grant of enforcement authority with respect to discharge violations in any region of the seas is qualified by a series of provisions designed to 'safeguard' the interests of maritime states.[46] Enforcement of violations within or damaging only to another state's waters may only occur upon the request of such state.[47] Similarly, any enforcement proceedings with respect to violations beyond the port state's territorial sea must be suspended upon the commencement of enforcement proceedings by the flag state, unless (*a*) the port state itself experienced major damage or (*b*) the flag state has 'repeatedly disregarded its obligation to enforce effectively the applicable international rules and standards in respect of violations committed by its vessels.'[48] Article 226 defines certain rules and standards for physical inspection and requires release in the event a violation is detected, subject to reasonable bonding or security procedures.[49] In an apparent effort to

Articles on the Enforcement of the Provisions for the Protection of the Marine Environment, UN Doc. A/Conf. 62/C.3/L.5, 29 July 1974, at art. 6.

[43] Belgium, Bulgaria, Denmark, German Democratic Republic, Federal Republic of Germany, Greece, Netherlands, Poland, and United Kingdom: Draft Articles on the Prevention, Reduction and Control of Marine Pollution, UN Doc. A/CONF.62/C.3/L.24, 1 Mar. 1975, at art. 3. See generally *Canadian Foreign Policy and the Law of the Sea* (Johnson and Zacher eds. 1977), at 145–6; Hakapaa, *supra* ch. 5 n. 57, at 174; Hsia, *supra* n. 24, at 126.

[44] Summary of Statement of Delegate from New Zealand at 20th Meeting of Committee III, 10 April 1975, in 4 *Official Records* 89, at 90 (1976). See also criticisms of the approach by Tanzania, India, Canada, Senegal, and US set forth at 84–7 *id.*

[45] LOS Convention, *supra* ch. 5 n. 17, art. 218(1). See generally Boyle, *supra* ch. 5 n. 51, at 365.

[46] These provisions are set forth in articles 223–33 of the Convention. For a useful discussion, see Bernhardt, *supra* ch. 10 n. 54, at 297–301.

[47] LOS Convention, *supra* ch. 5 n. 17, art. 218(1).

[48] *Id.*, art. 228.

[49] *Id.*, art. 226.

preclude arrest of responsible individuals and the attendant interference with navigation, Article 230 adds that only monetary penalties may be imposed for violations beyond the territorial sea.[50] Finally, Article 232 provides that states shall be liable for loss occasioned by enforcement measures in excess of those reasonable under the circumstances and permitted under the Convention.[51]

The relevant question for the present inquiry is whether the foregoing regime of 'port state' enforcement authority represents an expression, expansion, or diminution of customary internal waters' authority. As noted above, a state may enforce any prescription, territorial or extraterritorial, in such waters. To the extent that a port state possesses the customary authority to apply a prescription to the specific conduct violative of an international standard, therefore, the Convention adds nothing to custom. To the contrary, when prescriptive authority is so possessed, e.g. over a discharge in internal waters, the Convention works only to reduce the port state's correlative enforcement authority by imposing the 'safeguards' described above.

It is not intended here to anticipate the conclusions of the following chapters with respect to the ambit of prescriptive authority in regions beyond internal waters. It will suffice to note that customary law does not recognize state authority to reach out with prescriptions to all matters affecting the marine environment regardless of the allegiance of the actor or the location of the conduct or its impact.[52] Yet, that is precisely the scope of the port state regime. Given that a state may only enforce that which it can prescribe, the 'port state' text may be viewed as a supplement to the state's *prescriptive* authority—it permits the state to apply prescriptions incorporating international rules to conduct customarily beyond the state's reach. The authority to enforce such prescriptions in the ports of the state follows as a matter of customary law.

It has been suggested that the creative use of the prescriptive jurisdiction of the state over internal waters may support the port state regime, without recourse to an expanded right to prescribe as to remote conduct. The British branch of the ILA noted in a 1974 report that if states would adopt laws

[50] *Id.*, art. 230(2). Environmentalists at LOS III fought vigorously for the retention of arrest powers, arguing that they represent the most effective weapon in a state's enforcement arsenal. See Bernhardt, *supra* ch. 10 n. 54, at 301. It has been argued that 'there is little merit in the argument for the arrest power, especially because only monetary penalties can aid effectively in restoring the coastal environment after an incident.' *Id.* This is not a particularly persuasive defense of the LOS III provision for several reasons: (*a*) the 'restoration' argument fails to address the need to enforce preventative, as distinct from post-incident punitive, regulations; (*b*) the assessment of monetary penalties sufficient to restore the environment and the exercise of arrest authority are in no sense mutually exclusive; (*c*) the truly operative question as to the 'reasonableness' of arrest, in terms of the importance to the coastal State of the protected interest, and the interference to the foreign vessel, is not addressed.

[51] *Id.*, art. 232. Additional 'safeguards' generally applicable to all enforcement authority include (*a*) notification to the flag state (art. 231), (*b*) nondiscrimination among flags (art. 227), and (*c*) exercise only by marked and identifiable government vessels (art. 225).

[52] See ch. 13.

prohibiting vessels' presence in port following, or with documents evidencing, a remote discharge, no extraterritorial prescription would be required since the offence defined occurs within the borders of the state.[53] A second suggestion, finding some support in state practice with respect to civil jurisdiction, is simply that states may condition entry to internal waters on submission to the authority of prescriptions concerning remote conduct that would otherwise be *ultra vires*.[54]

Each of these approaches has the merit of technical consistency with the principles of jurisdiction; yet, each works a strain on the logic of those principles. There is little question that the expansive territorial prescriptive competence vested in all states would support the tactical definition of offence suggested in the British paper. Similarly, the right to deny entry to the state's waters would seem to subsume a right to condition such entry upon acceptance of jurisdictional conditions. The result of these methods, however, is that each state may apply its laws to any conduct by any actor in any location, based solely on the eventual presence of the actor (or perhaps even an asset of the actor) within state territory.[55] This would be true even when the 'primary' conduct effectively subjected to the state's exercise, e.g. a remote discharge of pollution, clearly could not be reached directly by the state under any of the recognized bases of prescriptive authority.[56] If the principles of jurisdiction are to retain integrity and function, such tactical avoidances of the limits imposed should not be permitted. Port state jurisdiction over acts of pollution beyond the range of the state's direct prescriptive authority is best viewed as outside of existing (though perhaps affecting the content of future) customary law; it is appropriately defined as an expansion of prescriptive competence resting on the contractual agreement of the parties to the LOS Convention.[57]

[53] See ILA 56th British Branch Report, *supra* n. 36.

[54] See Burmester, *supra* ch. 10 n. 2, at 10–11 for description and criticism of the argument. The historical antecedents of the argument may be found in the opinion of Mariscal in the *Cutting* Case, Moore, ii *Digest of International Law*, 228–42, [1887] *US Digest of For. Rel.* 751. Consider also the expansive language of *Lauritzen* v. *Larsen*, 345 US 571, 592–3 (1953): 'We do not question the power of Congress to condition access to our ports by foreign-owned vessels upon submission to any liabilities it may consider good American policy to exact.' See also *Payne* v. *SS Tropic Breeze*, 423 F. 2d 236 (1st Cir. 1970), *cert. den.* 400 US 964 (1970).

[55] Note the similarity to 'universal' jurisdiction over conduct not characterized as *delicta juris gentium*. See ch. 9, at n. 52 *supra*. Under this approach 'port states' would not require recourse to the tactical use of territoriality to reach remote conduct. As noted, however, this expansive variation of universality is not accepted by states within the Anglo-American tradition.

[56] See ch. 9 generally.

[57] Vallarta, 'Protection and Preservation of the Marine Environment and Marine Scientific Research at the Third UN Conference on the Law of the Sea', in Symposium on The Law of the Sea: Where Now?, 4–6 *Law & Contemp Probs* 147, at 149 (1983). As to the interplay between custom and the LOS Convention and the progressive impact of the latter on the former, see Jennings, *supra* ch. 5 n. 2, at 59; Lee, *supra* ch. 5 n. 2, at 541; See also Chessman, 'On Treaties and Customs: A Comment on the Draft Restatement', 18 *Int'l Lawyer* 421 (1984).

D. STATE RESPONSIBILITY

The foregoing regime of authority completes the set of rules necessary to render decisions regarding environmental responsibility for matters relating to internal waters. Generally, the conclusions reached in earlier chapters with respect to responsibility for conduct in or affecting any portion of state territory apply with full force to these waters. Thus, the *sic utere tuo* preventive obligation identified in Chapter 5 operates to protect the component of territory consisting of internal waters. All states must endeavour to prevent environmental harm to the internal waters of other states.[58] A coastal state whose internal waters are affected by a violation of this duty clearly has full standing to raise an international claim for territorial injury.[59]

Conversely, as internal waters constitute state territory, the coastal state's preventive obligation with respect to conduct within such waters is basically that defined for conduct on land. With respect to the conduct of state organs, it is the obligation of the state to exercise self-control to prevent harm to other states or the environment beyond the exclusive zone of any state. Responsibility will arise for a negligent or intentional failure to prevent or, on a strict basis, if the conduct was ultrahazardous or (in the suggested formulation) particularly egregious.[60] As to the conduct of non-state actors the test is that applicable to all private territorial matters—due diligence. To fulfil this duty, the coastal state must diligently exercise the full measure of legal authority possessed over private conduct in internal waters to prevent external environmental harm. As discussed in Part II, the diligence required in the environmental context also may be elevated to a strict standard when private conduct within any part of such state territory is ultrahazardous or causes serious harm.[61] These general conclusions will now be examined in the context of the principal categories of internal waters polluting conduct: vessels and land-based activity.

i. Vessel Conduct

a. Determination of Responsibility

The presence of foreign vessels and their ship-users within internal waters complicates the responsibility analysis in many respects. In general, of course, the conduct of such actors is not attributable to the coastal state since foreign flag ships and their users are private individuals *vis-à-vis* the territorial state. Yet, as noted in this and the preceding chapter, such individuals are subject to a greater degree of foreign authority and, in certain cases, a lesser degree of

[58] See ch. 5 at nn. 20 ff.

[59] The damage is to exclusive territorial interests. There is no question of having to act to vindicate community interests. See ch. 6 at nn 62–91 *supra*.

[60] See ch. 8 at n. 102.

[61] *Id.*, at n. 106.

local authority than other private actors in state territory.[62] The interplay between foreign and local jurisdictions has several significant consequences for decisions regarding state responsibility. First, it may affect the standard of performance of the preventive obligation to which the respective states will be held. If the authority of the coastal or other state is materially diminished in the interaction, the general conclusion regarding the imposition of strict responsibility may need to be revised. Second, the concurrence of authority provides a fertile ground for situations of multiple state responsibility. These matters and the rules of decision regarding internal waters generally are best analysed by reference to specific examples.

Consider a circumstance in which an oil tanker flying the flag of state *A*, yet owned by private citizens of state *B*, enters the internal waters of state *C*. In navigating to anchor, the vessel strikes a charted harbour installation, resulting in a pierced hull and a large oil spill causing severe damage to the territorial resources of state *C* and adjacent state *D*. An investigation concludes that the vessel's out-of-date charts, inadequate navigational equipment, and fragile hull construction combined to explain the casualty. States *A*, *B*, and *C* each possessed a degree of legal authority over the conduct of the vessel and its ship-users. Each of these states was obligated to exercise such jurisdiction to prevent environmental harm to other states. The species of authority possessed and, thus, the standards of required performance, however, differed among the states.

Coastal state *C* enjoyed the broadest prescriptive and enforcement rights as the territorial authority. As noted above, the fact that a merchant vessel flies a foreign flag does not diminish such authority in an environmental context. Even in the minority French view, the coastal state's capacity to regulate matters on board a foreign vessel with an external impact, e.g. matters threatening the environment, is not questioned.[63] Hence, state *C*'s plenary territorial jurisdiction enabled it to prevent the incident by requiring adequate construction and equipment and arresting or denying entry to vessels not meeting such demands. If one assumes that the carriage of large quantities of oil is an ultrahazardous activity, the standard to which state *C* should be held with respect to this spill is that applicable to all such private conduct within a state's territorial borders: due diligence elevated to strict responsibility.[64]

The jurisdiction of state *A* with respect to matters aboard flag vessels operating in foreign waters was defined in the preceding chapter. Prescriptive authority is plenary. Enforcement authority is limited to on-board actions taken by the officers of the vessel; only when the vessel departs from the foreign waters may the flag state legally use external means to enforce its laws.[65] As noted, the key to determining the appropriate standard of

[62] See c. 3 at n. 146. Noting that, of course, immunities versus local jurisdiction may exist with respect to persons or sites on land teritory—e.g diplomatic immunity.

[63] See text at nn. 18–22 *supra*.

[64] See ch. 8 at nn. 112–13.

[65] See ch. 10 at nn. 29–34, 100 *supra*.

performance is whether the flag state has authority over the harmful conduct which bestows a capacity to control of a 'territorial' order.[66] The previous chapter alluded to Quentin-Baxter's view that the 'paramount' authority of the coastal state in internal waters releases the flag state from a strict standard since the vessel is not within the flag state's 'territory or control' while in a foreign port.[67] It is submitted, however, that the flag state may indeed possess sufficient authority to merit application of a strict regime, even though the vessel is subject to dominant coastal jurisdiction at the moment of the event. When, as in the present example, the harm-producing conduct relates to the vessel's pre-existing condition or function (e.g. when the injury is caused by an inherent ultrahazardous function or inadequacies of construction, design or equipment), the flag state has the capacity to foresee the risk of harm and the authority and opportunity to prevent the harm.[68] The strict responsibility of the flag state should not be diminished by the fact that the condition or function results in an injury in foreign waters, since the cause could have been prevented by exercise of the flag's jurisdiction at the time of registration or by prior enforcement measures outside of such waters.

The analysis is quite different, of course, if the event arises not out of such pre-existing characteristics but an on-board activity taking place within state *C*'s internal waters. A vessel might, for example, by design or negligence release waste into a port's waters in the course of operation. Flag state *A*'s enforcement authority, central to its capacity to control and prevent, is so limited with respect to conduct in a foreign port to fall below a level which supports strict responsibility. The standard in such circumstances, therefore, should remain one of normal due diligence regardless of the magnitude of the harm. The responsibility of state *A* would turn on whether or not it diligently exercised the power it did possess to prevent the conduct. Were the ship-users adequately trained? Was such conduct proscribed by the law of the flag state? Were the responsible individuals subsequently punished?[69]

If the foreign vessel is a state or public vessel, the distinct regimes of authority again suggest different conclusions as to responsibility. The flag state is invariably subject to the defined regime of strict responsibility for ultrahazards and extreme injury arising out of the conduct of such state organs, regardless of whether the event relates to the character of the vessel or spontaneous conduct in foreign waters.[70] Conversely, coastal state *C*'s enforcement authority, i.e. its capacity to control, is dramatically reduced as to warships and non-commercial public vessels since the only means of enforcement is to require departure. Hence, it would seem that strict

[66] See ch. 8 at nn. 7–8.

[67] Q-B, 3rd Rpt., *supra* ch. 5 n. 72, at 19, 20, 24. See also Q-B, 5th Rpt., *supra* ch. 10 n. 104, at 8.

[68] See text preceding ch. 10 n. 118 *supra*.

[69] See ch. 3, at nn. 110 ff.

[70] See ch. 10, at nn. 87–8 supra and ch. 8, at n. 111.

responsibility for the coastal state generally should yield in such circumstances to the normal test of due diligence.[71]

Responsibility is not necessarily limited to flag and coastal states. Chapter 10 identified the possibility of the responsibility of non-flag states, such as state *B*, arising out of their capacity to exercise nationality-based authority over the vessel's ship-users to prevent the injurious event.[72] Matters such as equipment, design, construction, and function are perfect examples of the type of matters generally subject to the direction and decision of the owners or operators.[73] As noted, however, the standard of performance of state *B*'s obligation to exercise authority to prevent is invariably normal (i.e., not elevated to strict) due diligence. No effective authority is possessed over the vessel itself to enforce state *B*'s prescriptions. Responsibility would occur, therefore, if state *B* failed to do what it could, by exercise of jurisdiction over the owners, to ensure the use of adequate construction, charts, and equipment.[74]

The final issue regarding the attribution of responsibility relates to the obligations of the coastal state purely as a 'port state', neither the victim nor the site of the injurious conduct. What would be the responsibility, for example, of a state *E* which let the vessel sail from its port to state *C* in the condition leading to the casualty? States do possess the authority to prescribe and enforce laws regarding the condition of foreign vessels in port relating to environmental safety.[75] The conclusions of Part II dictate that the port state has the duty to exercise such authority to prevent environmental injury. The standard of performance of this preventive obligation with respect to foreign vessels would seem to be standard due diligence. Although the authority of state *E* is territorial for the period of the vessel's presence, it is neither the proximate plenary authority of state *C* nor the continuing, expansive authority of state *A* over the vessel at the moment of the casualty. Moreover, as to ultrahazardous causes, imposition of strict responsibility based solely on prior presence in state *E* would be at once illogical and unfair. In practical terms, the result of a series of strictly liable states along the vessel's route is clearly undesirable. Only a failure of diligence should trigger responsibility. What was the condition of the vessel in the port? Did the state take reasonable

[71] A distinction might be made, however, between injury-producing activities and vessel conditions. As to the former, the lack of coastal enforcement authority on board suggests the impropriety of strict responsibility. Harm from vessel condition or equipment, e.g. ultrahazardous cargo, on the other hand, could arguably be prevented in internal waters by denial of entry. Hence, coastal state strict responsibility might apply as to such matters.

[72] See ch. 10, at nn. 11–24 *supra*.

[73] NB that the same conclusion might be reached with respect to the operators or other ship-users. The key is which individuals exercise material and effective control over the vessel and its operations.

[74] By, for example, prescriptive efforts with respect to the national's conduct and internal enforcement efforts against the national or the national's assets.

[75] See text at nn. 31, 36 ff., *supra*.

action, such as inspection and review of papers, to confirm that no environmental harm was threatened?[76]

b. Consequences

The foregoing demonstrates that several states may stand responsible for breach of international obligations arising out of an event of vessel pollution in internal waters.[77] The central conclusion of Chapter 4 was that each state in breach of duty in a given case bears responsibility to the state to which the duty was owed; distinctions as to the relative severity, causality, and blameworthiness will affect the consequences of, but not absolve responsibility for, each of the several breaches. In the principal example, described above, states *A*, *B*, *C*, and *E*, depending on the specific facts, might each stand responsible to injured state *D* for breach of the obligation to prevent environmental harm. The threshold question with respect to the consequences of each state's responsibility must be whether or not a causal relationship exists between the breach and the material injury to state *D*. If an obligation is breached but no such connection is present, the breach may nevertheless yield reparation duties unrelated to compensation for the material injury.[78] If, for example, state *B* had failed to take any measures at all to ensure that vessels controlled by its nationals are adequately equipped or constructed, the due diligence standard should be deemed violated. Yet, if it were demonstrated that the injury would have occurred even if state *B* had been diligent, the absence of a causal connection would free state *B* from the duty to compensate state *D* for the environmental injury suffered. Logically, however, state *B* would still owe state *D* other reparation for the moral or political injury suffered whenever any international obligation is breached, including cessation of the breaching conduct and satisfaction, guarantee, or apology.[79]

Among any states determined to have participated in the cause of the injury, the criteria of relative causation and blameworthiness defined in Chapter 4 should control the apportionment of the consequential duty to compensate.[80] Under either the suggested regime of joint and several responsibility for compensation, coupled with a right of contribution, or the alternative of proportional direct responsibility, the central inquiry is each state's overall

[76] Another possible source of responsibility for a port state would be for a failure to punish after an event of pollution outside of the state's waters. Again, in customary law there exists no authority over such matters; nor, therefore, does there arise any obligation to exercise authority. The LOS Convention did establish such authority contractually. It could be argued that an attendant obligation to act pursuant to the grant was created by the Convention. However, the Convention does not appear to contemplate responsibility rising out of the failure to take enforcement actions. The port State provision states only that the State 'may' exercise authority; the obligatory 'shall' present elsewhere in the text is noticeably absent.

[77] See Meyers, *supra* ch. 10 n. 3, at 243 for an expression of this conclusion.

[78] See ch. 4 at n. 11.

[79] See ch. 4, at nn. 30–3 and ch. 10 at nn. 117–18, *supra*.

[80] See ch. 4, at n. 111. Such states may also have other duties of reparation such as apology or guaranty. Each state will have the consequential obligation to cease the violative conduct.

capacity to have prevented the injury.[81] The greater such effective capacity, the greater the compensatory burden.

This inquiry involves a comparative analysis of the same variables of state authority considered in fixing the applicable standards of performance. Generally, it will follow that the more expansive the order of jurisdiction possessed, the greater the capacity to control and prevent and the obligation to compensate.[82] Thus, in the example given, this preliminary analysis would direct the greatest burden to territorial state *C*, less to flag state *A*, and still less to nationality state *B* and port state *E*.[83] The specific facts might, however, alter this apportionment result. It is quite possible that a state with a lesser degree of direct legal authority may exercise a greater degree of effective control over a vessel. It may certainly be argued plausibly, for example, that a flag state possesses no less a degree of effective control over the CDEM of a vessel in a foreign port than the coastal state which permitted entry with CDEM inadequacies. Chapter 10 noted another illustration of a developed state *B* with far greater opportunity and capacity to control the condition of its national's vessel than flag state A.[84] In either circumstance, the burden of compensation should shift from the initial placement.[85] In other words, the character of each state's jurisdiction is the preliminary guideline to apportionment of the compensation obligation; ultimately, decisions will turn on a weighing of the relative preventive capacity of the responsible states and the extent to which each performed to such capacity.[86]

ii. Land-based Sources

Harm arising out of pollution of internal waters from land-based sources here receives separate, albeit brief, treatment for two reasons. First, it is, by far, the largest single source of marine pollution, accounting for in excess of 80 per cent of aggregate pollution.[87] Second, it provides a perfect opportunity to touch on the problems of responsibility related to technology transfer.

In general, the rules deduced with respect to the coastal state's responsibility for vessel-source pollution in internal waters apply. Consider, for example, a situation in which a privately owned factory in state *A* discharges petrochemical industrial waste into state *A*'s internal waters, causing material damage to

[81] See ch. 4 at 108.

[82] See ch. 4 at 112–14.

[83] Assuming that state *B*'s failure of due diligence bore a causal connexion to the injury at all.

[84] See ch. 9 at nn. 11–12, *supra*.

[85] This is true even if one is based on strict responsibility and the other on a breach of due diligence. These standards determine whether or not a breach of obligation has occurred. The question of relative causation and blame is additional and independent.

[86] Note that if state *C* were to bring a claim against state *A*, *B*, or *E*, the question of whether state *C* is entitled to compensation would turn on the same factors—comparative blame and causation. See ch. 4 at n. 81.

[87] Johnston, 'Marine Pollution Control: Law, Science and Politics', 28 *Int'l J.* 69, at 70 (1972–3); du Pontavice, 'Pollution', in *The Future of the Law of the Sea*, 104, at 129 (Bouchez and Kaijen eds. 1972).

the environmental interests of adjacent state *B*. State *A* was clearly obligated to exercise its territorial jurisdiction over the polluting activity with due diligence to prevent such external injury. Moreover, if the activity had been conducted by state organs or representatives, or could be defined as ultrahazardous or, possibly, if the injury was extreme, state *A* should stand responsible on a strict basis.[88] Land-based pollution does not necessarily raise any new analytical issues.

Interesting questions arise, however, to the extent other states are implicated. Assume, for example, that the factory was owned and operated in developing state *A* by nationals of developed state *C* seeking lower taxes, labour costs, or environmental standards. Alternatively, assume representatives of state *C* itself transferred the injury-producing technology to developing State *A* for purposes of a joint or assisted venture with that state. In each case, state *C* possessed a measure of authority over the matters leading to the injury that it was obligated to exercise to prevent any environmental harm to another state. In the former example it enjoyed prescriptive jurisdiction over the conduct of its nationals in any location. In the latter, the authority was simple self-control.

The obligation of states in the position of state *C* to act to prevent environmental harm to state *A* and third states was specifically identified by members of the ILC in discussions regarding 'Liability for Injurious Consequences Arising out of Acts Not Prohibited by International Law.'[89] Quentin-Baxter, the Special Rapporteur, suggested that the superior administrative and technical skills of state *C* and the direction of ultimate economic benefits to that state might even make it appropriate to subject state *C* to the regime of strict liability.[90] The rules of decision outlined above would not necessarily yield this result. The authority of state *C* over its nationals operating abroad does not confer the absolute capacity to control that merits a strict test. The standard of performance of the preventive obligation with respect to such private activities, therefore, should remain simple due diligence.[91] If the state took all reasonable and available measures to prevent the injurious event, no responsibility would be triggered. State *C*'s administrative and technical sophistication, coupled with any awareness of state *A*'s lack of such sophistication, would combine, however, to suggest an elevated

[88] Whether one of the consequences of responsibility should be a cessation of the injurious activity should also touch on the seriousness of the injury. See ch. 8 at n. 88.

[89] See Comments of Sucharitkul, ILC, 1980 Sum. Rec., *supra* ch. 5 n. 72, at 246 and 1981 Sum. Rec., *supra* ch. 4 n. 35, at 224. See also iii *Manual on Space Law* 331 (Jasentuliyana and Lee eds. 1981); Handl, *supra* ch. 8 n. 63, at n. 110. See also Benrudi, 'State Responsibility and Hazardous Products Exports: A Solution to an International Problem', 13 *Cal. W. Int'l L.J.* 135 (1983), who argues that joint responsibility should lie with two states: the state from whose territory the material is exported and the state of nationality of the exporter.

[90] Q-B, 3rd Rpt., *supra* ch. 5 n. 72, at 20; Q-B, 5th Rpt., *supra* ch. 10 n. 104, at 9. But see Magraw, *supra* ch. 4 n. 13, at 325–6.

[91] See ch. 8 at nn. 103–10.

standard of diligence due.[92] Indeed, if any of the nationals' contributing conduct, e.g. export of technology, took place within state *C*, and state *C* knew or should have known of state *A*'s lack of expertise or will to prevent the harmful use of such technology, due diligence might require prohibition of export.

As to responsibility for the state's direct participation in the supply or operation of the injury-producing activity, the general rules as to the conduct of state organs and agents apply. If fault or negligence is established, by reference to many of the same questions as to the knowledge and care of the state addressed in the private actor due diligence inquiry, responsibility will lie. If the conduct of state *C* may be categorized as ultrahazardous or produces extreme injury, responsibility will arise strictly, even in the absence of fault.[93]

Assuming the responsibility of states *A* and *C* is established, the principles of multiple responsibility, comparing blame and causation, would determine the consequential obligations of these states to injured state *B*. The apportionment of the burden of compensation thus would rest on factors such as each state's degree of participation, capacity to prevent (in terms of theoretical legal authority and actual opportunity and skill), receipt of the benefits of the conduct, knowledge of the risk, and diligence exercised to prevent the injury.

[92] See ch. 3 at n. 134.
[93] As to the standard of responsibility for state conduct generally, see ch. 8 at n. 102.

12

The Territorial Sea

A. COASTAL STATE AUTHORITY

i. Status as Territory

State assertions of exclusive legal authority over regions of the sea beyond internal waters were practically unknown throughout antiquity and at least the first half of the Middle Ages.[1] At the close of the medieval period, however, claims of exclusive territorial authority over adjacent seas were rather common.[2] The measure of the assertions expanded with the growth of sea-borne commerce and the corollary economic significance of the control of navigation. The assertions of Spain and Portugal in 1493 represented the culmination of this process. Based upon Papal Bulls issued by Pope Alexander VI, these two states arrogated between them the Indian and Pacific oceans, the Gulf of Mexico, and the western and southern Atlantic.[3] The asserted territorial rights, including the right to exclude or control foreign navigation, would have translated into absolute commercial monopolies in the New World and the East. It was precisely this intolerable economic fact that precipitated the first and aggressive theoretical attack on the doctrinal basis of such marine territorial claims.[4]

The most influential of the criticisms levelled at the extensive assertions of territorial authority were those of Hugo de Groot, or Grotius, then counsel to the Dutch East India Company. Grotius' argument, expressed in *Mare liberum*, consisted of two steps.[5] First, he posited that the open seas were not susceptible to the acts of possession and occupancy requisite to render them

[1] Oppenheim, *supra* ch. 2 n. 37, at 582. Oppenheim here cites Ulpian: 'Mare quod natura omnibus patet' (L. 13, pr. D. viii. 4) and Celsus: 'Maris communem usum omnibus hominibus ut aeris' (L. 3, D. xliii. 8). *Id.*

[2] See Brierly, *supra* ch. 2 n. 41, at 304–5; Fulton, *The Sovereignty of the Sea* 339 (1911). For example, England claimed the Channel, the North Sea, and parts of the Atlantic; Venice the Adriatic; Genoa the Ligurian; Denmark/Norway the Northern Seas; and Sweden the Baltic. Brierly, at 304. Note that Colombos argues that England's claim dates back to the 10th-century reign of Edgar the Peaceful. Colombus, *supra* ch. 11 n. 23, at 48. Fulton, *contra*, at 28, describes this as 'monkish fable'.

[3] See Brierly, *supra* ch. 2 n. 41, at 305; Fulton, *supra* n. 2, at 339. In the division, Spain received the Western Atlantic, the Gulf of Mexico, and the Pacific; Portugal received the Indian Ocean and the Atlantic south of Morocco. *Id.*

[4] Fulton, *supra* n. 2, at 339. The earliest attacks were those of De Castro, *De potestate legis poenalis*, Lib. iii, c. 14; and Vasquius, *Controversiae illustres*, lib. ii (1564). *Id.*, at 341. The absolutist perspective of sovereign authority admitted of no qualification to such authority.

[5] See Grotius, *Mare liberum* (1609).

property. Then, reflecting the current philosophical perspective, Grotius argued that in the absence of such a proprietary interest no state may exercise authority over a region of the seas.[6]

The responses to Grotius' argument for 'freedom of the seas' were legion.[7] Representative of the respondents was J. Selden, an Englishman.[8] Selden's argument was a fusion of theology and history: God defined certain boundaries subject to a monarch's sovereign authority; the balance of the seas were distributed on the basis of a type of historical occupancy well established as to the 'English' seas.[9] The theological component of Selden's argument lost popular support by the close of the seventeenth century. The historical element simply succumbed over time to consensus acceptance of Grotius' perspective of the open sea as an area not susceptible to occupancy or possession.[10]

The doctrine of the freedom of the seas did not, however, deny all claims to territorial authority over the seas. Even Grotius acknowledged that states could effectively possess a narrow adjacent sea; it was the scale of the contemporary claims that rendered them theoretically unsound.[11] To the extent that the state could physically control activities at sea from its land territory, the sea could appropriately be defined as in the state's possession and, consequently, subject to the regime of state territory.[12]

[6] As noted in ch. 9, the exercise of the authority of the state, was associated from the outset with the possession of territory. The implication for the assertion of legal authority over the seas was patent. The equation of sovereign authority with territory meant that if a state were to possess any authority over the seas, it must possess the seas themselves. 'If, according to the current philosophy, *imperium* and *dominium* could exist only in conjunction, so that the power to rule and to legislate, which is the power of *imperium*, could extend only so far as the ruler and legislator possessed *dominium*, or the rights of an owner, then foreign ships would be beyond the grasp of authority of the coastal State when outside the boundaries of its territory.' O'Connell, 'The Juridical Nature of the Territorial Sea', 45 *Brit. Yb. Int'l L.* 303, at 309–10 (1971). Hence, states desiring to exercise any measure of authority over marginal seas were jurisprudentially dependent on the definition of such seas as state property. As to Grotius' argument see Brierly, ch. 2 *supra* n. 41, at 305; O'Connell, 'Juridical Nature', at 306–14; Jessup, *supra* ch. 11 n. 14, at 5; Schneider, *supra* ch. 5 n. 36, at 147–52.

[7] Respondents included: Gentilis, *Avocatio hispanica* (1613); Welwood, *De Dominio maris* (1613); Boroughs, *The Sovereignty of the British Seas Proved by Records, History, and the Municipal Laws of this Kingdom* (written 1633, publ. 1651); Sarpi, *Del Dominio de mare adriatico* (1676); De Freitas, *De Justo imperio lusitanorum asiatic* (1625). See Oppenheim, *supra* ch. 2, n. 37, at 585.

[8] Selden, *Mare clausum seu de dominio maris* (written 1618, publ. 1635). Selden explained the delay in publication as a function of King James's concern not to offend the Danish king, from whom he wished to extract a loan. Fulton, *supra* n. 2, at 366. Fulton also asserts that Grotius himself joined the advocates of *Mare clausum* once Holland had established a trade with the East Indies and desired exclusivity. *Id.*, at 340–1.

[9] See O'Connell, *supra* n. 6, at 314.

[10] See Brierly, *supra* ch. 2 n. 41, at 305–6; Fulton, *supra* n. 2, at 336, 537; Schneider, *supra* ch. 5 n. 36, at 147–9; *id.*

[11] See Jessup, *supra* ch. 11 n. 14, at 5; Fulton, *supra* n. 2, at 347; O'Connell, *supra* n. 6, at 313; Schneider, *supra* ch. 10 n. 107, at 161.

[12] 'It remained for a Judge of the Supreme Court of Appeal of Holland, Cornelius Van Bynkershoek, to translate this idea into a maxim which seemed to capture the imagination and

The recognition of the extension of territorial jurisdiction over the proximate marginal sea endured without significant debate until the disjunction of the concepts of *dominium* and *imperium* in the middle of the nineteenth century. As described by O'Connell:

> Territory ceased to be regarded as something owned and came to be regarded as a spatial area within which the faculties of sovereignty could be exercised. Police powers could be exercised outside this spatial area to the extent international law permitted, and hence jurisdiction ceased to be spatially coterminous with territory. It now became possible to speak of 'jurisdiction' over coastal waters without imparting the notion of property or territory to justify it.[13]

With this development, exercise of coastal state authority in the marginal seas no longer required a 'territorial' definition of such waters. It became a popular view among publicists seeking to maximize maritime freedoms that states possessed only a set of specific, circumscribed, jurisdictional rights in the marginal sea, i.e. that these waters did not constitute state territory.[14]

Doctrinal debate on the issue continued unabated well into the twentieth century.[15] Conclusive evidence of community rejection of the bundle of rights approach in favour of a 'territorial' sea came at the 1930 Conference on the Codification of International Law held in The Hague.[16] Drawing extensively upon the advance work of several independent groups of publicists and the Conference's own preparatory survey of state attitudes, the Conference produced as part of its Final Act a statement entitled 'The Legal Status of the Territorial Sea'.[17] As to perhaps its principal objective—reaching agreement on the extent of the marginal sea—the 1930 Conference clearly failed.[18] On the other hand, the conferees managed to achieve a resolution of the dispute

convince the intellect: "Imperium terrae finitur armorum potestas." ' Jessup, *supra* ch. 11 n. 14, at 607, quoting van Bynkershoek, *Questiones juris publici* (1737), lib. 1, cap. viii.

13 *Id.*, at 325.

14 Proponents of the perspective included such notables as Lapradelle, *Revue générale de droit international public* 264 (1898); Ortolan, *Règles internationales et diplomatie de la mer* (1845); Twiss, *Law of Nations*, (2nd rev. edn. 1884). See also *R.* v. *Keyn*, (1876) L.R. 2 Ex. D. 63.

15 See generally the exceptionally comprehensive research into the pattern of publicists' opinions in O'Connell, *supra* n. 6, *passim*.

16 The Conference, convened by the Council of the League of Nations, was attended by forty-two states, with Russia as an observer.

17 Final Act, Conference for the Codification of International Law: The Legal Status of the Territorial Sea, League of Nations Pub. No. C. 228 M. 115 (1930) (hereinafter cited as League of Nations Final Act). See generally O'Connell, *supra* n. 6, at 348–50. For preparation efforts see Harv. Res. Territorial Waters, *supra* ch. 11 n. 35, at 243; Amended Draft Convention Communicated to Various Governments by the League of Nations Committee of Experts for the Progressive Codification of International Law, 29 Jan. 1926 (League of Nations Doc. C. 196 M. 70 1927 V at 72); 'Projet de règlement relatif à la mer territoriale en temps de paix', L'Institut de droit international, Stockholm (1928), reprinted in Harv. Res. Territorial Waters, *id.*, at 368–70.

18 The 1930 Conference apparently failed to adopt a compromise 3-mile territorial sea with a 9-mile contiguous zone due to British resistance to the concept of any contiguous zone. Brierly, *supra* ch. 2 n. 41, at 206. As to the failure of the 1958 Conference, see McDougal and Burke, *supra* ch. 6 n. 4, at 529–39.

regarding the character of authority in that zone; Article 1 clearly defined the band of coastal waters as state territory.[19] The consensus evidenced in 1930 was finally and formally codified in the 1958 Convention on the Territorial Sea and the Contiguous Zone.[20] Article 1 of the Convention states that: 'The sovereignty of a State extends beyond its land territory and its internal waters to a belt of sea adjacent to its coast, described as the territorial sea.'[21]

The breadth of this zone of now clearly territorial waters remained highly controversial.[22] Neither the 1958 Convention nor the 1960 UN Conference on the Law of the Sea produced agreement on the issue.[23] State practice has been extremely erratic; a 1977 UN survey identified nineteen 3-mile claims, seventy-three 12-mile claims, fourteen 200-mile claims, and the balance in the interstices.[24] Only in the package negotiations of LOS III has a resolution finally emerged. Article 3 of the 1982 Convention provides that '[e]very State has the right to establish the breadth of its territorial sea up to a limit not exceeding 12 nautical miles, measured from baselines determined in accordance with this Convention.'[25]

The territorial definition bestowed upon the marginal sea of up to twelve miles vests the coastal state with the same expansive prescriptive and enforcement competence enjoyed over any region within the bounds of the state.[26] The Hague Conference reports observed 'that the power exercised by the State over this belt is in its nature in no way different from the power which the State exercises over its domain on land.'[27] In this respect, the territorial sea does not differ from internal waters, the other marine component of state

[19] Art. 1, League of Nations Final Act, *supra* n. 17, at 184.

[20] Territorial Sea Convention, *supra* ch. 10 n. 70. Brierly defined this effort as 'the nearest thing that there is to an agreed statement of the modern law governing internal and territorial waters and the contiguous zone'. Brierly, *supra* ch. 2 n. 41, at 194.

[21] Territorial Sea Convention, *supra* ch. 10 n. 70. See also LOS Convention, *supra* ch. 5 n. 17, art. 2.

[22] By the term 'territorial sea' this work and contemporary jurisprudence refer to the surface, water column, seabed, and subsoil. For a discussion of the incremental development of the now unitary concept see Marston, 'The Evolution of the Concept of Sovereignty over the Bed and Subsoil of the Territorial Sea', 48 *Brit. Yb. Int'l L.* 321 (1976–7). For particularly useful treatments of the subject of the dispute regarding the breadth of the marginal sea see Brownlie, *supra* ch. 2 n. 52, at 186–203; McDougal and Burke *supra* ch. 6 n. 4, at 305–561.

[23] The subsequent failure at the 1960 conference is chronicled in Bowett, 'The Second United Nations Conference on the Law of the Sea', 54 *Am. J. Int'l L.* 751, at 779–81 (1960); McDougal and Burke, *supra* ch. 6 n. 4, at 540–8.

[24] Breadth of National Jurisdiction with Dates of Entry Into Force, UN Dept. of Pub. Info. Ref. Paper no. 18 (1978), at 59–54, reprinted in *New Directions in the Law of the Sea* 478 (Churchill *et al.* eds 1977). By 1981 the number of 12-mile territorial sea claims had increased to eighty. US Department of State, Office of the Geographer, National Claims to Maritime Jurisdiction 8 (Limits in the Seas, no. 36, 4th Rev. 1981). As to the relationship between codification and unilateral expansion see Apollis, *supra* ch. 10 n. 53, at 119–21.

[25] LOS Convention, *supra* ch. 5 n. 17, art. 3.

[26] O'Connell writes that the use of the term 'sovereignty' in the 1958 definition was designed to concede to the coastal state plenary power to regulate events in the territorial sea. O'Connell, *supra* n. 6, at 797. Apollis, *supra* ch. 10 n. 53, at 51–3.

[27] Observations to Art. 1, Second Comm. Rpt., Final Act. *supra* n. 17, at 239.

territory.[28] Subject to one caveat, the definition of the ambit of the coastal state's jurisdiction over environmental matters set forth in the preceding chapter serves equally to describe that applicable to the territorial sea.[29] Most states have in fact exercised such plenary jurisdiction, endeavouring to prevent conduct in territorial waters injurious to the marine environment.[30]

The significant distinction between the coastal state's environmental authority in internal and territorial waters turns, of course, on foreign vessels' right of 'innocent passage'. The host of complicated issues which arise as to the content of that right and its impact on flag and coastal authority and responsibility with respect to environmental matters must now be considered in detail.

ii. Innocent Passage

a. Evolution

It was not until the middle of the nineteenth century that the concept of a *right* of 'innocent passage' in the marginal sea was articulated. Prior to that period, there was some recognition in the literature that non-threatening passage ought to be tolerated by the coastal state.[31] Nevertheless, the contemporary absolutist definition of sovereign prerogative dictated that passage in territorial waters remain subject to coastal state discretion.[32]

The 'bundle of rights' alternative to the territorial definition of the marginal sea provided the first theoretical foundation for a right of passage.[33] Proponents of this view simply argued that authority to interfere with vessels in innocent passage was not among the limited jurisdictional rights vested in the coastal state.[34] With the advent of the doctrine of relative sovereignty, however, recourse to a non-territorial definition was no longer required. The acknowledgement of navigational rights as a qualification to state authority even in a territorial sea was not inconsistent with the relativist perspective of the character of sovereignty. Hence, in 1927, Philip Jessup could declare that within the marginal sea:

> a State may, under international law, exercise any jurisdiction and do any act which it may lawfully do upon its own land territory. Exception must be made to this general statement only in favor of the servitude known as the right of innocent passage.

[28] See Brierly, *supra* ch. 2 n. 41, at 237; Jessup, *supra* ch. 11 n. 14, at 123–33; Harv. Res. Territorial Waters, *supra* ch. 11 n. 35, at 299; Thommen, *supra* ch. 11 n. 18, at 68–70.

[29] See ch. 11 at nn. 5–28 *supra*.

[30] See e.g. Canada Shipping Act of 1970, *Can. Rev. Stat.* c. 5–9 (1970); Oman Marine Pollution Control Law (1974); Swedish Act of 2 June 1972 concerning Measures to Prevent the Pollution of Water by Vessels, Swed. Code of Stat. 15 June 1972; Decision no. 118 of 14 Feb. 1974 of the Council of Ministers of the USSR Relating to Greater Efforts to Counter Pollution of the Sea by Substances Harmful to Human Health or to the Living Resources of the Sea, reprinted in Ruster and Simma, *supra* ch. 11 n. 8, vol. iii at 1231; UK Prevention of Oil Pollution Act, 1971, c. 60, 27 July 1971; US Clean Water Act of 1977, 33 USC §§ 1251–376 (1977).

[31] O'Connell, *supra* n. 6, at 324–5.

[32] See ch. 5 at n. 5.

[33] See text at n. 14 *supra*.

[34] See authorities cited at n. 14 *supra*.

. . . [T]he existence of such a servitude is not inconsistent with sovereignty . . . International law itself is a restriction upon a denial of absolute sovereignty.[35]

The consensus at the 1930 Hague Conference on the territorial definition of the marginal sea rested precisely on the premise of relativism. The conferees emphasized that '[o]bviously, sovereignty over the territorial sea, like sovereignty over the domain on land, can only be exercised subject to the conditions laid down by international law.'[36] Principal among the identified conditions was the right of innocent passage. Article 4 of the Conference text prohibited the imposition by the coastal state of obstacles to the exercise of innocent passage.[37] 'Passage is not *innocent* when a vessel makes use of the territorial sea of a Coastal State for the purpose of doing any act prejudicial to the security, to the public policy or to the fiscal interests of that State.'[38] The comments published with the Conference text explained:

It is immaterial whether or not the intention to do such an act existed at the time when the vessel entered the territorial sea, provided that the act is in fact committed in that sea. In other words, the passage ceases to be innocent if the right accorded by international law and defined in the present Convention is abused and in that event the Coastal State resumes its liberty of action.[39]

Even vessels exercising the right of innocent passage were not, however, to be immune from coastal authority. To the contrary, the Conference text specifically provided (*a*) that coastal states may verify a vessel's innocence and take steps to protect against prejudicial acts[40] and (*b*) that vessels exercising innocent passage must nevertheless comply with 'laws and regulations enacted in conformity with international usage.'[41] Among the several species of coastal state regulation specifically enumerated as conforming with international practice were laws related to 'the protection of the waters of the Coastal State against pollution of any kind caused by vessels' and 'the protection of the products of the territorial sea'.[42] Implicitly, vessels violating such regulations forfeited some measure of the immunity from local authority otherwise conferred by innocent passage; the extent and import of such forfeiture were nowhere clarified in the text.

The Hague conferees in fact seem to have recognized that the definition of a territorial sea carried with it a presumptive grant of plenary legal authority over all matters within the region.[43] The innocent passage provisions did not suggest immunity from the exercise of all species of coastal authority other than those enumerated. To the contrary, the comments to the Hague text appear to presume the existence of *prescriptive* authority over any matters or

[35] See Jessup, *supra* n. 14, at xxxiv.
[36] Observations to Art. 1, Second Comm. Rpt., Final Act, *supra* n. 16, at 239.
[37] *Id.*, art. 4, at 185.
[38] *Id.*, art, 3, at 185.
[39] Observations to Art. 3, Second Comm. Rpt., *id.*, at 241.
[40] *Id.*, art. 5, at 185. See Observations to Art. 5, Second Comm. Rpt., *id.*, at 241.
[41] *Id.*, art. 6, at 185.
[42] *Id.*
[43] See Observations to Art. 8, Second Comm. Rpt., *id.*, at 243.

conduct in the territorial sea. The tactic engaged at the Hague Conference to safeguard innocent passage was to articulate constraints with respect to the *enforcement* of such prescriptions. Hence, Article 8 limited the coastal state's authority 'to arrest any person or to conduct any investigation' regarding a crime committed during passage unless (*a*) 'the consequences of the crime extend beyond the vessel'; (*b*) 'the crime is of a kind to disturb the peace of the country or the good order of the territorial sea'; or (*c*) 'the vessel or its flag State requests arrest'.[44] Pursuant to the same logic, the text prohibited such interference for the exercise of civil jurisdiction against any person on board a vessel in innocent passage or against the vessel itself, unless the action against the vessel was related to the current passage.[45]

The text generated by the Hague Conference, as outlined above, set forth a basic structure for the regime of innocent passage that still endures. It was not, however, a binding instrument.[46] The incentives, therefore, to the clarification of the effect of its specific provisions were limited. It was really not until the Geneva Conference, almost thirty years later, that a host of questions regarding the definition of innocence, the relationship of coastal regulation to that definition and the constraints on coastal prerogatives were addressed in any comprehensive fashion. Three events in the intervening period materially affected, directly or indirectly, the subsequent efforts to clarify the character of the regime.

The first was the 1933 decision of the United States–Panama Claims Commission in the matter of the *David*.[47] The charge to the Commission was to determine the legitimacy of the seizure for civil proceedings before a US court of a vessel of Panamanian registry navigating allegedly American territorial waters off the Canal Zone. The event giving rise to the proceedings was a collision which had occurred during an earlier passage in the same waters. In direct contradiction of the Hague text's restrictions on enforcement authority, the Commission held the seizure lawful.

> There is a clear preponderance of authority to the effect that this sovereignty [over the territorial sea] is qualified by what is known as the right of innocent passage, and that this qualification forbids the sovereign actually to prohibit the innocent passage of alien merchant vessels through its territorial waters.
>
> There is no clear preponderance of authority to the effect that such vessels when passing through territorial waters are exempt from civil arrest.[48]

[44] Final Act, *supra* n. 26, art. 8 at 186.

[45] *Id.*, art. 9.

[46] Indeed, a Canadian court denied the force of innocent passage in 1931 with a holding 'that each nation has the absolute right to prescribe the conditions upon which the vessels of another nation will be permitted to enter its territorial waters'. *SS May* v. *The King*, [1931] 3 DLR 15, at 20, quoted in O'Connell, *supra* n. 6, at 355.

[47] The *David* (1933) (*Panama* v. *United States*), United States–Panama Claims Commission, 52 *Ann. Dig.* 137, 6 R. Int'l Arb. Awards 382 (1933). See Jessup, 'Civil Jurisdiction over Ships in Innocent Passage', 27 *Am. J. Int'l L.* 747 (1933).

[48] *Id.*

The conclusion in the *David* decision was endorsed and reinforced, prior to the 1958 Geneva Convention, in the text of the International Convention Relating to the Arrest of Seagoing Ships done in Brussels in 1952.[49] Article 2 of that Convention expressly permits the arrest for civil proceedings relating to maritime claims of any vessel within a state's 'jurisdiction'.[50] No limitation with respect to vessels in innocent passage was articulated.[51]

The third, and certainly most important, of the three principal intervening events was the opinion issued by the International Court of Justice in the *Corfu Channel* Case.[52] In 1946, two warships of the United Kingdom entering the territorial waters of Albania in the strait between Albania and the Greek island of Corfu were fired upon by Albanian shore batteries. Following a process of diplomatic exchanges in which the United Kingdom asserted a violation of the right of innocent passage, British warships returned to and entered the strait with the announced intention of exercising and testing that right, and if necessary returning Albanian fire. Two of the vessels were damaged by uncharted mines located in the strait. Three weeks later British naval minesweepers entered the channel and removed the remaining mines.

In the litigation before the International Court arising out of these incidents, Britain asserted Albanian responsibility for the damage to its naval vessels; Albania countered, in part, with an assertion of British liability for the violation of Albanian sovereignty attendant to the entry of the vessels into territorial waters without consent.[53] The Albanian position rested on alternative premises: either (*a*) no right of innocent passage exists with respect to warships; or (*b*) the passage of the British vessels which encountered the mines was, in any case, not innocent. The Court rejected each of these premises. As to the first, the Court concluded that a right of innocent passage applicable to warships does indeed apply, at least with respect to straits utilized for international navigation such as the Corfu Channel.[54] As to the second contention, the opinion incorporated an extensive discussion of the manner of the passage of the warships, considering the number, type, and

[49] Signed at Brussels, 10 May 1952, registered 2 Oct. 1962, reprinted in 439 UNTS 192 (1963).

[50] *Id.*, art. 2, at 197.

[51] Interestingly, a companion treaty provided that states possess no authority to arrest or detain non-flag vessels even for investigation when the penal or disciplinary responsibility of individuals is the subject matter of the action. Art. 2, International Convention of the Unification of Certain Rules Relating to Penal Jurisdiction on matters of Collision or Other Incidents of Navigation, signed at Brussels, 10 May 1952, registered 2 Oct. 1962, reprinted in 439 UNTS 233 (1963). Art. 3 excepts from this restriction the state's internal waters, and explicitly acknowledges the right of parties to reserve its application to territorial waters. *Id.*, at 237. Critically, most states did express this reservation. *Id.*, at 242–8.

[52] The *Corfu Channel* Case (*UK* v *Albania*), [1949] ICJ 4 (Merits).

[53] *Id.*

[54] *Id.*, at 28. The Albanian argument that warships do not possess a right of innocent passage because, by definition, they 'prejudice' or threaten the coastal state was then and remains supported by considerable authority. See Argument of Elihu Root, North Atlantic Coast Fisheries Arbitration (1912), Hague Ct. Rep. (Scott), at 141; Brownlie, *supra* ch. 2 n. 52, at 206–7; McDougal and Burke, *supra* ch. 6 n. 4, at 199–208.

formation of ships, and the posture of weapons and gun crews.[55] Interpreting these facts in light of the vessels' express intent to assert the right of innocent passage, the Court concluded that the passage was, indeed, innocent.[56]

Following this decision, there could be little question that a right of innocent passage had risen to the dignity of a rule of international law. Yet, the decision only directly affirmed the existence of a right with respect to passage in international straits—zones of crucial navigational significance. Moreover, the analysis engaged by the Court raised a subsidiary set of questions as to the criteria of 'innocence'. Certain commentators ascribed the Court's inquiry into the manner of the vessels' passage to the conclusion that manner is the determinant of innocence.[57] Others voiced the broader perspective that the Court only defined otherwise patently threatening warship passage as innocent due to the unique facts with respect to motivation; but for the evidence that the British intent was only to test the right, the manner of the passage would not have been deemed innocent.[58] The *Corfu Channel* decision, then, illuminated, without solution, certain of the basic uncertainties in the definition and interpretation of the right of innocent passage.

b. The 1958 Geneva Convention

The first multilateral forum for the resolution of such uncertainties was the 1958 Geneva conference; having confirmed a regime of sovereignty, the conferees were compelled to define the qualifications to that regime. Article 14 of the Convention sets forth the basic rule that 'ships of all States, whether coastal or not, shall enjoy the right of innocent passage through the territorial sea.'[59] 'Passage' is then defined as 'navigation through the territorial sea for the purpose either of traversing that sea without entering internal waters, or of proceeding to internal waters, or of making for the high seas from internal waters.'[60] Passage is to be conferred the privileges of 'innocence' 'so long as it is not prejudicial to the peace, good order or security of the coastal State.'[61]

Notably, the language of the 1930 draft requiring a 'use' of the sea with the 'purpose' committing a 'prejudicial act' was not incorporated in the definition of innocence.[62] Fitzmaurice, of the British delegation, has clearly indicated

[55] The *Corfu Channel* Case *(UK v Albania)*, [1949] ICJ 4 (Merits), at 30–31.

[56] *Id.*

[57] See e.g. Fitzmaurice, 'The Law and Procedures of the International Court of Justice: General Principles and Substantive Law', 27 *Brit. Yb. Int'l L.* 1, at 28 (1950).

[58] See e.g. McDougal and Burke, *supra* ch. 6 n. 4, at 244–6.

[59] Territorial Sea Convention, *supra* ch. 10 n. 70, art. 14(1).

[60] *Id.*, art. 14(2). Thus, vessels stopped or at anchor are not in passage unless their position is 'incidental to ordinary navigation' or compelled by *force majeure*. Id., art. 14(3).

[61] *Id.*, art. 14(4). Certain of the participants wanted to limit the definition of non-innocence to acts of 'military menace' against the sovereignty of the state. The language actually used was a compromise proffered by the Indian representative. See Emanuelli, 'La Pollution maritime et la notion de passage innoffensif', 11 *Can. Yb. Int'l L.* 13, at 21 (1973).

[62] See text at n. 37 *supra*.

that a vessel's objective was nevertheless viewed by the draftsmen as one determinant of innocence.[63] Presumably, then, the rationale of the deletion of 'purpose' was to codify the propriety of the inquiry into *both* manner and purpose of passage suggested, under its most persuasive interpretation, by the *Corfu Channel* decision.[64] Furthermore, by deletion of the references to 'use' and 'prejudicial act', the Geneva text had the apparent intent to expand the bounds of the analysis of innocence even beyond consideration of actual conduct and its purpose engaged by the ICJ.[65] Activity was no longer a requisite component of the definition of 'prejudice' to the coastal state. Hence, the broad language of the Convention generally has been interpreted as establishing the relevance of, and the legitimacy of an inquiry into, additional passive characteristics such as species of cargo and destination.[66]

Article 15 supports the preceding general grant of a right of innocent passage with the statement that '[t]he coastal State must not hamper innocent passage.'[67] As with the parallel 1930 provisions, this prohibition was not intended to suggest the absence of coastal state regulatory authority. To the contrary, Article 16 clearly acknowledges the state's authority to take any action to prevent non-innocent passage.[68] Moreover, Article 17 recognizes the coastal state's right to regulate the passage of even innocent vessels with the admonition that 'vessels exercising the right of innocent passage shall comply with the laws and regulations of the coastal State enacted in conformity with these Articles and other rules of international law.'[69]

One of the principal drafting objectives of these provisions was 'to disassociate the idea of non-innocence of passage from that of infringements of local laws.'[70] In other words, the intent of the participants, not expressed in the text, was to establish an objective definition of innocence.[71] In the words of Fitzmaurice:

> If a vessel infringes such a [local] law or regulation, she may indeed be liable to a fine or other penalty. But her passage does not, merely on that account, cease to be innocent, or become liable to be prevented or denied entirely . . . To render a passage non-innocent, there must be something more than a mere infringement of a local law or

[63] Fitzmaurice, 'Some Results of the Geneva Conference on the Law of the Sea', 8 *Int'l & Comp. L.Q.* (72, at 96 (1979). The author did, however, view this as a deviation from the perspective of 'innocence' suggested by the *Corfu Channel* Case. See text at n. 57 *supra.*

[64] See discussion at nn. 57–8 *supra.*

[65] Note that the preparatory materials of the International Law Commission had suggested adoption of the language utilized in 1930. See McDougal and Burke, *supra* ch. 6 n. 4, at 258.

[66] See Fitzmaurice, *supra* n. 63, at 96; Legault, *supra* note ch. 5 n. 45, at 220; McDougal and Burke, *supra* ch. 6, n. 4, at 258. *Contra* Brownlie, *supra* ch. 2 n. 52, at 205.

[67] Territorial Sea Convention, *supra* n. 158, art. 15(1). Article 16(3) does provide that the coastal state may suspend innocent passage temporarily in specific areas if 'essential for the protection of its security.' This right does not apply in straits from one part of the high seas to another or to a foreign territorial sea. *Id.*, art. 16(4).

[68] *Id.*, art. 16(1).

[69] *Id.*, art. 17.

[70] Fitzmaurice, *supra* n. 63, at 94.

[71] See *id.*

regulation. There must really be something going beyond the existence of local laws and regulations as such—something that could be considered as tainting the passage even if there happened not to be any specific domestic law or regulation under which it was logically illegal.[72]

A violation of law, therefore, justifies prohibition of passage only to the extent that the coastal state law or regulation which has been transgressed reflects the objective definition. McDougal and Burke have succinctly summarized the object and effect of the disassociation:

For violation of coastal prescriptions . . . relating to interests broadly formulated as 'peace, good order, or security,' the coastal State would be competent to prohibit passage as non-innocent. For failure to comply with other coastal laws, however, passing vessels could not be excluded from the territorial sea but they could be subject to other forms of coastal authority.[73]

The basic issues unresolved by the Convention's approach relate precisely to the character of authority retained by the coastal state with respect to matters which do not rise to the level of implicating innocence itself. With respect to environmental matters, it is quite clear, from the comments prepared in conjunction with the Convention itself and the predecessor 1930 text, that coastal state authority to prescribe and enforce regulations designed to protect the environment against vessels in innocent passage was indeed contemplated by the Geneva participants.[74] Yet, that competence, together with all other coastal state authority, is expressly subject to the rule that innocent passage shall not be 'hampered.' The interpretative problem, of course, is that any exercise of coastal state legal authority may, to some degree, hamper passage. The very existence of a prescription which requires compliance of all actors within the territorial sea may have a chilling effect on the exercise of the right of innocent passage. This is true even in the absence of any enforcement action taken by the coastal state which physically interferes with innocent passage itself. The penalty for a violation of a coastal regulation may be enforced at another opportunity by methods or actions other than direct physical interference with the navigation of an offending vessel.[75] Hence, the simple presence of rules subject to such subsequent enforcement would constitute an impediment to the exercise of innocent passage by any vessel that might anticipate a violation; the threat of incurring liability may effectively impede the exercise of navigational rights.

[72] *Id.*, at 94–5.

[73] McDougal and Burke, *supra* ch. 6 n. 4, at 254. This conclusion rests both on the logic of the thing and the specific comments of participants. See Sorenson, 'The Law of the Sea', 520 *Int'l Conc.* 195, at 234 (1958); Verzijl, 'The United Nations Conference on the Law of the Sea, Geneva 1958', 6 *Nederlands tijdschrift voor international recht* 1, at 29 (1959).

[74] See Final Act, *supra* n. 17, art. 6(*b*); ILC Report to the General Assembly, UN Doc. A/3159 (1956); Teclaff, *supra* ch. 10 n. 53, at 120. See also Apollis, *supra* ch. 10 n. 53, at 234–5.

[75] For example when the same vessel next enters internal waters or ceases 'passage' in territorial waters or, in appropriate circumstances, against other related vessels, assets, or individuals present within state territory.

The utility of the restriction against hampering passage may be found, however, in its logical implication: a test of proportionality or reasonableness. It is submitted that the object of the 'hampering' language must be to strike an appropriate balance among (*a*) the signifiance of the interest which the coastal state seeks to protect or advance, (*b*) the threat to such interest in the absence of prescriptive authority and (*c*) the character and magnitude of the attendant interference with the exercise of innocent passage. Expressed in its most abstract form, the rule of decision that will lead to such a balance must be one of 'reasonableness.'[76] Coastal state prescriptions designed to protect minor interests which materially impair navigational rights (by, for example, creating standards and liabilities which render passage economically difficult) ought not to be tolerated. Such regulations would not survive scrutiny under a test of reasonableness. As unreasonable prescriptions, they must be deemed to 'hamper' the exercise of innocent passage. On the other hand, the same degree of hindrance to foreign vessels might well be defined as reasonable in connection with the application of a prescription designed to safeguard a seriously threatened interest of greater significance. Notwithstanding their practical effect, such prescriptions should not be viewed as impermissibly 'hampering' to passage.

The parallel between the foregoing interpretation and the consensus regime with respect to the right of coastal states to exercise authority on the high seas to protect environmental interests is sufficiently striking to demand notation. As chapter 13 will discuss, the 1969 International Convention Relating to Intervention on the High Seas in Cases of Oil Pollution Casualties acknowledges a coastal state's right to take measures on the high seas to protect itself from environmental injury following a maritime casualty. In the exercise of such authority the coastal state is constrained, pursuant to other provisions of the Convention, by a standard of proportionality, balancing the interests threatened, the probability of success and the interference or damage to the foreign vessel occasioned by the exercise. There is then a very recent model for the utilization of a rule of reason for assessing the propriety of the exercise of coastal state legal authority. The suggested interpretation of the 'hampering' prohibition does suffer from the same infirmity as the 1969 convention and all other abstract rules of decision. The outcome of a decision-maker's evaluation of the 'reasonableness' of a given prescription may not be predicted with certainty. Yet, certainty does not constitute the principal objective of this, or any, legal regime. Rather, a rule must first be formulated which serves effectively as a vehicle for accommodating the competing interests of the

[76] It should be noted that, in fact, the whole of the regime of innocent passage may be viewed as representing an expression of this approach. The definition of innocence is simply a crystallization of the community's conclusion that certain state interests are of sufficient dignity that any exercise of prescriptive authority, including denial of entry, is reasonable. On the other hand, prescriptions not relating to matters 'prejudicial to the peace, good order or security of the coastal state' must be subjected independently to a test of reasonableness to determine whether they impermissibly 'hamper'.

coastal state and the community. It is submitted that the prohibition against "hampering"–with its subsumed test of reasonableness—achieves that objective. Certainty will follow inevitably with the development of a body of decisional interpretative law.[77]

The reconciliation of the coastal state's right to regulate vessels in innocent passage and the imperative not to hamper such passage is even more difficult in the context of enforcement authority. Even a minor enforcement action, such as detention for inspection, taken against a vessel in innocent passage, directly interferes with the course of its navigation. Indeed, McDougal and Burke, in a critique following the 1958 Convention, persuasively argue that denial of entry to the territorial sea represents a far less intrusive or hampering exercise of enforcement authority than do other acts such as arrest, seizure, or judicial sale.[78] They submit, therefore, that the 1958 provisions which preclude only prohibitions of innocent passage fail to impose limits on enforcement actions of even greater detriment to the enjoyment of navigational rights.[79]

The latter conclusion, however, fails to recognize the applicability of the provision forbidding acts which hamper innocent passage to the exercise of coastal state enforcement authority. The subsumed test of reasonableness would dictate that the degree of interference attendant to any enforcement act must be proportionate to the interests of the coastal state, including the importance of the interest protected, the nature of the prescription violated, the risk of harm in the absence of enforcement, etc. It may indeed be appropriate to immunize a vessel from direct interference with passage caused by the enforcement of a rule forbidding the introduction of pollution, when the violation consists of the discard of a small bin of garbage.[80] On the other hand, a discharge of oil, although perhaps not rising to the level of 'serious' pollution, may merit a limited enforcement response such as inspection and brief detention. The prohibition against 'hampering' thus provides a flexible rule of decision for determining the reasonableness, i.e. legality, of any exercise of enforcement authority.

Abuse of enforcement, however, represents such a threat to innocent passage that the 1958 Convention text set forth a series of guidelines as to when a coastal state may take *any* action to enforce a prescription against a vessel in passage. Article 19 first provides that a state 'should not' conduct an arrest or investigation on board such a vessel for the commission of a crime during passage unless: (*a*) 'the consequences of the crime extend to the coastal State'; (*b*) 'the crime is of a kind to disturb the peace of the country or the good order of the territorial sea; (*c*) requested to do so by the captain or the flag state's consul; or (*d*) 'it is necessary for the suppression of illicit traffic in

[77] See ch. 13 *infra* at nn. 18–28.

[78] McDougal and Burke, *supra* ch. 6 n. 4, at 260–1.

[79] *Id.*

[80] That is not to suggest that the prescription so violated may not be enforced in a different fashion or at another opportunity.

narcotic drugs.'[81] Article 20 then states that a passing vessel 'should not' be stopped or diverted in innocent passage for the exercise of civil jurisdiction over a person on board and 'may not' be so interfered with for the exercise of civil jurisdiction over the vessel itself for liabilities not related to the current passage.[82] Finally, coastal states are precluded from enforcing extraterritorial prescriptions against vessels in innocent passage not on their way to internal waters; no arrest may be made for crimes committed prior to entry into the territorial sea.[83] It is noteworthy that only the text regarding arrest for prior or extraterritorial crimes and civil jurisdiction is unequivocally mandatory.[84] Although the conclusion is not without its critics, most commentators have concluded that the 'should not' language in the balance of Articles 19 and 20 was 'intended to reflect the fact that the rule enunciated represents standard international practice rather than strict international law.'[85]

c. *The LOS III Regime*

1. Definition of 'Innocence'

In basic structure, the regime of innocent passage defined in the 1982 LOS Convention closely parallels that described in the provisions of the 1958 Convention. Article 17 commences with a statement of the affirmative right of

[81] *Id.*, art. 19(1). Note that these restrictions are not applicable to vessels in passage from internal waters.

[82] *Id.*, art. 20(1) and (2). Again, these provisions are not applicable to vessels proceeding from internal waters.

[83] *Id.*, art. 19(5). See Brierly, *supra* ch. 2 n. 41, at 239–40; Brownlie, *supra* ch. 2 n. 52, at 208; McDougal and Burke, *supra* ch. 6 n. 4, at 273–81. A common logic may be discerned with respect to the foregoing provisions. Each denies an aspect of enforcement of legal authority otherwise within the ambit of the general territorial authority of the coastal state because to do so does not directly impair the capacity of the state to act to protect its interests in the territorial sea. In the absence of an occurrence or violation during passage which affects the coastal state, the harm or threat to the state's interests is not sufficiently immediate to merit interference with innocent passage. From another perspective, enforcement actions against a vessel in innocent passage for the type of violations enumerated would neither diminish nor prevent an adverse impact upon the coastal state. It is true, of course, that the authority to enforce any prescription against vessels in innocent passage would indirectly contribute to the protection of the coastal state's interests: the right to utilize the enforcement process in any context translates into enhanced respect for and future compliance with the state's laws. Yet, it must be recognized that the provisions in question do not deny authority to enforce a legitimate prescription. They only operate to forbid enforcement actions against vessels currently exercising the right of innocent passage. Enforcement action may be taken at another opportunity or in another fashion. The sacrifice by the coastal state is, then, only of an indirect means of fostering its interests in the territorial sea; enforcement authority is retained (subject to certain other qualifications) with respect to all aspects of a vessel's passage which do directly affect those interests.

[84] These provisions nevertheless run directly counter to both the *David* and the 1952 Brussels Convention. See text at nn. 47 and 50 *supra*. In response to the patent conflict with the 1952 text, the ILC's comments to the draft 1958 provisions stated the view that the 1952 Convention's reference to authority to arrest within 'the full jurisdiction of the State' must mean only internal waters. UN Doc. Supp. no. 9 A/3159 (1956). See Fitzmaurice, *supra* n. 63, at 108.

[85] Fitzmaurice, *supra* n. 63, at 104; Lee, 'Jurisdiction over Foreign Merchant Ships in the Territorial Sea: An Analysis of the Geneva Convention on the Law of the Sea', 55 *Am. J. Int'l L.* 77, at 84 (1961). For the contrary view see McDougal and Burke, *supra* ch. 6 n. 4, at 279–81.

innocent passage through the territorial sea.[86] Article 18 recites, with certain expansion, the definition of 'passage' articulated in 1958.[87] Article 19(1) continues with familiar language as to the meaning of 'innocence': 'Passage is innocent so long as it is not prejudicial to the peace, good order or security of the coastal State.'[88] The Convention then seeks to reduce the level of abstraction of this definition. Article 19(2) provides:

Passage of a foreign ship shall be considered to be prejudicial to the peace, good order or security of the coastal State if in the territorial sea it engages in any of the following activities: .... (*h*) any act of wilful and serious pollution contrary to the Convention; .... (*l*) any other activity not having a direct bearing on passage.[89]

In a number of respects this elaboration represents a deviation from custom and the 1958 text.

First, Article 19 would deny to the coastal state the legal authority to prohibit passage or exercise plenary authority with respect to vessels discharging pollution unless that discharge is 'wilful'. There would seem little question that the 1958 Convention contemplated coastal competence to prevent passage to polluting vessels as non-innocent.[90] Indeed, it is difficult to comprehend an argument that the preservation of aesthetic and recreational amenities, resource productivity, related general economic welfare, and the physical well-being of the population does not constitute a core interest embraced in the language 'peace, good order or security'. The Convention's introduction of a standard of intent is, therefore, perplexing.[91] The polluter's

[86] LOS Convention, *supra* ch. 5, n. 17, art. 31.

[87] Art. 18 provides:

1. Passage means navigation through the territorial sea for the purpose of: (*a*) traversing that sea without entering internal waters or calling at a roadstead or port facility. (*b*) proceeding to or from internal waters or a call at such roadstead or port facility.

2. Passage shall be continuous and expeditious. However, passage includes stopping and anchoring, but only in so far as the same are incidental to ordinary navigation or are rendered necessary for the purpose of rendering assistance to persons, ships or aircraft in danger or distress (*Id.*, art. 18).

[88] *Id.*, art. 19(1).

[89] The full list of Art 19 activities is as follows: (*a*) any threat or use of force against the sovereignty, territorial integrity or poltical independence of the coastal state, or in any other manner in violation of the principles of international law embodied in the Charter of the United Nations; (*b*) any exercise or practice with weapons of any kind; (*c*) any act aimed at collecting information to the prejudice of the defence or security of the coastal State; (*d*) any act of propaganda aimed at affecting the defense or security of the coastal state; (*e*) the launching, landing or taking on board of any aircraft; (*f*) the launching, landing or taking on board of any military device; (*g*) the loading or unloading of any commodity, currency or person contrary to the customs, fiscal, immigration or sanitary laws and regulations of the coastal state; (*h*) any act of wilful and serious pollution contrary to the Convention; (*i*) any fishing activities; (*j*) the carrying out of research or survey activities; (*k*) any act aimed at interfering with any systems of communications or any other facilities or installations of the coastal state; (*l*) any other activity not having a direct bearing on passage.

[90] See Teclaff, *supra* ch. 6 n. 33, at 120.

[91] It is true that the element of intent is common to each of the enumerated species of conduct defined in Art. 19 as tainting the innocence of passage. Yet, critically, it is an *inherent* aspect of each of the other activities listed (e.g., weapons exercise, the launching, landing or taking on board of aircraft or military devices, fishing, and scientific research). Obviously, these activities may occur only when the actor so intends. Pollution presents a threat of a very different order; it may

state of mind would not seem relevant to the issue of the magnitude and character of the threat to the coastal state. As one commentator has succinctly put it: '[t]he consequences, including harm to marine resources, amenities, and other coastal resource interests, can be just as prejudicial if a foreign ship "with gross negligence," or merely "accidentally" or "inadvertently," causes them.'[92] In short, the *mens rea* component of the Convention's definition of innocence is consistent with neither the underlying logic nor the current state of the customary regime.

The use of the adjective 'serious' in the definition, on the other hand, seems a laudable clarification of custom. A vessel's innocence, i.e. right of passage, ought not be denied absent an act or threat of pollution which materially affects, or threatens materially to affect, the coastal state's interests. Less consequential incidents of pollution simply merit less intrusive exercises of coastal state authority than denial of passage. The problem, however, is in what constitutes 'serious' pollution. It would seem, first, that the consequences of a given act or threat of pollution must not be considered in isolation from their incremental or synergistic effects.[93] Second, the analysis of seriousness should be conducted from the specific perspective and in light of the specific circumstances of the coastal state.[94] Finally, the scientific uncertainties with respect to the consequences of pollution suggest that the burden of establishing that pollution is not 'serious' ought to rest with the state asserting the innocence of its vessel.[95]

clearly occur, together with its prejudicial impacts, without any element of such intent. Note that the *Corfu Channel* Decision does represent authority for the proposition that the intent or purpose of a foreign vessel's actions in passage is relevant to the determination of innocence. Yet, as noted above, intent was by no means the exclusive subject of the analysis of the Court in that case. To the contrary, the manner or character of the British vessels' passage in Albanian waters was subjected to an equal or, perhaps, greater measure of scrutiny. See text at nn. 55–8 *supra*. Hence, intent may contribute to a determination of the prejudicial character of an act; it ought not, however, to be requisite to finding of prejudice.

[92] Schneider, *supra* ch. 5 n. 36, at 158. See also Hakapaa, *supra* ch. 5, n. 57.

[93] A single incident of pollution may alone appear of *de minimus* signficance. Yet, it may represent the proverbial 'last straw' which finally overtaxes the regional sea's assimilative capacity. Similarly, the substance introduced may alone be perfectly safe; in combination with other substances occurring in the natural marine environment or introduced by other polluters it may be severely damaging. Inquiry into the effect of an act of pollution in light of its addition to existing pollution and combination with diverse other substances is, therefore, a requisite element of any meaningful determination of seriousness.

[94] The diversity of coastal states' interests must be recognized in any determination of the propriety of denying a given state the legal authority to protect those interests. Clearly, the impact of oil spills in a sensitive fishery of a coastal state culturally and economically dependent on a fishing industry or in the vicinity of an important recreational area of a state reliant upon tourism constitute threats of quite different magnitude than precisely the same spills in a territorial sea devoid of such critical significance to its coastal state.

[95] Consider the language of one marine ecologist: 'In matters such as environmental pollution it is not safe to wait for conclusive proof of damage before acting to control it. Disturbance of biological systems has widespread repercussions and they are generally slow to manifest their full effects. By the time damage has been demonstrated to everyone's satisfaction and control measures instituted, the damage may well be irreversible on any reasonable human scale. This is a

The final component of the definition of 'innocence' set forth in the Convention which demands comment is the effective declaration that only prejudicial *activities* deny a vessel the right of innocent passage. On the basis of the LOS III text, passive characteristics such as cargo or Construction, design, equipment and maintenance would not be deemed relevant to the determination of innocence.[96] Yet, one may readily demonstrate the correlation between the incidence and seriousness of marine pollution and factors such as vessel cargo and CDEM.[97] There can be little question that it is the very presence of a vessel carrying a hazardous cargo with CDEM inadequate to the task which threatens the environmental interests of the coastal state. The LOS III formulation, in effect, denies this.

It should be noted that the argument of prejudice by passive characteristics does echo the traditional logic of those opposing warship and, more recently, fishing vessel innocent passage.[98] In each case, it is the character of the vessel in passage that has been identified as so inherently threatening to the coastal state as to justify a denial of a right of passage. Yet, an important distinction exists; the environmental argument ought not to be dismissed with the others. With respect to both warships and fishing vessels, the character of the vessel alone is not sufficient to damage the coastal state. Rather, it is only when there is a conjunction of the presence of the vessel with some intentional activity (i.e. military aggression or fishing) that the coastal state is harmed. It may be appropriate and effective, therefore to protect the coastal state from these risks by denying the innocence of such vessels only when the threatening intentional activity itself occurs.

The harm with which a vessel with inherently hazardous cargo or inadequate CDEM threatens the coastal state may occur, on the other hand,

situation in which legislation must often be in advance of firm scientific knowledge and great attention must be paid to the first tentative evidence that a dangerous situation may exist. Clark, 'The Biological Consequences of Oil Pollution of the Sea' in *Water Pollution as a World Problem: The Legal, Scientific and Political Aspects* 53, at 71 (David Davies Memorial Institute of International Studies 1971). Many of the disruptive effects of pollution are, then, either imperfectly understood or simply may not manifest themselves for extended periods following the pollution incident. It does not appear either equitable or consistent with the logic of innocent passage that the coastal state should bear the risk that time will disclose a more severe detriment to its resources than that demonstrable at the moment of the incident. Rather, it is the state of the vessel creating the risk by committing or threatening pollution that should bear the risk. This is readily accomplished by allocating the burden of denying the 'serious' character of pollution's impacts, or threatened impacts, to the flag state.

[96] This conclusion is bolstered by implication by Art. 22(2) which confers a very limited right to prescribe sea lanes for the innocent passage of 'tankers, nuclear-powered ships and ships carrying nuclear or other inherently dangerous or noxious substances or materials.' See Boyle, *supra* ch. 6, n. 51, at 360–1.

[97] See Burmester, *supra* ch. 10 n. 2, at 1–2; US Senate Hearings Before the Comm. on Commerce, Recent Tanker Accidents, 95th Cong., 1st Sess. 349 (1977), [1981 Current Reports] *Int'l Envir. Rep.* (BNA), at 935.

[98] See Argument of Elihu Root, North Atlantic Coast Fisheries Arbitration (1912), Hague Ct. Rep. (Scott), at 141; Brownlie, *supra* ch. 2 n. 52, at 206–7; McDougal and Burke, *supra* ch. 6 n. 4, at 199–208.

absent any intentional activity or even any human agency whatsoever. Accidents do happen. The prejudice to coastal state interests occurs, therefore, merely with presence. Hence the only opportunity the coastal state has to prevent the threat or the actual harm is to deny the right to such presence. It is true that actual harm to the coastal state from the vessel's presence is but a contingency. Yet, the experiencing of harm is not an element of most of Article 19's enumerated 'prejudicial' activities. For example, neither weapons exercise nor survey activity directly harms the state—it is only their potential for occasioning such harm that renders them prejudicial. In sum, there does not appear to be any consistent analytical justification for the categorical exclusion of all passive characteristics such as vessel CDEM from the definition of innocence in the Convention.

Notably, the LOS III approach is clearly contradictory to the 1958 Convention which purposefully deleted the 1930 Hague Conference text's reference to 'acts' in the definition of innocence.[99] It also runs directly counter to the specific conclusion of the Institute of International Law with respect to the issue of CDEM authority. At its 1969 meetings the Institute unequivocally resolved that vessels not conforming to CDEM standards may be prohibited entry to the territorial sea by the coastal state.[100] Moreover, the Convention provision stands in certain opposition to practice and the assertions of such authority by a variety of states.[101] Most importantly, however, the position taken at LOS III is inconsistent with one of the premises of the regime of innocent passage. The coastal state is not to be denied the competence necessary to protect its vital interests by prohibiting entry into its territory of vessels possessing characteristics which render them a material threat.

2. Prescriptive Authority

The LOS Convention treats the issue of the prescriptive authority of the coastal state over vessels in innocent passage in substantially the same fashion

[99] See text at n. 62 *supra*.

[100] See Resolutions adopted by the Institute at the Session at Edinburgh, 4–13 Sept. 1969: Measures Concerning Accidental Pollutions of the Seas, ii *Annuaire institut de droit international* 380 (1969) (hereinafter cited as ILI, Edinburgh Session), at 382. Consider too the prescient response of the United Kingdom to a 1930 Hague Conference questionnaire regarding the character of innocent passage: a 'vessel cannot claim to transport through territorial waters persons or goods whose presence there is prejudicial to the safety, good order or revenues of the State.' Quoted in Legault, *supra* ch. 5 n. 45, at 220.

[101] See e.g. Ports and Waterways Safety Act of 1972, Title I, 33 USC § 1221, Title II, 46 USC § 391a; 33 CFR 164 (1977); 33 CFR 157 (1976) (United States); Arctic Waters Pollution Prevention Act, *Can. Rev. Stat.* c. 2, § 12(1) (1st Supp. 1970); An Act to Amend the Canada Shipping Act, *Can Rev. Stat.* c. 27, (2d Supp. 1970-71-72) (Canada). See generally Burmester, *supra* ch. 10 n. 2, at 29; Legault, *supra* ch. 5 n. 45, at 220; McGonigle and Zacher, 'Canadian Foreign Policy and the Control of Marine Pollution', *Canadian Foreign Policy and the Law of the Sea* 100 (Johnson and Zacher eds. 1977); Pharand, 'Innocent Passage in the Arctic', 6 *Can. Yb. Int'l L.* 3 (1968); Schachter and Serwer, 'Marine Pollution Problems and Remedies', 65 *Am. J. Int'l L.* 84, at 93 (1971): Schneider, *supra* ch. 5 n. 36, at 159; Wulf, '"Comment" in Symposium: The Law of The Sea—Where Now?', 46 *Law & Contemp. Probs* 155, at 162 (1983).

as the 1958 text. Article 21(1) recites the authority of the coastal state to prescribe laws and regulations in connection with the exercise of innocent passage with respect to a substantial list of matters, including 'the preservation of the environment of the coastal State and the prevention, reduction and control of pollution thereof'.[102] The provision of the text relating exclusively to the protection of the marine environment underscore this prescriptive right: 'Coastal States may, in the exercise of their sovereignty within their territorial sea, adopt laws and regulations for the prevention, reduction and control of marine pollution from foreign vessels, including vessels exercising the right of innocent passage.'[103] Finally, the Convention states explicitly the correlative: '[f]oreign ships exercising the right of innocent passage through the territorial sea shall comply with all such laws and regulations.'[104]

As in the 1958 text, the basic qualification to this grant of coastal state prescriptive authority is the prohibition against 'hampering' innocent passage.[105] With one exception, no provision either elaborates on the definition of hampering or suggests any limitation to coastal state environmental prescriptions. That exception is a requirement that coastal state laws applicable to vessels in innocent passage 'shall not apply to the design, construction, manning or equipment of foreign ships unless they are giving effect to generally accepted international rules or standards.'[106]

Prescriptive authority over CDEM in the territorial sea has been a controversial issue in international dialogue for some time.[107] Opponents of any measure of coastal authority have argued that it would translate into a patchwork of extreme and inconsistent regulations rendering compliance technically or economically impractical, and therefore a disaster for maritime trade.[108] The debate found a forum, but no resolution, in the proceedings

[102] LOS Convention, *supra* ch. 5, n 17, art. 21(1)(*f*).

[103] *Id.*, art. 211(4).

[104] *Id.*, art. 21(4).

[105] Article 24 states unequivocally that: 'The coastal State shall not hamper the innocent passage of foreign ships through the territorial sea except in accordance with this Convention. In particular, in the application of this Convention or of any laws or regulations adopted in conformity with this Convention, the coastal State shall not: (*a*) impose requirements on foreign ships which have the practical effect of denying or impairing the right of innocent passage; . . .' (*Id.*, art. 24(1)) The prohibition against 'hampering' of innocent passage is echoed in Article 211 (4) of the Committee III text. *Id.*, art. 211 (4).

[106] LOS Convention, *supra* ch. 5 n. 17, art. 21(2). It should be emphasized that this unequivocal constraint does only relate to vessels in innocent passage; the Convention articulates no such limit with respect to other vessels situated in the territorial sea. See Oxman, 'The Third United Nations Conference on the Law of the Sea; The Seventh Session (1978)', 73 *Am. J. Int'l L. 1, at 25 (1979). Note further that Article 25 provides explicitly that the coastal state may take in the territorial sea 'necessary steps to prevent any breach of the conditions to which admission of [foreign] ships to internal waters . . . is subject.' Therefore internal waters CDEM rules may be applied to vessels in innocent passage proceeding to those internal waters.*

[107] *See e.g. Anderson, supra* ch. 11 n. 26, at 1009. Comment, 'Unilateral Action Versus Universal Evolution of Safety and Environmental Protection Standards in Maritime Shipping of Hazardous Cargoes,' 20 *Harv. Int'l L.J.* 127, at 144–5 (1979).

[108] See e.g. Statement of the International Chamber of Shipping quoted in Timagenis, *supra* ch. 5 n. 1, at 492; Statement of Collins (Liberia), Committee III 4th Meeting, 16 July 1974, in 2

leading to the 1973 Convention.[109] A number of states have adopted aggressive, unilateral CDEM prescriptions, notwithstanding the dispute.[110]

The LOS Convention approach to the resolution of the issue would amend the customary flexible standard by categorically defining all CDEM prescriptions not expressing 'generally accepted international rules or standards' as 'hampering' to passage. The impact of this rule depends, of course, on the character of such international rules; unfortunately, the Convention provides no real guidance on the appropriate standard.[111] In any event, the text clearly precludes CDEM prescriptive initiatives in advance of the definition of such rules or, critically, in excess of even patently inadequate rules. For several reasons, it is submitted that this inflexible approach finds support in neither logic nor necessity and thus will not likely be elevated to custom.

First, the articulated fears of a 'patchwork' of regulations appear apocryphal. Even variant CDEM standards are not, in fact, inconsistent; they are merely more or less stringent.[112] Hence, the only 'impediment' to navigation would be the cost of compliance with the highest promulgated standard. There would not likely occur the sort of conflicts, hypothesized by opponents of municipal CDEM prescription, which would preclude compliance with the rules of diverse coastal states for technical reasons.

Second, it is extremely unlikely that any state would produce CDEM prescriptions so stringent as to involve costs prohibitive to compliance and, therefore, navigation.[113] The rational self-interest of states dictates this

Official Records 315 (1974); Kiselev, 'The Freedom of Navigation and the Problem of Pollution of the Marine Environment', 6 *Ga. J. Int'l & Comp. L.* 93, at 102 (1976).

[109] See Sweeney, *supra* ch. 11 n. 38, at 301; Timagenis, *supra* ch. 5 n. 1, at 492.

[110] See legislative material cited in n. 101 *supra*. Numerous states supported CDEM regulation by coastal states at the LOS III Conference. See e.g. Statement of Petherbridge (Australia), Committee III 3rd Meeting, 15 July 1974, in 2 *Off. Rec.* 314 (1974); Statement of Legault (Canada), Committee III 4th Meeting, 16 July 1974, in 2 *Off. Rec.* 317 (1974). See generally Burmester, *supra* ch. 10 n. 2, at 17; Livingston, *supra* ch. 6 n. 30, at 12–13.

[111] One author has suggested four alternative definitions for qualifying rules: (*a*) adoption by international conference; (*b*) entry into force in international convention; (*c*) extensive ratification in international convention in excess of the minimum; or (*d*) binding on the particular state by ratification or succession to customary law. Timagenis, *supra* ch. 5 n. 1 at 605–6. See also Boyle *supra* ch. 6 n. 51, at 355–6; Burmester, *supra* ch. 10 n. 2, at 17–19.

[112] Consider the cynical, and persuasive, response of Frank to the argument in the context of a panel discussion: 'Mr Becker suggests that coastal State regulation would result in series of conflicting standards. I think the Petroleum Institute used the term "patchwork of conflicting standards". Keep in mind that port States now have the right to establish standards. And I ask Mr Becker to indicate one conflicting standard that has ever been put into force—just one conflicting standard. It is true that coastal states and some port States will adopt *higher* standards. But name one *conflicting* standard. One State does not go around saying, "The bottoms shall be purple"; while another State says "The bottoms shall be red", so that a vessel cannot comply. But some States do adopt higher standards, and what the oil companies are concerned about is those higher standards.' Reprinted in Panel Discussion, 'Law of the Sea: From Caracas to Geneva—A Time for Decision', 14 *Colum. J. Transnat'l L.* 1, at 73–4 (1975). See also Kingham, 'Marine Resource Management in the North Pacific Rim and Problems of Environmental Protection' in *Regionalization of the Law of the Sea* 161–2 (Johnson ed. 1978).

[113] See Statement of Petherbridge (Australia), Committee III 3rd Meeting, 15 July 1974, in 2 *Off. Rec.* 314 (1974).

conclusion. Every state, particularly a coastal state, experiences the benefits of sea-borne commerce. No state would rationally jeopardize such benefits by creating rules so strict as to dissuade or preclude vessels from commercial intercourse with the state. The history of United States' and Canadian CDEM legislative efforts bears strong witness to the credibility of this economic self-restraint argument.[114] In each state, legislation established a general mandate for the development of extensive unlateral CDEM regulation.[115] In the administrative process engaged for the promulgation of specific regulations, the realities of navigation, economics, and international relations were well and frequently voiced.[116] The draconian rules forecast by opponents of municipal CDEM prescription were simply not forthcoming. Constrained by economic factors, each state produced standards generally acknowledged as restrained and commercially workable.[117]

Perhaps more significantly, the customary, flexible standard of reasonableness would seem to suffice to protect vessels in innocent passage. If a coastal state's law were excessive in terms of its interference with innocent passage, it would be defined as unreasonable and violative of the 'hampering' rule. The reasonableness test would suffice, for example, to prevent the application of CDEM prescriptions that might be reasonable with respect to vessels with radioactive cargo to mere grain carriers. Similarly, unless 'peace, good order, or security' were implicated, regulations so stringent as to preclude, for economic or technical reasons, the effective excercise of innocent passage would not be permitted. On the other hand, the logic of the innocent passage regime mandates the preservation of coastal state authority to enact prescriptions reasonable in light of the nature of the protected interest, the threat to that interest, and the consequential interference with passage. The Convention acknowledges such authority only to the extent that prescriptions incorporate 'generally accepted international rules or standards.' Conformity to such standards certainly should raise a presumption that a prescription is reasonable. However, non-conformity should not necessarily dictate a contrary conclusion. That determination is, logically, a function of the content of the rule, the effect on passage, and the other specific facts of the case. In the absence of any or adequate international rules, a non-conforming municipal prescription might indeed satisfy a reasonableness standard. The Convention's categorical approach, therefore, seems unfortunate.

This conclusion seems particularly clear in light of the several subsidiary legal constraints which further diminish the risk that coastal CDEM

[114] Schneider, *supra* ch. 5 n. 36, at 159. [115] See materials cited at n. 101 *supra*.

[116] See Burmester, *supra* ch. 10 n. 2, at 45–6; McGonigle and Zacher, *supra* n. 101, at 122. See also Note, 'The Clean Water Act of 1977: Expanded Competence over Vessel-source Pollution', 18 *Va. J. Int'l L.* 289, *passim* (1978).

[117] *Id.* For an excellent discussion of (*a*) the economic truths that lead inevitably to reasonable regulation and (*b*) the cost–benefit analysis supportive of CDEM regulation see Cummins *et al.* 'Oil Tanker Pollution Control: Design Criteria *vs.* Effective Liability Assessment', 7 *J. Mar. L. & Com.* 169 (1975–6).

regulation will unreasonably interfere with innocent passage. Subsumed in the reasonableness standard is a further and most relevant requirement: the content of a prescription must bear a reasonable relationship to the end it is designed to achieve. Absent such a relationship, the fact of the significance of the protected interest or the magnitude of the threat to the interest could not logically justify interference with innocent passage. Any CDEM standard which did not in fact demonstrably contribute to environmental protection (e.g. requirements for equipment of duplicative function or design criteria with no material correlation to pollution prevention) could not, therefore, legitimately be applied to vessels in innocent passage.

A second effective check on coastal abuse is the specific prohibition against discrimination in the exercise of environmental duties set forth in Article 227 of the LOS Convention itself. By denying the right to discriminate against foreign vessels generally, this provision works to prohibit discrimination both among foreign vessels *and* between foreign and domestic vessels in the context of environmental regulation. States are thus precluded from enacting prescriptions which impose costs upon foreign vessels' navigation from which flag vessels are to be immune. Hence, there exists a patent and effective economic disincentive to overburdensome environmental regulations—the detriment to vessels and the maritime industry of the state's own flag.

The type of environmental legislation which discriminates for economic reasons may in fact be subject to the final legal constraint—the doctrine of 'abuse of rights'. As noted in Part II, it has been suggested that 'abuse of rights' represents at least a limit upon the exercise of a right by a state for a purpose contrary to or inconsistent with that for which the right is possessed.[118] In the context of CDEM regulation, a state would be in violation of this formulation of the abuse of rights principle if it were to adopt CDEM regulations for other than purely environmental reasons. Legislation intended to achieve an extraneous economic or political end by means of the exercise of CDEM authority would, therefore, constitute an international offence.

3. Enforcement Authority

The LOS Convention's fundamental qualification to the authority of the coastal state to take enforcement actions against vessels in innocent passage is, as in 1958, the prohibition against the hampering of innocent passage.[119] The participants of LOS III were, however, faced with the continuing problem of how to define that prohibition in light of the truism that all enforcement hampers. In response, the Convention adopts much of the 1958 text's explanatory language and, particularly with respect to the enforcement of environmental prescriptions, incorporates a number of material innovations.

The text first incorporates, in Articles 27 and 28, precisely the language of

[118] See ch. 5 at nn. 99–108.

[119] LOS Convention, *supra* ch. 5 n. 17, art. 24(1).

Articles 19 and 20 of the 1958 Convention which defines when a coastal state may take any enforcement action against a vessel in innocent passage.[120] The material expansion of the definition of 'hampering' enforcement occurs in those sections of the Convention devoted exclusively to issues related to the 'Protection and Preservation of the Marine Environment'.[121] Article 220(2) sets forth the basic structure of coastal state authority to enforce environmental prescriptions in the territorial sea:

> Where there are clear grounds for believing that a vessel navigating in the territorial sea of a State has, during its passage therein, violated laws and regulations of that State adopted in accordance with this Convention or applicable international rules and standards for the prevention, reduction and control of pollution from vessels, that State, without prejudice to the application of the relevant provisions of Part II, section 3 may undertake physical inspection of the vessel relating to the violation and may, where the evidence so warrants, institute proceedings, including detention of the vessel, in accordance with its laws subject to the provisions of section 7.[122]

Part II, section 3 provisions referred to in this paragraph set forth the rules of innocent passage. Hence the legal authority here acknowledged is expressly subordinate to the general prohibition against the hampering of innocent passage and the subsidiary rules of Articles 27 and 28 as to when any enforcement action may be taken. Notably, Article 220(2) itself refers specifically only to a vessel's violations 'during its passage' in the territorial sea. This further underscores the prohibition against enforcement of prior or extraterritorial prescriptions included in the innocent passage provisions of both the LOS Convention and the 1958 Convention.[123]

[120] *Id.*, arts. 27 and 28. The restatement of these provisions without alteration reinforces the conclusion that they have at least now come to represent consensus as to a definition of non-hampering enforcement. Yet, by wholesale adoption of the 1958 text's language, the Convention fails to resolve the controversy as to whether certain of the rules set forth are obligatory laws or merely discretionary principles of comity. Note, further, that the Convention does vary in one rather material aspect. Article 27(5) excepts from the prohibitions against enforcement any authority specifically granted by the articles relating to marine pollution. This is particularly germane to the enforcement of EEZ violations.

[121] This portion of the LOS Convention was developed by Committee II of the Conference and is set forth as Part XII of the Convention.

[122] LOS Convention, *supra* ch 5 n. 17, art. 222(2).

[123] Two comments are in order with respect to this conclusion. First, this provision of the LOS III text appears operative as a statement of the scope of enforcement authority with respect to *all* vessels navigating in the territorial sea—not only those in innocent passage. In this light, it represents a new and rather radical constraint of customary enforcement authority. Second, the conclusion with respect to enforcement of prior or extraterritorial violations of state prescriptions is subject to one new and significant exception. Article 220(3) provides that states may require information of vessels as to identity, flag and port of destination when there exist 'clear grounds' for belief that a violation of environmental rules has occurred in a state's 'exclusive economic zone'. Moreover, Article 220(6) specifically acknowledges the coastal state's authority to 'institute proceedings, including detention of the vessel, in accordance with its laws' when 'objective evidence' exists of a discharge violation 'causing major damage or threat of major damage to the coastline or related interests of the coastal State, or to any resources of its territorial

Article 220(2) does go beyond the 1958 Convention in limiting enforcement *vis-à-vis* vessels in the territorial sea in a number of respects. First, the provision expressly requires 'clear grounds' for believing that a territorial sea violation has occurred before any enforcement may be taken. Second, by reference to Section 7, the text subjects coastal state enforcement to the 'safeguard' provisions discussed above—including standards and procedures for inspection, detention, arrest, penalties, and judicial proceedings.[124] Finally, Article 220(2) operates to restrict enforcement actions against *all* vessels in the territorial sea, not only vessels in innocent passage.

4. Transit Passage

The LOS Convention diverges from innocent passage custom in one additional respect—the innovation of an elevated right of unimpeded 'transit passage' through international straits 'solely for the purpose of continuous and expeditious transit.'[125] The maritime states at the Conference sought and achieved a straits regime of diminished coastal authority far more protective of military and economic navigational interests than the rules of innocent passage. The capacity of the coastal state to interfere with navigation in exercise of jurisdiction over environmental matters was specifically targeted for and subjected to reduction.

Transiting vessels are expressly required to refrain from the threat or use of force against the coastal state, scientific research, and any other activity not incidental to transit, and to comply with 'generally accepted international regulations, procedures and practices for the prevention, reduction and control of pollution from ships.'[126] There is interpretative debate as to the consequences of a breach of these duties: Reisman argues that the coastal state must possess the correlative right to prescribe and enforce laws with respect to the breach and that in any event an act in breach would deny the vessel the immunities of transit; Moore responds that the drafting intent was to deny any right to interrupt transit for breach, and to vest only a right to seek *ex post*

sea or exclusive economic zone.' Subject to the substantial qualifications set forth, then, these provisions as to the exclusive economic zone do represent a divergence from the 1958 text's absolute prohibition of enforcement of extraterritorial violations against vessels in innocent passage.

[124] See ch. 11 at nn. 46–51 *supra*. Note well, however, that Article 228, the flag state provision captioned 'Suspension and Restriction of Institution of Proceedings', does *not* apply to enforcement of territorial sea prescriptions. In addition, the restriction in Article 230(2) to monetary penalties for environmental violations in the territorial sea does not apply if the violation is a 'wilful and serious act'. Given that a pollution violation by 'wilful and serious act' would, under the innocent passage provisions of the Convention, deny a vessel the status and attendant immunities of innocence, the import of this provision is that only monetary penalties may be imposed on vessels exercising innocent passage.

[125] *Id.*, art. 38. 'International straits' are defined as 'straits which are used for international navigation between one part of the high seas or an exclusive economic zone and another part of the high seas or an exclusive economic zone.' Art 38. Note in Art. 16(4) of the 1958 Territorial Sea Convention no suspension of innocent passage in international straits was permitted.

[126] *Id.*, arts. 39(1) (2), 40.

facto redress through diplomatic or dispute settlement procedures.[127] An element of textual ambiguity seems difficult to deny. In the environmental context, however, two specific provisions confirm the limited prerogatives of the coastal state. Article 42, which enumerates the few topics of coastal regulation (other than sea lanes and traffic schemes) with which vessels in transit must comply, limits environmental rules to those 'giving effect to applicable international regulations regarding the discharge of oil, oily wastes and other noxious substances in the strait.'[128] In contrast with the general duty provision, compliance is required only with respect to discharge, not CDEM, rules. Even discharge regulations are limited to prescribed international standards. The enforcement authority of the coastal state as to environmental matters parallels this narrow definition. Article 233 generally excepts straits from the provisions governing environmental protection and limits enforcement against vessels in transit to violations of traffic or discharge regulations 'causing or threatening major damage' to the strait's environment.[129] In short, the coastal state's jurisdiction over the condition and character of vessels in straits' transit is non-existent; jurisdiction over affirmative conduct affecting the environment is much diminished.

B. STATE RESPONSIBILITY

The definition of the marginal sea as a component of state territory yields the two basic rules governing environmental responsibility. First, harm to the territorial sea environment constitutes harm to the exclusive interests of the coastal state. It is, therefore, the obligation of all states to prevent such harm. Moreover, the coastal state possesses undeniable standing to bring an international claim for any breach of this preventive obligation.

The second fundamental conclusion is that the coastal state's obligation to prevent environmental harm to other states arising out of conduct in the territorial sea is generally the same, in terms of the standards and consequences of responsibility, as that defined with respect to any other region of the state's territory. This conclusion is subject, however, to the caveat that the specific rules of decision regarding environmental responsibility must reflect

[127] Reisman, 'The Regime of Straits and National Security', 74 *Am. J. Int'l L.* 48 (1980); Moore, 'The Regime of Straits and the Third United Nations Conference on the Law of the Sea', 74 *Am. J. Int'l L.* 77 (1980). For the latter perspective see Harlow 'International Straits: A Perspective on State Practice and UNCLOS III', Prepared Remarks of B. Harlow for Symposium on the Law of the Sea at the Univ. of California, Berkeley, 20 Feb. 1982. Note that certain activities (e.g. armed attack or intentional dumping) constituting a breach of one of the defined duties also would appear violative of the requirement of navigation 'solely' for transit. Such violations would thus seem to place the vessel in 'nontransit' and remove the limitations of the regime. Similarly, Art. 38(3) states that 'any activity which is not an exercise of the right of transit passage through a strait remains subject to the other applicable provisions of this convention.' Yet, authority over such activities is tantamount to the denied authority over breaches of the enumerated duties—one of which is precisely to refrain from incidental activities.

[128] *Id.*, art. 42. Note that Art. 42(2) prohibits the 'practical effect of denying, hampering or impairing the right of transit passage.'

[129] *Id.*, art. 43.

any variations in the regime of legal authority. As noted in the preceding chapter, the presence of foreign vessels in a state's waters produces an intersection of jurisdictions affecting both the standard of performance of the preventive obligation and the consequences of breach. The distinct juridical characteristic of the territorial sea relating to foreign vessels is, of course, the regime of innocent passage. The following analysis will consider first the rules of decision pertaining to the conduct of actors not exercising the right of innocent passage, and thereafter the rules relating to ships in such passage.

i. General Rules

The regime of state jurisdiction in the territorial sea with respect to vessels and other actors not in innocent passage is basically that applicable to internal waters.[130] It follows that the rules of environmental responsibility in internal waters discussed in detail in Chapter 11 apply fully to matters in the territorial sea which do not implicate the right of innocent passage. Hence, a coastal state generally should bear responsibility for such conduct in the territorial sea detrimental to another state's environment if (*a*) a state organ or representative negligently or intentionally produced the harm, (*b*) the conduct was ultrahazardous or the harm particularly serious (and the actor was not a foreign warship or non-commercial public vessel), or (*c*) the state failed to exercise due diligence to prevent the harm. The flag state of a polluting vessel not in innocent passage should stand responsible for any failure of due diligence to prevent and on a strict basis for harm arising out of pre-existing ultrahazardous functions, inadequacies of construction, design, or equipment causing serious harm, and the negligent or intentional conduct of warships and similar non-commercial public vessels.

Quentin-Baxter, echoing his view of responsibility for internal waters, has submitted that only the coastal state, with its 'paramount' control, should bear strict responsibility for vessels not in innocent passage.[131] He later suggests, however, that both the flag state and the coastal state may be strictly responsible when the ship is in innocent passage, since authority is 'evenly shared' by the two states.[132] If, indeed, the authority of the flag state over a vessel in innocent passage merits strict responsibility, it is difficult to see why the strict standard ought not to apply when the vessel ceases passage. Innocent passage only reduces the coastal state's authority; the measure of flag state jurisdiction is unaffected by the mantle of innocent passage. The fact that another state may possess even greater jurisidiction should alter the

[130] The only qualifications to this assertion are those enforcement 'safeguards' set forth in the Convention applicable to measures in the territorial sea but not in internal waters. See text at n. 151 *infra*. Note well that neither the text's conclusion nor the separate treatment of vessels in innocent passage should imply the absence of coastal jurisdiction or responsibility with respect to such vessels. 'Innocence' is not an absolute shield against either coastal authority or responsibility. As section *ii* immediately below will confirm, the coastal state may indeed bear responsibility for the conduct of vessels in innocent passage.

[131] Q-B, 3rd Rpt., *supra* ch. 5 n. 72, at 20, 24. As to internal waters see ch. 11 n. 67 *supra*.

[132] Q-B, 3rd Rpt., *supra* ch. 5 n. 72, at 24.

consequences of responsibility, not the *standard* of responsibility to which the state will be held.[133]

In any event, Quentin-Baxter's conclusion does not distinguish between different types of vessel conduct. As noted with respect to internal waters, it is probably not appropriate to hold flag states strictly responsible for spontaneous conduct arising in foreign territorial waters since the flag's enforcement capacity is too limited to merit the strict regime.[134] On the other hand, when the polluting incident relates to matters such as ultrahazardous function or vessel construction, design, and equipment, over which the flag state possesses original and continuing authority and control, strict responsibility may be in order.[135]

In a recent work, Handl has considered this distinction precisely in the context of the territorial sea.[136] He concludes first that flag state strict responsibility is proper, and only proper, when the incident arises out of an ultrahazardous use foreseeable and preventable by the flag. 'Upon registry of an oil tanker or a nuclear-powered vessel, the flag-state authorities are well aware that they authorize the creation of a significant transnational risk.'[137] 'The maritime carriage of bulk dangerous substances in special tanks or cargo spaces which are a structural part of the ship, may be an activity the risks of which flag-state authorities should have been aware of upon registering the vessel or upon authorizing subsequent structural changes.'[138] The author then notes that such responsibility should not lie for

> an accident involving a general purpose freighter which subsequent to registration has been used for say, transporting between ports of third countries hazardous or toxic substances in packaged form. The eventual hazardous use to which the freighter is being put was not specifically envisaged by the flag-state authorities at the time of registration. Nor can it be maintained that the state authorities had control over the freighter's subsequent utilization.[139]

Handl thus affirms the basic distinction described above in fixing flag state strict responsibility in the territorial sea. Moreover, the qualification in the foregoing quotation reflects the underlying logic of that distinction: the flag state should only be strictly accountable for matters subject to its effective authority and control. 'Spontaneous' ultrahazardous conduct thus should not yield application of the strict standard. On the other hand, the implicit

[133] As to multiple responsibility when several states are in a position of strict responsibility, see the guidelines set forth in ch. 4 at nn. 109–15.

[134] See ch. 11 at nn. 67–9 *supra*. Except if the actor is a state organ. *Id.*, at nn. 70–1.

[135] See ch. 11 at nn. 67–9 *supra*. Jenks uses the same dichotomy in referring to the types of territorial sea responsibility: flag state responsibility for CDEM matters, and coastal responsibility for conduct. Comments of Jenks, 53 *Ann. inst. droit int'l* 288 (1969). It is unclear whether these comments relate only to the source of strict, not all, responsibility. Certainly the possibility of responsibility arising out of the due diligence failure of either state must not be excluded.

[136] Handl, *supra* ch. 10, n. 108, at 111–15.

[137] *Id.*, at 112. [138] *Id.*, at n. 115. [139] *Id.*, at 112–13.

limitation of the strict regime to circumstances in which the flag state has specifically authorized, at or following registration, construction or design indicating an ultrahazardous purpose is perhaps too restrictive. As Handl's final reference suggests, the question is whether the flag state possessed authority to prevent the harm-producing, pre-existing condition. If so, the diminution of authority over the vessel in foreign waters at the moment and the site of the resultant injury does not deny the logic of imposing strict responsibility. Deterioration of vessel condition, the maintenance of inadequate safety equipment and a prior course of ultrahazardous conduct, reasonably detectable but unrelated to any structural change, represent examples of pre-existing conditions which might support strict responsibility based on the flag state's meaningful prior opportunity to prevent.[140]

An illustration considered by Handl presents the circumstance of multiple state responsibility in the context of actors not in innocent passage. Approximately eight years prior to Handl's comments a merchant ship of Yugoslavian registry, the *Cavtat*, had sunk in Italian territorial waters with a cargo of tanks containing toxic lead derivatives.[141] In considering the hypothetical issue of responsibility for a delayed escape of the toxic material, Handl reasoned:

> Had a subsequent corrosion of the containers resulted in a significant contamination of the transnational environment, international liability on the part of both Italy, as the coastal state within whose territorial waters the wreck had come to lie, and Yugoslavia as the flag-state, seemingly might have been at issue. . . . However, upon closer examination it is obvious that in a situation of this sort flag-state control over the sunk vessel is purely nominal. Its jurisdiction yields to that of the coastal state which must be deemed to exercise control over the wreck. In other words, Italy's rather than Yugoslavia's international liability might have been at issue *vis-à-vis* third countries as Italy's control over the sunk vessel would have been material to the prevention of any serious degradation of the marine environment.[142]

The logic underlying this view is compelling: Italy's jurisdiction over the vessel and opportunity to prevent the injury during the period of corrosion places it in the better or proximate position to prevent the injury. The exculpation of Yugoslavia, however, does not necessarily follow. As the discussion in Chapter 4 demonstrated, more than one state may bear responsibility for a single incident. The fact that one state's breach bears a greater causal connection to or renders it more blameworthy for the injury than that of a second state should not eliminate the responsibility of the latter for its breach.

[140] There certainly could be examples in which ultrahazardous conditions might not support strict responsibility. For example, Handl's hypothetical of a package of toxic material taken on board on a single occasion for transport from one foreign port to another through foreign territorial seas. *Id.*, at 112.

[141] *Id.*, at 113; Sand, 'The Domestic Procedures in Transnational Environmental Disputes', in OECD, *Legal Aspects of Transfrontier Pollution* 146, at 197 (1977).

[142] Handl, 'International Liability', *supra* ch. 10 n. 108 at 114.

Such factors properly determine the apportionment of the burden of compensation; they ought not to excuse a state committing a 'lesser' breach from the other consequences of the condition of responsibility.[143] Hence, in the example of the *Cavtat*, both Italy, for failure to exercise territorial authority to prevent the injury, and Yugoslavia, for condoning the creation of the ultrahazard, ought to bear responsibility to any third, injured state. The consequences of that responsibility, i.e. the division of the compensation burden and the types of reparation required, would properly reflect comparative causation and blame.

ii. Innocent Passage

The rules of decision with respect to the territorial sea are, then, no different than those applicable to internal waters—except when the right of innocent passage is implicated. That right, particularly in the LOS Convention formulation, may significantly diminish the legal authority of the coastal state to prevent an incident adversely affecting the environment. As the preceding chapters have made quite clear, attendant to any variation in the regime of authority are changes in the analysis of state responsibility. How, then, does innocent passage affect the rules for deciding responsibility with respect to the territorial sea?

The threshold question in each case, of course, must be whether or not the vessel was in fact in innocent passage. As noted above, the definition of innocence embraced by custom and conventions prior to the LOS III Conference and that adopted in the LOS Convention are quite different. Specifically, neither acts of accidental or negligent pollution nor passive vessel characteristics such as ultrahazardous cargo or CDEM deficiencies may deprive a ship of innocence in the latter.[144] For present purposes it is only necessary to reiterate that when a vessel is not in innocent passage, however defined, the internal waters rules of coastal authority and correlative guidelines of responsibility apply.

As to vessels in innocent passage, the coastal state's prescriptive and enforcement authority over, and therefore responsibility for, an incident of pollution will vary with the character of that incident. Consider, for example, a vessel of flag state *A* navigating the territorial waters of state *B*. If the ship commences a course of purposeful discharge of waste, the shield of innocence would itself disappear. The coastal state would possess the full measure of authority over the vessel possessed over other territorial actors.[145] Hence, the rules for determining the responsibility of the flag, coastal, or other state for

[143] See ch. 4, text at nn. 111–15.

[144] See text at nn. 96–101 *supra*. For the purposes of analyzing coastal responsibility, it should be underscored that the determination of 'innocence' is objective, not based upon the subjective classification of the coastal state.

[145] Subject only to the several LOS Convention safeguards appliable to enforcement against foreign vessels. See ch. 11 at nn. 46–51.

injury to a third state arising out of such discharge would again mirror the rules deduced with respect to internal waters.[146]

Even if the vessel retains its 'innocence', however, it is essential to recognize that state *B* retains a significant degree of jurisdiction to prevent environmentally harmful conduct. There is little question under customary or conventional law of state *B*'s authority, for example, to prescribe and enforce laws governing the negligent or even purely accidental introduction of pollution into the territorial sea by vessels in innocent passage.[147] A failure to exercise such authority with due diligence to prevent the polluting conduct should certainly place state *B*, together with flag state *A* if it has not exercised its authority to the requisite standard, in a position of responsibility to any injured third state.

The more challenging question is whether the jurisdiction possessed over acts of pollution by vessels in innocent passage bestows sufficiently effective control to merit the application of a standard of strict responsibility with respect to ultrahazards or, following the suggested approach, serious injuries. Under the customary regime of innocent passage, the answer might well be yes. The limitations imposed on coastal jurisdiction over vessels in innocent passage customarily have not significantly diminished the state's capacity to prevent environmental injury. Neither the constraint of reasonableness imposed by the 'no hampering' rule nor the specific checks on enforcement measures operate to prevent the state from taking effective preventive steps. Most importantly, under the customary definition of innocence, the coastal state may prohibit entry to a vessel engaged in conduct or of a character that threatens material environmental injury.[148]

Under the LOS Convention, this final conclusion is altered; passive characteristics, however threatening, do not justify the denial of entry for non-innocence.[149] Thus, the coastal state would not be in a position to prohibit an ultrahazardous activity, e.g. the transport of highly toxic substances or the use of nuclear power, from taking place within its territory. The capacity to forbid ultrahazards is, of course, a premise of the regime of strict responsibility for such activities within the state's territory.[150] It would seem inappropriate to impose strict responsibility for an ultrahazard introduced to the state without the leave or authorization of the state. Responsibility should follow, therefore, only from the coastal state's failure to exercise diligently the authority it does

[146] Note well that if only state *B* is injured, state *B*'s failure of due diligence should not exculpate the flag state. The analysis of the appropriate reparation should reflect the comparative blame or causation of the two states. See ch. 4 at nn. 41–8.

[147] See text at nn. 102–3 *supra*.

[148] On the other hand, one could argue cogently that strict liability should not lie for a vessel entering by right of innocent passage. Even though the coastal state may possess authority over the vessel, the presence of the vessel is not (like other actors in state territory) based on the permission of the state.

[149] See text at nn. 96–101 *supra*.

[150] See generally ch. 8 text at nn. 57–69.

possess to prescribe and enforce laws, stopping short of prohibition, designed to prevent injuries arising out of the ultrahazard.

The general conclusion that simple due diligence is the proper standard with respect to vessels in innocent passage under the regime defined in the LOS Convention is bolstered by two further aspects of the text. The first is the set of 'safeguard' provisions which diminish the enforcement authority of the coastal state.[151] The second, and far more significant, is the provision denying to the coastal state the right to prescribe any laws relating to ship CDEM in excess or in lieu of international standards.[152] It will be recalled that the only constraint on such regulation imposed by custom and pre-LOS III conventional law has been the rule against hampering innocent passage. If a prescription is reasonable, in light of a balancing of the impact on passage, the threat addressed by the law, the efficacy of the law, and similar factors, it likely would be deemed permissible.[153] Under the LOS Convention regime such prescriptions are categorically prohibited. Only flag states (or perhaps states of other ship-users) are free to prescribe and enforce CDEM rules beyond international minima. This diminution in coastal jurisdiction again suggests the impropriety of the application of a strict regime; certainly a state should not be held strictly accountable for the consequences of the inadequate CDEM of ships in innocent passage when its jurisdiction over such matters is severely circumscribed. In summary, the question to be asked is whether the coastal state has exercised with due diligence that authority which it does possess over vessels in innocent passage to prevent environmental injury. If it has not, the coastal state will stand responsible, together with any other states in breach (e.g. the flag state), to the injured state.

iii. Transit Passage

A final variation in the responsibility analysis arises out of the diminished jurisdiction of the coastal state over environmental matters relating to vessels in 'transit passage' through international straits. As noted above, the states bordering a strait are permitted no CDEM regulations, no discharge regulations in excess of international standards, and enforcement measures only when a violation of discharge rules causes or threatens 'major' environmental injury. The coastal state's capacity to control conduct and effectively prevent environmental injury is, therefore, materially less than that enjoyed even over vessels in innocent passage. It follows that the standard to which strait states should be held in assessing their performance of environmental duties is simple due diligence, not the elevated test of strict responsibility.

[151] See text at nn. 121–4 *supra*.
[152] See text at nn. 106–18 *supra*.
[153] See text at nn. 76–7 *supra*.

13

The High Seas and the Exclusive Economic Zone

A. APPORTIONMENT OF AUTHORITY

i. The Tradition of Flag State Primacy

The 1958 Convention on the High Seas defined the high seas as 'all parts of the sea that are not included in the territorial seas or in the internal waters of a State.'[1] Since the doctrinal victory of the Grotian *mare liberum*, the pattern of state jurisidiction over the region has been forged subject to the 'cardinal rule' of the law of the sea:[2]

> Vessels on the high seas are subject to no authority except that of the State whose flag they fly. In virtue of the principle of the freedom of the seas, that is to say the absence of any territorial sovereignty upon the high seas, no State may exercise any kind of jurisdiction over foreign vessels upon them.[3]

This general rule has dictated that only flag states possess authority to prescribe or enforce laws pertaining to conduct by or on board vessels beyond the territorial sea affecting the environment. As discussed in Chapter 10, the international obligation of the flag to exercise such authority to prevent injury to the environment of other states' waters or the high seas itself is now well established.[4] The tradition of the exclusivity of such authority and correlative obligation is manifest in the major multilateral environmental conventions' reliance on the exercise of flag state jurisdiction.[5]

Activities beyond the territorial sea are not, however, only subject to the authority of vessels' flag states. Not all conduct outside state territory occurs on board a vessel. Moreover, the customary principle of extraterritorial flag exclusivity clearly admits of certain significant qualifications. None works to diminish the expansive, 'quasi-territorial' authority of the flag with respect to vessels outside territorial waters; each, on the other hand, identifies a measure of concurrent jurisdiction vested in non-flag states. The balance of this section

[1] High Seas Convention, *supra* ch. 6 n. 2, art. 1.

[2] Brierly, *supra* ch. 2 n. 41, at 307.

[3] *SS Lotus*, [1927] PCIJ, ser. A, no. 10, at 25. See also The *Louis*, 2 Dodson 210 (1817); The *Antelope*, 10 Wheaton 66 (1825). See generally Brierly, *supra* ch. 2 n. 41, at 307; Brownlie, *supra* ch. 2 n. 52, at 279; McDougal, Burke and Vlasic, *supra* ch. 10 n. 19, at 26–7, 66–8.

[4] See ch. 10 nn. 49–57 *supra*.

[5] For a discussion of the tactical alternative of expanded 'port state' authority see ch. 11 commencing at n. 36 *supra*.

will consider such additional jurisdiction over environmental matters beyond the territorial sea before turning finally to the issues of consequential responsibility.

ii. *Coastal and other State Jurisdiction*

a. *Customary Prescriptive Rights*

As noted, the doctrine of flag exclusivity on the high seas rests on the absence of state territory, other than the territory-by-metaphor of vessels, upon which to base an assertion of jurisdiction. This does not, in logic or practice, preclude the exercise of authority over conduct beyond state territorial waters based upon one of the customary bases of extraterritorial prescriptive jurisdiction. These bases will support the penetration of a state's laws into foreign land territory; they certainly will serve as well to extend prescriptive authority to matters within quasi-territorial foreign vessels.

Nationality, for example, will always support extraterritorial prescriptive assertions. Each state may enact laws governing the activities of nationals in *any* region—including within the precincts of a foreign vessel on the high seas.[6] Similarly, the doctrine of objective territoriality logically could subject activities beyond the territorial sea directly and adversely affecting the territorial environment to coastal state prescriptive competence.[7] Pollution discharged by a vessel well outside the territorial sea of any state certainly may penetrate and degrade the environment of neighbouring state territory. If the adverse effects meet the emerging tests of materiality, proximate relationship to the extraterritorial conduct, and perhaps forseeability, the objective territorial principle would seem to support the application of coastal state law to the remote vessel.[8] With respect to conduct which may be defined as *delicta juris gentium*, the universal basis of jurisdiction will support such extraterritorial prescriptions. As noted, however, universality does not yet operate in an environmental context. Polluting conduct, though perhaps emerging as a violation of an obligation *erga omnes*, has not been assimilated to the *delicta juris gentium* regime.[9] The port state provisions at LOS III do not negate this conclusion. The extension of coastal prescriptive authority to activities beyond and without direct impact upon state territory is best defined as a contractual, reciprocal grant of authority.[10] State practice on the basis of the

6 See ch. 10 at n. 35 *supra*.

7 See ch. 9 at nn. 17–25 *supra*; McDougal, Burke and Vlasic, *supra* ch. 10 n. 19, at 82 n. 159. The problem of 'pirate' broadcasting from the high seas has highlighted the issue of the applicability of objective territoriality to the high seas. See Hunnings, 'Pirate Broadcasting in European Waters', 14 *Int'l & Comp. L.Q.* 410 (1965); Van Panhuys and Boas, 'Legal Aspects of Pirate Broadcasting', 60 *Am. J. Int'l L.* 303 (1966); Woodliffe, 'Some Legal Aspects of Pirate Broadcasting in the North Sea', 12 *Nederlands tijdschrift int'l recht* 365 (1965); LOS Convention, *supra* ch. 5 n. 17, art. 109.

8 As to these emerging requirements see ch. 9 at nn. 21–35 *supra*.

9 See ch. 6 n. 78 with respect to *erga omnes* status. See generally ch. 9 at nn. 48–51. Piracy is, of course, the best example of *delicta juris gentium*. See ch. 9 at n. 49.

10 See ch. 11 at n. 57.

Convention may indeed affect the ultimate contours of custom; at present, universality, unlike nationality and objective territoriality, will not likely support the extraterritorial reach of environmental laws.[11]

b. Hot Pursuit

The general principle of the limitation of a state's enforcement authority to its own territory operates to impose a general prohibition against enforcement measures beyond the territorial sea by other than the flag state. As noted in Chapter 9, however, the rule against extraterritorial enforcement does not apply with same vigour on the high seas as it does in the territory of other states.[12] The lesser intrusion of enforcement beyond the boundaries of any state is, in certain circumstances, tolerated in international law. Such non-flag state enforcement authority beyond the territorial sea is generally coupled and co-extensive with the zones of extraterritorial prescriptive authority to be identified below. The principal exception is the right of 'hot pursuit'.[13]

Under the customary doctrine of hot pursuit a coastal state may continue onto the high seas in the uninterrupted pursuit of a foreign vessel commenced immediately following an offence within state territory.[14] The principal disputes with respect to the doctrine have related to its application to incidents occurring in extraterritorial zones of coastal state authority.[15] The logic of hot pursuit, effective administration, suggests that if a state possesses prescriptive and enforcement authority over a region, hot pursuit should be allowed to commence within that region for offences against laws applicable to that region.[16] This was apparently precisely the conclusion of the LOS III participants; the LOS Convention confirms that hot pursuit may commence

[11] See Brownlie, *supra* ch. 6 n. 66, at 5. But see for a rare view *contra* Klotz, 'Are Ocean Polluters Subject to Universal Jurisdiction: Canada Breaks the Ice', 6 *Int'l Law* 706 (1972).

[12] See ch. 9 at n. 74 *supra*.

[13] See generally Brownlie, *supra* ch. 2 n. 52, at 250–3; McDougal and Burke, *supra* ch. 6 n. 4, at 893–923; Poulantzas, *The Right of Hot Pursuit in International Law* (1969). A second exception is the right of 'visit'—the right to board in limited circumstances such as suspected piracy, unauthorized broadcasting, and slave trade. See LOS Convention, *supra* ch. 5 n. 17, art. 110. Other rights of enforcement may be conceded by contact. See Carroz and Roche, 'The International Policing of High Seas Fisheries', 60 *Can. Yb. Int'l L.* 61 (1968); Koers, 'The Enforcement of International Fisheries Agreements', 1 *Neth. Yb. Int'l* L. 1 (1970).

[14] Poulantzas, *supra* no. 13, at 39. 'Where the offender escapes into neighbouring territory the situation is quite different, because to follow him involves an offence to the neighbouring sovereign. . . . When pursuit enters the high seas, however, there is no sovereign to be affronted.' O'Connell, *supra* Introd. n. 1, at 722.

[15] Fitzmaurice, for example, argued that the 1958 High Seas Convention only permits hot pursuit following a violation in territorial waters, not following a violation in the contiguous zone. Fitzmaurice, *supra* ch. 11 n. 5, at 112–17. Most commentators do not agree. See Brownlie, *supra* ch. 2 n. 52, at 252; McDougal and Burke, *supra* ch. 6 n. 4, at 906–13; Poulantzas, *supra* n. 13, at 163–4.

[16] This follows from the 1958 debates; see Poulantzas, *supra* n. 13, at 183–5.

and relate to violations within any of the zones of expanded coastal jurisdiction recognized in the text.[17]

c. Intervention

The intentional destruction of the *Torrey Canyon* on the high seas off the United Kingdom's coast in 1967 raised a host of questions with respect to the right of a state to exercise authority over foreign vessels on the high seas in a condition or engaging in conduct which constitutes an imminent threat to its territorial environmental interests.[18] The two states directly affected by the incident, Britain and France, sought and secured the convening of a multilateral conference under the auspices of IMCO to consider the matter. The 1969 Brussels 'Intervention' Convention responded with a codification of the right of coastal states to:

> take such measures on the high seas as may be necessary to prevent, mitigate or eliminate grave and imminent danger to their coastline or related interests from pollution or threat of pollution of the sea by oil, following upon a maritime casualty or acts related to such a casualty which may reasonably be expected to result in major harmful consequences.[19]

In exercise of such authority, states are constrained by a standard of proportionality, balancing the interests threatened, the probability of success, and the interference occasioned by exercise.[20] This right was extended to threats from maritime casualties involving substances other than oil by a Protocol which entered into force in 1983.[21] The same basic structure has

[17] LOS Convention, *supra* ch. 5 n. 17, art. 111. A variation of the doctrine of 'hot pursuit' permits states to exercise enforcement authority against vessels lying in the high seas which are involved in offences within zones of prescriptive and enforcement authority. This rule of 'constructive presence' treats such vessels as within the territorial limits of enforcement authority by allowing 'hot pursuit' out to the vessel when one of the vessel's small boats ('simple constructive presence') or small boats from shore operating in conjunction with the vessel ('extensive constructive presence') commits an offense within such limits. Article 23 of the 1958 High Seas Convention text expressly endorsed this extension of enforcement authority. Note, however, that subparagraph (1) seems to limit endorsement to the 'simple' formulation. Subparagraph (2), on the other hand, clearly endorses the 'extensive' form. See generally Jessup, *supra* ch. 11 n. 14, at 111–12. 242–75; Poulantzas, *supra* n. 13, at 71–90; 243–51; The *Araunah* (1888), reprinted in McNair, i *International Law Opinions* 245 (1956); The *Grace and Ruby*, 283 F. 475 (1922); The *Henry L. Marshall*, 292 F. 486 (1923); The *Tenyu Maru*, 4 Alaska Rpts. 136 (1910).

[18] For a description of the *Torrey Canyon* episode in some detail, see Cowan, *Oil and Water: The Torrey Canyon Disaster* (1969). Note that the Torrey Canyon was in fact within twelve miles of the UK coast. It nevertheless raised the issue of extra-contiguous zone rights simply because Britain made no claim to a contiguous zone. The authority at issue is perhaps best described as a hybrid of prescriptive and enforcement rights: it comprehends the authority both to enact and enforce rules regarding the presence of danger.

[19] International Convention on Intervention on the High Seas in Cases of Oil Pollution Casualties, done at Brussels 29 Nov. 1969, entry into force 6 May 1975, TIAS no. 8068, art. i(1). This general provision does not apply to public non-commercial vessels. Art. i(2).

[20] *Id.*, art. v, If action is taken in excess of this standard, compensation for damages occasioned is due. *Id.*, art. vi.

[21] Protocol relating to Intervention on the High Seas in Case of Marine Pollution by

since found expression in several regional conventions,[22] coastal initiatives[23] and the LOS Convention.[24] One may now conclude that the specific rights set forth in the Intervention Convention have risen to the dignity of customary law.[25]

The question of whether intervention on the high seas may rest independently on a general customary rule remains controversial. Certain commentators have asserted that no customary principle supported the innovation at Brussels.[26] Others have suggested the customary justification of self-defence as an explanation of the intervention right.[27] This view has been consistently and persuasively criticized on the basis of the absence of the 'intentional hostile attack' required for invocation of self-defence under the UN Charter.[28] The 1980 session of the ILC produced the conclusion that the *Torrey Canyon* action was an expression of the doctrine of 'necessity', which would excuse unlawful conduct engaged to prevent damage to the 'vital interests' of the state outweighing the damage attendant to the breach.[29] Article 33 of the Commission's draft text on state responsibility denies the wrongfulness of a 'situation of a State whose sole means of safeguarding an

Substances Other than Oil, done 2 Nov. 1973, entry into force 30 Mar. 1983, reprinted in 13 *Int'l Legal Materials* 605 (1974). The original Convention was limited to oil pollution due to a combination of forces concerning rejection by major shipping states and the impact on maritime insurance. Brown, *supra* ch. 6 n. 39, at 194.

[22] See Barcelona Convention, *supra* ch. 6 n. 42; Protocol Concerning Cooperation in Combating Pollution of the Mediterranean Sea by Oil and Other Harmful Substances in Cases of Emergency, reprinted in 15 *Int'l Legal Materials* 285 (1976); Kuwait Convention, *supra* ch. 6 n. 42; Protocol concerning Regional Co-operation in Combating Pollution by Oil and Other Harmful Substances in Cases of Emergency, reprinted in Ruster and Simma, *supra* ch. 11 n. 8, vol. xix at 9551.

[23] See Bissell, 'Intervention on the High Seas: An American Approach Employing Community Standards', 7 *J. Mar. L. & Com.* 718 (1975–6). For examples of municipal legislation see (UK) Prevention of Oil Pollution Act, 1971, c. 21; (US) Intervention on the High Seas Act, 33 USC 1471–87 (1974). See also the *Caro Cambanos* incident involving France's destruction of a Greek tanker, as described in Rousseau, 'Chronique des faits internationaux', 86 *RGDIP* 152 (1982).

[24] LOS Convention, *supra* ch. 5 n. 17, art. 221.

[25] See Bissell, *supra* n. 23, at 718; Caflisch, *supra* ch. 10 n. 29, at 27; Goldie, 'A General View of International Environmental Law', *supra* ch. 5 n. 45, at 41–2; Hakapaa, *supra* ch. 5 n. 57, at 270–1.

[26] See e.g. Observations of Bishop, Edinburgh Session, *supra* ch. 12 n. 100, at 617; De Smet, 'Policing on the High Seas: With special reference to the North Sea' in iii *New Directions in the Law of the Sea* 193, at 201. (Churchill *et al.* eds. 1973); and Douay, 'Le Droit de la mer et la préservation du milieu marin', in *Le Nouveau droit international de la mer* 231 (Bardonnet and Virally eds. 1983).

[27] See e.g. Observations of McWhinney, Edinburgh Session, *supra* ch. 12 n. 100, at 629. As to the application of the concept of self-defence on the high seas generally see Bowett, *Self-defence in International Law* (1958), at 105; Jennings, 'The *Caroline* and *McLeod* Cases', 32 *Am. J. Int'l L.* 82 (1938).

[28] See Ago, 8th Rpt, supra ch. 2 n. 89, at 51; Apollis, *supra* ch. 10 n. 53, at 229; Brierly, *supra* ch. 2 n. 41, at 415; Brown, *supra* ch. 6 n. 39, at 142; Caflisch, *supra* ch. 10 n. 38, at 18–21; Observations of de Visscher, Edinburgh Session, *supra* ch. 12 n. 100, at 652. But see Comments of Quentin-Baxter, ILC, 1980 Sum. Rec., *supra* ch. 5 n. 72, at 167.

[29] ILC, Report to the General Assembly, ii *Yb. Int'l L. Comm'n* 35 (1980), UN Doc. A/CN. 4/Ser.A/1980/Add.1 (Pt. 2).

essential interest threatened by a grave and imminent peril is to adopt conduct not in conformity with what is required of it by an international obligation to another State.'[30] The comments note specifically the possible invocation of the doctrine in the context of environmental protection.[31] The logic of the approach is one of proportionality. As expressed in a cited work by Cheng: 'a socially important interest shall not perish for the sake of respect for an objectively minor right.'[32] The Commission took care to deny the existence of any independent *right* based on this analysis; necessity only constitutes an extraordinary circumstance precluding wrongfulness.[33]

Other commentators disagree. Bowett and others have described an affirmative right of self-protection arising out of 'customary international law; its basis is found in the general practice of states rather than the exceptional right of self-defence . . . the legality and normality of the jurisdiction make an appeal to this exceptional right unnecessary in this age.'[34] Hydeman and Berman were able to conclude as early as 1960 that: '[a] rule of international law seems to have emerged which permits a coastal State to make reasonable assertions of jurisdiction and control in areas of the high seas contiguous to its territorial sea in order to protect vital interests in its territory or territorial waters.'[35] Goldie has described this customary right of extraterritorial environmental protection as a component of a general principle of 'self-help'.[36] Noting the problem of 'self-serving subjective appraisals by each State,' the author underscores that the exercise of the right is subject to the objective constraints of proportionality.[37] De Visscher identified the same customary right in the 1969 session of the International Law Institute, asserting the existence of each State's 'droit irreductible à l'autoprotection.'[38] Although the terms vary, each of these authors views the extraterritorial exercise of authority to protect environmental interests, by conduct proportional to the threat and the harm to any other state, to be a lawful act—

[30] *Id.*, at 34.

[31] *Id.*, at 35.

[32] Cheng, *supra* ch. 1 n. 6, at 29.

[33] As to the distinction between international rights and excuse see Bowett, *supra* n. 27, at 66–70; Brown, *supra* ch. 6 n. 39, at 143. The Commission reserved the possibility that compensation may be due following an exercise of necessity. ILC, 1980 Rpt., *supra* n. 29, at 51.

[34] Utton, 'The Arctic Waters Pollution Prevention Act and the Right of Self-protection', in *International Environmental Law* (Teclaff and Utton eds. 1974), referring to Bowett, *supra* n. 27.

[35] Hydeman and Berman, *supra* ch. 2 n. 80, at 236.

[36] Goldie, *supra* ch. 5 n. 45, at 47. Goldie argues, on the other hand that 'self-preservation' is an 'instinct', not a right, without legal function. *Id.*, at 41. See also Ago 8th Rpt., *supra* ch. 2 n. 89, at 56. There is generally great semantic confusion in the literature with respect to the terms 'self-defence', 'self-protection', 'necessity', 'self-help' and 'self-preservation'. The terms chosen in the text do seem to reflect the dominant (though not invariable) usages.

[37] Goldie, *supra* n. 36, at 47.

[38] Observations of de Visscher, Edinburgh Session, *supra* ch. 12 n. 100, at 652. See also Apollis, *supra* ch. 10 n. 53, at 224.

juridically quite distinct from an unlawful act excused by necessity. Hence, the Intervention Convention's central grant of authority is viewed as a crystallization of pre-existing customary rights.

d. Contiguous Pollution Zones

State assertions of jurisdiction beyond the territorial sea are more often spatially defined; there is a substantial pattern of claims to prescriptive and enforcement authority in zones contiguous to the territorial sea designed to protect territorial interests.[39] The rationale of such zones is essentially objective territoriality: conduct in regions adjacent to state territory affects, and therefore must be controlled to achieve, order within the state.[40] The first expression of the place of the contiguous zone in international law occurred in the 1958 Territorial Sea Convention.[41] Article 24 of the Convention provides that the coastal state may exercise in a contiguous zone not greater than twelve miles from the baseline of the territorial sea 'control necessary to: (*a*) prevent infringement of customs, fiscal, immigration or sanitary regulations within its territory or territorial sea; (*b*) punish infringement of the above regulations committed within its territory or territorial sea.'[42] Fitzmaurice has argued that this language conferred only a limited right of control to prevent or enforce infringements of law within the state's territory:

> It must follow—and this is the important point—that foreign vessels in the contiguous zone are not basically *subject* to the laws of the coastal State, or bound to conform to them, as they would be if it were the territorial sea; nor are they, in principle, obliged to submit to the control of the authorities of the coastal State, as they would be in the territorial sea. International practice allows, or—more probably— tolerates, that the coastal State should exercise certain limited powers of control in the contiguous zone in order to enable it to prevent *eventual* infringement *within its territory or territorial waters* of certain of its laws.[43]

The majority perspective, based upon both the records of the Conference and the weight of state practice, seems, however, to be that jurisdiction within the

[39] It is customary to trace such assertions to the British Hovering Acts, A. Geo. 2, c. 35 (1736). See Jessup, supra ch. 11 n. 14, at 77–9; Masterson, *Jurisdiction in Marginal Seas* 26 (1929). For an interesting example of a most recent assertion, See Barston and Birnie, 'The Falkland Islands/ Islas Malvinas Conflict', 7 *Marine Poly* 14 (1983). Note that this section considers the claim of zonal authority unrelated to any extraterritorial proprietary claim.

[40] See McDougal and Burke, *supra* ch. 6 n. 4, at 566–7 and 573–4. See also Apollis, *supra* ch. 10 n. 53, at 62 who sees the 'unité ecologique' of the coastal environment and the 'solidarité' of human activities on land in the proximate regions of the sea as the explanation of the contiguous zone.

[41] As to the 1958 negotiations on the subject, see Dean 'The Geneva Conference on the Law of the Sea: What was Accomplished', 52 *Am. J. Int'l L.* 607, at 623–25 (1958); Fitzmaurice, *supra* ch. 11 n. 5, at 110–20; Oda, 'The Concept of the Contiguous Zone', 11 *Int'l & Comp. L.Q.* 131 (1962).

[42] Territorial Sea Convention, *supra* ch. 9 n. 49, art. 24.

[43] Fitzmaurice, *supra* ch. 11 n. 5, at 112–14. See also Fitzmaurice, 'The Law and Procedure of the International Court of Justice, 1951–54: Points of Substantive Law—I', [1954] *Brit. Yb. Int'l L.* 371, at 378–79 (1954).

contiguous zone for the enumerated purposes is equivalent to that applicable to territorial waters.[44] There is continuing dispute, on the other hand, as to whether the term 'sanitary' comprehends marine pollution regulations. Indeed, it may be argued plausibly that the draftsmen at Geneva did not contemplate or consider such a reference.[45] Yet, most commentators now conclude that states do possess authority to prescribe and enforce laws with respect to pollution of the contiguous zone itself.[46]

The contiguous zone of Article 24 to which these conclusions apply was, of course, categorically limited to twelve miles. In 1970, Canada dramatically challenged this spatial restriction with its Arctic Waters Pollution Prevention Act.[47] This legislation prohibited waste discharge and mandated extensive CDEM regulations within a zone extending 100 nautical miles from the Canadian northern coast.[48] In response to a wave of international criticism, Canada asserted essentially a contiguous zone argument:

> A State may exercise special authority in areas of the sea adjacent to its territorial waters where functional controls of a continuing nature are necessary for the effective prevention of pollution which could cause damage or injury to the land or marine environment under its exclusive or sovereign authority.[49]

As with the established 12-mile zone and the right of case-by-case intervention, recourse is to the orthodoxy of objective territoriality: to protect territorial interests, it is essential to exercise extraterritorial jurisdiction.[50] The

[44] Brownlie, *supra* ch. 9 n. 52 at 217; McDougal and Burke, *supra* ch. 6 n. 4, at 612–21; Oda, *supra* no. 41, *passim*.

[45] See Brown, *supra* ch. 6 n. 39, at 145; Hakapaa, *supra* ch. 5 n. 145, at 212; Wulf, 'Contiguous Zones for Pollution Control: An Appraisal under International Law', Sea Grant Bulletin no. 13 (March 1971), at 133–58.

[46] See Brownlie, *supra* ch. 2 n. 92, at 221; Caflisch, *supra* ch. 10 n. 29, at 11; Poulantzas, *supra* n. 21, at 138–9, Teclaff, *supra* ch. 6 n. 33, at 126, Timagenis, *supra* ch. 5 n. 1, at 35; US S. Rep. no. 91–351, 91st Cong., 1st Sess. (1969), at 66 (justifying US anti-pollution legislation extending to contiguous zone violations on the basis of Article 24 of the Territorial Sea Convention).

[47] *Can. Rev. Stat.*, c. 2 (1st Supp. 1970). At the time of this legislation Canada tactically amended its submission to ICJ jurisdiction to except disputes relating to marine environmental jurisdiction. Letter of Notification to the United Nations from Ambassador Beaulne, reprinted in 9 *Int'l Legal Materials* 498 (1970).

[48] Arctic Act, Section 3(i). With respect to the legislation and its status in international law see Bilder, 'Canadian Arctic Waters Pollution Prevention Act: New Stresses on the Law of the Sea', 69 *Mich. L. Rev.* 1 (1970); Henkin, 'Arctic Anti-pollution: Does Canada Make—or Break—International Law?' 65 *Am J. Int'l L.* 131 (1971): Pharand, *The Law of the Sea of the Arctic* (1973).

[49] Canadian Working Paper on the Preservation of the Marine Environment, UN Doc A/AC.138/C.III/L.26 (1972). For the US and Canadian correspondence regarding the validity of this argument see US Dept. State Press Release no. 121, 15 Apr. 1970, 52 *Dept. State Bull.* 610 (1970) and Canadian Reply to the US Government, reprinted in 9 *Int'l Legal Materials* 607 (1970). For echoes of the same language see Principles Submitted by Spain (Working Paper A/CONF. 18 IWCMP. II/WP.VIII/Add. 1) in the Report of the Intergovernmental Working Group on Marine Pollution on its Second Session, UN Doc. A/CONF.48/IWCMP. II/5, Annex, IV; Governmental Statement of Chile for the Record, Convention on the Prevention of Marine Pollution by Dumping of Wastes and Other Matters, reprinted in *Envt'l L. Rep.* 40332 (1973).

[50] See Beesley, *supra* ch. 6 n. 61, at 8; Pharand, *supra* n. 48, at 260. It should be noted that the status of the Canadian assertion is confused by two factors: (*a*) Canada's diplomatic and

state may extend its enforcement authority to complement its external prescriptive rights due to the absence of any conflicting territorial authority over the high seas.[51]

To supplement this argument a number of authors have submitted that the pollution prevention zone rests on the right and correlative obligation of each state to act as the 'custodian' for the international community of the environment of proximate seas.[52] This may be viewed, in essence, as an extraterritorial application of Scelle's concept of 'dédoublement fonctionnel'. Pursuant to this notion, the state is vested with authority to act in its private interest; it must simultaneously exercise such authority to safeguard international interests.[53] Jennings succinctly summarizes the Canadian 'custodianship' variation:

> [T]he idea of a right of the coastal state is in the same moment linked with the idea of the responsibility of the coastal state to the international community generally; thus, the right of the coastal state to defend its own shores and territorial sea is made part and parcel of its responsibility, stemming from its proximity to the danger, to the international community to prevent pollution of the high seas.[54]

The logic of the argument is well expressed by Apollis: 'il apparait nettement que si l'État côtier est le plus exposé aux risques de pollution, il est, simultanement, l'autorité publique la mieux placée pour la combattre, non seulement dans son propre intérêt mais aussi dans l'intérêt commun de l'ensemble des nations.'[55]

Several states have followed Canada's lead in asserting the authority so explained to protect the environment in expansive contiguous zones.[56] Neither such limited practice nor 'the reason of the thing', however, elevates pollution prevention zones to international law.[57] To the contrary, there

academic defenses of the Arctic Act have been laced with language expressing the 'unique vulnerability' of the Arctic environment; and (*b*) Canada may indeed claim territorial rights over much of the Arctic Ocean on the basis of an amalgam of archipelagic, historic waters and sector claims. See *id.*, B. Smith, 'Canadian and Soviet Arctic Policy: An Icy Reception for the Law of the Sea?', 16 *Va. J. Int'l L.* 609 (1976); Reid, 'The Canadian Claim to Sovereignty over the Waters of the Arctic', 12 *Can. Yb. Int'l L.* 111 (1974).

[51] See ch. 5 at n. 85 *supra*.

[52] See e.g. Gotlieb and Dalfen, 'National Jurisdiction and International Responsibility: New Canadian Approaches to International Law', 67 *Am. J. Int'l L.* 229, at 249–50 (1973): Legault, 'Maritime Claims', in *Canadian Perspectives on International Law and Organization* 377 (MacDonald, *et al.* eds. 1974). See also Schneider, *supra* ch. 5 n. 36, at 183–5; Observations of de Visscher, Edinburgh Session, *supra* ch. 12 n. 100, at 28; Goldie *supra* ch. 5 n. 45, at 50.

[53] See ch. 11 at nn. 11–12.

[54] Jennings, *supra* ch. 7 n. 29, at 44.

[55] Apollis, *supra* ch. 10 n. 53, at 232.

[56] See e.g. (Oman) Marine Pollution Control Law of 1974, reprinted in UN Leg. Ser. St/LEG/Ser. B/18 at 74; (Bangladesh) Territorial Waters and Maritime Zones Act of 1974, reprinted in UN Leg. Ser. ST/LEG/Ser. B/19 at 4; (Sri Lanka) Maritime Zones Law no. 22 of 1976, reprinted in *id.*, at 120. It has also been noted that the language of the US Clean Water Act with respect to conduct which 'may affect' US interests may represent an assertion of authority over vessels well beyond the spatial limits of US resource claims. See Note, *supra* ch. 12 n. 116, at 292.

[57] Jennings, *supra* ch. 7 n. 29, at 44.

would seem little question of the validity of the US Draft Restatement's conclusion that '[i]nternational law has not recognized coastal state assertions of extensive zones to protect security or environment.'[58]

e. The Continental Shelf

The foregoing conclusion is limited to assertions of environmental authority unrelated to extraterritorial resource claims. In fact, international law does acknowledge coastal jurisdiction over environmental matters far beyond the 12-mile continguous zone when linked to co-extensive rights of exclusive resource exploitation. The earliest claims to such rights, and to attendant environmental authority, related to the continental shelf beyond territorial waters. Pursuant to the Truman Proclamation of 1945, generally regarded as the catalyst to extraterritorial resource claims, the United States claimed 'jurisdiction and control' with respect to the natural resources of the seabed and subsoil of its continental shelf.[59] State practice mirroring this assertion was sufficient by 1958 to characterize those provisions of the Convention on the Continental Shelf, reciting the state's 'sovereign rights' over the shelf 'for the purpose of exploring it and exploiting its natural resources' as declaratory of customary law.[60]

The precise definition of the continental shelf remained in question following 1958.[61] After vigorous negotiations at the LOS III Conference, the 1982 LOS Convention codified a resolution.[62] Subject to certain limits applicable to unusual physical circumstances, Article 76 defines the state's shelf as extending to the more distant of 'the natural prolongation of its land territory to the outer edge of the continental margin, or . . . a distance of 200 nautical miles' from the territorial baseline.[63]

The language of both the 1958 and 1982 Conventions treads gingerly in the definition of a state's 'sovereign rights' as opposed to 'sovereignty' over the shelf.[64] A number of factors suggest that the shelf might be viewed as

[58] 1982 Draft Rest., *supra* ch. 9 n. 4, § 511 Comment (i).

[59] Presidential Proclamation No. 2667, 3 CFR 67 (1943–8 Compil.) and companion Executive Order no. 9633, 3 CFR, 437 (1943–8 Compil.), reprinted in 40 *Am. J. Int'l L.* 45 (Suppl. 1946). See generally Brownlie, *supra* ch. 2 n. 52 at 223; Hollick, 'US Oceans Policy: The Truman Proclamations', 17 *Va. J. Int'l L.* 23 (1976); McDougal and Burke, *supra* ch. 6 n. 4, at 365.

[60] Convention on the Continental Shelf, done at Geneva 29 Apr. 1958, entry into force 10 June 1964, arts. 2(1) and 2(3), respectively. See the *North Sea Continental Shelf* Case, [1969] ICJ 3.

[61] See Brown, *supra* ch. 6 n. 39, at 3–73; Friedmann, 'The North Sea Continental Shelf Cases: A Critique', 18 *Int'l L & Comp. L.Q.* 819 (1969); Hedberg, 'Relation of Political Boundaries on the Ocean Floor to the Continental Margin', 17 *Va. J. Int'l L.* 57 (1976); Lauterpacht, 'Sovereignty over Submarine Areas', 27 *Brit. Yb. Int'l L.* 376 (1950); McDougal and Burke, *supra* ch. 6 n. 4, at 630–3; Moulton, *The Continental Shelf* (1952); Eustis, 'Method and Basis of Seaward Delimination of Continental Shelf Jurisdiction', 17 *Va. J. Int'l L.* 107 (1976).

[62] See Oxman, 'The Third United Nations Conference on the Law of the Sea: The Ninth Session (1980)', 75 *Am. J. Int'l L.* 211, at 229 (1981).

[63] Art. 76(1), LOS Convention, *supra* ch. 5 n. 17. The continental margin ends at the reach of the slope and rise of the shelf, excluding the deep floor.

[64] Continental Shelf Convention, *supra* n. 60, art 2(1), LOS Convention, *supra* ch. 5 n. 17, art. 77.

juridically indistinguishable from state territory: (*a*) the term sovereignty seems to have been avoided only to emphasize the absence of territorial authority over superadjacent waters; (*b*) the concept of shelf rights adopted was premised upon the continuity or natural prolongation of land territory; (*c*) continental shelf rights are inherent, i.e. they do not depend upon the affirmative claim of the coastal state as do lesser 'jurisdictional' contiguous rights; and (*d*) the rights granted compare in scope with territorial rights—the fact of subjection to limitations inherent in the location below high seas no more precludes territorial status than does innocent passage with respect to the territorial sea.[65] Yet, Brownlie, articulating the consensus position, notes that the language of 'sovereign rights' reflects the fact that authority over the shelf is *sui generis*—neither territorial nor merely jurisdictional.[66]

In any event, it is clear that states possess jurisidiction over conduct on the shelf which is tantamount to that enjoyed over territorial activity.[67] In exercise of such plenary authority, numerous states have restricted or prohibited pollution arising out of shelf activities.[68] A similar order of exclusive coastal jurisdiction is generally acknowledged with respect to artificial islands, installations, and structures engaged in shelf resource exploration or exploitation.[69] The LOS Convention specifically vests the shelf

[65] As to the first point see McDougal and Burke, *supra* ch. 6 n. 4, at 699–703. The second point was emphasized by the ICJ in the *North Sea Continental Shelf* Case, [1969] ICJ 3, at 31. See also Apollis, *supra* ch. 10 n. 53, at 54–67; the Truman Proclamation's language of 'extension of the land-mass of the coastal nation.' Presidential Proclamation no. 2667, 3 CFR 67, at 68 (1943–8 Compil.). Note, however, that prior to the Outer Continental Shelf Lands Act, as amended by The Outer Continental Shelf Lands Act Amendments of 1978, 43 USC § 1331–56, the United States' claim to jurisdiction over the shelf may have been limited to the mineral resources. See *Treasure Salvors, Inc.* v. *Abandoned Sailing Vessel*, 408 F. Supp. 907 (1976). Sect. 1333 of the OCS Act did extend 'the civil and political jurisdiction of the United States' to the subsoil and sea-bed of the shelf. For the third point, see Brownlie, *supra* ch. 9 n. 3 at 210, 226.

[66] Brownlie, *supra* ch. 2 n. 52, at 111, 226.

[67] The right to exclude others from resource exploitation is an essential component of this right. Continental Shelf Convention, *supra* n. 60, art. 2(2). N.B. The presence of the specific shelf regime does not pre-empt application of the general extraterritorial prescriptive rights described in subsection a. above.

[68] See e.g. (Finland) Law no. 146 Concerning The Prevention of Pollution of the Sea, 5 Mar. 1965, art. 1, reprinted in Ruster and Simma, *supra* ch. 11 n. 8, vol. iii at 1041; (France) Loi no. 68–1181, 30 Dec. 1968, Relative à l'exploration du plateau continental et à l'exploitation de ses resources naturelles, reprinted in Ruster and Simma, *supra* ch. 11 n. 8, vol. xix at 9965, (UK) Continental Shelf Act, 1964, c. 29.

[69] See LOS Convention, *supra* ch. 5 n. 17, arts. 60 and 80; 1982 Draft Rest. *supra* ch. 9 n. 4, § 514 comment (*f.*); McDougal and Burke, *supra* ch. 6 n. 4, at 710. There is no consensus, however, as to the precise juridical character of such resource installations or of the deep water ports constructed above the shelf beyond the territorial sea. Attachment may render them effectively part of the shelf; on the other hand, they may be deemed assimilated to the quasi-territoriality of vessels. Commentators have suggested that to avoid such issues permission to use such facilities should be conditioned on consent to jurisdiction. See US Deepwater Port Act of 1974, 33 USC §§ 1501–24, at Sect. 19(*c*). See generally Anderson, *supra* ch. 11 n. 26, at 1045; De Mestral, 'The Prevention of Pollution of the Marine Environment Arising from Offshore Mining and Drilling', 20 *Harv. Int'l L.J.* 469 (1979); International Law Association Report of the 57th Conference in Madrid (1976), Report of the Law of the Sea Committee on Artificial Islands and Offshore Installations, at 396.

state with prescriptive and enforcement competence over polluting conduct on such surface installations.[70]

The more perplexing issue is the measure of coastal authority over vessels navigating over the shelf engaged in conduct affecting shelf resources. The Continental Shelf Convention recognizes that shelf activities may disturb navigation in its prohibition only of 'unjustifiable interference'.[71] The shelf state, moreover, is granted and obligated to exercise jurisdiction to preserve the environment within a limited safety zone around shelf installations.[72] There is no recognition in the Convention, however, of general coastal authority over vessels above the shelf with respect to environmental matters. Consensus could not be achieved as to such jurisdiction in several multilateral anti-pollution conferences in the 1970s.[73] The LOS Convention expressed a partial resolution. The text recites the shelf state's authority to prescribe and enforce against foreign vessels laws to prevent dumping of pollution over the shelf.[74] On the other hand, no jurisdiction over vessels passing above the shelf is identified with respect to operational discharge or CDEM conditions which threaten accidental discharge. In any event, such questions as to shelf jurisdiction have been largely overwhelmed by the development of an exclusive economic zone which to a significant extent envelopes the shelf.[75]

f. The Exclusive Economic Zone

Without question, coastal state authority over the economic resources of zones beyond and contiguous to the territorial sea (in addition to shelf resources) constitutes the most radical departure from the orthodoxy of flag state exclusive authority. The earliest claims were modest attempts to establish exclusive fishery rights within twelve miles of the coastal baseline.[76] The 1945 US proclamation of a 200-mile fishery conservation zone marked the beginning of the dramatic expansion of contiguous resource claims.[77] The

[70] LOS Convention, *supra* ch. 5 n. 7, arts. 209 and 214. See also 1973 Convention, *supra* ch. 6 n. 37, art. 2(5).

[71] Continental Shelf Convention, *supra* n. 70, art. 5(1).

[72] *Id.*, arts. 5(2), (3), (7).

[73] For discussions of the debate in the negotiation of the Barcelona Convention, the London Dumping Convention, and the 1973 Convention see Timagenis, *supra* ch. 5 n. 1, at 286–7, 238–42, and 294. See also de Yturriaga, *supra* ch. 5 n. 1, at 270–2.

[74] LOS Convention, *supra* ch. 5 n. 17, arts. 210 and 216. See Hakapaa, *supra* ch. 5 n. 57, at 229.

[75] To the extent the EEZ overlays the shelf, issues of jurisdiction are subsumed within the EEZ regime.

[76] See Brownlie, *supra* ch. 2 n. 52, at 214. The *Fisheries Jurisdiction* Case (*UK* v. *Iceland*), [1974] ICJ 3, 23.

[77] The catalyst to such claims has again been identified as a US assertion of fishery conservation zone rights: Presidential Proclamation no. 2668, 3 CFR 68 (1943–48 Compil.) and companion Excecutive Order no. 9634, 3 CFR 437 (1943–8 Compil.). Ironically, it was not until 1976 that any effort was made in the US 'to implement the fisheries proclamation either via legislation or executive action.' Hollick, 'US Oceans Policy: The Truman Proclamations', 17 *Va. J. Int'l L.* 23, at 4 (1976). The 1976 legislation represents an example of the extensive conservation zone assertion. Fishery Conservation and Management Act of 1976, 16 USC §§ 1801–82 (1976). It should be noted that Articles 6 and 7 of the 1958 Convention on Fishing and Conservation of the Living Resources of the High Seas, done at Geneva 29 Apr. 1958, entry into force 20 Mar. 1966, TIAS no. 39 (1966), vest in coastal states the right to impose conservation measures in adjacent

content of such assertions varied greatly, ranging from mere exercises of jurisdiction to impose conservation measures to claims of plenary territorial rights subject only to rights of navigation.[78] By the mid-1970s and the commencement of the LOS III negotiations, however, practice and opinion had focused on a 200-mile zone of exclusive resource rights—the 'patrimonial sea' or 'exclusive economic zone' (EEZ).[79] By 1982, consensus was sufficiently advanced with respect to this concept for the ICJ to observe that the EEZ had indeed become part of 'modern international law'.[80] Noting the customary status of the EEZ, the United States joined the list of nations claiming such a zone in 1983.[81] It seems appropriate to conclude, with the US Draft Restatement, that '[r]ecent practice of States, supported by the broad consensus achieved at the Third Law of the Sea Conference, has effectively established the concept of the exclusive economic zone, and the general principles governing it, as customary law . . .'[82]

The LOS Convention defines the EEZ as a zone extending not more than 200 miles from the territorial baseline within which the coastal state enjoys

> sovereign rights for the purpose of exploring and exploiting, conserving and managing the natural resources, whether living or non-living, of the waters superjacent to the seabed and of the seabed and its subsoil, and with regard to other activities for the economic exploitation and exploration of the zone, such as the production of energy from the water, currents and winds.[83]

Notwithstanding substantial debate at the negotiations and continuing disclaimers outside the Conference, the Convention text *excludes* from the 'high seas' all areas within any such zone of sovereign rights.[84] The EEZ is

areas of the high seas subject to objective criteria regarding necessity, scientific basis and non-discrimination.

[78] See as to the latter Panama's Law no. 31 of 2 Feb. 1967, Gac. Off. 14 Feb. 1967; Brazil's Law no. 1.098 of 25 Mar. 1970, Reg. Off. 2 Apr. 1971. See Garcia-Amador, 'The Latin American Contribution to the Development of the Law of the Sea', 68 *Am. J. Int'l L.* 33, at 39 (1974).

[79] See Declaration of Santa Domingo, UN Doc. A/AC. 138/79 (1972), 11 *Int'l Legal Materials* 892 (1972); 1970 Declaration of Montevideo, 64 *Am. J. Int'l L.* 1021 (1970); 1970 Declaration of Lima, 10 *Int'l Legal Materials* 207 (1971); Declaration of Addis Ababa, UN Doc. A/CONF. 62/33 (1974). See generally Attard, *The Exclusive Economic Zone in International Law* (1987) Brownlie, *supra* ch. 2 n. 52 at 218; Extavour, *The Exclusive Economic Zone: A Study of the Evolution and Progressive Development of the International Law of the Sea* (1979); Kronfel, 'The Exclusive Economic Zone: A Critique of Contemporary Law of the Sea', 9 *J. Mar. L. & Com* 461 (1977-8); Phillips, 'The Economic Resources Zone: Progress for the Developing Coastal States', 11 *J. Mar. L. & Com.* 349 (1980).

[80] *Case concerning the Continental Shelf* (*Tunisia* v. *Libya*), [1982] ICJ 18.

[81] Presid. Proc. No. 5030, 10 Mar. 1983, 48 Fed. Reg. 10605, 14 Mar. 1983, reprinted with related statements in 22 *Int'l Legal Materials* 461 (1983). See Peirce, 'Selective Adoption of the New Law of the Sea: The United States Proclaims its Exclusive Economic Zone', 23 *Va. J. Int'l L.* 581 (1983).

[82] 1982 Draft Rest., *supra* ch. 9 n. 4, § 514 Comment (*a*).

[83] LOS Convention, *supra* ch. 5 n. 17, art. 56(1)(*a*). The limits of breadth are defined in Article 57. Article 56 also bestows jurisdiction over artificial islands and installations and marine scientific research. See Apollis, *supra* ch. 10 n. 53, at 183–90 for a definition of zonal resources.

[84] As to the debates, see Oxman, 'The Third United Nations Conference on the Law of the Sea: The 1977 New York Session', 72 *Am. J. Int'l L.* 57, at 67–75 (1978); Stevenson and Oxman, 'The Third United Nations Conference on the Law of the Sea: The 1975 Geneva Session', 64 *Am. J.*

thus codified as a distinct *sui generis* juridical region, not merely a contiguous zone qualification to the regime of the high seas.

The principal tension in the EEZ regime is, in any case, between the coastal state's authority to protect and enjoy its exclusive resource interests and the community's exercise of traditional non-resource freedoms. Article 58 of the Convention retains explicitly the freedoms of 'navigation and overflight and of laying submarine cables and pipelines, and other internationally lawful uses of the sea related to these freedoms . . .'[85] Other elements of the regime of the high seas are to be applied to the EEZ to the extent 'not incompatible' with EEZ coastal rights.[86] Article 87, which describes the basic freedoms of the high seas, including fishing, artificial installations, and scientific research, and those articles concerning high seas resources are, however, excluded from application to the EEZ for reasons of inherent incompatibility. In summary, it is principally the core freedoms of communication and transportation which are preserved in the EEZ.[87] As in the territorial sea, these navigational freedoms and coastal state competence in the EEZ may stand in conflict. The LOS Convention responds to this interaction first by clearly subordinating the exercise of common rights in the EEZ to laws of the coastal state enacted and enforced in conformity with the Convention.[88] The text then defines a rule for resolving conflicts: all states must exercise rights in the EEZ with 'due regard to the rights and duties' of others.[89] Finally, as to one of the most vexing areas of conflict, environmental matters, the text ventures to define specific rules of coastal authority in the EEZ.

Prior to turning to the Convention's regime, it is important to note that outside of the context of the Conference, authority to prescribe and enforce anti-pollution laws has been asserted consistently as a corollary to EEZ resource rights. Practice, in the form of both abstract declaration[90] and specific legislation,[91] has established protection of the environment as a

Int'l L. 763, at 774–81 (1975). The 1982 Draft Rest. states that many states conceded the technical definition but still view the EEZ as a part of the high seas. § 514, Rpt. n. 1.

[85] LOS Convention, *supra* ch. 5 n. 17, art. 58(1).

[86] *Id.*, art. 58(2).

[87] See e.g. the articles re: peaceful use of region (art. 88); exclusive flag jurisdiction (art. 92); public vessel immunities (arts. 95–6); flag penal jurisdiction over collisions (art. 97); liability for seizure (art. 106).

[88] *Id.*, art. 58(3). The general extraterritorial prescriptive authority reiterated in subsection a. continues to operate within the EEZ. To the extent that EEZ regime constraints on coastal jurisdiction rise to custom, however, any more expansive aspects of general prescriptive authority are likely qualified.

[89] *Id.*, art. 58(3) (as to EEZ use by other than the coastal state) and art. 56(2) (as to EEZ use by the coastal state).

[90] See materials cited at nn. 79, 81 *supra*.

[91] See e.g. (Canada) Part XX of Canada Shipping Act (An Act to Amend the Canada Shipping Act, Can. Stat. 1970–71–72, c. 27 (2nd Suppl.)); (Sri Lanka) Article 7 Maritime Zones Law, no. 22 of 1976 and Maritime Zones Proclamation of 15 Jan. 1977, reprinted in *New Directions*, at 322–3; (US) Section 311 (*b*) (1) of the Federal Water Pollution Control Act, 33 USC § 1321 (*b*) (1) (Supp. 1977). The US legislation asserted authority over all pollution 'which may affect natural resources belonging to, appertaining to, or under the exclusive management authority of the United States . . .'. *Id.* See Hakaapa, *supra* ch. 5 n. 57, at 238.

legitimate subject of coastal state EEZ jurisdiction. The principle of such authority has risen with the EEZ itself to the dignity of custom.[92] The limits to such authority, required at the intersection with community freedoms, on the other hand, have been ill-defined in state practice.

The provisions of the LOS Convention defining such positive coastal authority over EEZ environmental matters and the circumscribing rules proved highly controversial. The general recognition of coastal jurisdiction in the EEZ with regard to the 'protection and preservation of the marine environment' did not elicit great resistance.[93] The conflict between 'maritime' and 'coastal' states and interest groups, however, made the translation of the abstraction into specific rules exceedingly difficult.[94] In terms of prescriptive authority, jurisdiction over 'vessel source' pollution (i.e. accidental and operational discharge), as distinct from pollution arising out of dumping or sea-bed activities, was the principal subject of debate. The right to regulate conduct relating to the latter sources was not perceived as a sufficiently serious threat to navigational freedom to require circumscription.[95] Articles 208 and 210, expressing the coastal state's prescriptive environmental authority over

[92] Notwithstanding broad interpretive language in the literature, the *Behring Sea Fur Seal* Arbitrations of 1893 and 1902 did not articulate a conflicting principle denying extraterritorial authority to protect exclusive resource interests. See Moore, i *Digest Int'l L.* ¶¶ 172, 173. The first of the decisions involved American arrests of Canadian sealers on the high seas who were endangering seal stocks by aggressive harvesting of pregnant females. The second related to Russian arrests of American sealers engaged in similar detrimental harvesting practices. The orthodox perspective on the impact of the arbitral decisions is summarized by Brierly: 'In both these cases the Tribunal rejected the idea that a coastal state has a right to apply conservation to foreign vessels in areas of the high seas adjacent to its coasts for the purpose of safeguarding valuable natural resources against selfish and wasteful exploitation and confirmed that, in the absence of a treaty, a coastal State could only apply conservation measures to vessels of its own flag.' Brierly, *supra* ch. 2 n. 41, at 308. This broad interpretation fails, however, to reflect a critical qualifying element of the rationale of the decisions. It was the specific legal conclusion of the tribunal in the former of the arbitrations that 'the United States has not any right of protection or property in the fur-seals frequenting the islands of the United States in Behring Sea, when such seals are found outside the ordinary three-mile limit.' Hence, the decision may indeed represent authority for the proposition that no right of protection exists with respect to resources in which the state possesses no cognizable property interest. One commentator has submitted that 'the decision indicates only that the interests of the US were not of a sufficiently vital nature to support a plea of self-defence.' Bowett, *supra* n. 27, at 80. In any case, it is clear that the arbitrations may not be interpreted as categorically denying extraterritorial measures to protect resource interests. The *Fur Seal* Opinions quite simply never addressed the circumstances of a threat to resources in which the state does possess an acknowledged property interest, e.g. those resources situated within the EEZ.

[93] LOS Convention, *supra* ch. 5 n. 17, art. 56(1)(*b*)(iii). See Douay, *supra* n. 26, at 253–65.

[94] See generally Extavour, *supra* n. 79, at 215; Alexander and Hodgson, 'The Impact of the 200-mile Economic Zone on the Law of the Sea', 12 *San Diego L. Rev.* 569, at 595 (1975).

[95] 'The view of those States advocating the so-called "international" approach was that in the case of land-based pollution, dumping, and exploration and exploitation of the sea-bed and subsoil, fewer problems were presented because these were ". . . static and susceptible to national control and to enforcement in conjunction with other States." With respect to vessel-generated pollution, however, the interests of all nations were involved so that an international approach was best suited to secure the necessary consistency.' Extavour, *supra* n. 79, at 215.

sea-bed activities and dumping in the EEZ, respectively, thus achieved an early consensus.[96]

The provisions treating jurisdiction over vessel-generated pollution, on the other hand, were the product of extensive negotiation. Early proposals submitted by certain maritime states basically denied any coastal authority and sought to maintain exclusive flag state jurisdiction.[97] A number of developing and environmentally aggressive developed coastal states on the other hand advocated effectively territorial coastal state prescriptive rights with respect to environmental matters.[98] A formula for compromise was suggested in draft articles submitted by Canada, Fiji, Ghana, and others: the coastal state generally should possess prescriptive jurisdition only to implement international standards; in the absence of international rules or in special circumstances, however, the state should have a right to exercise its 'residual' authority to prescribe.[99]

The Convention reflects this basic approach. Article 211(5) recites the limited right of the EEZ state to 'adopt laws and regulations for the prevention, reduction and control of pollution from vessels conforming to and giving effect to generally accepted international rules and standards established through the competent international organization or general diplomatic conference.'[100] The 'residual' environmental authority concept is embodied in two provisions. Article 211(6) provides that any state, upon 'reasonable grounds', may request the 'competent international organization' to acknowledge the inadequacy of international rules with respect to specifically defined areas of the state's EEZ.[101] If, and only if, such

[96] LOS Convention, *supra* ch. 5 n. 17, arts. 208 and 210. See Oxman, *supra* n. 84, at 2

[97] See e.g. Federal Republic of Germany: Draft Articles—Enforcement of Regulations Concerning the Protection of the Marine Environment Against Vessel-source Pollution, A/CONF. 62/C.3/L.7, 1 Aug. 1974. See Alexander and Hodgson, *supra* n. 94, at 595; Apollis, *supra* ch. 10 n. 53, at 218.

[98] See e.g. Ecuador, El Salvador, Panama, Peru, and Uruguay: Preservation of the Marine Environment (Working Paper), UN Doc.A/AC.138/SC.III/L.47, 24 July 1973, at art. 8; Kenya: Draft Articles on the Exclusive Economic Zone Concept, UN Doc.A/AC.138/SCII/L.10, at art. 11; Nigeria: Draft Article, UN Doc.A/CONF.62/C.2/L.21/Rev.1. See also Statement of New Zealand, iv *Off. Rec.* 20th Mfg. Comm. III, 10 Apr. 1975, at 90; Statement of Canada, ii *Off. Rec.* 4th Mtg. Comm. III, 16 July 1974, at 317–18.

[99] Canada, Fiji, Ghana, *et al.*: Draft Articles on a Zonal Approach to the Preservation of the Marine Environment, UN Doc.A/CONF./62/C.3/L.6, 31 July 1974. As to the concept of 'residual authority', see Canada: Working Paper on the Preservation of the Marine Environment, A/AC. 138/SC III/L.26, in Report of the Committee on the Peaceful Uses of the Sea-bed and the Ocean Floor Beyond the Limits of National Jurisdiction, 27 UN GAOR Supp. (no. 21) 213, UN Doc.A/8721 (1972).

[100] LOS Convention, *supra* ch. 5 n. 17, art. 211(5). The language of this provision states that the right is 'for the purpose of enforcement.' Presumably, the purpose of the expression is to emphasize the linkage and limitation to international rules. It is, however, a rather awkward means of accomplishing this end—it only confuses the distinction between prescription and enforcement.

[101] As to IMCO's identification as the 'competent organization' see Kindt, *supra* ch. 7 n. 43, at n. 123.

acknowledgment is forthcoming, the coastal state may (*a*) enact supplementary laws implementing any of the body of rules and standards applicable to such 'special areas' which the competent international organization may have defined, and (*b*) enact additional laws and regulations for the special areas with respect to discharges and navigational practices; additional CDEM restrictions are expressly forbidden.[102] Article 234, the second concession to residual authority and a direct response to Canadian demands, acknowledges coastal prescriptive authority to protect environmentally fragile 'ice-covered areas' in the EEZ without reference to international standards or CDEM limits.[103] The sole check on such jurisdiction is the requirement that coastal initiatives have 'due regard for navigation' and a basis in the 'best available scientific evidence'.[104]

The provisions governing coastal enforcement in the EEZ again reflect the maritime interests' greater tolerance of jurisdiction over dumping and pollution from sea-bed activities than that over vessel-source pollution. The Convention clearly acknowledges the coastal state's right to take measures in the EEZ to enforce laws pertaining to the former matters.[105] The text regarding enforcement steps against polluting vessels is not nearly as unqualified in its grant of jurisdiction.[106] As noted in Chapter 11, the coastal state's authority to enforce EEZ prescriptions by actions against vessels in port received greater emphasis in the Convention.[107] Such 'port state' authority was viewed by maritime states as an acceptable alternative to extensive enforcement rights in the EEZ itself.[108] Outside of the port, therefore, jurisdiction to enforce EEZ rules is much circumscribed.

[102] LOS Convention, *supra* ch. 5 n. 17, art. 211(6).

[103] *Id.*, art. 234. See B. Smith, *supra* n. 30, at 628.

[104] *Id.* Note that Art. 234 appears applicable even to international straits. Art. 233 does *not* include Art. 234 among the environmental provisions subordinated to the regime of international straits.

[105] *Id.* arts. 214 and 216.

[106] Art. 73 does provide in blanket terms that the coastal state may take necessary measures 'including boarding, inspection, arrest and judicial proceedings' to ensure compliance with prescriptions related to its right 'to explore, exploit, conserve and manage the EEZ's living resources.' This language appears broad enough to comprehend the enforcement of laws designed to prevent detriment to those resources from pollution. The placement of Art. 73 in the EEZ paragraphs focusing on fisheries conservation and management and the clear inconsistency of its expansive grant with the limited specific provisions of the marine pollution chapter combine, however, to deny this conclusion. Either the provision (*a*) applies only to fisheries exploitation rules or (*b*) stands subordinate to the subsequent Committee III text.

[107] See ch. 11 n. 36 ff. *supra*.

[108] See Stevenson and Oxman, *supra* n. 84, at 791; Kiselev, *supra* ch. 12 n. 108, at 104. Kiselev articulates the view: 'Proceeding from the interests of navigation, a coastal State should be entitled to exercise a right to investigate such infringements only in cases where ships alleged to have discharged prohibited pollutants enter ports or offshore terminals of the coastal State.' Note again that port state jurisdiction is not an expansion of enforcement authority. States always possess authority to enforce prescriptions within territory. The expansion is in the reach of prescriptions into the EEZ.

Article 220 provides that if there are 'clear grounds' for suspicion of any EEZ violation, the coastal state may impede navigation in the EEZ or territorial sea to require information from the vessel with respect to its identity, registration, destination, and other matters relevant to the violation.[109] Physical inspection may only occur if (*a*) the violation includes a 'substantial discharge causing or threatening significant pollution', or the vessel has refused the requested information or the information is manifestly false, and (*b*) the circumstances justify inspection.[110] The full measure of enforcement authority as to EEZ violations, including detention and institution of proceedings, may only be exercised with respect to vessels navigating the EEZ or the territorial sea on the basis of 'clear objective evidence' of a discharge violation causing or threatening 'major damage' to the coastal or resource interests of the state.[111]

Several subtle aspects to the Convention's EEZ vessel-source enforcement provisions require notation. First, enforcement in the territorial sea of EEZ violations constitutes an exception to the general prohibition against interference with innocent passage for pre-passage violations.[112] Second, the coastal state possesses *no* authority outside of its ports to take enforcement measures, other than information request, for violations of CDEM rules in the absence of actual discharge. Finally, the contiguous zone of the 1958 Convention is extended to a maximum of twelve miles beyond the limits of the territorial sea.[113] Although this zone is embraced within the larger EEZ, its juridical status remains distinct. Thus, the authority of the coastal state within the EEZ is an overlay to the contiguous zone rights described above.[114]

In any case, enforcement actions against vessels with respect to both vessel-source and dumping violations in the EEZ, regardless of the zone in which the actions are taken, are subject to the 'safeguard' provisions described above.[115] Thus, the standards for investigation and detention of foreign

[109] LOS Convention, *supra* ch. 5 n. 17, art. 220(3).

[110] *Id.*, art. 220(5).

[111] *Id.*, art. 220(6). The rationale for this linkage to coastal damage is explained as follows: '[D]etention of a foreign ship in the economic zone for purposes of proceedings by a coastal State (that is not necessarily the State of destination) entails greater risks to freedom of navigation; such risks are thought to be justified only if the coastal state's resources or territory have been subjected to major damage or a threat of major damage by the discharge.' Oxman, *supra* ch. 12 n. 106, at 26–7. It could be argued that this entire structure of restrictions applies equally to enforcement of EEZ dumping violations. Indeed, the language of Art. 220 does refer broadly to enforcement of laws to prevent 'pollution from vessels.' Yet, several factors combine to suggest that enforcement of dumping laws is not so limited: (*a*) the absence of any limiting reference to Art. 220 in the general grant of enforcement authority over dumping in Art. 216; (*b*) the use of the same 'pollution from vessels' language to describe specifically vessel-source pollution (as distinct from dumping) in Art. 211; (*c*) the references to 'discharges' in Art. 220 suggestive only of vessel-source pollution; and (*d*) Art. 220's failure to express any limits to the authority to enforce prescriptions relating to dumping on the continental shelf beyond the EEZ.

[112] See ch. 12 nn. 83, 120 *supra*.

[113] LOS Convention, *supra* ch. 5 n. 17, art. 33.

[114] See text at n. 41 *supra*.

[115] See ch. 11 at n. 46 *supra*.

vessels in port, in the territorial sea, or in the EEZ are directly applicable to such EEZ violations.[116] Similarly, Article 232's imposition of liability for excessive enforcement is operative.[117] In addition, only monetary penalties may be imposed for such EEZ violations; no exception is made, however, with respect to 'wilful and serious acts of pollution' as in the territorial sea.[118]

The final component of the 'safeguard' provisions applicable to the EEZ relates to flag-state pre-emption of legal proceedings. Article 228 provides:

> Proceedings to impose penalties in respect of any violation of applicable laws and regulations or international rules and standards relating to the prevention, reduction and control of pollution from vessels committed by a foreign vessel beyond the territorial sea of the State instituting proceedings shall be suspended upon the taking of proceedings to impose penalties under corresponding charges by the flag State within six months of the first institution of proceedings, unless those proceedings relate to a case of major damage to the coastal State or the flag State in question has repeatedly disregarded its obligations to enforce effectively the applicable international rules and standards in respect of violations committed by its vessels. . . .When proceedings of the flag State have been brought to a conclusion, the suspended proceedings shall be terminated.[119]

This provision was heatedly debated at the Conference. Flag states saw pre-emption as a requisite complement to their concession of exclusive authority over flag vessels.[120] On the other hand, many states, including the United States, were concerned that the provision might effectively emasculate coastal state authority, and therefore aggressively sought to deny pre-emption of proceedings for violations in the state's own EEZ.[121] The qualifications with respect to major damage to the coasal state and repeated disregard of flag obligations represent the Conference's resolution of the conflict. Yet, the potential for abuse of the pre-emption right by flag states and the attendant

[116] LOS Convention, *supra* ch. 5 n. 17, art. 226(1).

[117] *Id.*, art. 232.

[118] *Id.*, art. 230(1). See ch. 12 n. 124 *supra*. As this provision relates to 'pollution from vessels', it may be argued that it does not apply to dumping violations.

[119] *Id.*, art. 228(1). The following subparagraph adds a three-year statute of limitations from the date of the violation to the date of the imposition of penalties. The applicability of the provision to dumping violations in the EEZ is not certain. As noted above, the language 'pollution from vessels' does generally suggest only non-dumping vessel-source pollution. Significantly, the other safeguard provisions refer either to all enforcement actions against foreign vessels or to enforcement of rules concerning 'pollution of the marine environment' generally. These facts suggest that flag pre-emption does not apply to dumping enforcement proceedings. Certain ambiguity does unfortunately remain.

[120] See e.g. Federal Republic of Germany: Draft Article: Enforcement of Regulations concerning the Protection of the Marine Environment against Vessel-source Pollution, UN Doc. A/CONF. 62/C. 3/L. 7, 1 Aug. 1974.

[121] See Reports of the Committees and Negotiating Groups on Negotiations at the Seventh Session (distr. 19 May 1978) (GE 78-858800), 88, 94. For a discussion of the negotiations see Phillips, *supra* n. 79, at 363.

diminution of coastal enforcement authority has triggered serious criticism in the literature.[122]

The broader criticism that may be directed at the foregoing regime is precisely that discussed above with respect to the Convention's innocent passage provisions: rigidity. The problem in each context is the accommodation of the rights of the community with those of the coastal state. The character of respective rights differ in the two zones; the structural challenge for international law is the same. It was submitted in Chapter 12 that the Convention imposed unnecessary limits on the effective and flexible standard of proportionality implicit in the customary regime of innocent passage.[123] The same logic applies to the EEZ. The Convention text would deny categorically the state's right to prescribe laws beyond international standards (without submission to an uncertain and lengthy international process), to prevent pollution by arrest in the EEZ for CDEM violations prior to discharge, and to impose monetary penalties.[124] A preferable rule with respect to each of these matters, it is submitted, would be a flexible rule of reason based on 'due regard' standard, inquiring into the balance of the nature of the protected interest, the significance of the risk, and the degree of attendant interference.[125] In short, the rights of foreign states in the EEZ might be subsumed under, and qualified by, a general right of 'innocent presence' analogous to the right of innocent passage. Customary law spurred by practice may yet take the course of such a flexible rule of decision.

g. *The Sea-bed Authority*

The final species of non-flag state authority over environmental matters beyond the territorial sea was generated in the negotiations at the LOS III Conference regarding the regime of the deep sea-bed. The challenge has been

[122] See e.g. Bernhardt, *supra* ch. 10 n. 54, at 297; Johnson and Zacher (eds.), *supra* ch. 11 n. 43, at 145. Livingston, *supra* ch. 11 n. 24, at 17.

[123] See ch. 12 at nn. 111–18 *supra*.

[124] As to the limits of international rules, it is noteworthy that there inevitably exists a substantial time lag between the identification by the international community of a 'reasonable' norm and the elevation of that norm to the dignified status of an 'international' norm. Moreover, those same law-making processes are often subject to extraneous political, ideological, economic, and institutional influences. Hence, the norms defined by those processes may not even accurately represent the balance between the specific interests of states in the EEZ. Finally, international law-making—particularly in an institutional context—may simply require the consensus of states with a dominant commercial maritime orientation. The tempering impact of such states on the environmental law-making process is patent; environmental rules (not uniquely) tend not to advance beyond the lowest common point of consensus.

[125] For example, it indeed may be the case that most CDEM offences do not present a measure of imminent threat that justifies the extreme interference with navigation that would occur with arrest. Yet, a patently unseaworthy vessel with a hazardous cargo surely may imminently threaten an important fishery. This is an issue of degree which is again best treated through the application of an objective and flexible standard. For an opinion that practice will erode the rigid rules of the Convention to permit coastal state regulations of CDEM and cargo see Wulf, *supra* ch. 12 n. 101, at 165.

to define a legal order which reflects both developed and developing state perceptions of the import of the deep sea-bed's status as the 'common heritage of mankind'.[126] The regime of the high seas as articulated in the 1958 Convention imposed no limit, beyond the 'reasonable regard' standard, on any state's exploitation of high seas' sea-bed resources, including by means of the construction of artificial islands and installations. Flag states would presumably enjoy their traditional jurisdiction over vessels engaged in such activities. Jurisdiction over structures has not long been an issue; the technology of high seas installations is relatively recent. It does appear, however, that the 'flag' or authorizing state would possess spatial jurisdiction over such installations parallel to that enjoyed over similar extraterritorial shelf facilities.[127]

This conclusion finds support (and the attendant obligation to exercise such jurisdiction to protect the environment is evidenced) in recent state practice. A number of industrialized states, responding to the uncertain status and prospects of LOS Convention provisions on the subject, have enacted domestic laws asserting jurisdiction over and authorizing nationals' exploitation of deep sea-bed resources; in each case, the laws seek to prevent environmental harm.[128] Japan, the United States, and six European states have established a further regime ensuring the reciprocal recognition of the legitimacy of such authorized resource activities.[129] Significantly, the Memorandum implementing this regime states that '[e]ach Party will take all necessary measures so that deep seabed operations under its control . . . will include efforts to protect the quality of the environment and will not result in significant adverse effects on the environment; . . .'[130]

[126] See Declaration of Principles Governing the Sea-bed and the Ocean Floor Beyond the Limits of National Jurisdiction, GA Res. 2749 (XXV), 23 UN GAOR Supp. (no. 28) 24, UN Doc. A/8028 (1970); Amerasinghe, 'Basic Principles relating to the International Regime of the Oceans', 6 *J. Mar. L. & Comm.* 213 (1975); Bowett, 'Deep Sea-bed Resources: A Major Challenge', [1972] *Camb. L.J.* 50; Danzig, 'A Funny Thing Happened to the Common Heritage on the Way to the Law of the Sea', 12 *San Diego L. Rev.* 655 (1975); Gorove, 'The Concept of Common Heritage of Mankind: A Political, Moral or Legal Innovation?', 9 *San Diego L. Rev.* 340 (1972); Pardo, *supra* ch. 1 n. 6, at 216.

[127] ILA *supra* n. 69, at 399–410 (1976); 1982 Draft Rest, *supra* ch. 9 n. 4, § 521, comment (*g*). Note that without a flag or authorizing state, a structure would likely be assimilated to a regime parallel to that of a stateless vessel.

[128] See e.g. (France) Art. 14(*c*) Law no. 81-1135 of 23 Dec. 1981 on the Exploration and the Exploitation of the Mineral Resources of the Deep Seabed, 1981 JO 3499, reprinted in 21 *Int'l Legal Materials* 808 (1982); (UK) sect. 5, Deep Sea Mining (Temporary Provisions) Act, 1981, ch. 53, reprinted in 20 *Int'l Legal Materials* 1217 (1981); (USSR) parag. 14, Edict on Provisional Measures to Regulate Soviet Enterprise for the Exploration and Exploitation of Mineral Resources, USSR Presidium 17 Apr. 1982, reprinted in 21 *Int'l Legal Materials* 551 (1982).

[129] Belgium, France, Federal Republic of Germany, Italy, Japan, Netherlands, United Kingdom, and United States: Provisional Understanding Regarding Deep Sea-bed Matters, done at Geneva, 3 Aug. 1984, entered into force 2 Sept. 1984, reprinted in *Int'l Legal Materials* 1354 (1984).

[130] Art. 3, Memorandum on the Implementation of the Provisional Understanding Regarding Deep Sea-bed Matters, done at Geneva, 3 Aug. 1984, reprinted in 23 *Int'l Legal Materials* 1358 (1984).

The 'reciprocating states regime' and the problems which the LOS Convention itself has encountered are, in large measure, a reaction to the Convention's imposition of the authority of a new international body on these areas customarily within the exclusive jurisdiction of the flag state. To resolve the 'common heritage' debate, the Convention created an International Seabed Authority to organize, manage and control all activities relating to the resources of the sea-bed and subsoil beyond the EEZ or continental shelf of any state 'on behalf of mankind as a whole'.[131]

To perform this general task, the Authority is specifically endowed with authority to adopt rules, regulations, and procedures to protect the marine environment. The scope of this authority is described in a Convention Annex:

> Rules and regulations shall be drawn up in order to secure effective protection of the marine environment from harmful effects directly resulting from activities in the Area or from shipboard processing immediately above a mine site of minerals derived from that mine site, taking into account the extent to which such harmful effects may directly result from drilling, dredging, coring and excavations and from disposal, dumping and discharge into the marine environment of sediment, wastes or other effluents.[132]

Attendant to this prescriptive jurisdiction is a set of enforcement rights. The Authority generally 'shall exercise such control over activities in the Area as is necessary for the purpose of securing compliance' with its prescriptions.[133] It may inspect resource activities and require adjustment or suspension of operations to 'prevent serious harm to the marine environment', and in the event of 'serious, persistent and wilful' non-compliance, may suspend or terminate resource activities in the area.[134] For lesser offences, or in lieu of such suspension or termination, monetary penalties 'proportionate to the seriousness of the violation' may be imposed.[135]

In fact, certain states in the early days of the Conference proposed a far broader measure of jurisdiction for the Authority; drafts submitted would have vested authority in the international body over all environmental matters beyond regions of national jurisdictions.[136] The Convention, of

[131] LOS Convention, *supra* ch. 5 n. 17, art. 145.

[132] *Id.*, Annex III, art. 17(2) (*f*). For notation of the environmental risks associated with deep sea-bed mining see Pruitt, 'Unilateral Deep Sea-bed Mining and Environmental Standards: A Risky Venture', 8 *Brooklyn J. Int'l* 345, at 350–3 (1982).

[133] *Id.*, art. 153(4).

[134] *Id.*, art. 162(2)(2), Annex III, art. 18(2) and Annex III, art. 18(1)(*a*).

[135] *Id.*, Annex III, art. 18(2). Any dispute with respect to such violations or the enforcement measures of the Authority may be subjected to proceedings before a Sea-bed Disputes Chamber of the International Tribunal for the Law of the Sea. Arts. 186–91. Finally, any state found by this Chamber to have 'grossly and persistently' violated the provisions with respect to activity in the area may be suspended from exercising the important rights of membership in the supreme legislative organ of the Authority, the Assembly. Art. 185.

[136] See e.g. Kenya: Draft Articles for the Preservation and the Protection of the Marine environment for Inclusion in the Convention on the Law of the Sea, UN Doc. A/CONF. 62/C. 3/L. 2, 23 July 1974, at Arts. 2, 3, and 9; Malta: Draft Articles on the Preservation of the Marine Environment, *inter alia*, the Prevention of Pollution, UN Doc. A/AC. 138/SC. III/L. 33, 16 Mar. 1973, at Art. 6.

course, does not venture that far. First, the subject 'Area' consists only of the sea-bed and subsoil beneath the high seas.[137] Second, the Authority's competence is limited to resource activities in the Area.[138] This jurisdiction does extend to surface installations and ship-board processing above a mine site; it is doubtful that it extends to remote activities less intimately related to the primary sea-bed activity, such as vessel transport of minerals.[139] Moreover, the Convention seems to deny the Authority any right to prevent pollution from sources unrelated to resource exploitation, regardless of the impact of such pollution on the marine environment or on resource activities themselves.[140]

Notwithstanding such limitations, the creation of any international jurisdiction over high seas matters constitutes a rather radical departure from the traditional rule of flag exclusivity. There is certainly no basis in customary law for such authority. The concession of flag prerogatives by treaty, on the other hand, is innovative but not juridically troubling. Among the party-states, the Authority's jurisdiction simply finds its source in contract. Application of the environmental rules of the Authority to non-parties must, however, be seriously questioned: '[a] treaty does not create either obligations or rights for a third State without its consent.'[141]

[137] Article 135 emphasizes that the regime has no effect on the 'legal status' of the water column or the 'superadjacent' surface.

[138] Art. 145 uses the language 'with respect to activities in the Area.' The Annex III text at Art. 17(2)(*f*) speaks of prescriptions to avoid harm to the environment 'directly resulting from activities in the Area.' Note that Article 1(3) defines 'activities in the Area' as resource exploration and exploitation activities only.

[139] The lists of activities which are to be regulated, set forth in Art. 145 and the Annex provision, underscore the limitation to sea-bed resource explorative and exploitive conduct. They include drilling, dredging, excavation, disposal of sediment and other wastes, and maintenance of installations and pipelines related to sea-bed resource activities.

[140] The second sentence of Art. 145 does provide that the Authority should adopt rules and regulations for: 'The protection and conservation of the natural resources of the Area and the preservation of damage to the flora and fauna of the marine environment.' Yet, this expansive language must be read as qualified by the first sentence limitations to harm from 'activities in the Area.' It is noteworthy in this regard that no permission from the Authority is required by the general anti-dumping provision for the dumping of wastes within or onto the area. See LOS Convention, *supra* ch. 5, n. 17, art. 210.

[141] Vienna Convention on the Law of Treaties, done at Vienna, 23 May 1969, not yet in force, reprinted in 8 *Int'l Legal Materials* 679 (1969),. Although not all provisions of this Convention do represent customary law, this general rule—expressed in the maxim *pacta tertiis nec nocent nec prosunt*—is firmly established as a customary rule. See Brownlie, *supra* ch. 2 n. 52, at 619–20. The arguments that certain treaties may qualify as exceptions to this rule and create 'objective regimes' binding on all states remains highly controversial, highly relevant to the issue of the deep sea-bed, but beyond the scope of this effort. It may be noted, however, that the lack of consensus at the Convention would seem to undercut an 'objective' definition with respect to the deep sea-bed provisions. For notations of this problem see Bowett, *supra* n. 126, at 56; Jennings, *supra* ch. 7 n. 29, at 40; Jennings, *supra* ch. 5 n. 2, 11 n. 57, at 85–7; Lee, *supra* ch. 5 n. 2, at 541. For one opinion that the Convention sea-bed provisions represent customary law see Macrae, 'Customary International Law and The United Nations' Law of the Sea Treaty', 13 *Cal. W. Int'l L.J.* 181, at 221 (1983).

B. STATE RESPONSIBILITY

Previous chapters have demonstrated that the rules of decision for environmental responsibility reflect the regime of authority applicable to the polluting conduct and the affected region. Two distinct zones of authority have now been identified beyond the territorial sea of any state: the EEZ and the high seas beyond. It is appropriate, therefore, to consider issues of responsibility pertaining to the two zones independently.

i. The EEZ

Chapter 6 discussed the fact that environmental injury to resources within zones of exclusive coastal authority beyond the territorial sea is as much the subject of the *sic utere tuo* obligation as territorial injury.[142] Each state is obligated to exercise its authority to prevent harm to the exclusive environmental interests of other states, even if those interests are extraterritorial. This conclusion applies directly, of course, to the EEZ, and the continental shelf within and beyond the EEZ, newly defined as distinct from the high seas. Harm to the resources of these zones from conduct within the jurisdiction and control of another state constitutes a 'transboundary' injury for the purpose of eliciting responsibility.[143] There is no question of the standing of the coastal state; a failure to perform the preventive obligation which occasions harm to an EEZ clearly constitutes an actionable international wrong.

Conversely, the exclusive authority of the coastal state over such resource zones carries with it a measure of responsibility for the environmental consequences of conduct within such zones. The international obligation deduced in Part II requires each state to exercise authority possessed, whether territorial or extraterritorial, to prevent environmental harm to other states. Analysis of the application of this imperative in the context of EEZ jurisdiction is best approached by considering in turn the two *loci* of EEZ conduct: sea-bed installations and vessels.

a. Sea-bed Activities and Structures

As to the former, it was noted above that the coastal state's prescriptive and enforcement jurisdiction over structures, installations, and artificial islands engaged in resource activities in the EEZ, or over the continental shelf beyond, is well established in state practice and specifically identified in the LOS Convention.[144] It follows from the general principles of environmental responsibility that the state must exercise such authority to prevent environmental harm. The LOS Convention text certainly supports this conclusion in

[142] See ch. 6 at nn. 5 ff.

[143] See Observations of H. Chiu, Rpt. of the ILA 59th, *supra* ch. 5 n. 39, at 571–2; ILA 55th, *supra* ch. 9 n. 20, at 100; Q-B, 3rd Rpt, *supra* ch. 10 n. 104, at 24 (region within 'jurisdiction and control'); Stein, *supra* ch. 5 n. 45, at 41.

[144] See text at nn. 69-70.

its choice of mandatory language with respect to the adoption and enforcement of laws to prevent pollution from sea-bed activities and surface installations.[145] Certain earlier conventions had considered codifying the preventive obligation with respect to dumping from such sources; in each case neutral language was chosen pending the LOS III Conference's definition of the ambit of coastal authority.[146] With that clearly accomplished, the dumping treaties now constitute evidence of the preventive duty. One commentator has expressed well the rationale of such an application of *sic utere tuo* principles with respect to mineral resource activities within the EEZ or shelf:

> [I]f the coastal states do enjoy in these areas the same rights to explore and exploit the mineral resources as in the territorial sea, it follows logically that they must use these rights in a way which does not impair the rights of other states and bear the responsibility for any violation of these rights.[147]

The same logic applies, of course, to installation and sea-bed conduct unrelated to mineral resources. International law has recognized exclusive coastal rights with respect to all such matters; correlative to the grant of such rights is the duty to prevent harm to others arising out of their exercise.

The question that remains is the appropriate standard of performance to which the coastal state should be held. As in internal and territorial waters, if the polluting conduct is that of the state itself, performance of the preventive obligation is a matter of self-control. In such circumstances it has been determined that responsibility should arise for an intentional or negligent failure to prevent, and on a strict basis if the activity was ultrahazardous or, pursuant to the proposed regime, if the harm is particularly serious.[148] The principles applicable to private conduct, it will be recalled, depend very much on the character of the state's authority over such conduct; the closer authority and the attendant opportunity to control moves to the level enjoyed over state territory, the more appropriate the imposition of a strict conception of the due diligence standard for ultrahazards or extreme injury.[149] The jurisdiction enjoyed by the coastal state over the activities in question is in fact tantamout to territorial jurisdiction. As noted, the continental shelf is probably best defined as a component of state territory.[150] In the limited

[145] LOS Convention, *supra* ch. 5 n. 17, arts. 208 and 214. See also 1976 London Convention on Civil Liability for Oil Pollution Damage resulting from Exploration for and Exploitation of Sea-bed Mineral Resources, opened for signature 1 May 1977, reprinted in 121 *Int'l Env. Rep.* 601 (1978). See Vallarta, *supra*, ch. 11 n. 57, at 149, for the conclusion that the Convention codifies custom in this area.

[146] As to the 1972 London Dumping Convention and the anti-dumping protocol to the Barcelona Mediterranean Convention see de Yturriaga, *supra* ch. 5 n. 1 at 371–2; Timagenis, *supra* ch 5 n. 1, at 239, 294.

[147] Kwiatkowska-Czechowska, *supra* ch. 6 n. 56, at 160–1.

[148] See ch. 11 at n. 60.

[149] See ch. 12 at n. 131.

[150] See text at n. 66 *supra*.

context of the quality of coastal jurisdiction, shelf installations, structures and artificial islands are assimilated to the same regime. One may reason, therefore, that the standard of coastal state responsibility for private conduct in such locations should parallel that applicable in territorial waters: due diligence, elevated to strict responsibility for ultrahazardous conduct or extraordinary harm.[151] Notably, this equation of territorial and offshore sites would appear consistent with each of the principal variations of the strict regime discussed above.[152]

Prior to considering the more complex issue of responsibility for vessel conduct, it is appropriate to note a characteristic of the EEZ which affects the analysis of coastal obligation regardless of the source of pollution. Chapter 7 determined that, although adequate theoretical bases may be identified, no obligation to prevent environmental harm limited to the state's own territory yet exists in international law. One might reasonably conclude that the same conclusion would deny the responsibility of the coastal state for a failure to prevent harm limited to its own EEZ environment. The LOS Convention's EEZ regime provides, however, that not only the coastal state possesses a particularized interest in the quality of the EEZ environment. Both land-locked and geographically disadvantaged states have an affirmative 'right to participate, on an equitable basis, in the exploitation of an appropriate part of the surplus of the living resources of the exclusive economic zones of coastal States of the same sub-region or region . . .'[153] To the extent such a surplus exists or may exist, it would seem that the legal interest in the quality of the EEZ environment is not exclusively that of the coastal state. Indeed, a failure to prevent harm to the private (i.e. not common to all states) resources interests of other states would seem squarely to violate the *sic utere tuo* principle. Moreover, unlike a circumstance of injury to the common resources of the high seas, it would seem that a state whose interests in the EEZ of another state are so injured would possess standing to initiate a claim against the coastal state.[154]

b. Vessels

Turning to the issue of responsibility for vessel conduct in the EEZ, one encounters analytic complexity for two reasons: the character of coastal state

[151] Note that if other states or even nationals of other states are the private actors engaged in offshore activities with the authorization of the coastal state, a circumstance of multiple responsibility may arise.

[152] Consider the application of the strict regime with respect to extraterritorial matters 'within the territory or control' of the state (Q-B, 3rd Rpt., *supra* ch. 5 n. 72, at 24, and Q-B, 5th Rpt., *supra* ch. 10 n. 104, at 1–7); 'within its jurisdiction or undertaken on its behalf or with its authority' (Jenks, *supra* ch. 5 n. 51, at 194); foreseeable based upon state authorization (Handl, *supra* ch. 8 n. 63, *passim*).

[153] LOS Convention, *supra* ch. 5 n. 17, arts. 69–70.

[154] This conclusion, of course, also means that the land-locked or geographically disadvantaged state may bring a claim if the EEZ injury is the responsibility of a third state alone or with the coastal state.

jurisdiction and the interplay between coastal and flag authority. The fact of certain limited coastal authority over environmental matters in the EEZ, based upon both custom and convention, has been established. As noted repeatedly, the obligation to prevent environmental harm described in Part II generally requires the exercise of all authority possessed by the state; each state must utilize the full measure of its jurisdiction to perform its preventive duty.[155] Yet, it must be noted that the LOS Convention text acknowledging coastal environmental authority over vessel source pollution is couched in distinctly discretionary terms: the state 'may' enact and enforce EEZ anti-pollution laws.[156] Avoidance of the term 'shall', used in all other contexts including jurisdiction over EEZ dumping, may be explained as a concession to both flag states seeking to minimize coastal initiatives and developing states desiring to avoid international environmental minima.[157] Nevertheless, the choice of non-obligatory language does seem inconsistent with the implications of the customary rules of environmental responsibility.

In fact, at least two commentators, Messrs Lammers and Moreno in the sessions of the ILA and the ILC, respectively, have observed that the normal rules of responsibility may not apply in the EEZ.[158] In light of the language and the context, however, these comments are perhaps most accurately characterized as denials of the application of territorial standards of responsibility to the EEZ. Given the significant distinctions in coastal jurisdiction in the two regions, this is certainly a proper conclusion. The weight of the logic of environmental responsibility suggests that the wholesale rejection of coastal obligations, hence responsibility, with respect to EEZ environmental authority would not be proper.

It has been noted that several pre-LOS Convention multilateral efforts used neutral language referring to areas 'within jurisdiction' to describe the extent of specified anti-pollution obligations of the party-states.[159] As with sea-bed installations, the LOS Convention's expression of coastal jurisdiction over dumping by vessels now confirms the applicability of the earlier treaty obligations to the EEZ.[160] Similar neutral language in the 1973 Convention, describing the range of coastal state obligations with respect to the imposition of penalties and commencement of proceedings for vessel source pollution, would seem to have been given meaning and application to the EEZ by the LOS Convention's recognition of coastal authority.[161] In fact, much of the literature of environmental responsibility, ranging from the Stockholm

[155] See ch. 10 at nn. 35–47.

[156] LOS Convention, *supra* ch. 5 n. 17, arts. 211(5) and 220(3).

[157] As to dumping, see arts. 210(1) and 216(1) (*a*). See Frank, *supra* ch. 7 n. 43, at 75.

[158] Observations of Lammers, ILA 59th *supra* n. 141, at 569; Comments of Moreno, ILC Sum. Rec., *supra* ch. 3 n. 133, at 53.

[159] See materials cited at n. 146 *supra*.

[160] See Timagenis, *supra* ch. 5 n. 1, at 617.

[161] The language of Arts. 4(1) and 9(3) of the 1973 Convention was designed as a compromise between conflicting perspectives of coastal jurisdiction. The neutral reference to 'jurisdiction' as

Declaration to the work of publicists such as Jenks and Handl, utilizes such general references to the limits of jurisdiction and control to define the boundaries of environmental obligation.[162] The logic of this flexible approach is simply that duty will follow authority beyond the borders of state territory.[163] All of such works support the conclusion, therefore, that the preventive obligation does apply to require exercise of EEZ authority.[164] The specific conclusion that international responsibility may arise out of a failure to prevent environmental harm caused by EEZ activities subject to coastal jurisdiction has been reached by the very few commentators considering the issue.[165]

The general rules of environmental responsibility do apply then to coastal authority in the EEZ. In light of the nature of such coastal jurisdiction, what is the appropriate standard to which the state should be held in performance of the obligation to prevent pollution from vessels? If the actor is an organ of the state, the answer is the same as that deduced with respect to conduct in other regions. Responsibility for harm to other states occasioned by the acts of the state's own vessels in the EEZ may be premised upon intention, negligence, ultrahazard or extraordinary harm.[166] If, on the other hand, the vessel is properly characterized as private, whether of domestic or foreign registry, the invariable standard is due diligence.[167] In state territory or as to matters over which the state enjoys effectively 'territorial'-quality jurisdiction and control, the diligence due may be elevated, however, to that necessary *strictly* to prevent injury from ultrahazardous sources or of particularly serious consequence.[168] In the EEZ there appear to be two levels of coastal environmental authority over vessels: one applicable to dumping of wastes, the other applicable to all other polluting conduct. Coastal state jurisdiction with respect to the former is not significantly less expansive than that applicable in territorial waters with respect to vessels not in innocent passage.[169] No dumping in the EEZ may occur without the authorization of

defined by international law contemplated resolution at the LOS III Conference. For the several drafts submitted on the subject see IMCO Doc. MP/CONF.C. 1/WP. 20.

[162] See Principle 21, Declaration of the United Nations Conference on the Human Environment, adopted 16 June 1972, UN Doc. A/CONF. 48/14 and Corr. 1; Handl, *supra* ch. 2 n. 82, at 527–9; Jenks, supra ch. 5 n. 51, at 180, 194.

[163] See ch. 3 at n. 145 and ch. 8 at n. 105.

[164] Note that the 'custodianship' doctrine championed by Canada at the Conference links EEZ resource and environmental rights to correlative duties; rights must be exercised to protect the interests of the community. See e.g. Gotlieb and Dalfen, *supra* n. 52, at 249–50; Stanford, 'Canadian Perspectives on the Future Enforcement of the Exclusive Economic Zone: A Paper in Diplomacy and the Law of the Sea', 5 *Dalhousie L.J.* 73, at 103 (1979).

[165] Q-B, 3rd Rpt., *supra* ch. 5 n. 72, at 20; Q-B, 5th Rpt., *supra* ch. 10 n. 104, at 1; Kwiatkowska-Czechowska, *supra* ch. 6 n. 55, at 160–1. See also Comments of Chiu, ILA 59th Session, *supra* ch. 5 n. 39, at 569.

[166] See ch. 11 at n. 60 and ch. 12 at n. 131 *supra*.

[167] See ch. 3 at n. 106 *supra*.

[168] See ch. 3 at n. 140 *supra*.

[169] See text at n. 96 *supra*.

the coastal state.[170] Hence, in the LOS Convention, the coastal state's prescriptive authority is constrained only by a 'due regard' standard; enforcement is checked only by the same standard and certain of the general 'safeguards' applicable to measures against foreign vessels in any region.[171] It would seem appropriate, therefore, to conclude that, in the limited context of dumping, the coastal state should be held to the strict standard, i.e. stand responsible for the consequences of dumping in the EEZ when such conduct may be defined as ultrahazardous or causes exceptional injury.[172]

EEZ prescriptive and enforcement jurisdiction over other vessel environmental matters, on the other hand, is quite restricted. The customary boundaries of such authority are ill-defined. Under the LOS Convention, no laws may exceed approved international standards without the consent of a governing international institution—no consent will be given to additional CDEM laws.[173] Enforcement actions are subject to Article 220's procedures and standards,[174] the implicit prohibition against any measure to enforce CDEM violations at sea in advance of actual discharge, the 'safegards' applicable to violations in other regions (with the added limitation that only monetary penalties may be assessed even if the discharge is 'wilful and serious')[175] and the flag state pre-emption provision. In light of such limitations, it is difficult to characterize coastal authority over vessel-source pollution in the EEZ as bestowing a degree of effective control at all comparable to territorial control. The limited capacity to prevent afforded the coastal state seems to dictate the propriety of the simple due diligence standard in assessing coastal responsibility for vessel conduct in the EEZ.

State responsibility for flag vessels acting in the EEZ of another state may be analysed in much the same terms as in the territorial sea. The single distinction in flag authority between the two zones is that the prohibition against enforcement actions in foreign territory does not operate in the EEZ.[176] The flag state would seem free, therefore, to take any enforcement measure against its vessels in a foreign EEZ that it deems appropriate.[177] It might be argued that this distinction renders flag authority outside foreign territorial waters so expansive as to merit application of a strict view of diligence in all cases. For practical reasons, this would not seem appropriate.

In preceding chapters it has been concluded that the proper standard for flag responsibility with respect to private conduct in foreign territory is due

[170] LOS Convention, *supra* ch. 5 n. 17, art. 210(5).

[171] *Id.*, art. 56(2). See ch. 11 at nn. 46–51 and ch. 12 at n. 124. But as to the application of the monetary penalties restriction, see n. 118 *supra*.

[172] See ch. 12 at n. 131 *supra*.

[173] See text at n. 102 *supra*.

[174] See text at n. 109 *supra*.

[175] LOS Convention, *supra* ch. 5 n. 17, art. 430. See n. 124 *supra*.

[176] See ch. 9 at n. 66 *supra*.

[177] Subject, of course, to the Art. 58 requirement that any action take 'due regard' of the interests of the coastal State.

diligence, elevated to a strict test when the flag possesses meaningful authority over the violative conduct.[178] The rationale of this perspective is that strict responsibility should only be imposed when the violation arises out of matters inherent or pre-existing, and thus susceptible to prior and effective flag state preventive action. Only regular due diligence should apply to spontaneous conduct, i.e. conduct over which the flag state did not possess meaningful authority or control.[179]

The foregoing conclusions were reached, however, in light of the flag state's incapacity to exercise the full range of enforcement jurisdiction in foreign territory. Although that constraint is not technically applicable in the EEZ, it is submitted that the standard of flag state responsibility ought to be the same. The capacity of flag states to police and prevent spontaneous decisions and conduct on board vessels beyond the state's own waters is of a limited character, notwithstanding the fact of a legal right to exercise such authority. In fact, no state possesses unlimited administrative capacity. It is believed, therefore, that the logic of strict responsibility is better served by again requiring an analysis in each case of the character of the vessel's polluting conduct in the EEZ. If the violation involves ultrahazardous conduct (other than the type of spontaneous ultrahazardous acts noted by Handl) or serious injury from vessel design, equipment, or condition, a strict standard should be employed.[180] In other words, flag state authority over and capacity to prevent such pre-existing matters should be treated as 'effectively territorial' for the purpose of fixing a standard of responsibility.[181] If, on the other hand, the violation arises out of matters over which a flag state would not have had a comparable prior and effective opportunity to exercise preventive authority, the test should be simple due diligence.

To examine the interplay between the foregoing rules of decision for flag and coastal state responsibility, it may be helpful to consider two examples. Assume that a private vessel of flag state *A* loads containers of industrial waste in the port of state *B*. The vessel then proceeds to dump its cargo in the EEZ of state *C*. In the unloading process several of the containers crack and the discharged waste causes material injury to the fishery in the EEZ of adjacent state *D*. How is responsibility for such environmental injury to be determined?

As deduced above, state *C*'s standard of performance of the preventive

[178] See ch. 10 at nn. 102–9, ch. 11 at nn. 66–8 and ch. 12 at nn. 134–40 *supra*.

[179] *Id.*

[180] As to Handl's point, see ch. 12 at n. 139 *supra*.

[181] NB that the introduction of such practical considerations should not suggest a subjective test. Rather, an objective determination of whether the opportunity to exercise authority was adequate to support the strict standard is advocated. If the character of the conduct was such that reasonable flag diligence, in an objective sense, could have detected the threat and prevented the injury, strict responsibility would apply. If the objective test is not met, i.e. due diligence is determined to be the appropriate performance standard, the fact that the particular flag state possesses extraordinary administrative capacity will affect the analysis of the level of diligence due.

obligation with respect to dumping in the EEZ is due diligence elevated to its strict formulation.[182] Whether state *C* authorized the dumping or failed adequately to exercise its plenary jurisdiction over such conduct, it stands responsible to state *D*. Whether state *A* also bears responsibility demands further inquiry into the facts. If the vessel had been designed for hazardous waste disposal or had engaged in a regular course of such conduct and inadequacies of equipment caused the accident, then the preceding analysis would dictate imposition of a strict standard. Absent such pre-existing characteristics, responsibility would arise only if state *A* failed to act with due diligence to prevent the incident. Finally, the position of state *B vis-à-vis* state *D* must be considered. The obligation of state *B* to exercise its port/territorial jurisdiction to prevent injury from dumping clearly follows from the general principles of environmental responsibility; it is specifically noted in the LOS Convention and evidenced in prior anti-dumping initiatives.[183] Chapter 11 concluded that a port state's responsibility for allowing an unseaworthy vessel to sail should be measured by its due diligence.[184] As in that case, although state *B* here had territorial authority over the loading, the authority was both temporary (unlike the flag state's) and remote to the event (unlike the coastal state's). Following the earlier reasoning, the proper inquiry would be whether state *B* took due measures to prevent the injurious event, such as equipment inspection, review of permits, and assessment of the degree of danger in disposal of the particular waste. Yet, the character of dumping suggests that this prior logic may be inapposite. State *B* did not merely tolerate the continuation of a pollution-threatening situation during the temporary stay of the vessel in port. Rather, it had the authority to control and permitted the creation of the threat, much as a flag state does in authorizing an ultrahazardous activity by registration for such purpose. Indeed, in the context of dumping, the state's authority may be even more immediate to the injury since the causal event may be viewed as commencing at the point of loading. The ultimate act of intentional dumping is the direct, certain, and foreseeable culmination of the process begun in state *B*. The case is even stronger with respect to dumping without containers or with other than permanent containers. Tolerance of such acts is tolerance of the actual introduction of pollution into the environment, not merely the creation of a risk of such introduction. In light of such factors indicating the effective control of state *B* over the polluting conduct, it seems more appropriate to impose a strict standard as to ultrahazards and incidents of extreme harm.

Several states might then be in a position of responsibility to state *D*. Applying the principles of multiple state responsibility determined in Chapter

[182] See text at nn. 169–71 *supra*.

[183] See LOS Convention, *supra* ch. 5 n. 17, art. 216(1) (*c*); London Dumping Convention, *supra* ch. 10 n. 2, art. VIII(1) (*b*); Barcelona Convention, *supra* ch. 6 n. 42; Protocol for the Prevention of Pollution of the Mediterranean Sea by Dumping from Ships and Aircraft, art. 11(1) (*b*).

[184] See ch. 11 at nn. 75–6 *supra*.

4, each state found to have violated the preventive obligation would bear responsibility to state *D*.[185] The consequences of such responsibility would turn first upon whether the state's violation bore a causal connection to the injury.[186] Without such a connection, the breaching state's obligations to state *D* would not directly relate to the environmental injury itself; reparation, in forms such as apology, satisfaction, and guarantee, would be due only for the political or moral injury attendant to every breach of an international obligation.[187] As to those states found to have participated causally, it was suggested in Chapter 4 that a regime of joint and several liability for compensating state *D* might be properly imposed.[188] A weighing of relative causation and blameworthiness would determine the proper allocation of the burden of compensation, either through the process of contribution among wrongdoers or directly through proportional liability.[189] The principal guideline in this analysis is the relative authority of the several states over the event; hence, state *C* would, solely on this theoretical basis, bear the dominant burden. This conclusion may be altered greatly, however, by the facts. If, for example, a dumping of radioactive waste was not authorized by state *C*, and state *A* or *B* knew or should have known, based upon due inquiry, of the magnitude of the hazard, the inadequacy of the vessel's equipment, and the absence of authorization, the burden would surely shift. As discussed in previous chapters, it is the preventive capacity of each state in light of all facts, including the character of jurisdiction and the extent to which that capacity was utilized, which must ultimately be weighed.

Turning to a second example, consider the responsibility of flag state *A* and coastal state *B* arising out of the grounding of a private tanker and a consequential oil spill in state *B*'s EEZ which severely injures tourist beaches and fishery resources of states *B* and *C*. Assume other salient facts to parallel the *Argo Merchant* incident: the vessel was twenty-eight kilometres off course when it ran aground; it had a history of oil spillage (eleven times in two years); the charts were six years out of date; the compass was broken; the radio direction finder was outdated; and the helmsman was untrained.[190]

As noted, the responsibility of state *B* to state *C* would depend upon the diligence with which state *B* exercised its EEZ authority to prevent the incident. The test of due diligence, it should be reiterated, refers to an international minimum standard elevated in light of any greater capacity or practice of diligence of the subject state.[191] In the example, then, the inquiry into state *B*'s responsibility should begin with a decision as to whether the

[185] See ch. 3 at nn. 143 ff.

[186] For example, if state *A* had failed to perform the preventive obligation with due diligence, but the injurious conduct would have occurred even if state *A* had been duly diligent.

[187] See ch. 3 at nn. 173–6.

[188] See ch. 4 at n. 99.

[189] See ch. 4 at nn. 102–9 *supra*.

[190] See [1977] *Marine Pollution Bull.* 124, 171.

[191] See ch. 3 at nn. 117–34.

state acted with at least minimum diligence to perform its preventive obligation. Were laws incorporating international CDEM standards enacted? Did the state employ minimum standard enforcement procedures such as radio checks and inspection? Was punishment imposed for this incident?[192] If the overall answer is yes, responsibility may still lie if the state possessed and did not utilize a markedly higher capacity to prevent than the norm.

The facts presented are a classic example of circumstances in which holding state *A* to a strict standard is both logical and dictated by the rules described above. By registration of an oil tanker, flag state *A* authorized and could foresee use for ultrahazardous purposes.[193] The catastrophe may be traced directly to pre-existing inadequacies of vessel equipment and manning. The vessel's pattern of prior spills provided adequate prior evidence that it constituted an environmental threat. Any one of these facts would seem to support the imposition of a strict standard; for each reason, state *A* possessed the requisite capacity or opportunity to exercise its expansive flag jurisdiction to control the causes and prevent the incident.[194]

The consequences of the responsibility of states *A* and *B* (assuming state *B* did not act with due diligence) to state *C* should be decided utilizing the same rules outlined above. The threshold question is whether the respective breaches may be defined as causal. If, for example, state *B* had failed to exercise its authority with due diligence in circumstances in which the casualty would have occurred anyway, e.g. by a failure to punish, no causal connection exists.[195] State *B* would owe state *C* only appropriate non-compensatory forms of reparation; the burden of compensation would fall squarely and solely on state *A*. On the other and, if state *B*'s conduct constituted a participating cause, the duty of compensation would be apportioned between the two states on the familiar bases of relative causation and blame, weighing the authority and capacity of each state to have prevented the injury.[196]

Several concluding notes regarding EEZ environmental responsibility are in order. It must be underscored that the preceding examples should not suggest that only flag and coastal states may bear responsibility for the conduct of vessels in the EEZ. To the contrary, all of the conclusions of earlier chapters with respect to the responsibility of other states, for example, states exercising nationality-based jurisdiction over the owners or operators of

[192] See c. 4 at nn. 9–12 for a discussion of the failure to punish as a breach of the preventive obligation and the consequences.

[193] See Handl, *supra* ch. 12 n. 136, *re* the significance of foreseeability.

[194] In a case such as the *Argo Merchant*, the patent lack of administrative attention to the condition of the vessel and its crew and equipment would seem to violate even the orthodox due diligence standard.

[195] See ch. 4 at nn. 9–12.

[196] Apportionment would occur either through the process of contribution following the suggested joint and several compensation liability to state *C* or the alternative of direct proportional liability to state *C*.

vessels, apply with full force to events within the EEZ.[197] Similarly, it may be recalled that the fact that state *B* in the preceding example is found to have contributed causally to the event would not preclude state *B*'s recovery from state *A* for injury to state *B*'s EEZ. In circumstances of such contributory conduct by the injured state, responsibility is not absolved. Rather, the compensation burdern may be reduced, based on the same test of relative causation and blame employed in apportioning compensation to a third state.[198] Finally, it should be reiterated that harm to an EEZ environment and its resources may constitute harm to the interests of states other than just the coastal state. Hence, in the final example, any land-locked state with a vested interest in the injured fishery of state B's EEZ might enter as an additional claimant.[199]

ii. The High Seas

It was the central conclusion of Chapter 6 that the obligation to prevent environmental injury does apply to the environment of the high seas beyond the limits of any exclusive coastal jurisdiction.[200] It was further determined, however, that no present basis exists in international law for any state to bring a claim for a violation of this obligation.[201] Standing based upon *actio popularis* certainly has both judicial and scholarly advocates.[202] Moreover, Chapter 6 noted the theoretical argument that a breach of the preventive obligation with respect to the high seas represents a breach of a bilateral obligation owed each state, as distinct from an obligation owed the personified community. It was suggested, therefore, that recourse to *actio popularis* should not be necessary.[203] It is quite clear, though, that neither the concept of actions by states on behalf of the community nor this alternative thesis has yet found a place in law.

The foregoing does not mean that conduct on the high seas causing environmental harm will not yield state responsibility. Chapter 6 noted that injury experienced by other users of the high seas is juridically tantamount to 'transboundary' injury.[204] Similarly, any harm arising out of high seas conduct suffered in a state's territory or EEZ will support an assertion of responsibility. The remaining task then is to define the rules for determining responsibility for such violative and actionable conduct on the high seas.

The initial paragraphs of this chapter defined the 'cardinal rule' of the high seas that only flag states possess authority over vessels, the principal actors on

[197] See ch. 10 at nn. 110–24 *supra*.
[198] See ch. 4 at nn. 9–12
[199] See text at nn. 153–4 *supra*.
[200] See ch. 6 at nn. 24–61.
[201] *Id*., at nn. 53–78.
[202] *Id*., at nn. 65–77.
[203] *Id*., at nn. 70–5.
[204] See ch. 5 at nn. 105–15.

the high seas. Certain qualifications have been enumerated. Yet, it certainly remains a valid general truth that beyond the EEZ flag jurisdiction is pre-eminent; it follows that responsibility for vessel pollution beyond the EEZ will be principally that of the flag state. The standard to which the flag ought to be held in performance of the preventive obligation would seem to be that suggested with respect to vessel conduct in the EEZ. In each zone the prescriptive and enforcement authority of the flag state over environmental matters is the same: juridically unfettered, but of diminished effectiveness due to the realities of remoteness. Applying the conclusions reached above, responsibility for high seas conduct of the state's public vessels should lie in the event of negligence, intent, ultrahazardous conduct or, in the suggested regime, extraordinary harm. The standard applicable to private flag vessels is, of course, due diligence. The standard of diligence required may be strict, however, in circumstances in which the injurious conduct was foreseeable (and thus subject to effective preventive measures), due to pre-existing characteristics such as inadequate vessel condition or ultrahazardous function or behaviour.

Flag authority over the activities of vessels on the high seas, although invariable and dominant, is not exclusive. The fact of overlapping and often effective nationality-based jurisdiction over ship-users has been identified at several points in this work.[205] All of the conclusions reached with respect to the consequential responsibility of such non-flag states and its interaction with flag state responsibility apply fully to high seas matters.[206]

The second principal form of overlapping jurisidiction, the right of coastal 'intervention', presents new issues of responsibility. The threshold question, of course, is whether intervention is in any sense obligatory. Is it an authority which must be exercised pursuant to the general duty to prevent environmental injury? To the extent intervention is characterized as an extraordinary justification or excuse for an otherwise unlawful act, the imposition of a duty to act is certainly not logical. As discussed, however, intervention is more properly viewed as an affirmative right recognized in international law.[207] In its codified form, the right has been expressed in terms of the protection of the coastal state's interests—not those of other states or the community.[208] Yet, certain notable commentators have underscored the obligatory aspect of intervention: de Visscher characterized it as 'un devoir exercé dans l'intérêt de la communauté internationale'; Goldie described the right as a matter of 'custodial privilege'.[209] Indeed, the logic of the advocates of 'custodianship'

[205] See ch. 10 at nn. 110–24 and ch. 11 at nn. 73–4 *supra*.

[206] *Id.*

[207] See text at nn. 34–8 *supra*.

[208] See text at nn. 19, 22, 24 *supra*.

[209] Comments of de Visscher, Edinburgh Session, *supra* ch. 12 n. 100, at 284; Goldie, *supra* ch. 5 n. 45, at 50. See also Comments of Jenks, Edinburgh Session, at 288.

or 'dedoublement fonctionnel' as the basis of extraterritorial environmental zones generally seems apt in the intervention context.[210] The authority of the coastal state to protect its own interests must be exercised to prevent harm to the interests of others. This is, it may be suggested, the not inappropriate result of applying to intervention the basic environmental imperative to exercise any authority possessed to prevent injury.

To assess the consequences of this conclusion, consider an example drawn from the incident of the *Mont-Louis*, a private French freighter which sank off the Belgian coast with a cargo of cylinders of radioactive material following a collision with a passenger ferry.[211] French authorities, aware of the hazardous cargo, responded promptly by sending divers to recover the containers. Assume, however, that such remedial action had not been taken in timely fashion by the flag state, no measures were taken by Belgium and the radioactive material leaked out following corrosion of the cylinders, injuring passing ship-users and Belgian and neighbouring coastal state resources.[212]

Belgium clearly possessed the authority to intervene by taking remedial measures, including the immediate salvage of the containers. Evaluation of the possible responsibility of Belgium to other injured states would seem to be an issue of normal due diligence. The right of intervention itself is defined by the constraints of proportionality and due response; the coastal state is not vested with territorial control and discretion in the exercise of jurisdiction. Imposition of a strict standard, therefore, would seem improper. Given the assumption that Belgium took no action to recover the containers prior to corrosion, a conclusion is probable that the right to intervene was not exercised with due diligence. This decision would be affected, of course, by factors such as the time involved, reasonable expectations of risk, available information, and French representations. If Belgian responsibility were determined to exist for a failure of due diligence, it would in any case be shared with the flag state, applying the strict standard based on the flag's cognizance of the ultrahazardous character of the voyage, and, possibly, other coastal states failing to exercise a right to intervene to prevent the injury.[213] The consequences of such multiple state responsibility, in terms of both the type and apportionment of reparation duties, would be decided on the basis of the rules outlined.[214]

210 See text at nn. 52–5 *supra* and ch. 7 at nn. 24–5.

211 See extract from *Le Monde*, *Manchester Guardian Weekly*, 9 Sept. 1984, at p. 11, col. 1. See also *Manchester Guardian Weekly*, 9 Sept. 1984, at p. 3, col. 4 *re* the debate concerning such transport of radioactive materials.

212 Also assume that the sinking takes place on the high seas beyond the EEZ. The *Mont-Louis* sunk approximately 16 kilometres off the Belgian coast.

213 The possibility of nationality-based responsibility is, of course, always present. The flag or other states with authority over the conduct of the ferry might also bear some responsibility for the event. Neither would likely bear a causal connection to the injury, however, given that the immediate cause was a failure to recover the cylinders prior to corrosion.

214 Note particularly that the duty to compensate would be assessed among any states failing

Vessels are not necessarily the only actors on the high seas. Activities on the sea-bed and surface structures beyond the EEZ present both a potentially material source of pollution and certain distinct juridical issues. To the extent such conduct occurs on the portion of a state's continental shelf extending beyond its EEZ, the coastal state possesses the plenary shelf authority discussed above; the rules of responsibility with respect to such conduct would track, therefore, those described for similar EEZ activities.[215] The same standards of responsibility might be applied to conduct on artificial islands and installations in any region of the high seas beyond the shelf over which the 'flag' or authorizing state would likely possess comparable quasi-territorial authority.[216] Yet, as with flag responsibility for vessels, considerations of administrative capacity suggest that responsibility for private conduct in such remote locations should be imposed strictly only when it is clear that the state had a meaningful opportunity to exercise its jurisdiction.[217] Hence, the strict regime should apply when the injury arises out of the ultrahazardous function of the structure or other pre-existing conditions (e.g. equipment or staff inadequacies); otherwise, simple due diligence should be the test.

The innovation of the International Seabed Authority in the LOS Convention established, at least with respect to the parties, an additional layer of jurisdiction over any of such sea-bed or surface installation activities relating to sea-bed resource exploitation.[218] Indeed, no such activity may take place unless the operator, a state or 'natural or juridical persons which possess the nationality of States Parties or are effectively controlled by them or their nationals, when sponsored by such States', applies to, is approved by, and complies with the regulations of the Authority.[219] This regime raises two questions of consequential responsibility. Does the Convention alter the preceding conclusions regarding the responsibility of authorizing states? May the Authority bear international responsibility for failure to prevent environmental harm?

As to the first question, the Convention in no way disturbs the fact of responsibility of authorizing states for the conduct of the users of resource installations:

> States Parties shall have the responsibility to ensure that activities in the Area, whether carried out by States Parties, or state enterprises or natural or juridical persons which possess the nationality of States Parties or are effectively controlled by them or their nationals, shall be carried out in conformity with this part.[220]

to intervene on the basis of comparative and contributory responsibility—weighing relative diligence and capacity to prevent.

215 See text at nn. 144–52 *supra*.

216 See text at nn. 127–30 *supra*.

217 For a discussion of such conclusions regarding vessels, see text at nn. 179–80 *supra*.

218 As to the universal application of sea-bed provisions see n. 141 *supra*.

219 LOS Convention, *supra* ch. 5 n. 17, art. 153(2) (*b*). See also *id.*, Annex III.

220 *Id.*, art. 139(1).

A failure to fulfil such responsibility is to elicit liability for damages.[221] The standard to which states are to be held with respect to private conduct is specifically identified as due diligence. Article 4 of Annex III provides:

> A sponsoring State shall not, however, be liable for damage caused by any failure of a contractor sponsored by it to comply with its obligations if that State Party has adopted laws and regulations and taken administrative measures which are, within the framework of its legal system, reasonably appropriate for securing compliance by persons under its jurisdiction.[222]

In this respect alone, then, the Convention diverges from the principles outlined above. If the injury-producing activity is defined as ultrahazardous or the cause of serious harm was otherwise foreseeable, based on pre-existing conditions, the suggested rules would elevate the diligence due to a strict standard. The regime adopted in the Convention requires only simple due diligence.

The answer to the second question is a simple no. The general principle of the linkage of jurisdiction and responsibility might suggest that an institution with prescriptive and enforcement authority over environmental matters should bear responsibility for a failure to exercise such authority to prevent injury.[223] There is, however, no language in the Convention to this effect. Rather, the treaty appears to limit the responsibility of the Authority to two circumstances. The text acknowledges the responsibility of the Authority for 'wrongful acts in the exercise of its powers and functions', citing the example of disclosure of confidential information.[224] An earlier provision confirms the responsibility of the 'Enterprise', the organ of the Authority intended to engage directly in resource activities in the Area, for its own violations of Convention obligations.[225]

[221] *Id.*, art. 139(2).

[222] *Id.*, Annex III, art. 4(4). See also *id.*, art. 139(2).

[223] A Kenyan proposal would have imposed precisely such responsibility: 'The Authority shall be responsible for damage caused by polluton to the marine environment by its activities or by the activities of those who the Authority permits to undertake exploration and exploitation of the marine resources in areas beyond the limits of national jurisdiction.' Kenya: Draft Articles for the Preservation and Protection of the Marine Environment for inclusion in the Convention on the Law of the Sea, UN Doc. A/CONF. 62/C. 3/L. 2 of 23 July 1974.

[224] LOS Convention, *supra* ch. 5 n. 17, Annex III, art. 22.

[225] *Id.*, art. 139. Note that the Statute of the Enterprise provides that (*a*) the Authority is not responsible for the obligations of the Enterprise, and (*b*) except certain specified obligations to contribute capital, members of the Authority shall bear no responsibility for Enterprise obligations based simply upon such membership. Annex IV, arts. 2(3) and 3.

Conclusion

In the introduction to this work two levels of inquiry were projected: an examination of the 'secondary' rules of state responsibility, the 'primary' rules of state environmental obligation, and the pattern of state legal authority over the seas; and an analysis of the intersection of these three bodies of law to deduce the rules governing marine environmental responsibility. Each of these tasks is now complete. The systematic exposition of the content of and the relations among the component regimes did indeed yield the anticipated rules of decision.

The system of rules defined is, of course, quite complex; the examples of its operation were, in contrast, somewhat simple. The actual circumstances of marine pollution may produce an infinite variety of intricate fact patterns, based upon variables of pollution source and the roles, identities, and relationships of multiple actors. The intent here has been only to identify and illustrate, in summary form, a basic set of rules present in or suggested by customary international law to meet the complex demands of interstate environmental dispute settlement. The definition of a set of such rules for deciding issues of international responsibility would seem imperative to safeguard the order of the marine environment.

Perhaps the single most significant conclusion to be drawn from the analysis is that the seeds of the requisite developed regime of marine environmental responsibility are present in the contemporary international system. Certainly, there were interstices manifest in existing customary law which required extensive and progressive development in the text. The effort, however, was generally one of expansion and interpretation of existing principles, not one of pure creation. In summary, the international legal order currently possesses a perfectly adequate foundation for an equitable and effective regime of state responsibility for marine environmental injury; final progress to that end awaits only the will of the community.

Bibliography

Abecassis, 'The Law and Practice Relating to Oil Pollution From Ships', Ph.D. diss., Cambridge Univ. (1978).

Académie de Droit International de La Haye, Colloque 1973. 'The Protection of the Environment and International Law' (1975).

Accioly, 'Principes généraux de la responsabilité internationale d'apres la doctrine et la jurisprudence', 96 *Recueil des cours* 353 (1959).

'An Acid Rain Perspective, Canadian Perspective', 'National Coal Association', 'Environmentalist', 'Practical Perspectives', 14 *Nat Res. L. Newsl.* No. 4 (1982).

Adede, 'United Nations Efforts toward the Development of an Environmental Code of Conduct for States concerning Harmonious Utilization of Shared Natural Resources', 43 *Albany L. Rev.* 485 (1979).

Ago, First Report on State Responsibility, ii *Yb. Int'l L. Comm'n* 125, UN Doc. A/CN.4/217 and Add. 1 (1969).

—— Second Report on State Responsibility, ii *Yb. Int'l L. Comm'n* 177, UN Doc. A/CN.4/233 (1970).

—— Third Report on State Responsibility, ii *Yb. Int'l L. Comm'n* 193, UN Doc. A/CN.4/246 and Add 1–3 (1971).

—— Fourth Report on State Responsibility, ii *Yb. Int'l L. Comm'n* 71, UN Doc. A/CN.4/264 and Add. 1 (1972).

—— Fifth Report on State Responsibility, ii *Yb. Int'l L. Comm'n* 3, UN Doc. A/CN.4/291 and Add. 1–2 (1976).

—— Sixth Report on State Responsibility, ii *Yb. Int'l L. Comm'n* 3, UN Doc. A/CN.4/302 and Add. 1–3 (1977).

—— Seventh Report on State Responsibility, ii *Yb. Int'l L. Comm'n* 31, UN Doc. A/CN.4/307 and Add. 1–2 (1978).

—— Eighth Report on State Responsibility, ii *Yb. Int'l L. Comm'n* 3, UN Doc. A/CN.4/318 and Add. 1–4 (1979).

Akehurst, 'Jurisdiction in International Law', 46 *Brit. Yb. Int'l L.* 145 (1972–3).

Alexander and Hodgson, 'The Impact of the 200-Mile Economic Zone on the Law of the Sea', 12 *San Diego L. Rev.* 569 (1975).

Allott, 'Language, Method and the Nature of International Law', 45 *Brit. Yb. Int'l L.* 79 (1971).

—— 'Power Sharing in the Law of the Sea', 77 *Am. J. Int'l L.* 1 (1983).

Amerasinghe, 'Imputability in the Law of State Responsibility for Injuries to Aliens', 22 *R. Égyptienne de droit int'l* 91 (1966).

—— *State Responsibility for Injury to Aliens* (1967).

—— 'Basic Principles relating to the International Regime of the Oceans', 6 *J. Mar. L. & Com.* 213 (1975).

American Law Institute, Restatement of the Foreign Relations Law of the United

States (Revised), Tentative Draft no. 3, 15 Mar. 1982.

Anand, 'Equitable Use and Sharing of the Common Heritage of Mankind', in *LOS Needs and Interests of Developing Countries*, Proc. Seventh Annual Conf., Law of the Sea Institute (1972).

Anderson, 'National and International Efforts to Prevent Traumatic Vessel-source Oil Pollution', 30 *U. Miami L. Rev.* 985 (1976).

—— 'A Return to Ocean Dumping?' *City of New York* v. *US Environmental Protection Agency*, 14 *Nat. Res. L. Newsl.* 3, no. 3 (1982).

Andrassy, 'Les Relations internationales de voisinage', ii *Recueil des cours* 88 (1951).

Anzilotti, *Teoria generale della responsabilita dello stato nel diritto internazionale* (1902).

—— 'La Responsabilité internationale des états à raison des dommages soufferts par des étrangers', 13 *RGDIP* 5 (1906).

—— *Cours de droit international* (Gidel trans. 6th edn. 1929).

Apollis, *L'Emprise maritime de l'état côtier* (1981).

Attard, D., *The Exclusive Economic Zone in International Law* (1987).

Ballschmiter, 'Pollutants in the Environment: A Global Experiment', 23 *Universitas* 131 (1981).

Barboza, Preliminary Report on International Liability for Injurious Consequences Arising out of Acts Not Published by International Law, UN Doc. A/CN. 4/394 (1985).

Barros and Johnston (eds.), *The International Law of Pollution* (1974).

Barston and Birnie, 'The Falkland Islands/Islas Malvinas Conflict', 7 *Marine Pol'y* 14 (1983).

Beckett, 'The Exercise of Criminal Jurisdiction over Foreigners', 6 *Brit. Yb. Int'l L.* 44 (1925).

Beesley, 'Rights and Responsibilities of Arctic Coastal States: The Canadian View', 3 *J. Mar. L. & Com.* 1 (1971–2).

—— 'The Canadian Approach to International Environmental Law', 11 *Can. Yb. Int'l L.* 3 (1973).

Benrudi, 'State Responsibility and Hazardous Products Exports: A Solution to an International Problem', 13 *Cal. W. Int'l L.J.* 135 (1983).

Bergman, 'No-fault Liability for Oil Pollution Damage', 5 *J. Mar. L. & Com.* 1 (1973).

Bernhardt, 'A Schematic Analysis of Vessel-source Pollution: Prescriptive and Enforcement Regimes in the Law of the Sea Conference', 20 *Va. J. Int'l L.* 265 (1980).

Bilder, 'The Canadian Arctic Waters Pollution Prevention Act: New Stresses on the Law of the Sea', 69 *Mich. L. Rev.* 1 (1970–1).

Bishop, 'New US Policy Limiting Sovereign Immunity', 47 *Am. J. Int'l L.* 93 (1953).

Bissell, 'Intervention on the High Seas: An American Approach employing Community Standards', 7 *J. Mar. L. & Com.* 718 (1975–6).

Boczek, *Flags of Convenience* (1962).

—— 'International Protection of the Baltic Sea Environment against Pollution: A Study in Marine Environment', 72 *Am. J. Int'l L.* 782 (1978).

Boehmer-Christiansen, 'Limits to the International Control of Marine Pollution' (Ph.D. diss., Univ. Sussex 1981).

—— 'Dumping Nuclear Waste into the Sea', 7 *Marine Pol'y* 25 (1983).

Bollecker-Stern, *Le préjudice dans la théorie de la responsabilité internationale* (1973).
Booth, 'International Ship Pollution Law', 4 *Marine Pol'y* 215 (1980).
Borchard, *The Diplomatic Protection of Citizens Abroad* (1915).
—— 'Theoretical Aspects of the International Responsibility of States', 1 *Zeitschrift für Aüsland* Pt. 1, 223 (1929).
Borghese, 'The New International Economic Order and the Law of the Sea', 14 *San Diego L. Rev.* 584 (1977).
Bothe, 'International Legal Problems of Industrial Siting in Border Areas and National Environmental Policies', in OECD, *Transfrontier Pollution and the Role of States* 79 (1981).
Bourne, 'International Law and Pollution of International Rivers and Lakes', 21 *U. Tor. L.J.* 82 (1971).
Bouvé, 'The National Boycott as an International Delinquency', 28 *Am. J. Int'l L.* 19 (1934).
Bowett, *Self-defence in International Law* (1958).
—— 'The Second United Nations Conference on the Law of the Sea', 54 *Am. J. Int'l L.* 751 (1960).
—— *The Law of the Sea* (1967).
—— 'Nuclear and Thermal Waste Pollution: Some Legal Considerations', in *Water Pollution as a World Problem: The Legal, Scientific and Political Aspects* 22 (The David Davies Memorial Institute of International Studies 1971).
—— 'Deep Sea-bed Resources: A Major Challenge', 31 *Cam. L.J.* 50 (1972).
—— *The Law of International Institutions* (4th edn. 1982).
Boyle, 'Marine Pollution under the Law of the Sea Convention', 79 *Am. J. Int'l L.* 347 (1985).
Bramsen, 'Transnational Pollution and International Law', 42 *Nordisk tidsskrift for int'l ret.* 153 (1972).
Brendel, 'The Marijuana on the High Seas Act and Jurisdiction over Stateless Vessels', 25 *Will. & Mary L. Rev.* 313 (1983).
Brierly, 'The Theory of Implied State Complicity in International Claims', 9 *Brit. Yb. Int'l L.* 42 (1928).
—— 'Règles générales du droit de la Paix', iv *Receuil les cours* 5 (1936).
—— *The Law of Nations* (Waldock ed. 6th edn. 1963).
Britton, 'The South West Africa Decision', 22 *R. Égyptienne de droit int'l* 147 (1966).
Brown, *The Legal Regime of Hydrospace* (1971).
Brown, 'Maritime Zones: A Survey of Claims' in iii *New Directions in the Law of the Sea* 157 (Churchill, Lay, and Welch eds. 1973).
—— 'The Conventional Law of the Environment', in *International Environmental Law* (Teclaff and Utton eds. 1974).
Brown, S., Cornell, Fabian and Weiss, *Regimes for the Ocean, Outer Space and Weather* (1977).
Brownlie, 'International Law and the Activities of Armed Bands', 7 *Int'l & Comp. L.Q.* (1958).
—— *Basic Documents in International Law* (3rd ed., 1983).
—— *Basic Documents on Human Rights* (3rd ed., 1983).
—— *Principles of Public International Law* (3rd edn. 1979).
—— 'A Survey of International Customary Rules of Environmental Protection', in

International Environmental Law (Teclaff and Utton eds. 1974).

—— 'Causes of Action in the Law of Nations', 30 *Brit. Yb. Int'l L.* 13 (1979).

—— 'Legal Status of Natural Resources in International Law (Some Aspects), 162 *Recueil des cours* 244 (1979).

—— *System of the Law of Nations: State Responsibility*, Pt. I (1983).

Burke, 'Contemporary Law of the Sea: Transportation, Communication and Flight', Occasional Paper no. 28, Law of the Sea Institute, Univ. of Rhode Island (Nov. 1975).

Burmester, 'Vessel-source Pollution: The Integration of International and Domestic Responses in the Search for an Effective Legal Framework', *Oceans Policy Study* 1:6. Center for Oceans Law and Policy, Univ. of Virginia (June 1978).

Caflisch, 'International Law and Ocean Pollution: The Present and the Future', 8 *Rev. belge de droit int'l* 7 (1972).

—— 'Some Aspects of Oil Pollution from Merchant Ships', 4 *Annals of Int'l Stud.* 213 (1974).

Cahier, 'Le Problème de la responsabilité pour risque en droit international', in *International Relations in a Changing World* 411 (1977).

Calabresi, 'Some Thoughts on Risk Distribution and the Law of Torts', 70 *Yale L.J.* 499 (1961).

—— 'The Decision for Accidents: An Approach to Non-fault Allocation of Costs', 78 *Harv. L. Rev.* 713 (1965).

Caldwell, 'Concepts in Development of International Environmental Policies', in *International Environmental Law* (Teclaff and Utton eds. 1974).

Calvo, *Le Droit international théoretique et pratique* (5th edn. 1986).

Carroz and Roche, 'The International Policy of High Seas Fisheries', 60 *Can. Yb. Int'l L.* 61 (1968).

Charteris, 'The Legal Position of Merchantmen in Foreign Ports and National Waters', [1920–1] *Brit. Yb. Int'l L.* 45.

Cheng, *General Principles of Law as Applied by International Courts and Tribunals* (1953).

—— 'Crimes on Board Aircraft', 12 *Current Legal Probs* 177 (1959).

—— 'Convention on International Liability for Damage Caused by Space Objects', 1 *Manual on Space Law* 83 (Jasentuliyana and Lee eds. 1979).

Chessman, 'On Treaties and Custom: A Commentary on the Draft Restatement', 18 *Int'l Lawyer* 421 (1984).

Chorley and Giles, *Shipping Law* (Giles 7th edn. 1979).

Christol, 'International Liability for Damage caused by Space Objects', 74 *Am J. Intl'L.* 346 (1980).

Clark, P., 'Criminal Jurisdiction over Merchant Vessels engaged in International Trade', 11 *J. Marit. L. & Com.* 219 (1980).

Clark, R., 'The Biological Consequences of Oil Pollution of the Sea', in *Water Pollution as a World Problem: The Legal, Scientific and Political Aspects* (David Davies Memorial Institute of International Studies 1971).

Colombos, *The International Law of the Sea* (6th edn. 1967).

'Comment: The Convention for the Prevention of Marine Pollution from Land-based Sources: An Effective Method for Arbitrating International Effluent Pollution Disputes', 5 *Cal. W. Int'l L.J.* 350 (1975).

'Comment, The Participation of International Organizations in the Proposed International Agreement on Liability for Damage Caused by Objects Launched into Outer Space', 3 *Can. Yb. Int'l L.* 265 (1965).

'Comment, Unilateral Action *versus* Universal Evolution of Safety and Environmental Protection Standards in Martine Shipping of Hazardous Cargoes', 20 *Harv. Int'l L.J.* 127 (1979).

Contini and Sand, 'Methods to Expedite Environment Protection: International Ecostandards', 66 *Am. J. Int'l L.* 37 (1972).

Coppoc, 'The Environment: No Respecter of National Boundaries', 43 *Alb. L. Rev.* 520 (1979).

Council on Environmental Quality, 'Ocean Dumping: A National Policy. A Report to the President, 1970', reprinted in *The Pollution Crisis: Other Documents* 107 (Rubin and Schwarz eds. 1972).

Cowan, *Oil and Water: The Torrey Canyon Disaster* (1969).

Cowell, 'Oil Pollution of the Sea', in *Marine Pollution* 353 (Johnston ed. 1976).

Cummins, Logue, Tollison and Willett, 'Oil Tanker Pollution Control: Design Criteria *vs.* Effective Liability Assessment', 7 *J. Mar. L. & Com.* 169 (1975–6).

Curtis, 'The United States and the Law of the Sea: Marine Environmental Concerns', 63 *Oregon L. Rev.* 139 (1984).

Damrosch, 'Retaliation or Arbitration or Both? The 1978 United States–France Aviation Dispute', 74 *Am. J. Int'l L.* 785 (1980).

Danzig, 'A Funny Thing Happened to the Common Heritage on the way to the Law of the Sea', 12 *San Diego L. Rev.* 645 (1975), 340.

David Davies Memorial Institute of International Studies, *Water Pollution as a World Problem: The Legal, Scientific and Political Aspects*. Report of a Conference Held at the University College of Wales, Aberystwyth July 11–12, 1970 (1971).

Dean, 'The Geneva Conference on the Law of the Sea: What Was Accomplished', 52 *Am. J. Int'l L.* 607 (1958).

De Beus, *The Jurisprudence of the General Claims Commission: United States and Mexico* (1938).

Delupis, *International Law and the Independent State* (1974).

De Mestral, 'The Prevention of Pollution of the Marine Environment arising from Offshore Mining and Drilling', 20 *Harv. Int'l L.J.* 469 (1979).

de Mestral and Legault, 'Multilateral Negotiation: Canada and the Law of the Sea Conference', iii 35 *Int'l L.J.* 46 (1979–80).

de Smet, 'Policing on the High Seas: With special reference to the North Sea', in *New Directions in the Law of the Sea* 193 (Churchill, Simmonds, and Welch eds. 1973).

de Visscher, 'La Responsabilité des états', ii *Bibliotheca visseriana* 86 (1924).

—— *Theory and Reality in Public International Law* (Corbett trans. 1957).

de Yturriaga, 'Regional Conventions on the Protection of the Marine Environment', i *Recueil des cours* 244 (1979).

di Bari, 'International Legal Aspects of Marine Pollution', 97 *Quaderni de la ricerca scientifica* (1977).

Diederiks-Verschoor and Gormley, 'The Future Legal Status of Non-governmental Entities in Outer Space: Private Individuals and Companies as Subjects and Beneficiaries of International Space law', 5 *J. Space L.* 125 (1977).

Dinstein, 'Oil Pollution by Ships and Freedom of the High Seas', 3 *J. Mar. L. & Com.*

363 (1971–2).
Djordjevic, 'The Social Property of Mankind', in *Pacem in maribus* (Borghese ed. 1972).
Douay, 'Le Droit de la mer et la préservation du milieu Marin', in *Le Nouveau droit international de la mer* 231 (Bardonnet and Virally eds. 1983).
Dunn, *The Protection of Nationals* (1932).
Du Pontavice, 'Pollution', in *The Future of the Law of the Sea* (Bouchez and Kaijen eds. 1972).
—— 'Compensation for Transfrontier Pollution Damage', in OECD, *Legal Aspects of Transfrontier Pollution* 409 (1977).
Dupuy, 'Due Diligence in the International Law of Liability', in OECD, *Legal Aspects of Transfrontier Pollution* 369 (1977).
—— 'International Liability of States for Damage caused by Transfrontier Pollution', in OECD, *Legal Aspects of Transfrontier Pollution* 345 (1977).
—— *La Responsabilité internationale des états pour les dommages d'origine technologique et industrielle* (1976).
—— (ed.), *The Right to Health as a Human Right*, Académie de Droit International Colloque (1978).
Eagleton, 'Denial of Justice in International Law', 22 *Am. J. Int'l L.* 538 (1928).
—— *The Responsibility of States in International Law* (1928).
—— 'Measure of Damages in International Law', 39 *Yale L.J.* 52 (1929).
Eckert, *The Enclosure of Ocean Resources* (1979).
Elles, *International Provisions Protecting the Human Rights of Non-citizens*, UN Doc. E/CN.4/sub.2/392/Rev. 1 (1980).
Emmanuelli, 'La Pollution maritime et la notion de passage inoffensif', 11 *Can Yb. Int'l L.* 13 (1973).
Ereli, *The Environmental Regulation of the Sea and its Resources* (1972).
Eustathiades, 'La responsabilité internationale de l'état pour les actes des organes judiciaires et le probleme du deni de justice en droit international (1936).
Eustis, 'Method and Basis of Seaward Delimitation of Continental Shelf Jurisdiction', 17 *Va. J. Int'l L.* 107 (1976).
Extavour, *The Exclusive Economic Zone: A Study of the Evolution and Progressive Development of the International Law of the Sea* (1979).
Falk, 'The South West Africa Cases: An Appraisal', 21 *Int'l Org.* 1 (1967).
Falk and Black (eds.), *The Future of the International Legal Order* (1970).
Fauchille, *Traites Droit International Public* (1925).
—— 'Responsibilité des états à raison des dammages soufferts par des étrangers en cas d'emeute on de guerre civile' 18 *Annuaire Inst. Droit. Int'l* 234 (1900).
Fawcett, *International Law and the Uses of Outer Space* (1968).
Fitzmaurice, 'The Meaning of Denial of Justice', 13 *Brit. Yb. Int'l L.* 93 (1932).
—— 'The Law and Procedure of the International Court of Justice: General Principles and Substantive Law', 27 *Brit. Yb. Int'l L.* 1 (1950).
—— 'The Law and Procedure of the International Court of Justice, 1951–54: Points of Substantive Law—I', 31 *Brit. Yb. Int'l L.* 371 (1954).
—— 'The General Principles of International Law', ii *Recueil des cours* 2 (1957).
—— 'Some Results of the Geneva Conference on the Law of the Sea', 8 *Int'l & Comp. L.Q.*72 (1959).

Fleischer, 'Pollution from Seaborne Sources', in iii *New Directions in the Law of the Sea* (Churchill, Simmonds, and Welch eds. 1973).

Force Majeure (and 'Fortuitous Event' as Circumstances Precluding Wrongfulness: Survey of State Practice, International Judicial Decisions and Doctrine, UN Doc. A/CN.4/315, in ii *Yb. Int'l L. Comm'n* 51, at 190, UN Doc. A/CN.4/Ser.A/1978/Add 1 (Pt. 1) (1978).

Foster, 'The Convention on International Liability for Damage Caused by Space Objects', 10 *Can. Yb. Int'l L.* 137 (1972).

Frank, 'Protection of the Marine Environment from Pollution', 6 *Ga. J. Int'l & Comp. L.* 73 (1976).

Freeman, *The International Responsibility of States for Denial of Justice* (1938).

Friedmann, 'The Growth of State Control over the Individual and Its Effect upon the Rules of International State Responsibility', 19 *Brit. Yb. Int'l L.* 118 (1938).

—— 'The Uses of General Principles in the Development of International Law', 57 *Am. J. Int'l L.* 279 (1963).

—— 'The North Sea Continental Shelf Cases: A Critique', 18 *Int'l & Comp. L.Q.* 819 (1969).

—— 'Selden Redivivus: Towards a Partition of the Seas?', 65 *Am J. Int'l L.* 757 (1971).

Fulton, *The Sovereignty of the Sea* (1911).

Garcia-Amador, 'State Responsibility in the Light of the New Trends of International Law', 49 *Am. J. Int'l L.* 339 (1955).

—— First Report on the Responsibility of the State for Injuries caused in its Territory to the Person or Property of Aliens, ii *Yb. Int'l L. Comm'n* 173, UN Doc. A/CN. 4/96 (1956).

—— Second Report on the Responsibility of the State for Injuries caused in its Territory to the Person or Property of Aliens, ii *Yb. Int'l Comm'n*, 104, UN Doc. A/CN.4/106 (1957).

—— 'State Responsibility: Some New Problems', ii *Recueil des cours* 369 (1958).

—— Third Report on the Responsibility of the State for Injuries caused in its Territory to the Person or Property of Aliens, ii *Yb. Int'l L. Comm'n* 47, UN Doc. A/CN.4/111 (1958).

—— Fourth Report on the Responsibility of the State for Injuries caused in its Territory to the Person or Property of Aliens, ii *Yb. Int'l L. Comm'n* 1, UN Doc. A/CN.4/119 (1959).

—— Fifth Report on the Responsibility of the State for Injuries caused in its Territory to the Person or Property of Aliens, ii *Yb. Int'l L. Comm'n* 41, UN Doc. A/CN.4/125 (1960).

—— Sixth Report on the Responsibility of the State for Injuries caused in its Territory to the Person or Property of Aliens, ii *Yb. Int'l L. Comm'n* 1, UN Doc. A/CN.4/134 and Add. 1 (1961).

—— 'The Latin American Contribution to the Development of the Law of the Sea', 68 *Am. J. Int'l L.* 33 (1974).

Garcia-Amador, Sohn, and Baxter, *Recent Codification of the Law of State Responsibily for Injuries to Aliens* (1974).

Garcia-Mora, *International Responsibility for Hostile Acts of Private Persons against Foreign States* (1962).

George, 'Extraterritorial Application of Penal Legislation', 64 *Mich. L. Rev.* 609 (1966).

Gidel, *Le Droit international public de la mer* (1934).

Gilmore and Black, *The Law of Admiralty,* (2nd edn. 1975).

Ginsburg, 'The Lure of Tidewater: The Problem of the Interface between Land and Sea', in *Pacem in Maribus* 32 (Borghese ed. 1972).

Ginsburgs, 'The Soviet Union and the Biosphere', 28 *Int'l J.* 50 (1972–3).

Gold, 'Pollution of the Sea and International Law: A Canadian Perspective', 3 *J. Mar. L. & Com.* 13 (1971–2).

Goldberg, 'The Chemical Invasion of the Oceans by Man', in *Global Effects of Environmental Polluton* 178 (Singer ed. 1968).

Goldberg (ed.), *A Guide to Marine Pollution: Seminar in connection with the FAO Technical Conference on Marine Pollution and its Effects on Resources and Fishing* (1972).

Goldie, 'Liability for Damage and the Progressive Development of International Law', 14 *Int'l & Comp. L.Q.* 1189 (1965).

—— 'International Principles of Responsibility for Pollution', 9 *Colum. J. Transnat'l L.* 283 (1970).

—— 'The Management of Ocean Resources: Regimes for Structuring the Marine Environment', in iv *The Future of the International Legal Order* (Black and Falk eds. 1972).

—— 'A General View of International Environmental Law: A Survey of Capabilities, Trends and Limits', in *Academie de Droit International Colloque: The Protection of the Environment and International Law* (1973).

—— 'The Nuclear Tests Cases: Restraints on Environmental Harm', 5 *J. Mar. L. & Com.* 491 (1973–4).

—— 'International Impact Reports and the Conservation of the Ocean Environment', in *International Environmental Law* (Teclaff and Utton eds. 1974).

—— 'Responsibility and Liability in the Common Law', in OECD, *Legal Aspects of Transfrontier Pollution* 306 (1977).

Gordenker, 'Livelihood and Welfare', in *The Future of the International Legal Order* (Black and Falk eds. 1972).

Gorove, 'The Concept of the Common Heritage of Mankind: A Political, Moral or Legal Innovation?', 9 *San Diego L. Rev.* 340 (1972).

—— 'Development of an International Environmental Law: An Appraisal in Law', in *Institutions and the Global Environment* 108 (ed. Hargrove 1972).

Gotlieb and Dalfen, 'National Jurisdiction and International Responsibility: New Canadian Approaches to International Law', 67 *Am. J. Int'l L.* 229 (1973).

Grotius, 'De jure belli ac pacis', Libri Tres Vol ii 1625 (Kelsey trans.).

Guerrero (Rapporteur), *Report to the Council of the League of Nations on the Questions which Appear Ripe For International Regulation: Responsibility of States for Damage done in Their Territories to the Person or Property of Foreigners.* League of Nations Doc. C. 196 M.70 1927 v (1927).

Gustafson, 'PCBs: Prevalent and Persistent', [1970] *Envt'l Sci. & Tech.* 814.

Guzhenko, 'Soviet Merchant Marine and World Shipping', 1 *Marine Pol'y* 102 (1977).

Hakapaa, *Marine Pollution in International Law: Material Obligations and Jurisdiction* (1981).

Hall, *Treatise on International Law* (8th edn. 1924).

Hallman, *Towards an Environmentally Sound Law of the Sea* (1974).

Hambro and Rovine, *The Case Law of the International Court* (1976).

Hancock and Stone, 'Liability for Transnational Pollution caused by Offshore Oil Rigs', 5 *Hast. Int'l & Comp. L. Rev.* 377 (1982).

Handl, 'Balancing of Interests and International Liability for the Pollution of International Watercourses: Customary Principles of Law Revisited, 13 *Can. Yb. Int'l L.* 156 (1975).

—— 'Territorial Sovereignty and the Problem of Transnational Pollution', 69 *Am. J. Int'l L.* 50 (1976).

—— 'The Environment: International Rights and Responsibilities', in [1980] *Proc. Am. Soc. Int'l L.* 223.

—— 'State Liability for Accidental Transnational Environmental Damage by Private Persons', 74 *Am. J. Int'l L.* 525 (1980).

—— 'International Liability of States for Marine Pollution', 21 *Can Yb. Int'l L.* 85 (1983).

Hardy, 'Nuclear Liability: The General Principles of Law and Further Proposals', 36 *Brit. Yb. Int'l L.* 223 (1960).

—— 'The United Nations Environment Programme', 13 *Nat. Res. J.* 235 (1973).

Hargrove, *Law, Institutions and the Global Environment* (1972).

Harris, 'The Law On Air Pollution: International Aspects', in *Environmental Pollution Control: Technical, Economic and Legal Aspects* 77 (McKnight, Marstrand, and Sinclair eds. 1974).

Hayashi, 'Comparative National Legislation on Offshore Pollution', 1 *Syracuse J. Int'l L. & Com.* 252 (1973).

—— 'An International Machinery for the Management of the Sea-bed: Birth and Growth of the Idea', 4 *Annals of Int'l Stud* 251 (1974).

Hedberg, 'Relation of Political Boundaries on the Ocean Floor to the Continental Margin', 17 *Va. J. Int'l L.* 57 (1976).

Heine, *The Attitudes of the Asian-African States toward the Laws of State Responsibility* (1976).

Henkin, 'Arctic Anti-pollution: Does Canada Make—Or Break—International Law?', 65 *Am. J. Int'l L.* 131 (1971).

Heuston and Chambers (eds.), *Salmond and Heuston on the Law of Torts* (18th edn. 1981).

Hickey, 'Custom and Land-Based Pollution of the High Seas', 15 *San Diego L. Rev.* 409 (1978).

Ho, 'UN Recognition of the Human Right to Environmental Protection', 2 *Earth L.J.* 225 (1976).

Hoffman, 'State Responsibility in International Law and Transboundary Pollution Injuries', 25 *Int'l Comp. L.Q.* (1976).

Hohfeld, *Fundamental Legal Conceptions as applied in Judicial Reasoning* (1923).

Hoijer, La Responsabilité internationale des états en matière d'Actes législatifs, 4 RGDIP 577 (1929).

Hollick, 'US Oceans Policy: The Truman Proclamations', 17 *Va. J. Int'l L.* 23 (1976).

Hoult, 'Marine Pollution, Concentrating on the Effects of Hydrocarbons in Seawater', in *Canadian–US Maritime Problems* (Alexander and Hawkins eds. 1972).

Hsia, 'Some Jurisdictional Problems Arising from Ship-source Marine Pollution with special reference to Port State Jurisdiction' (M.Litt. diss., Oxford Univ. 1981).

Hudson, *Permanent Court of International Justice* 1920–1942 (1943).
Hunnings, 'Pirate Broadcasting in European Waters', 14 *Int'l & Comp. L.Q.* 410 (1965).
Hyde, i–ii *International Law* (2nd edn. 1945).
Hydeman and Berman, *International Control of Nuclear Maritime Activities* (1960).
International Law Association, Report on the 52nd Conference—Helsinki (1967), Helsinki Rules on the Uses of Waters of International Rivers.
—— Report on the 53rd Conference—Buenos Aires (1968), 'Draft Rules on Sea Pollution'.
—— Report of the 55th Conference—New York (1972), 'Report of the Committee on the Extraterritorial Application of Restrictive Trade Legislation'.
—— Report of the 55th Conference—New York (1972), Report of the Committee on International Water Resources Law, Marine Pollution of Continental Origin.
—— Report of the 56th Conference—New Delhi (1974), British Branch Committee on the Law of the Sea, The Concept of Port State Jurisdiction.
—— Report of the 56th Conference—New Delhi (1974), Haight, the UN Conference on the Law of the Sea (Caracas Session).
—— Report of the 57th Conference—Madrid (1976), Report of the Law of the Sea Committee on Artificial Islands and Offshore Installations.
—— Report of the 58th Conference—Manila (1978), Report of the Committee on Legal Aspects of the Conservation of the Environment.
—— Report of the 59th Conference—Belgrade 531 (1980), Report of the Committee on Legal Aspects of the Conservation of the Environment.
—— Report of the 60th Conference—Montreal (1982), Report of the Committee on Legal Aspects of the Conservation of the Environment.
International Law Commission, Reports to the General Assembly and Summary Records, *Yb. Int'l Comm'n* (1969–84).
Jackson, 'The Dimensions of International Pollution', 50 *Oreg. L. Rev.* 223 (1971).
James and Brown, *General Principles of the Law of Torts* (4th edn. 1978).
Jantscher, *Bread Upon The Waters: Federal Aids to the Maritime Industries* (1975).
Jasentuliyana and Lee (eds.), *Manual on Space Law* (1981).
Jenks, *Space Law* (1965).
—— 'Liability for Utrahazardous Activities in International Law', i *Recueil des cours* 100 (1966).
Jennings, 'The *Caroline* and *McLeod* Cases', 32 *Am. J. Int'l L.* 82 (1983).
—— *Extraterritorial Jurisdiction and the United States Antitrust Laws*, 33 *Brit. Yb. Int'l L.* 146 (1957).
—— *The Acquisition of Territory in International Law* (1963).
—— 'General Course of International Law', ii *Recueil des cours* 321 (1967).
—— 'Oil Pollution: The Law', in *Water Pollution as a World Problem: The Legal, Scientific and Political Aspects* 77 (David Davies Memorial Inst. of International Studies 1971).
—— 'A Changing International Law of the Sea', 31 *Camb. L.J.* 32 (1972).
—— 'What Is International Law and How Do We Tell It When We See It?' 36 *Swiss Yb. Int'l L.* 59 (1981).
Jessup, *The Law of Territorial Waters and Maritime Jurisdiction* (1927).
—— 'Civil Jurisdiction over Ships in Innocent Passage', 27 *Am. J. Int'l L.* 747 (1933).

Jiménez De Arechaga, 'International Responsibility', in Sørensen, *Manual of Public International Law* 531 (1968).
Johnson and Zacher (eds.), *Canadian Foreign Policy and the Law of the Sea* (1977).
Johnston, D., 'Law, Technology and the Sea', 55 *Cal. L. Rev.* 449 (1967).
—— 'Marine Pollution Control: Law, Science, and Politics', 28 *Int'l J.* 69 (1972–3).
—— 'The New Equity in the Law of the Sea', 31 *Int'l J.* 79 (Winter 1975–6).
Johnston, R., 'Mechanisms and Problems of Marine Pollution in Relation to Commercial Fisheries', in *Marine Pollution* 3 (Johnston ed. 1976).
—— (ed.), *Marine Pollution*, 1976.
Jolowicz, Lewis, and Harris (eds.), *Winfield and Jolowicz in Tort*, (9th edn. 1971).
Juda 'UNCLOS III and the New Economic Order', 7 *Ocean Dev. & Int'l L.* 221 (1974).
—— 'IMCO and the Regulation of Ocean Pollution from Ships', 26 *Int'l & Comp. L.Q.* 558 (1977).
Kelsen, *Principles of International Law* (2nd edn. 1966).
Kelson, 'State Responsibility and the Abnormally Dangerous Activity', 13 *Harv. J. Int'l L.* 197 (1972).
Kilgour, 'Effective United States Control?', 8 *J. Mar. L. & Com.* 337 (1976–7).
Kindt, 'The Effect of Claims by Developing Countries on LOS International Marine Pollution Negotiations', 20 *Va. J. Int'l L.* 313 (1980).
Kingham, 'Marine Resource Management in the North Pacific Rim and Problems of Environmental Protection', in *Regionalization of the Law of the Sea* 151 (Johnson ed. 1978).
Kingham and McRae, 'Competent International Organizations and the Law of the Sea', 3 *Marine Pol'y* 106 (1979).
Kiselev, 'The Freedom of Navigation and the Problem of Pollution of the Marine Environment', 6 *Ga. J. Int'l & Comp. L.* 93 (1976).
Kiss, *L'Abus de droit en droit international* (1953).
—— *La Notion de Patrimoine commun de L'Humanité*, ii *Recueil des cours* 109 (1982).
—— *Survey of Current Development in International Environmental Law*, IUCN Policy Paper no. 10 (1976).
Kitchen, *Labour Law and Offshore Oil* (1977).
Klotz, 'Are Ocean Polluters Subject to Universal Jurisdiction: Canada Breaks the Ice', 6 *Int'l Lawyer* 706 (1972).
Koers, 'The Enforcement of International Fisheries Agreements', 1 *Neth. Yb. Int'l L.* 1 (1970).
Kronfel, 'The Exclusive Economic Zone: A Critique of Contemporary Law of the Sea', 9 *J. Mar. L. & Com.* 461 (1977–8).
Kwasniewski, 'Shipping Policy of the Comecon Countries', 1 *Marine Pol'y* 110 (1977).
Kwiatkowska-Czechowska, 'States' Responsibility for Pollution Damage Resulting from the Exploration for and Exploitation of Sea-bed Mineral Resources', 10 *Polish Yb. Int'l L.* 157 (1980).
Lapradelle, *Revue genérale de droit international public* (1898).
Larson and Jenks, *Sovereignty within the Law* (1965).
Lasswell, 'Future Systems of Identity in the World Community', in iv *The Future of the International Order* (Black and Falk eds. 1972).
Lauterpacht, E. 'The Inevitability of Change in International Law and the Need For Adjustment of Interests', 51 *Austl. L.J.* 83 (1977).

Lauterpacht, Hersch, *Private Law Sources and Analogies of International Law* (1927).

—— 'Boycott in International Relations', 14 *Brit. Yb. Int'l L.* 125 (1933).

—— *The Function of Law in the International Community* (1933).

—— 'Allegiance, Diplomatic Protection and Criminal Jurisdiction over Aliens', 9 *Camb. L.J.* 330 (1947).

—— *International Law and Human Rights* (1950).

—— 'Sovereignty over Submarine Areas', 27 *Brit. Yb. Int'l L.* 376 (1950).

—— 'The Problem of Jurisdictional Immunities of Foreign States', 28 *Brit. Yb. Int'l L.* 220 (1951).

Lawson and Markesinis, *Tortious Liability for Unintentional Harm in the Common Law and the Civil Law* (1982).

Law of the Sea: From Caracas to Geneva A Time for Decision, 14 *Colum J. Transnat'l L.* 1 (1975) (Panel Discussion Transcript).

League of Nations, Committee of Experts for the Progressive Codification of International Law, Report to The Council of the League of Nations on the Questions which Appear Ripe for International Resolution, Adopted by Comm. 3rd Sess. Mar.–Apr. 1927, League of Nations Doc. C. 196 M. 70 1927 V. (*CPDI* 95 (2)). Sub-Committee on the Criminal Competence of States in respect of Offences Committed outside their Territory, 20 *Am. J. Int'l L.* 253 (Suppl. 1926).

Lee, 'Jurisdiction over Foreign Merchant Ships in the Territorial Sea: An Analysis of the Geneva Convention on the Law of the Sea', 55 *Am. J. Int'l L.* 77 (1961).

—— 'The Law of the Sea Convention and Third States', 77 *Am. J. Int'l L.* 541 (1983).

Legatski, 'Port State Jurisdiction over Vessel-source Marine Pollution', 2 *Harv. Env. L. Rev.* 448 (1977).

Legault, 'The Freedom of the Seas: A License to Pollute?', 21 *Univ. Tor. L.J.* 211 (1971).

Lenoble, 'Responsabilité internationale des états et controle territorial', 16 *Rev. belge droit int'l* (1981–2), 95.

Lillich, *International Law of State Responsibility for Injuries to Aliens* (1983).

Lillich and Paxman, 'State Responsibility for Injury to Aliens Occasioned by Terrorists', 26 *Am U.L. Rev.* 219 (1977).

Livingston: 'Science, Technology, and International Law: Present Trends and Future Developments', in iv *The Future of the International Legal Order* (Black and Falk eds. 1972).

—— 'Marine Pollution Articles in the Law of the Sea: Single Informal Negotiating Text', Occasional Paper no. 31 Law of the Sea Institute, Univ. of Rhode Island (June 1976).

Llewelyn-Davies, 'The Influence of Huber's *De Conflictu Legum* on English Private International Law', 18 *Brit. Yb. Int'l L.* 49 (1937).

Lundholm, 'The Oceans: Their Production and Pollution—The Baltic as a Case Study', in *Pacem in Maribus* 25 (Borghese ed. 1972).

Lowe, 'The Enforcement of Marine Pollution Regulations', 12 *San Diego L. Rev.* 624 (1975).

Lutz, 'The Law of Environmental Management: A Comparative Study', 24 *Am. J. Comp. L.* 447 (1976).

—— 'The Right of Entry into Maritime Ports in International Law', 14 *San Diego L. Rev.* 597 (1977).

Macrae, 'Customary International Law and the United Nations Law of the Sea Treaty', 13 *Cal. W. Int'l L.J.* 181 (1983).

Magraw, 'Transboundary Harm: The International Law Commission's Study of "International Liability"', 80 *Am. J. Int'l L.* 305 (1986).

Makovsky, 'Liability for Marine Environment Pollution Damage in Contemporary International Sea Law', 6 *Ga. J. Int'l & Comp. L.* 59 (1976).

Malik, 'Liability for Damage caused by Space Activities', 6 *Indian J. Int'l L.* 335 (1966).

Manca, *The Italian Code of Navigation* (1959).

Mann, 'The Doctrine of Jurisdiction in International Law', in *Studies in International Law* 1 (1973).

—— 'The Consequences of an International Wrong in International and National Law', 48 *Brit. Yb. Int'l L.* (1976–7).

Marston, 'The Evolution of the Concept of Sovereignty over the Bed and Subsoil of the Territorial Sea', 48 *Brit. Yb. Int'l L.* 321 (1976–7).

Marstrand, 'Pollution of the Seas', in *Environmental Pollution Control* 150–73 (McKnight, Marstrand, and Sinclair eds. 1974).

—— Crimes on Board Foreign Merchant Ships at Sea: Some Aspects of English Practice', 83 *L.Q. Rev.* 357 (1972).

Martens, 'Evolution of Coastal State Jurisdiction: A Conflict between Developed and Developing States', 5 *Ecology L.Q.* 531 (1976).

Martinez, 'The Third United Nations Conference on the Law of the Sea: Prospects, Expectations and Realities', 7 *J. Mar. L. & Com.* 253 (1975–6).

Masterson, *Jurisdiction in Marginal Seas* (1929).

Matsunami, *Immunity of State Ships* (1924).

McCaffrey, 'The 34th Session of the International Law Commission', 77 *Am. J. Int'l L.* 323 (1983).

Macdonald, Morris and Johnston (eds.) *Canadian Perspectives on International Law and Organisation* (1974).

McDougal, 'Jurisdiction', in 62 *International Law Studies* 634 (Lillich and Moore eds. 1980).

McDougal and Burke, *The Public Order of the Oceans: A Contemporary International Law of the Sea* (1962).

McDougal and Schneider, 'The Protection of The Environment and World Public Order: Some Recent Developments', 45 *Miss L. J.* 1085 (1974).

McDougal, Burke and Vlasic, 'The Maintenance of Public Order at Sea and the Nationality of Ships', 54 *Am. J. Int'l L.* 25 (1960).

McDougal, Lasswell and Vlasic, *Law and Public Order in Outer Space* (1964).

McDougal, Lasswell and Chen, *Human Rights and World Public Order* (1980).

McNair, 'Problems connected with the Position of the Merchant Vessel in Private International Law, with particular reference to the Power of Requisition', 31 *Transactions of the Grotius Society of 1945* 30 (1946).

Mendelsohn, 'Ocean Pollution and the 1972 United Nations Conference on the Environment', 3 *J. Mar. L. & Com.* (1971–2), 385.

Mensah, 'Avoidance and Adjustment of International Environmental Disputes', in Papers presented at the Bellagio Conference Organised by the American Society of International Law in July, 1974.

—— 'The Law relating to the Pollution of the Seas', in *Environmental Pollution Control* 174 (McKnight, Marstrand, and Sinclair eds. 1974).

Meron, 'International Responsibility of States for Unauthorized Acts of their Officials', 33 *Brit. Yb. Int'l L.* 84 (1957).
Meyer, *The Extent of Jurisdiction in Coastal Waters* (1937).
Meyers, *The Nationality of Ships* (1967).
Miller, 'Doomsday Politics: Prospects for International Cooperation', 28 *Int'l J.* 121 (1972–3).
Moore, 'Legal Aspects of Marine Pollution Control', in Johnston (ed.), *Marine Pollution* 589 (Johnston ed. 1976).
—— 'The Regime of Straits and the Third United Nations Conference of the Law of the Sea', 74 *Am. J. Int'l L.* 77 (1980).
Moskowitz, *Human Rights and World Order* (1958).
—— *The Politics and Dynamics of Human Rights* (1968).
Moulton, *The Continental Shelf* (1952).
Munton, 'Dependence and Interdependence in Transboundary Pollution', 36 *Int'l J.* 139 (1980–1).
Naess, *The Great Panlibhon Controversy* (1972).
Nanda, 'The Establishment of International Standards for Transnational Environmental Injury', 60 *Iowa L. Rev.* 1089 (1975).
Nanda and Ris, 'The Public Trust Doctrine: A Viable Approach to International Environmental Protection', 5 *Ecol. L.Q.* 291 (1976).
Nelson-Smith, *Oil Pollution and Marine Ecology* (1972).
Norris, *The Law of Seamen* (3rd edn. 1970).
Note, 'Continental Shelf Oil Disasters: Challenge to International Pollution Control', 55 *Cornell L. Rev.* 113 (1969).
—— 'Criminal Law: Jurisdiction to Punish for Crimes Committed by an Alien outside the United States', 45 *Cal. L. Rev.* 199 (1957).
—— 'No Dumping in This Ocean: Nearing the End of Ship Generated Pollution', 7 *NYU J. Int'l L. & Pol'y* 545 (1974).
—— 'The Protection of Maritime Environment by the Courts of Third States: Some Difficulties', 19 *McGill L.J.* (1973).
—— 'Reflection on Brussels: IMCO and the 1969 Pollution Conventions', 3 *Cornell Int'l L.J.* 161 (1970).
—— 'Saving A Dying Sea? The London Convention on Ocean Dumping', 7 *Cornell Int'l L.J.* 32 (1973).
—— 'Smoke on the Water: Coast Guard Authority to Seize Foreign Vessels beyond the Contiguous Zone', 13 *NYU J. Int'l L. & Pol'y* 249 (1980).
—— 'The Clean Water Act of 1977: Expanded Competence over Vessel-source Pollution', 18 *VA J. Int'l L.* 289 (1978).
O'Connell, i–ii *International Law* (1965).
—— 'The Juridical Nature of the Territorial Sea', 45 *Brit. Yb. Int'l L.* 303 (1971).
Oda, 'The Concept of the Contiguous Zone', 11 *Int'l & Comp. L.Q.* 131 (1962).
OECD, *Legal Aspects of Transfrontier Pollution* (1977).
—— *Transfrontier Pollution and the Role of States* (1981).
—— Environment Committee, 'Application of Information and Consultation Practices for Preventing Transfrontier Pollution', in OECD, *Transfrontier Pollution and the Role of the States* (1981).
Oppenheim, *International Law*, (8th edn., H. Lauterpacht ed. 1955).

Ortolan, *Règles internationales et diplomatie de la mer* (1845).
Osieke, 'Flags of Convenience Vessels: Recent Developments', 73 *Am. J. Int'l L.* 604 (1979).
Ostrovskii, 'International Legal Protection of the Seas from Pollution', 3 *Ocean Dev. & Int'l L.* 287 (1976).
Oxman, 'The Third United Nations Conference of the Law of the Sea: The 1976 New York Sessions', 71 *Am. J. Int'l L.* 247 (1977).
—— 'The Third United Nations Conference on the Law of the Sea: the 1977 New York Sessions', 72 *Am. J. Int'l L.* 57 (1978).
—— The Third United Nations Conference on the Law of the Sea: The Seventh Session (1978)', 73 *Am. J. Int'l L.* 1 (1979).
—— 'The Third United Nations Conference on the Law of the Sea: The Eighth Session (1979)', 74 *Am. J. Int'l L.* (1980).
—— 'The Third United Nations Conference of the Law of the Sea: The Ninth Session (1980)', 75 *Am. J. Int'l L.* 211 (1981).
Pardo, 'Whose is the Bed of the Sea?', 62 *Proc. Am. Soc. Int'l L.* 216 (1968).
Parry, 'Some Considerations upon the Protection of Individuals', ii *Recueil des cours* 657 (1956).
—— *The Sources and Evidence of International Law* (1965).
Peirce, 'Selective Adoption of the New Law of the Sea: The United States Proclaims its Exclusive Economic Zone', 23 *Va. J. Int'l L.* 581 (1983).
Personnaz, *La Réparation du préjudice en droit international public* (1939).
Pharand, 'Innocent Passage in the Arctic', 6 *Can. Yb. Int'l L.* 3 (1968).
—— 'Contiguous Zones of Pollution Prevention', 1 *Syracuse J. Int'l L. & Com.* 257 (1973).
—— *The Law of the Sea of the Arctic* (1973).
Phillips, 'The Economic Resources Zone: Progress for the Developing Coastal States', 11 *J. Mar. L. & Com.* 349 (1980).
Pinto, 'Problems of Developing States and their Effects on Decisions on LOS', in *LOS Needs and Interests of the Developing Countries*, Proc. 7th Annual Conf. Law of the Sea Institute, Univ. of Rhode Island (1972).
Pollard, 'The Exclusive Economic Zone: The Elusive Consensus', 12 *San Diego L. Rev.* 600 (1975).
Popp, *Voisinage et bon voisinage en droit international* (1980).
Poulantzas, *The Right of Hot Pursuit in International Law* (1969).
Prosser, *The Law of Torts* (4th edn. 1971).
—— 'Comparative Negligence', 51 *Mich. L. Rev.* (1953), 465, reprinted in *Selected Topics on the Law of Torts* 1 (1953).
Pruitt, 'Unilateral Deep Sea-Bed Mining and Environmental Standards: A Risky Venture', 8 *Brooklyn J. Int'l L.* 345 (1982).
Queneudec, *La Responsabilité internationale de l'état pour les fautes personelles de ses agents* (1966).
Quentin-Baxter, Preliminary Report on International Liability for Injurious Consequences of Acts Not Prohibited by International Law, 2 *Yb. Int'l L. Comm'n* 247 (1980), UN Doc. A/CN. 4/334 and Add. 1 and 2.
—— 'Second Report on International Liability for Injurious Consequences of Acts Not Prohibited by International Law', 2 *Yb. Int'l L. Comm'n* 247 (1980), UN Doc. A/CN, 4/346 (12 June 1981).

—— 'Third Report on International Liability for Injurious Consequences of Acts Not Prohibited by International Law', 2 *Yb. Int'l L. Comm'n* 247 (1980), UN Doc. A/CN. 4/360 (23 June 1982).

—— 'Fourth Report on International Liability for Injurious Consequences of Acts Not Prohibited by International Law', 2 *Yb. Int'l L. Comm'n* 247 (1980), UN Doc. A/CN 4/373 (27 June 1983).

—— 'Fifth Report on International Liability for Injurious Consequences of Acts Not Prohibited by International Law', 2 *Yb. Int'l L. Comm'n* 247 (1980), UN Doc. A/CN 4/303 (12 June 1984).

Ray, 'Ecology, Law and the Marine Revolution', in *Pacem in Maribus* (Borghese ed. 1972).

Read, 'The Trail Smelter Dispute', 1 *Can. Yb. Int'l L.* 213 (1963).

Reid, 'The Canadian Claim to Sovereignty over the Waters of the Arctic', 12 *Can Yb. Int'l L.* 111 (1974).

Reisman, 'The Regime of Straits and National Security', 74 *Am. J. Int'l L.* 48 (1980).

Research in International Law, Harvard Law School: Draft Convention and Comments on Territorial Waters, 23 *Am. J. Int'l L.* 243 (1929 Supp.).

Research in International Law, Under the Auspices of the Faculty of the Harvard Law School: Jurisdiction with Respect to Crime (Part II) Convention on Jurisdiction with Respect to Crime, 29 *Am. J. Int'l L.* 435 (1935 Supp.).

Rest, 'Convention on Compensation for Transfrontier Environmental Injuries'. Project of the Institute of International & Comparative Law of the Univ. of Cologne in collaboration with the IUCN Environmental Law Centre (1976).

Rienow, *The Test of the Nationality of a Merchant Vessel* (1937).

Riesenfeld, 'Sovereign Immunity of Foreign Vessels in Anglo-American Law: The Evolution of a Legal Doctrine', 25 *Minn. L. Rev.* 1 (1940).

Riphagen, Preliminary Report on the Content, Forms and Degrees of State Responsibility, 2 *Yb. Int'l L. Comm'n* 107 (1980), UN Doc. A/CN.4/330.

—— Second Report on the Content, Forms and Degrees of State Responsibility, UN Doc. A/CN.4/344 (1 May 1981).

—— Third Report on the Content, Forms and Degrees of State Responsibility, UN Doc. A/CN.4/354 and Add. 2 (5 May 1982).

—— Fourth Report on the Content, Forms and Degrees of State Responsibility, UN Doc. A/CN.4/366 (14 April 1983).

—— 'The Jurisdiction of the Coastal State', in *The Future of the Law of the Sea* (Bouchez and Kaijen eds. 1973).

Robol, 'Admiralty's Adjudicatory Jurisdiction over Alien Defendants: A Functional Analysis', 11 *J. Mar. L. & Com.* 395 (1980).

Rolin, 'Les Principes de droit international public', ii *Recueil des cours* 445 (1950).

Ross, 'National Sovereignty in International Environmental Decisions', 12 *Nat. Res. J.* 242 (1972).

—— *Oil Pollution as an International Problem: A Study of Puget Sound and the Strait of Georgia* (1973).

Rosenne, *The Law and Practice of the International Court* (1961).

—— *The World Court* (1973).

Rousseau, 'L' Indépendance de l'état dans l'ordre International', 73 *Recueil des cours* 171 (1948).

Rubin, 'Pollution by Analogy: The Trail Smelter Arbitration', 50 *Oreg. L. Rev.* 259 (1971).
Ruster and Simma (eds.), *International Protection of the Environment* (1974).
Ruivo (ed.), *Marine Pollution and Sea Life* (1972).
Sack, 'The Doctrine of Quasi-territoriality of Vessels and the Admiralty Jurisdiction over Crimes Committed on Board National Vessels in Foreign Ports', 12 *NYU L.Q. Rev.* 628 (1934–55) and 13 *NYU L.Q. Rev* 43 (1935–6).
Savioli, 'Les Règles générales de la Paix', 58 *Recueil des cours* 5 (1933).
Sax, 'The Public Trust Doctrine in Natural Resources Law', 68 *Mich L. Rev.* 471 (1969).
Scelle, *Droit international public* (1922).
Schachter, 'Scientific Advances and International Law Making', 55 *Cal. L. Rev.* 423 (1967).
Schachter and Serwer, 'Marine Pollution Problems and Remedies', 65 *Am. J. Int'l L.* 84 (1971).
Schellenberg, 'Proceedings against Two French Customs Officials in Switzerland', 9 *Int'l Bus. Law.* 139 (1981).
Schermers, *International Institutional Law* (1982).
Schneider, 'World Public Order of the Environment' (1979).
—— 'Something Old, Something New: Some Thoughts on Grotius and the Maritime Environment', 18 *Va. J. Int'l L.* 147 (1977).
Schoen, *Die Völkerrechtliche Haftung der Staaten aus Unerlaubten Handlungen* (1917).
Schram, 'The Case for Coastal State Jurisdiction', 44 *Nordisk Tiddsskrift for int'l ret.* 17 (1974–5).
Schwarzenberger, *International Law* (3rd edn. 1957).
Schwarzenberger and Brown, *A Manual of International Law* (6th edn. 1976).
Singh, *Maritime Flag and International Law* (1978).
—— (ed.) *International Conventions of Merchant Shipping* (2nd edn. 1973).
Smith, 'Canadian and Soviet Arctic Policy: An Icy Reception for the Law of the Sea?', 16 *Va. J. Int'l L.* 609 (1976).
—— 'Innocent Passage as a Rule of Decision: Navigation *v.* Environmental Protection', 21 *Colum. J. Transnat'l L.* 57 (1982).
Smith W. and A. Smith, *Minamata* (1975).
Sohn and Buergenthal, *Basic Documents on International Protection of Human Rights* (1973).
Sohn, 'The Stockholm Declaration on the Human Environment', 14 *Harv. Int'l L.J.* 423 (1973).
—— 'Interdiction of Vessels on the High Seas', 18 *Int'l Lawyer* 411 (1984).
Sohn and Baxter (eds.), *Recent Codification of the Law of State Responsibility for Injuries to Aliens* (1974).
Sorensen, *Manual of Public International Law* (1968).
—— 'Les Relations internationales de voisinage', ii *Recueil des cours*, 88 (1951).
Sorenson, 'The Law of the Sea', 520 *Int'l Conc.* 195 (1958).
Springer, *The International Law of Pollution* (1983).
—— 'Towards a Meaningful Concept of Pollution in International Law', 26 *Int'l Comp. L.Q.* 531 (1977).
Stanford, 'Canadian Perspectives on the Future Development of the Exclusive

Economic Zone: A Paper in Diplomacy and the Law of the Sea', 5 *Dalhousie L.J.* 73 (1979).

Starke, 'Imputability in International Delinquencies', 19 *Brit. Yb. Int'l L.* 104 (1938).

—— *An Introduction to International Law* (7th edn. 1972).

Stein, 'Responsibility and Liability for Harm to the Marine Environment', 6 *Ga. J. Int'l & Comp. L.* 41 (1976).

—— 'The OECD Guiding Principles on Transfrontier Pollution', 6 *Ga. J. Int'l & Comp. L.* 245 (1976).

Stevenson and Oxman, 'The Preparations for the Law of the Sea Conference', 68 *Am. J. Int'l L.* 1 (1974).

—— 'The Third United Nations Conference on the Law of the Sea: The 1974 Caracas Session', 69 *Am. J. Int'l L.* 1 (1975).

—— 'The Third United Nations Conference on the Law of the Sea: The 1975 Geneva Session', 69 *Am. J. Int'l L.* 763 (1975).

Story, *Conflict of Laws* (1834).

Strupp, *Éléments de droit international public universel, européen et americain* (1930).

Sucharitkul, *State Immunities and Trading Activities in International Law* (1959).

Swan, 'International and National Approaches to Oil Pollution Responsibility: An Emerging Regime for a Global Problem', 50 *Oreg. L. Rev.* 504 (1971).

Sweeney, 'Oil Pollution of the Oceans', 37 *Fordham L. Rev.* 155 (1968–9).

—— 'Environmental Protection by Coastal States: The Paradigm from Marine Transport of Petroleum', 4 *Ga. J. Int'l & Comp. L.* 278 (1974).

Szuk, *The Bombs of Palomares* (1967).

Tache, 'The Nationality of Ships: The Definitional Controversy and Enforcement of Genuine Link', 16 *Int'l Law* 301 (1982).

Taubenfeld, 'Modification of the Human Environment', in iv *The Future of the International Legal Order* (Black and Falk eds. 1972).

Taylor, 'The Content of the Rule against Abuse of Rights in International Law' 46 *Brit. Yb. Int'l L.* 323 (1972–3).

Teclaff, 'International Law and the Protection of the Oceans from Pollution', 40 *Fordham L. Rev.* 529 (1971–2).

—— 'International Law and the Protection of the Oceans from Pollution', in *International Environmental Law* (Teclaff and Utton eds. 1974).

Teclaff and Utton (eds.), *International Environmental Law* (1974).

Theraulaz, *Droit de l'espace et responsabilité* (1971).

Thommen, *Legal Status of Government Merchant Ships in International Law* (1962).

Timagenis, *International Control of Marine Pollution* (1980).

Topping, 'Sewage and the Sea', in *Marine Pollution* 303 (Johnston ed. 1976).

Train, 'Perspective: Environment, Energy, Economic Equity—Can We Balance these Vital Elements?' 6 *Envt'l Aff.* (1977).

Treves, 'Les Tendances récentes du droit conventionnel de la responsabilité et le nouveau droit de la mer', 21 *Annuaire français de droit int'l* 767 (1975).

Tribe, *American Constitutional Law* (1978).

Tunkin, *Theory of International Law*, (Butler trans. 1974).

Twiss, *Law of Nations* (2nd rev. ed. 1884).

UN Legislative Service, *Laws concerning the Nationality of Ships*, ST/LEG/SER. B (Nov. 1955).

US Congress, Senate Committee on Commerce and National Ocean Policy Study, *Soviet Oceans Development*, 94th Cong., 2nd Sess. Comm. Print (1976).

US Dept. of Justice, *The Regulated Ocean Shipping Industry* (Jan. 1977).

US Dept. of Public Information, 'Breadth of National Jurisdiction with Dates of Entry into Force', Reference Paper no. 18.

Utton, 'The Arctic Waters Pollution Prevention Act and the Right of Self-protection', in *International Environmental Law* 143 (Teclaff and Utton eds, 1974).

Váli, *Servitudes of International Law: A Study of Rights in Foreign Territory* (2nd edn. 1958).

Vallarta, 'Protection and Preservation of the Marine Environment and Marine Scientific Research at the Third UN Conference on the Law of the Sea', in 'Symposium on The Law of the Sea: Where Now?' 46 *Law & Contemp. Probs.* 147 (1983).

Van Gelder-Ottway and McKnight, 'A Review of World Oil Spillages 1960–75', in *Marine Ecology and Oil Pollution* 483–520 (Baker ed. 1976).

Van Lier, *Acid Rain and International Law* (1981).

Van Panhuys and Boas, 'Legal Aspects of Pirate Broadcasting', 60 *Am. J. Int'l L.* 303 (1966).

Vattel, *Le droit des gens ou principes de la loi Naturelle* (Fenwick trans. 1758 edn. 1916).

Verwey, 'The New Law of the Sea and the Establishment of a New International Economic Order: The Role of the Exclusive Economic Zone', in *The Management of Humanity's Resources: The Law of the Sea, Workshop*, Hague Academy of International Law (1981).

Verzijl, 'The United Nations Conference on the Law of the Sea: Geneva 1958', 6 *Nederlands tijdschrift voor international recht* 1 (1959).

—— *The Jurisprudence of the World Court* (1965).

Virally, 'Good Faith in Public International Law', 77 *Am. J. Int'l L.* 130 (1983).

Vlasic, 'The Space Treaty: A Preliminary Evaluation', 55 *Cal. L. Rev.* 507 (1967).

Waldock, 'General Course on Public International Law', ii *Recueil des cours* 1 (1962).

Watts, 'The Protection of Merchant Ships', 33 *Brit. Yb. Int'l L.* 52 (1957).

—— 'Review of F. Florio, Nazionalita della nave e legge Della Bandiera (1957)', 7 *Int'l & Comp. L.Q.* 399 (1958).

Wetstone, 'Air Pollution Control Laws in North America and the Problem of Acid Rain and Snow', 10 *Envt'l L. Rep.* 50001 (1980).

Whiteman, i–iii *Damages in International Law* (1937–43).

Wiewiorowska, 'Some Problems of State Responsibility in Outer Space Law', 7 *J. Space L.* 23 (1979).

Williams, *Joint Torts and Contributory Negligence* (1951).

Winfield, 'The Myth of Absolute Liability', 42 *L.Q. Rev.* 37 (1926).

Woodliffe, 'Some Legal Aspects of Pirate Broadcasting in the North Sea', 12 *Nederlands tijdschrift voor international recht* 365 (1965).

Wulf, 'Contiguous Zones for Pollution Control: An Appraisal Under International Law', *Sea Grant Technical Bulletin* No. 13 (March 1971).

—— 'Contiguous Zones for Pollution Control', 3 *J. Mar. L. & Com.* 537 (1971–2).

—— 'Comment, in Symposium, The Law of the Sea—Where Now?', 46 *Law & Contemp. Probs.* 155 (1983).

Yates, 'Unilateral and Multilateral Approaches to Environmental Problems', 21 *U. Tor. L.J.* 182 (1971).

Yuan, 'China's Offshore Petroleum Resources Law: A Critical and Interpretative Analysis', 16 *Int'l Law* 647 (1982).

Zoller, *La Bonne foi en droit international public* (1977).

Index